IPv6 Essentials

IPv6 Essentials

Silvia Hagen

O'REILLY®

Beijing · Cambridge · Farnham · Köln · Paris · Sebastopol · Taipei · Tokyo

IPv6 Essentials
by Silvia Hagen

Copyright © 2002 O'Reilly & Associates, Inc. All rights reserved.
Printed in the United States of America.

Published by O'Reilly & Associates, Inc., 1005 Gravenstein Highway North,
Sebastopol, CA 95472.

O'Reilly & Associates books may be purchased for educational, business, or sales pro-
motional use. Online editions are also available for most titles (*safari.oreilly.com*). For
more information, contact our corporate/institutional sales department: (800) 998-9938
or *corporate@oreilly.com*.

Editor:	Jim Sumser
Production Editor:	Claire Cloutier
Cover Designer:	Hanna Dyer
Interior Designer:	David Futato

Printing History:

July 2002:	First Edition.

Nutshell Handbook, the Nutshell Handbook logo, and the O'Reilly logo are registered
trademarks of O'Reilly & Associates, Inc. All Cisco-based trademarks are registered
trademarks of Cisco Systems, Inc. Many of the designations used by manufacturers and
sellers to distinguish their products are claimed as trademarks. Where those
designations appear in this book, and O'Reilly & Associates, Inc. was aware of a
trademark claim, the designations have been printed in caps or initial caps. The
association between the image of a rigatella snail and the topic of IPv6 is a trademark of
O'Reilly & Associates, Inc.

While every precaution has been taken in the preparation of this book, the publisher and
the author assume no responsibility for errors or omissions, or for damages resulting
from the use of the information contained herein.

Library of Congress Cataloging-in-Publication Data

Hagen, Silvia, 1965- .
    IPv6 Essentials/Silvia Hagen.
        p. cm.
    Includes index.
    ISBN 0-596-00125-8
    1. TCP/IP (Computer network protocol) I. Title.

TK5105.585 .H3397 2002
004.6'2—dc21   2002025285

ISBN: 0-596-00125-8   [10/02]
[M]

Table of Contents

Preface

This book is about the next generation Internet protocol. We have become familiar with the strengths and weaknesses of IPv4; we know how to design and configure it, and we have learned how to troubleshoot it. And now we have to learn a new protocol? Start from scratch? Not really. The designers of IPv6 have learned a lot from over 15 years of experience with IPv4, and they have been working on the new protocol since the early 1990s. They retained the strengths of IPv4, extended the address space from 32 bits to 128 bits, and added functionality that is missing in IPv4. They developed transition mechanisms that make IPv4 and IPv6 coexist peacefully and that guarantee a smooth transition between the protocols. In fact, this was one of the major requirements for the development of the new protocol version.

So you do not need to forget what you know about IPv4; many things will feel familiar with IPv6. When you get started, you will discover new features and functionalities that will make your life a lot easier. IPv6 has features that will be needed in tomorrow's networks—features that IPv4 does not provide. The day will come when our Personal Digital Assistants (PDAs) and mobile phones have an IP address. Aside from the fact that the IPv4 address space could never cover the demand for that number of IP addresses, imagine configuring those devices with the means we have today!

One of the coolest features built into IPv6 is autoconfiguration capability. Haven't we always been struggling with IP address assignment? The advent of DHCP made our lives a little easier, but now we need to maintain and troubleshoot the DHCP servers. And when our refrigerator, our PDA, and our TV all have an IP address, will we need a DHCP server at home? Not with autoconfiguration. If you have an IPv6-enabled host, you can plug it into your network, and it will configure automatically for a valid IPv6 address. Internet Control Message Protocol (ICMP), which is a networker's best friend, has become much more powerful with IPv6. Many of the new features of IPv6, such as autoconfiguration, optimized multicast routing and multicast group management, neighbor discovery, path MTU discovery, and Mobile IPv6, are based on ICMPv6.

Audience

This book covers a broad range of information about IPv6 and is an excellent resource for anybody who wants to understand or implement the protocol. This book is for system and network administrators, engineers, network designers, and IT managers. If you need to plan your corporate strategy for IPv6, you will be most interested in chapters 1, 4, 9, and 10. If you are a system or network administrator, all chapters are relevant: this book provides a foundation for IPv6 implementation and integration with IPv4. If you manage the infrastructure in your company, you will be especially interested in Chapters 7 and 8, which cover Layer 2 issues and routing, and in Chapter 10, which addresses interoperability.

About This Book

This book covers IPv6 in detail and explains all the new features and functions. It will show you how to plan for, design, and integrate IPv6 in your current IPv4 infrastructure. It also teaches you what you need to know to get started, to configure IPv6 on your hosts and routers, and to find the right applications that support IPv6.

Now that you know what this book is about, I should explain what this book does *not* cover. This book is not written for developers. This doesn't mean you should not be reading it if you are a developer. If you do, you will understand the implications of introducing IPv6 in your network and how important it is to develop cool applications for IPv6.

This book assumes that you have a good understanding of network issues in general, and that you are familiar with IPv4. It is beyond the scope of this book to discuss IPv4 concepts in detail. We refer to them when necessary. But if you want to learn more about IPv4, there are a lot of good books on the market. You can find a list of these books in the Appendix.

Organization

This book is organized so that a reader familiar with IPv4 can easily learn about the new features in IPv6 by reading Chapters 2 to 6. These chapters cover what you need to know about addressing, the new IPv6 header, ICMPv6, security, and quality of service (QoS). Chapters 7 to 10 cover such topics as networking aspects, support of different link-layer services, Mobile IPv6, routing, and the transition mechanisms that make IPv6 interoperable with IPv4. Chapter 11 is a quick-start guide and includes sample implementations of IPv6 stacks tested in my lab. Chapter 11 also offers a short description of how different operating systems are configured for IPv6. Here is a chapter-by-chapter breakdown of the book:

- Chapter 1, *IPv6 Versus IPv4*, briefly explains the history of IPv6, gives an overview of the new functionality, and describes some live test and production networks that are already using IPv6.

- Chapter 2, *The Structure of the IPv6 Protocol*, describes the new IPv6 header format, with a discussion of each field and a trace file example. It also describes what Extension headers are, what types of Extension headers have been defined, and how they are used.

- Chapter 3, *IPv6 Addressing*, explains everything you need to know about the new address format, address notation, address types, international registry services, and prefix allocation.

- Chapter 4, *ICMPv6*, describes the new ICMPv6 message format, the IMCPv6 Error messages and Informational messages, and the ICMPv6 header in a trace file. The chapter also discusses the extended functionality based on ICMPv6 such as neighbor discovery, autoconfiguration, path MTU discovery, and multicast group management. You will learn how ICMPv6 makes administration easier.

- Chapter 5, *Security in IPv6*, begins with a short discussion of basic security concepts, requirements, and current solutions. It then covers the IPSEC framework, security elements available in IPv6 for authentication and encryption, how they are used, and how they integrate with other elements such as NAT routers and autoconfiguration. This chapter was written by Hannes Lubich.

- Chapter 6, *Quality of Service in IPv6*, discusses basic requirements and types of QoS. We explain the QoS elements available in IPv6 and how they can be implemented. We also describe different QoS architectures and introduce further work in this area, primarily on resource reservation. This chapter was written by Hannes Lubich.

- Chapter 7, *Networking Aspects*, discusses Layer 2 support for IPv6 (Ethernet, Token Ring, ATM, frame relay, etc.); explains multicast support, multicast routing, and Mobile IPv6; and discusses some sample network designs that show how IPv6 can grow into our networks step-by-step, without interruption of our IPv4 services.

- Chapter 8, *Routing Protocols*, discusses the advanced routing features of IPv6 and covers the available routing protocols such as RIPng, OSPFv3 for IPv6, and BGP extensions for IPv6, IS-IS, and EIGRPv6. This chapter was written by Stefan Marzohl.

- Chapter 9, *Upper-Layer Protocols*, discusses what is going on above the IP layer, starting with changes for TCP and UDP and continuing with DHCPv6, DNS extensions for IPv6, SLPv2 in IPv6 networks, FTP, Telnet, and web servers.

- Chapter 10, *Interoperability*, discusses the different transition mechanisms that have been defined, such as dual-stack operation, tunneling, and translation techniques. It also shows how they can be used and combined to ensure peaceful coexistence and smooth transitions. The chapter also provides a list of vendor links that show what equipment, stacks, and software are currently available.

- Chapter 11, *Get Your Hands Dirty*, explains how to get started with IPv6 on different operating systems such as Sun Solaris, Linux, Windows 2000, Windows XP, and a Cisco router. The Chapter also explains what I did in my lab and provides examples of trace files.

- The *Appendix* includes a short introduction to the RFC process and authorities and provides a list of relevant RFCs for IPv6. The Appendix reflects the chapter organization of the book and provides summaries of all indexes, protocol numbers, message types, and address allocations. The Appendix is your best place for getting quick information if you are configuring or troubleshooting IPv6.

Conventions Used in This Book

I use the following font conventions in this book:

- *Italic* for commands, directory paths, filenames, and URLs.
- **Boldface** for names of GUI items such as window names, buttons, and menu choices.
- Constant Width for names and keywords in Java programs, including method names, variable names, and class names; IP and MAC addresses; and XML element tags.
- Constant width italic for replaceable text.
- **Constant width bold** for text that users should input.

Comments and Questions

Please address comments and questions concerning this book to the publisher:

O'Reilly & Associates, Inc.
1005 Gravenstein Highway North
Sebastopol, CA 95472
(800) 998-9938 (in the United States or Canada)
(707) 829-0515 (international or local)
(707) 829-0104 (fax)

There is a web page for this book, which lists errata, examples, or any additional information. You can access this page att:

http://www.oreilly.com/catalog/ipv6ess

To comment or ask technical questions about this book, send email to:

bookquestions@oreilly.com

For more information about books, conferences, Resource Centers, and the O'Reilly Network, see the O'Reilly web site at:

http://www.oreilly.com/

Acknowledgments

I want to thank all the people who have contributed to this book. First of all, I'd like to thank Hannes Lubich, who is responsible for IT security and architecture at a well-known Swiss private bank and who has taught courses on TCP/IP, Unix, IT security, and IPv6 at the Swiss Federal Institute of Technology for more than ten years. He is the author of Chapters 5 and 6. Also many thanks to Stefan Marzohl, who is a Cisco- and Nortel-certified instructor and the author of Chapter 8. A big thank you goes out to Anja Spittler (Maggy). She has spent hours, days, and weeks in our lab setting up SuSE Linux, getting BIND and other services to work, and writing parts of Chapter 9 and Chapter 11. I also want to thank the technical editors who have made this book much better with their invaluable comments, corrections, and clarifications. They were great resources when I was struggling with a topic and needed some answers. The technical reviewers were Patrick Grossetete, who works as a product manager for the Internet Technology Division (ITD) at Cisco, and Neil Cashell, who is a great TCP/IP guy at

Novell. He works for the worldwide connectivity support team. Last but not least, thanks to Brian McGehee from Native6Group, who has been working with IPv6 for over two years and has written numerous courses for IPv6. He did the final technical edits and added a lot of useful information to this book. I want to thank Axept AG, a professional Swiss integrator who sponsored this book and supported me in the writing process. Axept AG understands that getting familiar with IPv6 will be an important requirement in the near future. I'd like to thank Cisco for providing an updated router and access to their technical resources, the guys at SuSE for providing software and supporting us in getting our SuSE host ready for IPv6, Microsoft for providing software and information about their implementations, Network Associates for providing Sniffer Pro Software for the trace files, Bob Fink for running the 6Bone web site, Cricket Liu for answering my DNS questions, and Peter Bieringer for running a great Internet resource site and for answering my questions with lightning speed. I also want to thank all the guys at Cyberlink in Zurich. Cyberlink hosts my web site and is working hard to make it accessible over IPv6. So check back on my web site; soon you will find a link to the IPv6-accessible version. I also want to thank all the people in the international working groups. Without their visionary power, enthusiasm, and tireless work, we would not have IPv6 ready.

The events of September 11, 2001 hit the world during my writing of this book. I believe that ultimately, mankind can solve the problems in this world only by understanding that we are all one and that we are all connected. This understanding creates a genuine feeling of responsibility for everything and tolerance for other viewpoints. Connectedness manifests on different levels and in different realities. TCP/IP is the protocol that connects mankind on the physical level of the Internet, which opens the way to being in touch and sharing information and viewpoints all over the world. IPv6 will be the protocol that provides the scalability to take this connectedness and span it even further around the globe, to the countless people in parts of the world who today may not even have a telephone.

A special thank you goes to Jim Sumser at O'Reilly. He has been guiding me through the whole writing process with a lot of enthusiasm, patience, trust, and experience. Thank you, Jim, for being there and thank you for never hassling me when I was already struggling. You made a difference! I also want to thank all the other folks at O'Reilly who contributed to this book, especially Tim O'Reilly, for making this book possible.

I want to thank everybody who was involved when I got into writing books. They helped me get started with something new that now is an important and rewarding part of my business life. These people include Laura Chappell, founder of the Protocol Analysis Group; Stephanie Frank-Lewis, coauthor of my previous TCP/IP book; and Michael Ganser, from Cisco.

I thank my daughter Marina for being patient and supportive when I spent countless evenings and weekends hidden behind my computer and she had to cook her own meals. I wonder whether she is ever going to write a book. And I also thank all my friends and neighbors who were there when I needed them.

CHAPTER 1

IPv6 Versus IPv4

IPv6 is sometimes called the Next Generation Internet Protocol, or IPng. Even though the Internet is seen as a relatively new technology, the protocols and technologies that make it work were developed in the 1970s and 1980s. The current Internet and all our corporate and private intranets use IPv4. Now, with IPv6, the first major upgrade of the Internet protocol suite is on the horizon or maybe even closer. Close enough, anyway, to start taking it seriously.

The History of IPv6

The effort to develop a successor protocol to IPv4 was started in the early 1990s by the Internet Engineering Task Force (IETF). Several parallel efforts began simultaneously, all trying to solve the foreseen address space limitation as well as provide additional functionality. The IETF started the IPng area in 1993 to investigate the different proposals and to make recommendations for further procedures.

The IPng area directors of the IETF recommended the creation of IPv6 at the Toronto IETF meeting in 1994. Their recommendation is specified in RFC 1752, "The Recommendation for the IP Next Generation Protocol." The Directors formed an Address Lifetime Expectation (ALE) working group, whose job was to determine whether the expected lifetime for IPv4 would allow the development of a protocol with new functionality or if the remaining time would only allow for developing an address space solution. In 1994, the ALE working group projected the IPv4 address exhaustion to occur sometime between 2005 and 2011, based on the statistics that were available at that time.

For those of you who are interested in the different proposals, here's some more information about it (from RFC 1752). There were four main proposals called CNAT, IP Encaps, Nimrod, and Simple CLNP. Three more proposals followed: the P Internet Protocol (PIP), the Simple Internet Protocol (SIP), and TP/IX. After the March 1992 San Diego IETF meeting, Simple CLNP evolved into TCP and UDP with Bigger Addresses (TUBA) and IP Encaps evolved into IP Address Encapsulation (IPAE). IPAE merged with PIP and SIP and called itself Simple Internet Protocol Plus (SIPP). The TP/IX working group changed its name to Common Architecture for the Internet (CATNIP). The main proposals were now CATNIP, TUBA, and SIPP. For a short discussion of the proposals, refer to RFC 1752.

CATNIP is specified in RFC 1707, TUBA in RFC 1347, RFC 1526, and RFC 1561, and SIPP in RFC 1710.

The Internet Engineering Steering Group approved the IPv6 recommendation and drafted a Proposed Standard on November 17, 1994. The core set of IPv6 protocols became an IETF Draft Standard on August 10, 1998.

Why is the new protocol not IPv5? The version number 5 could not be used because it had been allocated to the experimental Stream Protocol.

Overview of Functionality

IPv6 is one of the most significant network and technology upgrades in history. It will slowly grow into your existing IPv4 infrastructure and positively impact your network. Reading this book will prepare you for the next step of networking technology evolution. IPv6 product development and implementation efforts are already underway all over the world. IPv6 is designed as an evolutionary step from IPv4. It is a natural increment to IPv4, can be installed as a normal software upgrade in most Internet devices, and is interoperable with the current IPv4. IPv6 is designed to run well on high performance networks like Gigabit Ethernet, ATM, and others, as well as low bandwidth networks (e.g., wireless). In addition, it provides a platform for new Internet functionality that will be required in the near future, such as extended addressing, better security, and quality of service (QoS) features.

IPv6 includes transition and interoperability mechanisms that are designed to allow users to adopt and deploy IPv6 step by step as needed and to provide direct interoperability between IPv4 and IPv6 hosts. The transition to a new version of the Internet Protocol (IP) must be incremental, with few or no critical interdependencies, if it is to succeed. The IPv6 transition allows users to upgrade their hosts to IPv6 and network operators to deploy IPv6 in routers with very little coordination between the two groups.

The main changes from IPv4 to IPv6 can be summarized as follows:

Expanded addressing capability and autoconfiguration mechanisms
The address size for IPv6 has been increased to 128 bits. This solves the problem of the limited address space of IPv4 and offers a deeper addressing hierarchy and simpler configuration. There will come a day when you will hardly remember how it felt to have only 32 bits in an IP address. Network administrators will love the autoconfiguration mechanisms built into the protocol. Multicast routing has been improved, with the multicast address being extended by a scope field. And a new address type has been introduced, called Anycast address, which can send a message to the nearest single member of a group.

Simplification of the header format
The IPv6 header has a fixed length of 40 bytes. This actually accommodates only an 8-byte header plus two 16-byte IP addresses (source and destination address). Some fields of the IPv4 header have been removed or become optional. This way, packets can be handled faster with lower processing costs.

Improved support for extensions and options
With IPv4, options were integrated into the basic IPv4 header. With IPv6, they are handled as *Extension headers*. Extension headers are optional and only inserted between the IPv6 header and the payload, if necessary. This way the IPv6 packet can be built very flexible and streamlined. Forwarding IPv6 packets is much more efficient. New options that will be defined in the future can be integrated easily.

Extensions for authentication and privacy
Support for authentication, and extensions for data integrity and data confidentiality, have been specified and are inherent.

Flow labeling capability
Packets belonging to the same traffic flow, requiring special handling or quality of service, can be labeled by the sender. Real-time service is an example where this would be used.

 For a current list of the standardization status of IPv6, you can refer to *http://playground.sun.com/pub/ipng/html/specs/ standards.html*.

Transition Aspects

Is IPv6 worth all the migration and upgrade headaches? Will it ever become the IP of the future? Can't IPv4 extensions offer all that functionality? After all, we have Network Address Translation (NAT) to solve address space problems and IPSEC to provide security.

The 128-bit address space is the most obvious feature of the new protocol, but it is not the only important change. The IPv6 package includes important features such as higher scalability, better data integrity, QoS features, autoconfiguration mechanisms that make it manageable even for high numbers of dynamically connecting devices, improved routing aggregation in the backbone, and improved multicast routing.

Extensions for IPv4 that have been widely deployed, such as NAT, should be viewed as good solutions but only for limited short-term scenarios. In the long term, nothing can replace IPv6's features for inherent secure end-to-end connectivity. Multimedia and interactive, transaction-oriented network applications require high levels of connectivity that can only be provided by IPv6. In the future, an unforeseeable number of new devices may want to connect to our networks, including devices such as Personal Digital Assistants (PDAs), mobile phones, smart set-top boxes with integrated web browsers, home entertainment systems, coffee machines, refrigerators, and car devices. The list is endless. Only IPv6, with its extended address space and advanced autoconfiguration and mobility features, can manage such devices. There is no comparable alternative technology in sight.

IPv6 Alive

There are already a surprising number of global test networks and even commercial networks running over IPv6. I discuss some interesting examples in the next sections. In order to describe what they are doing, I use some IPv6-specific terms that are probably not familiar to you yet. They are all explained in this book.

 In February 2002 over 120 production networks have been allocated IPv6 address prefixes. For a current list, refer to *http://www.dfn.de/service/ipv6/ipv6aggis.html*.

The 6Bone

The 6Bone started out as a network of IPv6 islands working over the existing IPv4 infrastructure of the Internet by tunneling IPv6 packets in IPv4 packets. The tunnels were mainly statically configured point-to-point links. The 6Bone became a reality in early 1996 as a result of an initiative of several research institutes. The first tunnels were established between the IPv6 laboratories of G6 in France, UNI-C in Denmark, and WIDE in Japan.

Structure of the 6Bone

The 6Bone is structured as a hierarchical network of two or more layers. The top layer consists of a set of backbone transit providers, called pseudo Top Level Aggregators (pTLAs), which use BGP4+ as a routing protocol. The bottom layer is comprised of leaf sites connected via the 6Bone. Zero or more intermediate layers, called pseudo Next Level Aggregators (pNLAs), interconnect leaf sites and the pTLA backbone networks.

Addressing

IPv6 unicast addressing of node interfaces (for both end systems and routers) is based on RFC 2374, which covers the Aggregatable Global Unicast address format. 6Bone backbone networks play the role of experimental TLAs, called pseudo TLAs (pTLAs), and assign address space to pseudo NLAs (pNLAs) and leaf sites. The prefix assigned to the 6Bone is 3ffe::/16 (RFC 2471). These pTLA backbone networks are currently allocated 32-bit prefixes (previously, 24- and 28-bit prefixes were allocated) that must be administered according to the rules defined for pTLAs. So every pTLA plays the role of an experimental top-level ISP and assigns chunks of its addressing space to directly connected transit and leaf sites without breaking aggregation inside the 6Bone backbone.

Growth

The 6Bone is growing fast. In December 1997 there were 43 backbone sites and 203 leaf sites registered. In December 1998 there were 51 backbone sites and 332 leaf sites. In January 2000 there were 67 backbone sites and 505 leaf sites.

I gave up on trying to find a nice picture of the world with the 6Bone backbone sites on it. The 6Bone has grown too big to display it in one screenshot. If you want to get a feeling for the size and workings of the 6Bone, go to *http://www.cs-ipv6.lancs.ac.uk/ipv6/6Bone* and look at the maps, statistics, and tools.

At the time of this writing, the number of nodes in the 6Bone has just reached 1000 nodes and grows daily. Find an updated list at *http://www.cs-ipv6.lancs.ac.uk/ipv6/6Bone/Whois/index.html#full*.

Joining the 6Bone

Membership in the 6Bone is open to anyone. Reasons for joining, besides the fun of it, would be to gain early experience working with IPv6, to build the expertise necessary to make decisions about when and how to use IPv6 for production networks, and to have working access to IPv6 servers and resources. Joining the 6Bone connects you with a cool crowd of people who want to be on top of technology and are willing to share their experience.

The 6Bone community spans the globe and is very active and enthusiastic. By joining, you not only gain access to the network and the common experience of those in it; you can also participate and help develop protocols, programs, and procedures.

 If you are interested in joining the 6Bone, here's the link: *http://www.6bone.net/6bone_hookup.html*.

There are different ways for you to connect to either the 6Bone or production IPv6 networks:

- Become an end site of an existing 6Bone ISP (which means you will get your 48-bit IPv6 external routing prefix from that ISP's TLA). You can also get temporary address allocations from tunnel broker sites (see the 6Bone home page for more information).

- Apply for your own 6Bone TLA (if you are an ISP) based on the 6Bone process.

- To get your first production IPv6 address, find a production IPv6 ISP (i.e., an ISP that has a sub-TLA) from which to get your prefix. Note that you can partially qualify for a sub-TLA production prefix if you have a 6Bone *pTLA* prefix (at least during the early phase of production prefix allocation).

- Use the "6to4" automatic tunneling mechanism. This allows you to specify the IPv4 address of your end user site router for an IPv6-over-IPv4 tunnel to reach your end user site. Addresses of this type have the first 16 bits of 2002::/16, with the next 32 bits containing the IPv4 address of a router on your site supporting this mechanism (thus making up the entire 48-bit external routing prefix). Refer to Chapter 10 for more information on the "6to4" automatic tunneling mechanism.

Now all you really need is a router and a host running IPv6 stacks. Almost all router vendors have either production stacks or beta stacks available. Refer to *http://playground.sun.com/pub/ipng/html/ipng-implementations.html* for a list of router and host implementations.

Obviously you need an entry point into the 6Bone. Try to find one that is close to your normal IPv4 path into the Internet. You can find a good 6Bone TLA on the 6Bone home page at *http://www.6bone.net/6bone_pTLA_list.html*. Use *traceroute* to determine the closest path.

IPv6 Commercial Networks

Since I started writing this book, a lot has happened in the development of IPv6. There are many production networks worldwide that have already been assigned IPv6 address prefixes. We picked four examples of companies that made their step into the future by offering IPv6 services.

vBNS+

vBNS+ is a specialized US IP network that supports high-performance, high-bandwidth applications. The vBNS+ network supports both native IPv6-over-ATM connections and tunneled IPv6-in-IPv4 connections. The vBNS+ service has been assigned its own sTLA from ARIN, as well as a pTLA for the 6Bone, and is delegating address space under these assignments to vBNS-attached sites. For more information, refer to their site at *http://www. vbns.net.*

Telia Sweden

In summer 2001, Telia, in Sweden, announced its intention to build a new generation Internet based on IPv6. By the end of 2001, connection points were installed in Stockholm, Farsta, Malmoe, Gothenburg (Sweden), Vasa (Finland), Oslo, Copenhagen, and London.

I spoke with the project manager at Telia because I thought that his early adopter input might be interesting for companies that consider going into IPv6. Telia's intent was to break through the lethargy of the chicken and the egg problem: vendors do not develop because the market is not asking for it, and the market doesn't ask for it because vendors don't develop. So Telia made the decision to create a market by building an IPv6 network and opening it to the public. Telia's hope is that, through the publicity of its endeavor, other companies will follow suit, and the acceptance and development of IPv6 will increase.

At the current stage of its rollout, Telia is keeping the IPv6 network separate from the existing IPv4 infrastructure. There were different reasons for this decision:

- It was easier to start by keeping the networks separate. Telia does not have to educate all of its IPv4 engineers to use IPv6 overnight.
- If there are problems with the IPv6 network, the IPv4 network is not affected in any way.
- It is less complex to configure if the networks are separate.

The new network is primarily built as a native IPv6 network. In some instances, tunnels over IPv4 are used. Currently, Telia is offering an IPv6 transport service to a limited number of customers. It will add features and gradually open the IPv6 network as a general service for everyone. Telia uses Hitachi routers that support IPv6 in hardware (versus software implementations).

After rolling out the first connection points, Telia concluded that market support for IPv6 was sufficient to get started. There are applications that will need to be ported to IPv6, but Telia recommends that companies and ISPs start right away. The foundation is here and when IPv6 is implemented on a broader range, vendors and application developers will be encouraged to speed up development.

Internet Initiative Japan

Another company that offers IPv6 transport services is Internet Initiative Japan (IIJ), Japan's leading Internet access and solutions provider, which targets high-end corporate customers. IIJ offers a trial IPv6 service (tunneling through IPv4) and a native IPv6 service that is independent from existing IPv4 networks. In December 2001 IIJ extended its IPv6 services to individual users connecting through IIJmio DSL/SF, an ADSL Internet service.

 For information about IIJ's services, refer to *http://www.iij. ad.jp/IPv6/index-e.html.*

NTT Communications Corporation

NTT Laboratories started one of the largest global IPv6 research networks in 1996. Trials of their global IPv6 network, using official IPv6 addresses, began in December 1999. Since spring 2001, NTT Communications has offered commercial IPv6 services.

In April 2001 the company started their commercial IPv6 Gateway Service. This native IPv6 backbone service connects sites in Japan to the NTT/ VERIO Global Tier1 IPv6 backbone deployed over Asia, the U.S., and Europe. Monitoring and operation continues 7 days a week, 24 hours a day, through NTT Communications NOC in Tokyo, Japan and Verio NOC in Dallas, US. Figure 1-1 shows the layout of the backbone.

The IPv6 Gateway Service offers native IPv6 transport. Also shown on the picture is the IPv6 Tunneling Service that NTT has offered since June 2001. It uses the existing IPv4 network to enable NTT's partners to access the IPv6 network, using IPv6-over-IPv4 tunneling techniques via dedicated lines. The

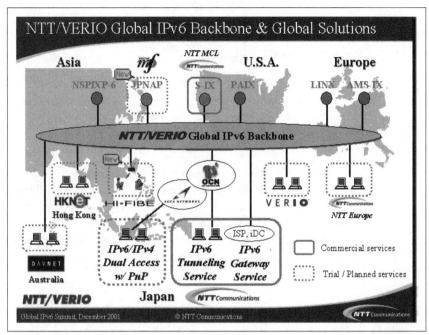

Figure 1-1. NTT/VERIO's global IPv6 backbone

newest addition is the IPv6/IPv4 Dual Access point with plug-and-play functionality, which became available in the first quarter of 2002. It is shown in dotted lines on Figure 1-1. The first customers to use the native backbone service were BIGLOBE/NEC Corporation, CHITA MEDIAS NETWORK INC., Toshiba, InfoSphere/NTTPC Communications, Fujitsu Matsushita Graphic Communication Systems, Inc., and MEX/Media Exchange, Inc. In June 2001, NTT demonstrated applications running over IPv6, including a remote control camera running over IPv6 and videoconferencing using IPv6.

The routing protocols used are BGP4+ and RIPng, IS-IS (which will be on the global backbone in the near future), and OSPFv3 (which is used at NTT's Japan domestic backbone). What NTT lacked was ICMPv6 polling in commercial operational tools. They utilize their own custom-developed router configuration tools and network management tools that support IPv6.

NTT offers Points Of Presence (POPs) all over the world, currently in London, Palo Alto, San Jose, Seattle, and Tokyo. They plan to extend their services throughout the world; the next POPs will be in Hong Kong and Australia. NTT's services include official IPv6 addresses from their *sTLA* block, IPv6 Internet connectivity, and DNS reverse zone delegation for the subscriber's IPv6 address space.

For an overview of NTT's global IPv6 services and how you can participate and connect, refer to *http://www.v6.ntt.net/ globe/index-e.html.*

Links to Other IPv6 Networks

There are a large number of international IPv6 test and research networks. You can find some interesting links in the following list:

The 6Ren

The 6Ren is a voluntary coordination initiative of research and education networks that provide production IPv6 transit service to facilitate high-quality, high-performance, and operationally robust IPv6 networks. Participation is free and open to all research and education networks that provide IPv6 service. Other profit and nonprofit IPv6 networks are also encouraged to participate. The 6Ren web site can be found at *http://www.6ren.net.*

The 6Net

The 6Net is a high-capacity IPv6 research network coordinated by Cisco, with more than 30 members. Their home page can be found at *http://www.sixnet.org.*

DRENv6

The Defense Research and Engineering Network (DREN) is a major component of the DoD High Performance Computing Modernization Program (HPCMP). Its purpose is to provide high-performance network connectivity to various communities of interest in the DoD, including research and development, modeling and simulation, and testing and evaluation. DREN also provides connectivity to other high-performance backbones and Federal networks to serve the needs of these communities. DREN is also a research network; it provides a test bed for testing new protocols and applications. DREN provides both ATM cell-based services and IP frame-based services. The DREN IPv6 network is one of the services provided as part of DREN. The DREN web site is at *http://www.v6.dren.net.*

CHAPTER 2

The Structure of the IPv6 Protocol

This chapter explains the structure of the IPv6 header and compares it to the IPv4 header. It also discusses Extension headers, which are new in IPv6.

The header structure of an IPv6 packet is specified in RFC 2460. The header has a fixed length of 40 bytes. The two fields for source and destination addresses each use 16 bytes (128 bits), so there are only 8 bytes for general header information.

General Header Structure

In IPv6, five fields from the IPv4 header have been removed:

- Header Length
- Identification
- Flags
- Fragment Offset
- Header Checksum

The Header Length field was removed because it is not needed in a header with a fixed length. In IPv4 the minimum header length is 20 bytes, but if options are added, it can be extended in 4-byte increments up to 60 bytes. Therefore, with IPv4, the information about the total length of the header is important. In IPv6 options are defined by Extension headers (covered later in this chapter).

The Identification field, the Flags field, and the Fragment Offset field handle fragmentation of a packet in the IPv4 header. Fragmentation happens if a large packet has to be sent over a network that only supports smaller packet sizes. In that case, the IPv4 router splits the packet into smaller slices and forwards multiple packets. The destination host collects the packets and reassembles them. If only one packet is missing or has an error, the whole transmission has to be redone; this is very inefficient. In IPv6, a host learns the Path Maximum Transmission Unit (MTU) size through a procedure called Path MTU Discovery. If a sending IPv6 host wants to fragment a packet, it will use an Extension header to do so. IPv6 routers along the path of a packet do not provide fragmentation, as they did with IPv4. So the Identification, Flags, and Fragment Offset fields were removed from the IPv6 header and will be inserted as an Extension header, if needed. Extension headers are explained later in this chapter.

Path MTU Discovery is explained in Chapter 4.

The Header Checksum field was removed to improve processing speed. If routers do not have to check and update checksums, processing becomes much faster. Checksumming is done at the media access level, too, and the risk for undetected errors and misrouted packets is minimal. There is a checksum field at the transport layer (UDP and TCP). IP is a best-effort delivery protocol; it is the responsibility of upper layer protocols to insure integrity.

The Type of Service field was replaced by the TrafficClass field. IPv6 has a different mechanism to handle preferences. Refer to Chapter 6 for more information. The Protocol Type and the Time-to-Live (TTL) fields were renamed and slightly modified. A Flow Label field was added.

The Fields in the IPv6 Header

By becoming familiar with the fields of the IPv6 header, you will better understand how IPv6 works.

For a detailed description of all the fields in an IPv4 header, refer to Novell's *Guide to Troubleshooting TCP/IP* (John Wiley & Sons) by Silvia Hagen and Stephanie Lewis.

Figure 2-1 provides an overview of the IPv6 header. The fields are discussed in detail in the following paragraphs.

Figure 2-1 shows that even though the header has a total size of 40 bytes, which is twice as long as a default IPv4 header, it has actually been streamlined because most of the header is taken by the two 16-byte IPv6 addresses. That leaves only 8 bytes for other header information.

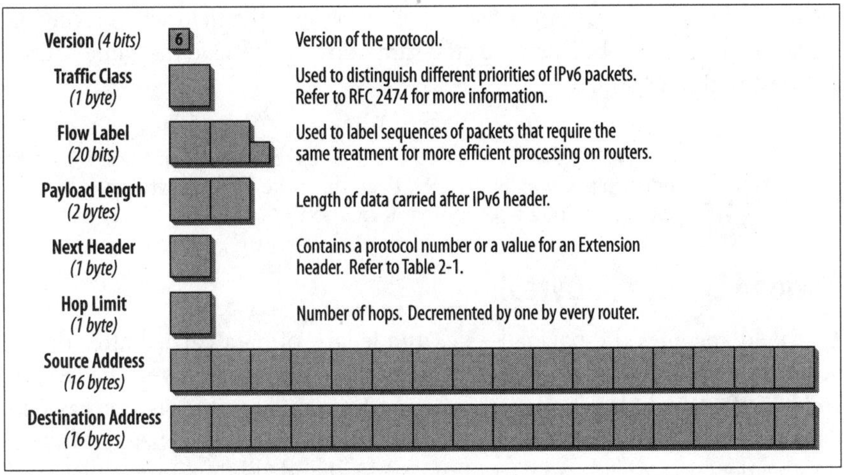

Figure 2-1. Fields in the IPv6 header

Version (4 Bits)

This is a 4-bit field and contains the version of the protocol. In the case of IPv6, the number is 6. The version number 5 could not be used because it had already been assigned an experimental stream protocol (ST2, RFC 1819).

Traffic Class (1 Byte)

This field replaces the Type of Service field in IPv4. This field facilitates the handling of real-time data and any other data that requires special handling. This field can be used by sending nodes and forwarding routers to identify and distinguish between different classes or priorities of IPv6 packets.

RFC 2474, "Definition of the Differentiated Services Field (DS Field) in the IPv4 and IPv6 Headers," explains how the Traffic Class field in IPv6 can be used. RFC 2474 uses the term DS Field to refer to the Type of Service field in the IPv4 header, as well as to the Traffic Class field in the IPv6 header.

Flow Label (20 Bits)

This field distinguishes packets that require the same treatment, in order to facilitate the handling of real-time traffic. A sending host can label sequences of packets with a set of options. Routers keep track of flows and can process packets belonging to the same flow more efficiently because they do not have to reprocess each packet's header. A flow is uniquely identified by the flow label and the address of the source node. Nodes that do not support the functions of the Flow Label field are required to pass the field unchanged when forwarding a packet and to ignore the field when receiving a packet. All packets belonging to the same flow must have the same source and destination IP address.

 The use of the Flow Label field is experimental and still under discussion at the IETF at the time of this writing. Refer to Chapter 6 for more information.

Payload Length (2 Bytes)

This field specifies the payload—i.e., the length of data carried after the IP header. The calculation in IPv6 is different from the one in IPv4. The Length Field in IPv4 includes the length of the IPv4 header, whereas the Payload Length field in IPv6 contains only the data following the IPv6 header. Extension headers are considered part of the payload and are therefore included in the calculation.

The fact that the Payload Length field has 2 bytes limits the maximum packet payload size to 64 KB. IPv6 has a Jumbogram Extension header, which supports bigger packet sizes, if needed. Jumbograms are relevant only when IPv6 nodes are attached to links that have a link MTU greater than 64 KB. Jumbograms are specified in RFC 2675.

Next Header (1 Byte)

In IPv4, this field is the Protocol Type field. It was renamed in IPv6 to reflect the new organization of IP packets. If the next header is UDP or TCP, this field will contain the same protocol numbers as in IPv4—for example, protocol number 6 for TCP or 17 for UDP. But if Extension headers are used with IPv6, this field contains the type of the next Extension header. That header is located between the IP header and the TCP or UDP header. Table 2-1 lists possible values in the Next Header field.

Table 2-1. Values in the Next Header field

Value	Description
0	In an IPv4 header: reserved and not used
	In an IPv6 header: Hop-by-Hop Option Header following
1	Internet Control Message Protocol (ICMPv4)—IPv4 support
2	Internet Group Management Protocol (IGMPv4)—IPv4 support
4	IP in IP (encapsulation)
6	TCP

Table 2-1. Values in the Next Header field (continued)

Value	Description
8	Exterior Gateway Protocol (EGP)
9	IGP - any private interior gateway (used by Cisco for their IGRP)
17	UDP
41	IPv6
43	Routing header
44	Fragmentation header
45	Interdomain Routing Protocol (IDRP)
46	Resource Reservation Protocol (RSVP)
50	Encrypted Security Payload header
51	Authentication header
58	ICMPv6
59	No Next Header for IPv6
60	Destination Options header
88	EIGRP
89	OSPF
108	IP Payload Compression Protocol
115	Layer 2 Tunneling Protocol (L2TP)
132	Stream Control Transmission Protocol (SCTP)
134-254	Unassigned
255	Reserved

Header type numbers derive from the same range of numbers as protocol type numbers and should therefore not conflict with them.

> The complete list of protocol numbers can be found in the appendix. For the most current list, go to IANA's web site at *http://www.iana.org/assignments/protocol-numbers*.

Hop Limit (1 Byte)

This field is analogous to the TTL field in IPv4. The TTL field contains a number of seconds, indicating how long a packet can remain in the network before being destroyed. Most routers simply decremented this value by one at each hop. This field was renamed to Hop Limit in IPv6. The value in this field now expresses a number of hops and not a number of seconds. Every forwarding node decrements the number by one.

Source Address (16 Bytes)

This field contains the IP address of the originator of the packet.

Destination Address (16 Bytes)

This field contains the IP address of the intended recipient of the packet. With IPv4, this field always contains the address of the ultimate destination of the packet. With IPv6, this field might not contain the IP address of the ultimate destination if a Routing header is present.

Figure 2-2 shows the IPv6 header in the trace file.

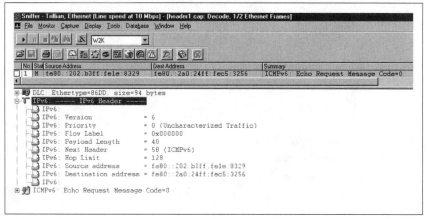

Figure 2-2. The IPv6 header in a trace file

This trace file shows all of the header fields I have discussed and how they are presented in a trace file. The Version field is set to 6 for IPv6. The Priority and the Flow Label fields are not used in this packet and are set to zero. The Payload Length is 40 and the Next Header value is set to 58 for ICMPv6. The Hop Limit is set to 128 and the Source and Destination addresses contain the link local addresses of my IPv6 nodes.

Extension Headers

The IPv4 header can be extended from a minimum of 20 bytes to 60 bytes in order to specify options such as Security Options, Source Routing, or Timestamping. This capacity has rarely been used because it causes a performance hit. For example, IPv4 hardware forwarding implementations have to pass the packet containing options to the main processor (software handling).

The simpler a packet header, the faster the processing. IPv6 has a new way to deal with options that has substantially improved processing. It handles options in additional headers called Extension headers.

The current IPv6 specification (RFC 2460) defines six Extension headers:

- Hop-by-Hop Options header
- Routing header
- Fragment header
- Destination Options header
- Authentication header
- Encrypted Security Payload header

There can be zero, one, or more than one Extension header between the IPv6 header and the upper-layer protocol header. Each Extension header is identified by the Next Header field in the preceding header. The Extension headers are examined or processed only by the node identified in the Destination Address field of the IPv6 header. If the address in the Destination Address field is a multicast address, the Extension headers are examined and processed by all the nodes belonging to that multicast group. Extension headers must be strictly processed in the order they appear in the packet header.

There is an exception to the above rule: only the destination node will process an Extension header. If the Extension header is a Hop-by-Hop Options header, the information it carries must be examined and processed by every node along the path of the packet. The Hop-by-Hop Options header, if present, must immediately follow the IPv6 header. It is indicated by the value zero in the Next Header field of the IPv6 header (see Table 2-1, earlier in this chapter).

 The first four Extension headers are described in RFC 2460. The Authentication header is described in RFC 2402 and the Encrypted Security Payload header in RFC 2406.

Figure 2-3 shows how Extension headers are used.

Each Extension header is a multiple of 8 octets long. That way, subsequent headers can always be aligned. If a node is required to process the Next Header but cannot identify the value in the Next Header field, it is required to discard the packet and send an ICMPv6 Parameter Problem message back to the source of the packet. For details on ICMPv6 messages, refer to Chapter 4.

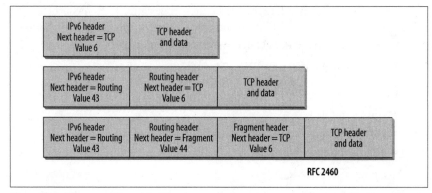

Figure 2-3. The use of Extension headers

If more than one Extension header is used in a single packet, the following header order should be used (RFC 2460):

1. IPv6 header
2. Hop-by-Hop Options header
3. Destination Options header (for options to be processed by the first destination that appears in the IPv6 Destination address field, plus subsequent destinations listed in the Routing header)
4. Routing header
5. Fragment header
6. Authentication header
7. Encapsulating Security Payload header
8. Destination Options header (for options to be processed only by the final destination of the packet)
9. Upper-Layer header

In cases when IPv6 is encapsulated in IPv4, the Upper-Layer header can be another IPv6 header and can contain Extension headers that have to follow the same rules.

Hop-by-Hop Options Header

The Hop-by-Hop Options Extension header carries optional information that must be examined by every node along the path of the packet. It must follow the IPv6 header immediately and is indicated by a Next Header value of zero. For example, the Router Alert (RFC 2711) uses the Hop-by-Hop Extension header for protocols like Resource Reservation Protocol (RSVP) or Multicast Listener Discovery (MLD) messages. With IPv4, the only way for a router to determine if it needs to examine a datagram is to, at least partially, parse upper layer data in all datagrams. This slows down the routing process substantially. With IPv6, in the absence of a Hop-by-Hop Extension header, a router knows that it does not need to process router-specific information and can route the packet immediately to the final destination. If there is a Hop-by-Hop Extension header, the router only needs to examine this header and not look further into the packet.

The format of the Hop-by-Hop Options header is shown in Figure 2-4.

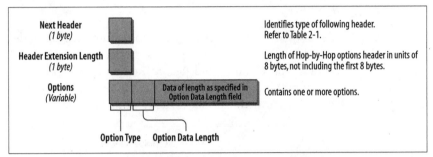

Figure 2-4. Format of the Hop-by-Hop Options header

The following list describes each field:

Next Header (1 byte)
> The Next Header field identifies the type of header that follows the Hop-by-Hop Options header. The Next Header field uses the values listed in Table 2-1, earlier in this chapter.

Header Extension Length (1 byte)
> This field identifies the length of the Hop-by-Hop Options header in 8-byte units. The length calculation does not include the first 8 bytes.

Options (variable size)
> There can be one or more options. The length of the options is variable and determined in the Header Extension Length field.

The Option Type Field, the first byte of the Options fields, contains information about how this option must be treated in case the processing node does not recognize the option. The value of the first two bits specifies the actions to be taken:

- Value 00: skip and continue processing.
- Value 01: discard the packet.

- Value 10: discard the packet and send ICMP Parameter Problem, Code 2 message to the packet's source address, pointing to the unrecognized option type.
- Value 11: discard the packet and send ICMP Parameter Problem, Code 2 message to the packet's source address only if the destination is not a multicast address.

The third bit of the Options Type field specifies whether the option information can change en route (value 01) or does not change en route (value 00).

Routing Header

The Routing header is used to give a list of one or more intermediate nodes that should be visited on the packet's path to its destination. In the IPv4 world, this is called the Loose Source and Record Route option. The Routing header is identified by a Next Header value of 43 in the immediately preceding header. Figure 2-5 shows the format of the Routing header.

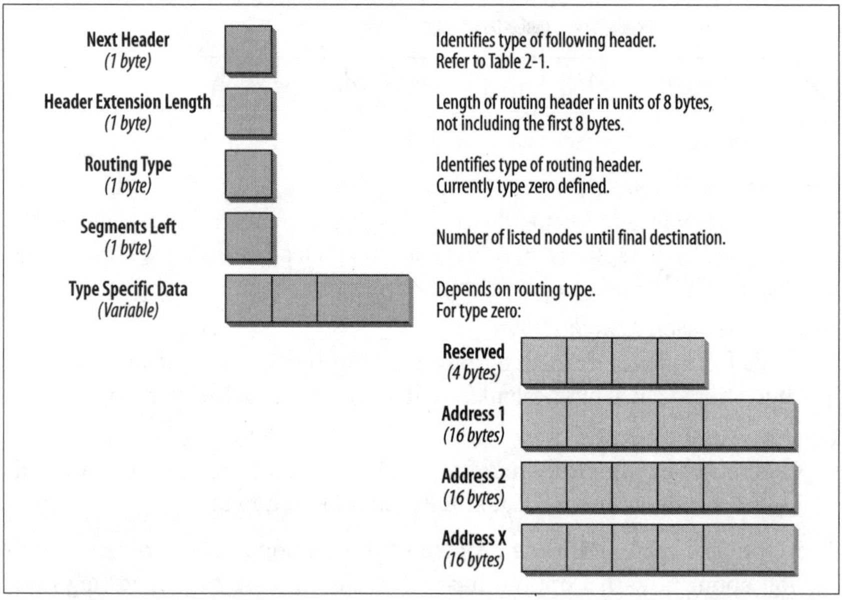

Figure 2-5. Format of the Routing header

The following list describes each field:

Next Header (1 byte)
    The Next Header field identifies the type of header that follows the Routing header. It uses the same values as the IPv4 Protocol Type field (see Table 2-1, earlier in this chapter).

Header Extension Length (1 byte)
This field identifies the length of the Routing header in 8-byte units. The length calculation does not include the first 8 bytes.

Routing Type (1 byte)
This field identifies the type of Routing header. RFC 2460 describes Routing Type zero.

Segments Left (1 byte)
This field identifies how many nodes are left to be visited before the packet reaches its final destination.

Type-Specific Data (Variable-length)
The length of this field depends on the Routing Type. The length will always make sure that this complete header is a multiple of 8 bytes.

If a node processing a Routing header cannot identify a Routing Type value, the action taken depends on the content of the Segments Left field. If the Segments Left field does not contain any nodes to be visited, the node must ignore the Routing header and process the next header in the packet, determined by the Next Header field value. If the Segments Left field is not zero, the node must discard the packet and send an ICMP Parameter Problem, Code 0 message to the packet's source address, pointing to the unrecognized Routing Type. If a forwarding node cannot process the packet because the next link MTU size is too small, it discards the packet and sends an ICMP Packet Too Big message back to the source of the packet.

The only Routing Type described in RFC 2460 is a Type Zero Routing header. The first node that processes the Routing header is the node addressed by the Destination address field in the IPv6 header. This node decrements the Segments Left field by one and inserts the next address field from within the Routing header in the IPv6 header Destination address field. Then the packet is forwarded to the next hop that will again process the Routing header as described until the final destination is reached. The final destination is the last address in the Routing Header Data field. For example, Mobile IPv6 uses the Routing header. Any node sending a packet to a mobile node will send the packet to the mobile node's care-of-address. It will include a Routing header with one entry, the mobile node's home address. The mobile node swaps the Destination address in the IPv6 header with the entry in the Routing header and will reply with its home address as a source address as if it received the packet attached to its home network. For further discussion and definition of terms regarding Mobile IPv6, refer to Chapter 7. Figure 2-6 shows the routing header in a trace file.

The Next Header field within the IPv6 header shows the value 43 for the Routing header. The Source and Destination addresses have the prefix 2002:,

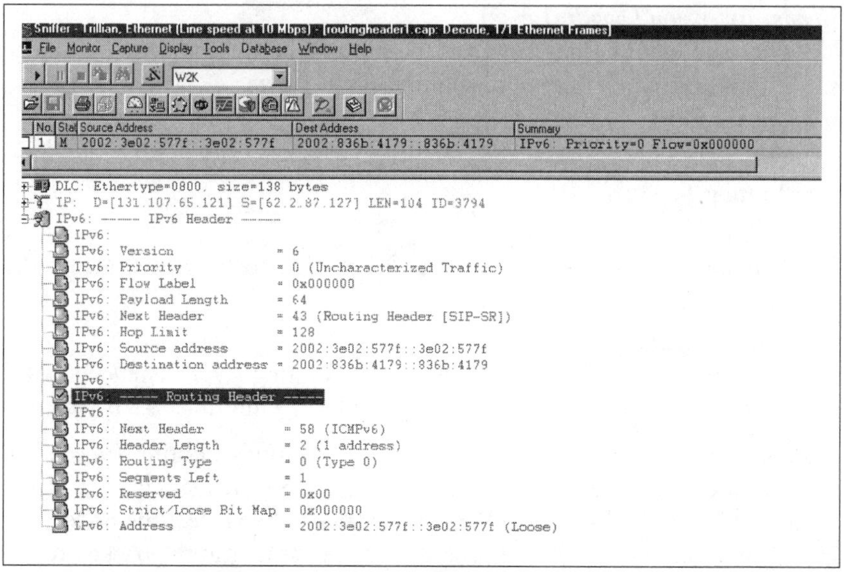

Figure 2-6. Routing header in a trace file

which is allocated to 6to4 sites. The Routing header contains the fields discussed earlier in this section. Next Header will be ICMPv6, value 58. The Header Length is two 8-byte units, which calculates to a total length of 16 bytes. The Segments Left field contains the value 1 because there is one address entry in the Options Fields. Finally, the Options field lists the addresses to be visited. In this case, there is only one entry. If a number of hosts is listed here, every forwarding node (that is, the destination IP address in the IPv6 header) takes the next entry from this host list, uses it as a new destination IP address in the IPv6 header, decrements the Segments Left field by one, and forwards the packet. This is done until the last host in the list is reached. Note that the Sniffer decode shows the Strict/loose Bit Map containing three bytes. This decode is not according to the latest specification in RFC 2460. Between 'segments left' and the first address entry there are four reserved bytes which have to be zero. RFC 2460 shows an example.

A source node S sends a packet to destination node D using a Routing header to send the packet through the intermediate nodes I1, I2, and I3. The Routing header changes are shown in Table 2-2.

Table 2-2. Processing the Routing header

	IPv6 Header	Routing Header
Packet from S to I1	Source address S	Segments Left 3
	Destination address I1	Address (1) = I2
		Address (2) = I3
		Address (3) = D

Table 2-2. Processing the Routing header (continued)

	IPv6 Header	**Routing Header**
Packet from I1 to I2	Source address S	Segments Left 2
	Destination address I2	Address (1) = I1
		Address (2) = I3
		Address (3) = D
Packet from I2 to I3	Source address S	Segments Left = 1
	Destination address I3	Address (1) = I1
		Address (2) = I2
		Address (3) = D
Packet from I3 to D	Source address S	Segments Left = 0
	Destination address D	Address (1) = I1
		Address (2) = I2
		Address (3) = I3

Fragment Header

An IPv6 host that wants to send a packet to an IPv6 destination uses Path MTU discovery to determine the maximum packet size that can be used on the path to that destination. If the packet to be sent is larger than the supported MTU, the source host fragments the packet. Unlike IPv4, with IPv6, a packet does not get fragmented by a router along the path. Fragmentation only occurs on the source host sending the packet. The destination host handles reassembly. A Fragment header is identified by a Next Header value of 44 in the preceding header. The format of the Fragment header is shown in Figure 2-7.

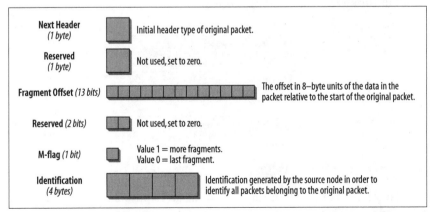

Figure 2-7. Format of the Fragment header

The following list describes each field:

Next Header (1 byte)
> The Next Header field identifies the type of header that follows the Fragment header. It uses the same values as the IPv4 Protocol Type field. (See Table 2-1).

Reserved (1 byte)
> Not used; set to zero.

Fragment Offset (13 bits)
> The offset in 8-byte units of the data in this packet relative to the start of the data in the original packet.

Reserved (2 bits)
> Not used; set to zero.

M-Flag (1 bit)
> Value 1 indicates more fragments; value zero indicates last fragment.

Identification (4 Bytes)
> Generated by the source host in order to identify all packets belonging to the original packet. This field is usually implemented as a counter, increasing by one for every packet that needs to be fragmented by the source host.

The initial unfragmented packet is referred to as the original packet. It has an unfragmentable part that consists of the IPv6 header, plus any Extension headers that must be processed by nodes along the path to the destination (i.e., Hop-by-Hop Options). The fragmentable part of the original packet consists of any Extension headers that need only to be processed by the final destination, plus the Upper-Layer headers and any data. Figure 2-8 (RFC 2460) illustrates the fragmenting process.

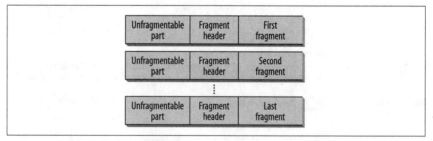

Figure 2-8. Fragmentation with IPv6

The unfragmentable part of the original packet appears in every fragment, followed by the Fragmentation header, and then the fragmentable data. The IPv6 header of the original packet has to be slightly modified. The length field reflects the length of the fragment (excluding the IPv6 header) and not the length of the original packet.

The destination node collects all the fragments and reassembles them. The fragments must have identical Source and Destination addresses and the same identification value in order to be reassembled. If all fragments do not arrive at the destination within 60 seconds after the first fragment, the destination will discard all packets. If the destination has received the first fragment (offset = zero), it sends back an ICMPv6 Fragment Reassembly Time Exceeded message to the source.

Figure 2-9 shows a Fragment header.

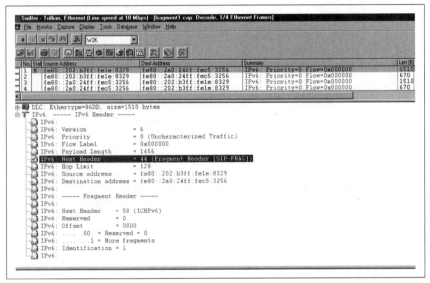

Figure 2-9. Fragment header in a trace file

I created this Fragment header by generating an oversized ping from *Marvin* to *Ford* (Win2000 to Linux). The whole fragment set consists of two packets, the first of which is shown in Figure 2-9. In the IPv6 header, the Payload Length field has a value of 1456, which is the length of the fragmentation header and this one fragment, not the length of the whole original packet. The Next Header field specifies the value 44, which is the value for the Fragment header. This field is followed by the Hop Limit field and by the Source and Destination IP addresses. The first field in the Fragment header is the Next Header field. Because this is a ping, it contains the value 58 for ICMPv6. And because this is the first packet in the fragment set, the value in the Offset field is zero and the M-Flag is set to one, which means there are more fragments to come. The Identification field is set to one and has to be identical in all packets belonging to this fragment set. Figure 2-10 shows the second packet of the fragment set.

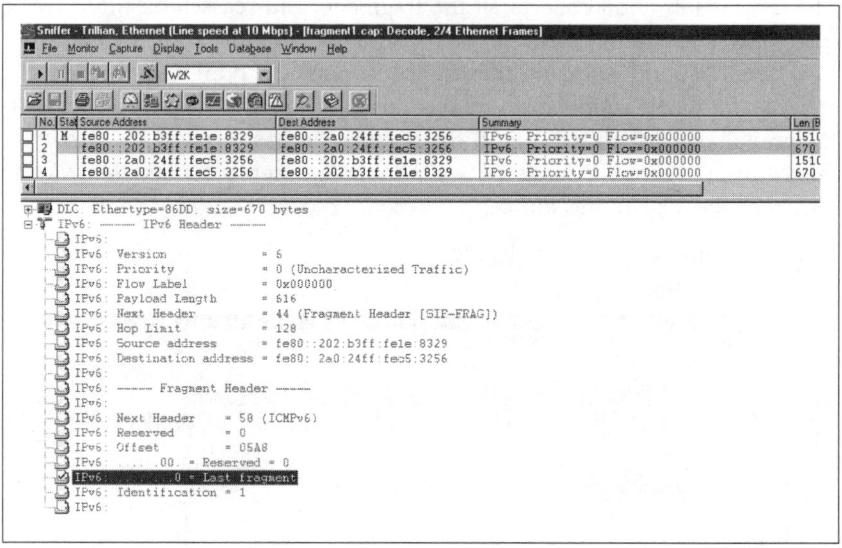

Figure 2-10. The last packet in the fragment set

The second and last packet of this fragment set has an Offset value of 0x05A8, which translates to 1448 in decimal, the length of the first fragment. The M-Flag is set to zero. This indicates that it is the last packet and tells the receiving host that it is time to reassemble the fragments. The Identification field is set to one in both packets.

Destination Options Header

A Destination Options header carries optional information that is examined by the destination node only. The Next Header value identifiying this type of header is the value 60. Figure 2-11 shows the format of the Destination Options header.

The following list describes each field:

Next Header (1 byte)
> The Next Header field identifies the type of header that follows the Destination Options header. It uses the same values listed in Table 2-1, earlier in this chapter.

Header Extension Length (1 byte)
> This field identifies the length of the Destination Options header in 8-byte units. The length calculation does not include the first 8 bytes.

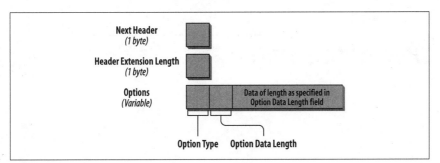

Figure 2-11. Format of the Destination Options header

Options (variable size)

There can be one or more options. The length of the options is variable and determined in the Header Extension Length field.

The Options field is used in the same way as the Hop-by-Hop Options header, which I discussed earlier in this chapter. An example of the Destination Options header is Mobile IPv6. A mobile IPv6 node connected to a foreign network can send packets with its care-of-address as a source address and its home address in a home address destination option. According to the current Mobile IPv6 draft, the ability to correctly process a home address in a Destination Option is required in all IPv6 nodes. For a detailed explanation of Mobile IPv6, refer to Chapter 7 or to the current draft of Mobile IPv6 at *http://www.ietf.org/internet-drafts/draft-ietf-mobileip-ipv6-17.txt*. Note that the draft number may have increased by one or more when you follow this link.

CHAPTER 3

IPv6 Addressing

An IPv4 address has 32 bits and is familiar. An IPv6 address has 128 bits and looks wild. Extending the address space was one of the driving reasons to develop IPv6, along with optimization of routing tables, especially on the Internet. This chapter will help you become familiar with the extended address space and will also explain how IPv6 addressing works and why it has been designed the way it is. The IPv6 addressing architecture is defined in RFC 2373, which obsoletes RFC 1884.

Address Types

IPv4 knows unicast, broadcast, and multicast addresses. With IPv6, the broadcast address is not used anymore; multicast addresses are used instead. This is good news because broadcasts are a problem in most networks. The *anycast* address, a new type of address introduced with RFC 1546, is now used with IPv6.

Unicast, Multicast, and Anycast Addresses

An IPv6 address can be classified into one of three categories:

Unicast
    A unicast address uniquely identifies an interface of an IPv6 node. A packet sent to a unicast address is delivered to the interface identified by that address.

Multicast
    A multicast address identifies a group of IPv6 interfaces. A packet sent to a multicast address is processed by all members of the multicast group.

Anycast

> An anycast address is assigned to multiple interfaces (usually on multiple nodes). A packet sent to an anycast address is delivered to only one of these interfaces, usually the nearest one.

Some General Rules

IPv6 addresses are assigned to interfaces, as in IPv4, not to nodes, as in OSI, so each interface of a node needs at least one unicast address. A single interface can also be assigned multiple IPv6 addresses of any type (unicast, multicast, anycast). A node can therefore be identified by the address of any of its interfaces. It is also possible to assign one unicast address to multiple interfaces for load-sharing reasons, but if you do this, you need to make sure that the hardware and the drivers support it. With IPv6, all zeros and ones are legal values for any field in an address, excluding some special combinations depending on address type (e.g., Subnet Router anycast address, RFC 2373). A typical IPv6 address consists of three parts—the *global routing prefix*, the *subnet ID,* and the *interface ID*—as shown in Figure 3-1.

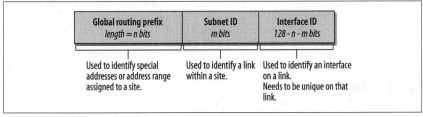

Figure 3-1. IPv6 general address format

The global routing prefix is used to identify a special address, such as multicast, or an address range assigned to a site. A subnet ID is used to identify a link within a site. (The subnet ID may also be referred to as subnet prefix or simply "subnet.") A subnet ID is associated with one link. Multiple subnet IDs may be assigned to one link. An interface ID is used to identify an interface on a link and needs to be unique on that link.

Address Notation

An IPv6 address has 128 bits, or 16 bytes. The address is divided into eight, 16-bit hexidecimal blocks, separated by colons. For example:

    FE80:0000:0000:0000:0202:B3FF:FE1E:8329

To make life easier, some abbreviations are possible. For instance, leading zeros in a 16-bit block can be skipped. The example address now looks like:

    FE80:0:0:0:202:B3FF:FE1E:8329

A double colon can replace consecutive zeros, or leading or trailing zeros, within the address. If we apply this rule, our address looks as follows:

```
FE80::202:B3FF:FE1E:8329
```

Note that the double colon can appear only once in an address. The reason for this rule is that the computer always uses a full 128-bit binary representation of the address, even if the displayed address is simplified. When the computer finds a double colon, it expands it with as many zeros as are needed to get 128 bits. If an address had two double colons, the computer would not know how many zeros to add for each. So the IPv6 address CAFF: CA01:0000:0056:0000:ABCD:EF12:1234 can be represented in the following ways (note the two possible positions for the double colon):

- CAFF:CA01:0000:0056:0000:ABCD:EF12:1234
- CAFF:CA01::56:0:ABCD:EF12:1234
- CAFF:CA01:0:56::ABCD:EF12:1234

In environments where IPv4 and IPv6 nodes are mixed, another convenient form of IPv6 address notation is to put the values of an IPv4 address into the four low-order byte pieces of the address. An IPv4 address of 192.168.0.2 can be represented by x:x:x:x:x:x:192.168.0.2 and an address of 0:0:0:0: 0:0:192.168.0.2 can be written as ::192.168.0.2. If you prefer, you can also write ::C0A8:2.

Prefix Notation

The notation for prefixes has also been specified in RFC 2373. A *format prefix* is the high-order bits of an IP address used to identify the subnet or a specific type of address (refer to Table 3-2). In newer drafts, it is called the global routing prefix. The prefix notation is very similar to the way IPv4 addresses are written in Classless Interdomain Routing (CIDR) notation, and it is also commonly used for subnetted IPv4 addresses. The notation appends the prefix length, written as a number of bits with a slash, which leads to the following format:

IPv6 address/prefix length

The prefix length specifies how many left-most bits of the address specify the prefix. This is another way of noting a subnet mask. Remember, a subnet mask specifies the bits of the IPv4 address that belong to the network ID. The prefix is used to identify the subnet that an interface belongs to and is used by routers for forwarding. The following example explains how the prefix is interpreted. Consider the IPv6 prefix notation 2E78:DA53:1200::/40. To understand this address, let's convert the hex into binary as shown in Table 3-1.

Table 3-1. *Understanding prefix notation*

Hex notation	Binary notation	Number of bits
2E 78	00101110 01111000	16 bits
DA 53	11011010 01010011	16 bits
12	00010010	8 bits, total 40 bits

The compressed notation (replacing a sequence of zeros with a double colon) is also applicable to the prefix representation. It should be used carefully, though, because there are often two or more ranges of zeros within an address, and only one can be compressed.

To play with the example in the previous section, look at the prefix notation. The address is CAFF:CA01:0000:0056:0000:ABCD:EF12:1234/64, but now we're just interested in the prefix of the address. Can we compress it as follows?

    CAFF:CA01::56/64

In order to verify this notation, we'll expand the address again. If we follow the notation rules, we end up with an address of CAFF:CA01:0000:0000:0000: 0000:0000:0056, with CAFF:CA01:0000:0000 for the 64-bit prefix. This is not the same as the original address and prefix. To make sure the address interpretation is unambiguous, we have to note it as CAFF:CA01:0:56::/64

Format Prefixes

RFC 2373 lists a number of format prefixes (also called global routing prefixes) that are used to identify special addresses, such as link-local addresses or multicast addresses. Table 3-2 outlines the initial assignment of reserved prefixes. The major part of the address space (over 80 percent) is unassigned, which leaves room for future assignments.

Table 3-2. *List of assigned prefixes*

Allocation	Prefix binary	Prefix hex	Fraction of address space
Reserved	0000 0000	::0/128	1/256
Reserved for NSAP allocation	0000 001		1/128
Reserved for IPX allocation (deprecated in later draft)	0000 010		1/128
Aggregatable global unicast addresses	001		1/8
Link-local unicast addresses	1111 1110 10	FE80::/10	1/1024
Site-local unicast addresses	1111 1110 11	FEC0::/10	1/1024
Multicast addresses	1111 1111	FF00::/8	1/256

Some special addresses are assigned out of the reserved address space with the binary prefix 0000 0000. These include the *unspecified address*, the *loopback address*, and IPv6 addresses with embedded IPv4 addresses, which will be discussed in detail later in this chapter. In drafts released after RFC 2373, the prefix for IPX has been removed. (The most recent draft, at the time of writing, is available at *http://www.ietf.org/internet-drafts/draft-ietf-ipngwg-addr-arch-v3-07.txt*.)

Unicast addresses can be distinguished from multicast addresses by their prefix. Globally unique unicast addresses have a high-order byte starting with 001. An IPv6 address with a high-order byte of 1111 1111 (FF in hex) is always a multicast address. For more information about multicast addresses, refer to the section "Multicast Address," later in this chapter.

Anycast addresses are taken from the unicast address space, so they can't be identified as anycast just by looking at the prefix. If you assign a unicast address to multiple interfaces, thereby making it an anycast address, you have to configure the interfaces so that they all know this address is an anycast address. For more information about anycast addresses, refer to the section "Anycast Address," later in this chapter.

Addresses in the prefix range 001 to 111 should use a 64-bit interface identifier that follows the EUI-64 (Extended Unique Identifier) format (except for multicast addresses with the prefix 1111 1111). The EUI-64 is a unique identifier defined by the Institute of Electrical and Electronics Engineers (IEEE); for more information, refer to *http://standards.ieee.org/regauth/oui/tutorials/EUI64.html*. Appendix A of RFC 2373 explains how to create EUI-64 identifiers, and more details can be found in the link-specific RFCs, such as "IPv6 over Ethernet" or "IPv6 over FDDI." Chapter 7 and this book's Appendix contain a short discussion and a complete list of these RFCs, respectively.

A host uses an identifier following the EUI-64 format during autoconfiguration. For example, when our Windows 2000 host Marvin autoconfigures for a link-local address on an Ethernet interface, the 64-bit interface identifier has to be created from the 48-bit (6-Byte) Ethernet MAC address. First, the hex digits 0xff-fe are inserted between the third and fourth bytes of the MAC address. Then the universal/local bit, the second low-order bit of 0x00 (the first Byte) of the MAC address, is complemented. The second low-order bit of 0x00 is 0, which, when complemented, becomes 1; as a result, the first Byte of the MAC address becomes 0x02. Therefore, the IPv6 interface identifier corresponding to the Ethernet MAC address 00-02-b3-1e-83-29 is 02-02-b3-ff-fe-1e-83-29. This example discusses only the EUI-64 creation process. Many other steps occur during autoconfiguration.

The link-local address of a node is the combination of the prefix fe80::/64 and a 64-bit interface identifier expressed in IPv6 colon-hexadecimal notation. Therefore, the link-local address of the previous example node, with prefix fe80::/64 and interface identifier 02-02-b3-ff-fe-1e-83-29, is fe80:: 202:b3ff:fe1e:8329. This process is described in RFC 2464, "Transmission of IPv6 Packets over Ethernet Networks."

To learn how IPv6 autoconfiguration works and what a stateless address is, refer to Chapter 4.

Address Privacy

The privacy of autoconfigured IPv6 addresses using the interface identifier is a major issue in the IETF. If an IPv6 address is built using the MAC identifier, your Internet access could be traced because this identifier is unique to your interface. Part of the concern is the result of a misunderstanding. An IPv6 node *can* have an address based on the interface identifier, but this is not a requirement. As an alternative, the IPv6 device can have an address like the ones currently used with IPv4, static and manually configured or dynamically assigned by a DHCP server. In early 2001, RFC 3041, "Privacy Extensions for Stateless Address Autoconfiguration in IPv6," was published; it introduces a new kind of address, available only in IPv6, that contains a random number in place of the factory-assigned serial number. This address can also change over time. An Internet device that is a target for IP communication—for instance, a web or FTP server—needs a unique and stable IP address. But a host running a browser or an FTP client does not need to have the same address every time it connects to the Internet. With the address architecture in IPv6, you can choose between two types of addresses:

Unique stable IP addresses
> Assigned through manual configuration, a DHCP server, or autoconfiguration using the interface identifier

Temporary transient IP addresses
> Assigned using a random number in place of the interface identifier

Link- and Site-Local Addresses

With IPv4, organizations often use IP addresses from the private range, as defined in RFC 1918. The addresses reserved for private use should never be forwarded over Internet routers, but should instead be confined to the organization's network. For connection to the Internet, Network Address Translation (NAT) maps internal private addresses to publicly registered IPv4 addresses.

IPv6 allocates two separate address spaces for link- and site-local use, both identified by their prefix. A *link-local* address is for use on a single link and should never be routed. It can be used for autoconfiguration mechanisms, for neighbor discovery, and on networks with no routers, so it is useful for creating temporary networks. Let's say you meet your friend in a conference room and you want to share files on your computers. You can connect your computers using a wireless network or a cross-cable between your Ethernet interfaces, and you can share files without any special configuration by using the link-local address. *Site-local* addresses contain subnet information within the address. They can be routed within a site, but routers should not forward them outside the site. Both address types can be used without a global prefix. The format of these two address types is shown in Figure 3-2.

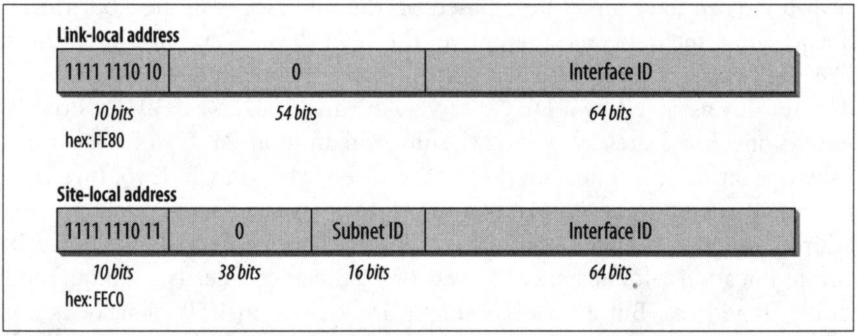

Link-local address

1111 1110 10	0	Interface ID
10 bits	54 bits	64 bits
hex: FE80		

Site-local address

1111 1110 11	0	Subnet ID	Interface ID
10 bits	38 bits	16 bits	64 bits
hex: FEC0			

Figure 3-2. Link- and site-local address format

In hexadecimal notation, a link-local address is identified by the prefix `fe80`; a site-local address is identified by the prefix `fec0`.

Aggregatable Global Unicast Address

Aggregatable global unicast addresses are identified by the prefix `001`, as shown earlier, in Table 3-2. The initial address specification defined *provider-based addresses*; the name has been changed to *aggregatable global unicast address*. The name change reflects the addition of an ISP-independent means of aggregation called *exchange-based aggregation*.

The prefix is followed by five components, as shown in Figure 3-3.

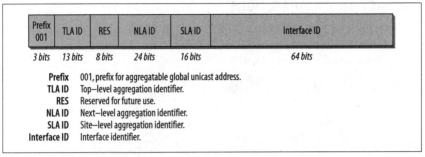

Prefix 001	TLA ID	RES	NLA ID	SLA ID	Interface ID
3 bits	13 bits	8 bits	24 bits	16 bits	64 bits

Prefix	001, prefix for aggregatable global unicast address.
TLA ID	Top–level aggregation identifier.
RES	Reserved for future use.
NLA ID	Next–level aggregation identifier.
SLA ID	Site–level aggregation identifier.
Interface ID	Interface identifier.

Figure 3-3. Format of the aggregatable global unicast address

The format prefix 001 is assigned to the aggregatable global unicast address range. The *top-level aggregation identifier (TLA)* contains the highest level of routing information about the address. Its size of 13 bits limits the number of top-level routes to 8192. In the earlier specification, the TLA was the provider-based identifier. It was assigned to the American Registry for Internet Numbers (ARIN) in North America, Réseau IP Européens (RIPE) Network Coordination Center in Europe, and Asia Pacific Network Information Center (APNIC). With this change in the specification, the commercial touch of the TLA has been removed and the focus is now on routing optimization; the TLA does not need to be a provider. At the core of the Internet, the routing tables need just one route entry per TLA, so the 13-bit TLA is large enough.

Providers and exchange points use the *next-level aggregation identifier (NLA)*. These network access providers are usually public, and they will further structure the address space assigned by the TLA with route topology optimization as a priority.

The *site-level aggregation identifier (SLA)* is the address space assigned to organizations, used for internal network structure. It can be subnetted further within the organization. The last part of the address is used for the 64-bit interface identifier, as discussed earlier in this chapter.

Many discussions have been going on in recent months, and the area of address assignment is still evolving. A number of clarifications are described in the Internet draft available at *http://www.ietf.org/internet-drafts/draft-ietf-ipngwg-addr-arch-v3-07.txt*. (Note that the draft number may have increased by one or more when you go there.)

International Registry Services and Current Address Allocations

Several TLA allocations have been made, as listed in Table 3-3.

Table 3-3. Current TLA allocations

Prefix	Allocation	RFC
2001::/16	Sub-TLA Assignments	RFC 2450
	ARIN 2001:0400::/29	
	RIPE NCC 2001:0600::/29	
	APNIC 2001:0200::/29	
2002::/16	6to4	RFC 3056
3FFE::/16	6Bone Testing	RFC 2471

 http://www.iana.org/ipaddress/ip-addresses.htm is a great entry point for global IP address services, current address allocations for both IPv4 and IPv6, and information about how to request IPv6 address services.

ISPs can use the following sites to access their regional registry for information about IPv6 address registration. For end users, IPv6 address allocation is managed by their ISP.

- ARIN Registration Services, *http://www.arin.net/library/guidelines/ ipv6_initial.html*
- RIPE-NCC Registration Services, *http://www.ripe.net/ripencc/ mem-services/registration/ipv6.html*
- APNIC Registration FAQ, *http://www.apnic.net/faq/IPv6-FAQ.html*

As I've already mentioned, address allocation is a work in progress. Information about the latest status, clarifications, and current practices can be found at *http://www.arin.net*. There is also an informational RFC called "IAB/IESG Recommendations on IPv6 Address Allocations to Sites," numbered RFC 3177.

Special Addresses

There are a number of special addresses that we need to discuss. The first part of the IPv6 address space with the prefix of 0000 0000 is reserved. Out of this prefix, special addresses have been defined as follows:

The unspecified address

The unspecified address has a value of 0:0:0:0:0:0:0:0 and is therefore also called the all-zeros address. It is comparable to 0.0.0.0 in IPv4. It indicates the absence of a valid address, and it can, for example, be used as a source address by a host during the boot process when it sends out a request for address configuration information. If you apply the notation conventions discussed earlier in this chapter, the unspecified address can also be abbreviated ::. It should never be statically or dynamically assigned to an interface, and it should not appear as a destination IP address or within an IPv6 routing header.

The loopback address

The IPv4 loopback address, 127.0.0.1, is probably familiar. It is helpful in troubleshooting and testing the IP stack because it can be used to send a packet to the protocol stack, without sending it out on the subnet. With IPv6, the loopback address works the same way and is represented as 0:0:0:0:0:0:0:1, abbreviated ::1. It should never be statically or dynamically assigned to an interface.

The next three sections describe three different types of addresses that have been specified to be used with different transition mechanisms. These virtual interfaces are called *pseudo-interfaces*.

IPv6 addresses with embedded IPv4 addresses

Because the transition to IPv6 will be gradual, two special types of addresses have been defined for backward compatibility with IPv4. Both are described in RFC 2373:

IPv4-compatible IPv6 address

This type of address is used to tunnel IPv6 packets dynamically over an IPv4 routing infrastructure. IPv6 nodes that use this technique are assigned a special IPv6 unicast address that carries an IPv4 address in the low-order 32 bits.

IPv4-mapped IPv6 address

This type of address is used to represent the addresses of IPv4-only nodes. This address can be used by an IPv6 node to send a packet to an IPv4-only node. The address also carries the IPv4 address in the low-order 32 bits of the address.

Figure 3-4 shows the format of both these addresses.

The two addresses are pretty much the same. The only difference is the 16 bits in the middle. When they are set to zero, the address is an IPv4-compatible IPv6 address; if these bits are set to one, it is an IPv4-mapped IPv6 address.

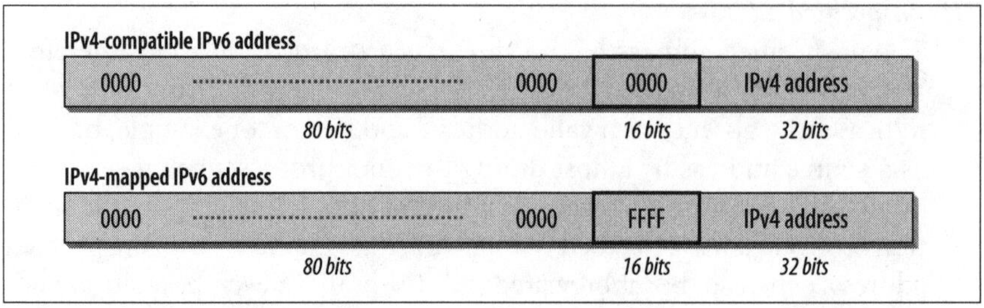

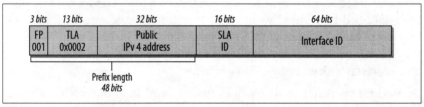

Figure 3-4. Format of IPv6 addresses with an embedded IPv4 address

6to4 addresses

The IANA has permanently assigned a 13-bit TLA identifier for 6to4 operations within the aggregatable global unicast address range (001). 6to4 is one
of the mechanisms defined to let IPv6 hosts or networks communicate over
an IPv4-only infrastructure without explicit tunnel setup. 6to4 is described
in Chapter 10 and in RFC 3056. The 6to4 TLA identifier is 0x0002. The
address format is shown in Figure 3-5.

Figure 3-5. Format of the 6to4 address

The prefix has a total length of 48 bits. The IPv4 address in the prefix must
be a public IPv4 address and is represented in hexadecimal notation. For
instance, if you configure an interface for 6to4 with an IPv4 address of 62.2.
84.115, the 6to4 address is 2002:3e02:5473::/48. Through this interface, all
IPv6 hosts on this link can tunnel their packets over the IPv4 infrastructure.

ISATAP addresses

A new automatic tunneling mechanism, called Intra-Site Automatic Tunnel
Addressing Protocol (ISATAP), is currently being defined. It is designed to
let IPv6 hosts communicate easily within an IPv4 infrastructure. It is still in
the draft stage, but it might become popular. Windows XP already includes
an implementation of ISATAP (described in Chapter 11). It uses a type identifier of 0xFE for specifying an IPv6 address with an embedded IPv4 address.
The format of an ISATAP address according to the current draft is shown in
Figure 3-6.

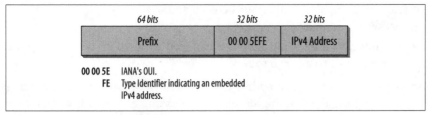

64 bits	32 bits	32 bits
Prefix	00 00 5EFE	IPv4 Address

00 00 5E	IANA's OUI.
FE	Type Identifier indicating an embedded IPv4 address.

Figure 3-6. Format of the ISATAP address

The first 64 bits follow the format of the aggregatable global unicast address. IANA owns the IEEE Organizationally Unique Identifier (OUI) 00 00 5E and specifies the EUI-48 format interface identifier assignments within that OUI. The next 8 bits are used for a type identifier to indicate that this is an IPv6 address with an embedded IPv4 address. The type identifier is 0xFE. The last 32 bits contain the embedded IPv4 address, which can be written in dotted decimal notation or in hexadecimal representation.

Assume we have a host with an IPv4 address of 192.168.0.1 and the host is assigned a 64-bit prefix of 3FFE:1a05:510:200::/64. The ISATAP address for this host is 3FFE:1a05:510:200:0:5EFE:192.168.0.1. Alternatively, you can use the hexadecimal representation for the IPv4 address, in which case the address is written 3FFE:1a05:510:200:0:5EFE:C0A8:1.

The link-local address for this host is FE80::5EFE:192.168.0.1 and the site-local address is FEC0::200:0:5EFE:192.168.0.1.

> To learn how IPv6 and IPv4 can coexist using these addresses, refer to Chapter 10.

Anycast Address

As already mentioned, anycast addresses are in the same address range as aggregatable global unicast addresses, and each participating interface must be configured as having an anycast address. Within the region where the interfaces containing the same anycast addresses are, each host must be advertised as a separate entry in the routing tables. If the anycast interfaces have no definable region, each anycast entry (in the worst case) has to be propagated throughout the Internet, which obviously does not scale. It is expected, therefore, that support for such global anycast addresses will be either unavailable or very restricted. Until there is more experience gained, the following restrictions are defined in RFC 2373.

- An anycast address must not be used as the source address of an IPv6 packet.

- An anycast address must not be assigned to an IPv6 host. It may be assigned only to an IPv6 router.

An expected use of anycast addresses is to identify a set of routers providing access to a particular routing domain. One example is the 6to4 relay anycast address that is specified in RFC 3068 and described in Chapter 10. Another possibility is to configure with a specific anycast address all the routers within a corporate network that provide access to the Internet. Whenever a packet is sent to that anycast address, it will be delivered to the closest router that provides Internet access.

A required anycast address is the *subnet-router anycast address*, which is defined in RFC 2373 and shown in Figure 3-7.

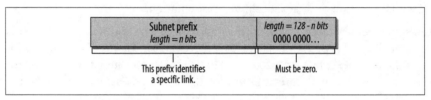

Figure 3-7. Format of the subnet-router anycast address

Basically, the address is like a regular unicast address with a prefix specifying the subnet and an identifier that is set to all zeros. A packet sent to this address will be delivered to one router on that subnet. All routers are required to support the subnet-router anycast address for subnets to which they have interfaces.

RFC 2526 provides more information about anycast address formats and specifies other reserved subnet anycast addresses and IDs. A reserved subnet anycast address can have one of two formats, as shown in Figure 3-8.

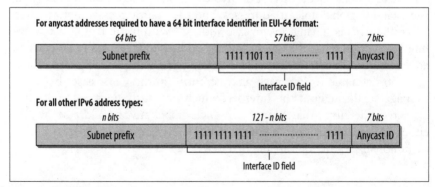

Figure 3-8. General format of anycast addresses

RFC 2526 specifies that within each subnet, the highest 128 interface identifier values are reserved for assignment as subnet anycast addresses. Currently, the anycast IDs listed in Table 3-4 have been reserved.

Table 3-4. Reserved anycast IDs

Decimal	Hexadecimal	Description
127	7F	Reserved
126	7E	Mobile IPv6 Home-Agents anycast
0-125	00-7D	Reserved

Multicast Address

A multicast address is an identifier for a group of nodes, identified by the high-order byte FF, or 1111 1111 in binary notation (refer to Table 3-2). A node can belong to more than one multicast group. Multicast exists in IPv4, but it has been redefined and improved for IPv6. The multicast address format is shown in Figure 3-9.

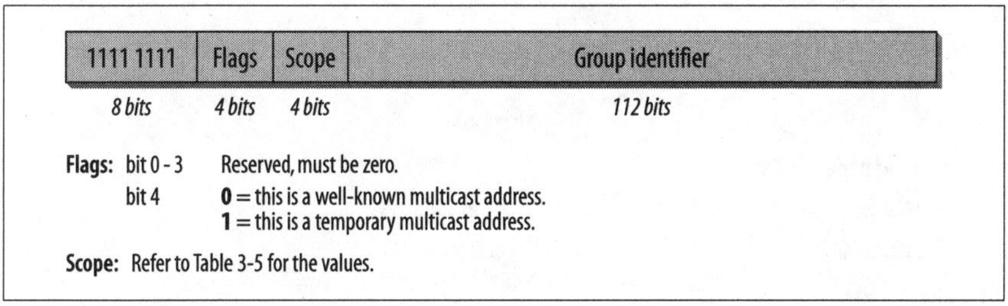

1111 1111	Flags	Scope	Group identifier
8 bits	4 bits	4 bits	112 bits

Flags: bit 0 - 3   Reserved, must be zero.
        bit 4   **0** = this is a well-known multicast address.
                 1 = this is a temporary multicast address.

Scope: Refer to Table 3-5 for the values.

Figure 3-9. Format of the multicast address

The first byte identifies the address as a multicast address. The next 4 bits are used for Flags, defined as follows: The first 3 bits of the Flag field must be zero; they are reserved for future use. The last bit of the Flag field indicates whether this address is permanently assigned—i.e., one of the well-known multicast addresses assigned by the IANA—or a temporary multicast address. A value of zero for the last bit defines a well-known address; a value of one indicates a temporary address. The Scope field is used to limit the scope of a multicast address. The possible values are shown in Table 3-5.

Table 3-5. Values for the Scope field

Value	Description
0	Reserved
1	Node-local scope (name changed to interface-local in new draft)
2	Link-local scope
3, 4	Unassigned

Table 3-5. Values for the Scope field (continued)

Value	Description
5	Site-local scope
6, 7	Unassigned
8	Organization-local scope
9, A, B, C, D	Unassigned
E	Global scope
F	Reserved

Well-Known Multicast Addresses

The last 112 bits of the address carry the multicast group ID. RFC 2375 defines the initial assignment of IPv6 multicast addresses that are permanently assigned. Some assignments are made for fixed scopes, and some assignments are valid over all scopes. Table 3-6 gives an overview of the addresses that have been assigned for fixed scopes. Note the scope values that you learned in Table 3-5 in the byte just following the multicast identifier of FF (first Byte).

Table 3-6. Well-known multicast addresses

Address	Description
Interface- or node-local scope	
FF01:0:0:0:0:0:0:1	All-nodes address
FF01:0:0:0:0:0:0:2	All-routers address
Link-local scope	
FF02:0:0:0:0:0:0:1	All-nodes address
FF02:0:0:0:0:0:0:2	All-routers address
FF02:0:0:0:0:0:0:3	Unassigned
FF02:0:0:0:0:0:0:4	DVMRP routers
FF02:0:0:0:0:0:0:5	OSPFIGP
FF02:0:0:0:0:0:0:6	OSPFIGP designated routers
FF02:0:0:0:0:0:0:7	ST routers
FF02:0:0:0:0:0:0:8	ST hosts
FF02:0:0:0:0:0:0:9	RIP routers
FF02:0:0:0:0:0:0:A	EIGRP routers
FF02:0:0:0:0:0:0:B	Mobile agents
FF02:0:0:0:0:0:0:D	All PIM routers
FF02:0:0:0:0:0:0:E	RSVP encapsulation
FF02:0:0:0:0:0:1:1	Link name
FF02:0:0:0:0:0:1:2	All DHCP agents
FF02:0:0:0:0:1:FFXX:XXXX	Solicited-node address

Table 3-6. Well-known multicast addresses (continued)

Address	Description
Site-local scope	
FF05:0:0:0:0:0:0:2	All-routers address
FF05:0:0:0:0:0:1:3	All DHCP servers
FF05:0:0:0:0:0:1:4	All DHCP relays
FF05:0:0:0:0:0:1:1000 to FF05:0:0:0:0:0:01:13FF	Service location

The term "node-local scope" from RFC 2375 has been changed to "interface-local scope" in later drafts, so you might encounter both terms. The list for the permanently assigned multicast addresses that are independent of scopes is long and is available in the Appendix or in RFC 2375. All those addresses are noted beginning with FF0X; X is the placeholder for a variable scope value.

As an example, let's look at the one described in RFC 2373. There is a multicast group ID defined for all NTP servers. The multicast group ID is 0x101. This group ID can be used with different scope values as follows:

FF01:0:0:0:0:0:0:101
  All NTP servers on the same node as the sender

FF02:0:0:0:0:0:0:101
  All NTP servers on the same link as the sender

FF05:0:0:0:0:0:0:101
  All NTP servers on the same site as the sender

FF0E:0:0:0:0:0:0:101
  All NTP servers in the Internet

Temporarily assigned multicast addresses are meaningful only within a defined scope.

> Multicast addresses should not be used as a source address in IPv6 packets or appear in any routing header.

To learn how multicast addresses are managed, refer to the section "Multicast Group Management" in Chapter 4.

Solicited-Node Multicast Address

The *solicited-node multicast address* is a multicast address that every node must join for every unicast and anycast address it is assigned. It is used in the Duplicate Address Detection (DAD) process, described in Chapter 4. RFC 2373 specifies the solicited-node multicast address.

This address is formed by taking the low-order 24 bits of an IPv6 address (the last part of the host ID) and appending those bits to the well-known prefix FF02:0:0:0:0:1:FF00::/104. Thus, the range for solicited-node multicast addresses goes from FF02:0:0:0:0:1:FF00:0000 to FF02:0:0:0:0:1:FFFF:FFFF.

For example, our host Marvin has the MAC address 00-02-B3-1E-83-29 and the IPv6 address fe80::202:b3ff:fe1e:8329. The corresponding solicited-node multicast address is FF02::1:ff1e:8329. If this host has other IPv6 unicast or anycast addresses, each one will have a corresponding solicited-node multicast address.

Required Addresses

The standard specifies that each host must assign the following addresses to identify itself:

- Its link-local address for each interface
- Any assigned unicast addresses
- The loopback address
- The all-nodes multicast address
- Solicited-node multicast address for each of its assigned unicast and anycast addresses
- Multicast addresses of all other groups to which the host belongs

A router needs to recognize all of the above plus the following:

- The subnet-router anycast address for the interfaces for which it is configured to act as a router on each link
- All anycast addresses with which the router has been configured
- The all-routers multicast address
- Multicast addresses of all other groups to which the router belongs

Now that we are familiar with the extended address space and the IPv6 address types, the next chapter introduces the advanced features of ICMPv6, which offer management functionality not known with ICMPv4.

CHAPTER 4

ICMPv6

If you are familiar with IPv4, the Internet Control Message Protocol (ICMP) for IPv4 is probably a good friend of yours: it gives important information about the health of the network. ICMPv6 is the version that works with IPv6. It reports errors if packets cannot be processed properly and sends informational messages about the status of the network. For example, if a router cannot forward a packet because it is too large to be sent out on another network, it sends back an ICMP message to the originating host. The source host can use this ICMP message to determine a better packet size and then resend the data. ICMP also performs diagnostic functions, such as the well-known ping, which uses ICMP Echo Request and Echo Reply messages to test availability of a node.

ICMPv6 is much more powerful than ICMPv4 and contains new functionality, as described in this chapter. For instance, the Internet Group Management Protocol (IGMP) function that manages multicast group memberships with IPv4 has been incorporated into ICMPv6. The same is true for the Address Resolution Protocol/Reverse Address Resolution Protocol (ARP/RARP) function that is used in IPv4 to map layer 2 addresses to IP addresses (and vice versa). Neighbor discovery (ND) is introduced; it uses ICMPv6 messages in order to determine link-layer addresses for neighbors attached to the same link, to find routers, to keep track of which neighbors are reachable, and to detect changed link-layer addresses. ICMPv6 also supports Mobile IPv6, which is described in Chapter 7. ICMPv6 is part of IPv6 and it must be implemented fully by every IPv6 node. It is defined in RFC 2463 (obsoletes RFC 1885). Neighbor discovery is defined in RFC 2461 (obsoletes RFC 1970).

General Message Format

There are two classes of ICMP messages:

ICMP error messages
Error messages have a zero in the high-order bit of their message Type field. ICMP error message types are therefore in the range 0 to 127.

ICMP informational messages
Informational messages have a one in the high-order bit of their message Type field. ICMP informational message types are therefore in the range 128 to 255.

An IPv6 header and zero or more extension headers precede every ICMPv6 message. The header just preceding the ICMP header has a next header value of 58. This value is different from the value for ICMPv4 (which has the value 1).

> The values for the next header field are discussed in Chapter 2.

The following message types are described in RFC 2463:

- ICMPv6 error messages
  - Destination Unreachable (message type 1)
  - Packet Too Big (message type 2)
  - Time Exceeded (message type 3)
  - Parameter Problem (message type 4)
- ICMPv6 informational messages
  - Echo Request (message type 128)
  - Echo Reply (message type 129)

> For the most current list of ICMPv6 message types, refer to the Internet Assigned Number Authority (IANA) at *http:// www.iana.org/assignments/icmpv6-parameters*. All IPv4 ICMP parameters can be found at *http://www.iana.org/ assignments/icmp-parameters*.

All ICMPv6 messages have the same general header structure, shown in Figure 4-1. Notice that the first three fields for type, code, and checksum have not changed from ICMPv4.

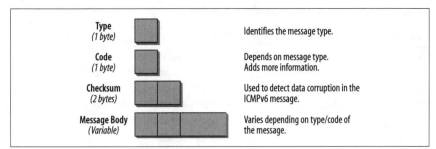

Type (1 byte)		Identifies the message type.
Code (1 byte)		Depends on message type. Adds more information.
Checksum (2 bytes)		Used to detect data corruption in the ICMPv6 message.
Message Body (Variable)		Varies depending on type/code of the message.

Figure 4-1. General ICMPv6 header format

Type (1 Byte)

This field specifies the type of message, which determines the format of the remainder of the message. Table 4-1 and Table 4-2 list ICMPv6 message types and message numbers.

Code (1 Byte)

The Code field depends on the message type and allows for more granular information in certain cases. Refer to Table 4-1 and Table 4-2 for a detailed list.

Checksum (2 Bytes)

The Checksum field is used to detect data corruption in the ICMPv6 header and in parts of the IPv6 header. In order to calculate the checksum, a node must determine the source and destination address in the IPv6 header. If the node has more than one unicast address, there are rules for choosing the address (refer to RFC 2463 for details). There is also a pseudoheader included in the checksum calculation, which is new with ICMPv6.

Message Body (Variable Size)

Depending on the type and code, the message body will hold different data. In the case of an error message, it will contain as much as possible of the packet that invoked the message to assist in troubleshooting. The total size of the ICMPv6 packet should not exceed the minimum IPv6 MTU, which is 1280 bytes. Table 4-1 and Table 4-2 provide an overview of the different message types, along with the additional code information, which depends on the message type.

Table 4-1. ICMPv6 error messages and code types

Message number	Message type	Code field
1	Destination Unreachable	0 = no route to destination
		1 = communication with destination administratively prohibited
		2 = beyond scope of source address (draft)
		3 = address unreachable
		4 = port unreachable
2	Packet Too Big	Code field set to 0 (zero) by the sender and ignored by the receiver
3	Time Exceeded	0 = hop limit exceeded in transit
		1 = fragment reassembly time exceeded
4	Parameter Problem	0 = erroneous header field encountered
		1 = unrecognized next header type encountered
		2 = unrecognized IPv6 option encountered
		The pointer field identifies the octet offset within the invoking packet where the error was detected. The pointer points beyond the end of the ICMPv6 packet if the field in error is beyond what can fit in the maximum size of an ICMPv6 error message.

Note that the message numbers and types have substantially changed compared to ICMPv4. ICMP for IPv6 is a different protocol, and the two versions of ICMP are not compatible. Your analyzer should properly decode all this information, so you do not have to worry memorizing it.

Table 4-2. ICMPv6 informational messages

Message number	Message type	Description
128	Echo Request	RFC 2463. Both used for the ping command.
129	Echo Reply	
130	Multicast Listener Query	RFC 2710. Used for multicast goup management (IPv4 uses IGMP for this functionality).
131	Multicast Listener Report	
132	Multicast Listener Done	
133	Router Solicitation	RFC 2461. Used for neighbor discovery and autoconfiguration.
134	Router Advertisement	
135	Neighbor Solicitation	
136	Neighbor Advertisement	
137	Redirect Message	

Table 4-2. ICMPv6 informational messages (continued)

Message number	Message type	Description
138	Router Renumbering	RFC 2894
139	ICMP Node Information Query	Draft number at the time of writing: *http://www.ietf.org/ internet-drafts/draft-ietf-ipngwg-icmp-name-lookups-09. txt.*
140	ICMP Node Information Response	
141	Inverse ND Solicitation	RFC 3122
142	Inverse ND Adv Message	RFC 3122
150	ICMP Home Agent Address Discovery Request Message	Experimental / Draft—ICMPv6 Messages for Mobile IPv6 Draft number at time of writing: *http://www.ietf.org/ internet-drafts/draft-ietf-mobileip-ipv6-17.txt.*
151	ICMP Home Agent Address Discovery Reply Message	Message numbers have not yet been assigned by IANA.
152	ICMP Mobile Prefix Solicitation Message Format	
153	ICMP Mobile Prefix Advertisement Message Format	

ICMP Error Messages

Every ICMP message can have a slightly different header depending on the kind of error report or information it carries. The following sections outline the structure of each type of ICMPv6 message.

Destination Unreachable

A Destination Unreachable message is generated if an IP datagram cannot be delivered. A Type field with the value 1 identifies this message. The ICMP message is sent to the source address of the invoking packet. The format of the Destination Unreachable message is shown in Figure 4-2.

The Type field is set to one, which is the value for the Destination Unreachable message. The Code field supplies more information about the reason why the datagram was not delivered. The possible codes are listed in Table 4-3. The data portion of the ICMP message contains parts of the original message—as much as will fit into the ICMP message.

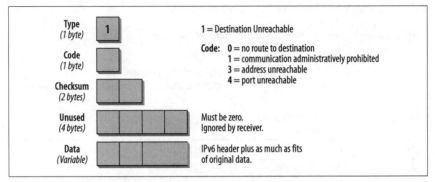

Figure 4-2. Format of the Destination Unreachable message

Table 4-3. Code values of the Destination Unreachable message (type 1)

Code	Description
0	No route to destination
	This message is generated if a router cannot forward a packet because it does not have a route in its table for a destination network. This can only happen if the router does not have an entry for a default route.
1	Communication with destination administratively prohibited
	This type of message can, for example, be sent by a firewall that cannot forward a packet to a host inside the firewall because of a packet filter. It might also be sent if a node is configured not to accept unauthenticated Echo Requests.
2	Beyond scope of source address
	This code is used when the multicast scope of the source address is smaller than the scope of the destination address. This code is a draft at the time of writing (*http://www.ietf.org/internet-drafts/draft-ietf-ipngwg-icmp-v3-02.txt*).
3	Address unreachable
	This code is used if a destination address cannot be resolved into a corresponding network address or if there is a data-link layer problem preventing the node from reaching the destination network.
4	Port unreachable
	This code is used if the transport protocol (e.g., UDP) has no listener and if there is no other means to inform the sender. For example, if a Domain Name System (DNS) query is sent to a host and the DNS server is not running, this type of message is generated.

If the destination is unreachable due to congestion, no ICMP message is generated. A host that receives a Destination Unreachable message must inform the upper-layer process.

Packet Too Big

If a router cannot forward a packet because it is larger than the MTU of the outgoing link, it will generate a Packet Too Big message (shown in

Figure 4-3). This ICMPv6 message type is used as part of the Path MTU discovery process discussed later in this chapter. The ICMP message is sent to the source address of the invoking packet.

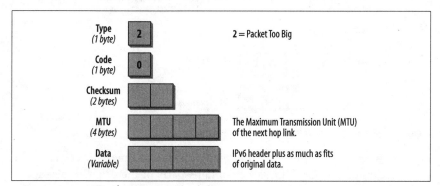

Figure 4-3. Format of the Packet Too Big message

The Type field has the value 2, which identifies the Packet Too Big message. In this case, the Code field is not used and is set to zero. The important information for this type of message is the MTU field, which contains the MTU size of the next hop link.

RFC 2463 states that an ICMPv6 message should not be generated as a response to a packet with an IPv6 multicast destination address, a link-layer multicast address, or a link-layer broadcast address. The Packet Too Big message is an exception to this rule. Because the ICMP message contains the supported MTU of the next hop link, the source host can determine the MTU that it should use for further communication. A host that receives a Packet Too Big message must inform the upper-layer process.

Time Exceeded

When a router forwards a packet, it always decrements the hop limit by one. Remember, the hop limit makes sure that a packet does not endlessly travel through a network. If a router receives a packet with a hop limit of one and decrements the limit to zero, it discards the packet, generates a Time Exceeded message with a code value of zero, and sends this message back to the source host. This error can indicate a routing loop or the fact that the sender's initial hop limit is too low. It can also tell you that someone used the *traceroute* utility, which is described later in the chapter. Figure 4-4 shows the format of the Time Exceeded message.

The Type field carries the value 3, specifying the Time Exceeded message. The Code field can be set to 0, which means hop limit exceeded in transit,

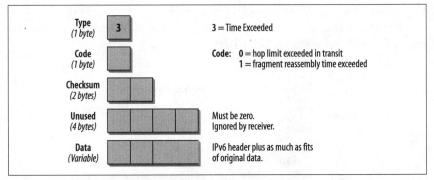

Figure 4-4. Format of the Time Exceeded message

or to 1, which means that the fragment reassembly time is exceeded. The data portion of the ICMP message contains parts of the original message—as much as fits into the ICMP message, depending on the MTU used.

An incoming Time Exceeded message must be passed to the upper-layer process. Table 4-4 shows the Code fields for the Time Exceeded message.

Table 4-4. Code values for Time Exceeded message (type 3)

Code	Description
0	Hop limit exceeded in transit.
	Possible causes: the initial hop limit value is too low, or there are routing loops.
1	Fragment reassembly time exceeded.
	If a fragmented packet is sent by using a fragment header (refer to Chapter 2 for more details) and the receiving host cannot reassemble all packets within a certain time, it notifies the sender by issuing this ICMP message.

The hop limit exceeded in transit message type is commonly used to do the *traceroute* function. *Traceroute* is helpful in determining the path that a packet takes when traveling through the network. In order to do this, a first packet is sent out with a hop limit of one. The first router in the path decrements the hop limit to zero, discards the packet, and sends back an ICMP message type three, code zero. The source host now knows the address of the first hop router. Next, it sends out a second packet with a hop limit of two. This packet is forwarded by the first router, which decrements the hop limit to one. The second router in the path decrements the hop limit to zero, discards the packet, and sends back an ICMP message type three, code zero. Now the source knows about the second router in the path. Raising the hop limit by one (with every packet sent until the packet reaches the final destination) continues this process. Every router in the path to the final destination sends an ICMP message back to the source host, thereby providing its

IP address. It is important to know that if there are redundant paths to the destination, *traceroute* does not necessarily show the same route for all tests because it might choose different paths.

Parameter Problem

If an IPv6 node cannot complete the processing of a packet because it has a problem identifying a field in the IPv6 header or in an Extension header, it must discard the packet and it should send an ICMP Parameter Problem message back to the source of the problem packet. This type of message is often used when an error that does not fit into any of the other categories is encountered. The format of this ICMP message is shown in Figure 4-5.

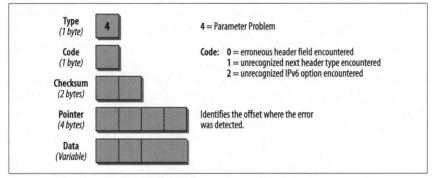

Figure 4-5. Format of the Parameter Problem message

The Type field has the value 4, which specifies the Parameter Problem message. The Code field can contain any of the three values described in Table 4-5. The Pointer field identifies at which byte in the original packet the error was detected. The ICMP message includes as much of the original data as fits up to the minimum IPv6 MTU. It is possible that the pointer points beyond the ICMPv6 message. This would be the case if the field in error was beyond what can fit in the maximum size of an ICMPv6 error message.

Table 4-5 shows the Code fields for the Parameter Problem message.

Table 4-5. Code values for Parameter Problem (type 4)

Code	Description
0	Erroneous header field encountered
1	Unrecognized next header type encountered
2	Unrecognized IPv6 option encountered

For example, if you see an ICMPv6 message of type 4 with a code value of 1 and a pointer set to 40, this indicates that the next header type in the header following the IPv6 header was unrecognized.

ICMP Informational Messages

In RFC 2463, two types of informational messages are defined: the Echo Request and the Echo Reply messages. Other ICMP informational messages are used for Path MTU Discovery and neighbor discovery. These messages are discussed at the end of this chapter and defined in RFC 2461, "Neighbor Discovery for IP Version 6," and RFC 1981, "Path MTU Discovery for IP version 6."

The Echo Request and Echo Reply messages are used for one of the most common TCP/IP utilities: Packet INternet Groper (ping). Ping is used to determine if a specified host is available on the network and ready to communicate. The source host issues an Echo Request message to the specified destination. The destination host, if available, responds with an Echo Reply message. In Chapter 11, you can find a screenshot that shows you what an IPv6 ping looks like in the trace file, as well as the command you need to ping over IPv6.

Echo Request Message

The format of the Echo Request message is shown in Figure 4-6.

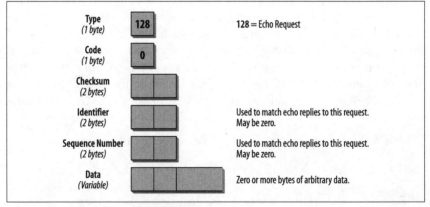

Figure 4-6. Format of the Echo Request message

The Type Field is set to 128, the value for the Echo Request. The Code Field is not used for this message and is therefore set to zero. The Identifier and Sequence Number fields are used to match requests with replies. The reply must always contain the same numbers as the request. Whether an identifier and a sequence number are used and what kind of arbitrary data is included in the Echo Request depends on the TCP/IP stack you are using. When you analyze trace files with Echo Request and Echo Reply messages and you are familiar with some stacks, you can determine the TCP/IP stack of the sender by looking at the arbitrary data. You can see an example of this in Figure 4-8, later in this chapter.

Echo Reply

The format of the Echo Reply message is very similar to that of the Echo Request, as shown in Figure 4-7.

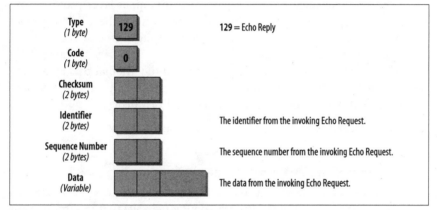

Figure 4-7. Format of the Echo Reply message

The Type field contains the value 129 for Echo Reply. The Code field is unused and set to zero. The Identifier and Sequence Number fields must match the fields in the request. The data of the Echo Request message must be copied into the reply entirely and unmodified. If an upper-layer process initiated the Echo Request, the reply must be passed to that process. If the Echo Request message was sent to a unicast address, the source address of the Echo Reply message must be the same as the destination address of the Echo Request message. If the Echo Request was sent to an IPv6 multicast address, the source address of the Echo Reply must be a unicast address of the interface on which the multicast Echo Request was received.

ICMPv6 Echo Request and Reply messages can be authenticated, using an IPv6 authentication header. This means that a node can be configured to ignore nonauthenticated ICMPv6 pings and provide protection against different sorts of ICMPv6 attacks.

Processing Rules

There are several rules that govern processing of ICMP packets. They can be found in RFC 2463 and are summarized as follows:

- If a node receives an ICMPv6 error message of unknown type, it must pass it to the upper layer.
- If a node receives an ICMPv6 informational message of unknown type, it must be silently discarded.
- As in ICMPv4, as much as possible of the packet that caused the ICMP error message will be included in the ICMP message body. The ICMP packet should not exceed the minimum IPv6 MTU.
- If the error message has to be passed to the upper-layer protocol, the protocol type is determined by extracting it from the original packet (present in the body of the ICMPv6 error message). In case the protocol type cannot be found in the body of the ICMPv6 message (because there were too many extension headers present in the original packet and the part of the header that contained the upper-layer protocol type was truncated), the ICMPv6 message is silently discarded.

An ICMPv6 message must not be sent in the following cases:

- As a result of an ICMPv6 error message.
- As a result of an ICMPv6 redirect message.
- As a result of a packet sent to an IPv6 multicast address. There are two exceptions to this rule: the Packet Too Big message that is used for Path MTU discovery and the Parameter Problem with the code value 2 for an unrecognized IPv6 option.
- As a result of a packet sent as a link-layer multicast (same exceptions as above apply).
- As a result of a packet sent as a link-layer broadcast (same exceptions as above apply).
- As a result of a packet whose source address does not uniquely identify a single node. This could be an IPv6 unspecified address, an IPv6 multicast address, or an IPv6 address known to be an anycast address.

Every IPv6 node must implement a rate-limiting function that limits the rate of ICMPv6 messages it sends. The configurable limit can be either timer- or bandwidth-based. If this function is implemented properly, it protects against denial-of-service attacks.

The ICMPv6 Header in a Trace File

After reading through all that dry information, you deserve something different. The following screenshot (Figure 4-8) shows what a ping looks like in the trace file and provides details of many of the fields we have discussed so far.

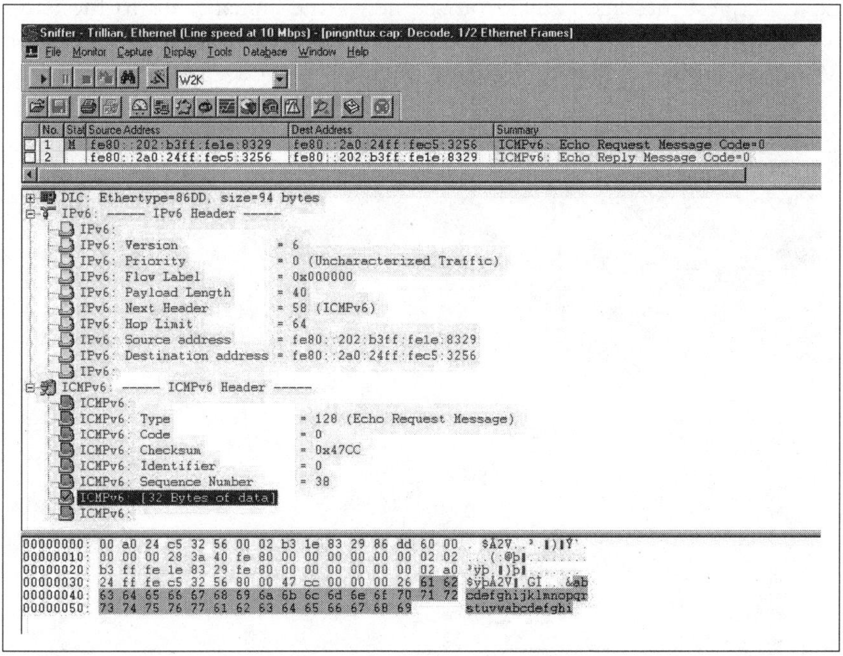

Figure 4-8. Echo Request in a trace file

The two frames in this trace file were captured when my Windows 2000 host issued a ping command to a Linux host. Note that the source address of the second frame, the Echo Reply, is the same as the destination address in the first frame, the Echo Request. The IPv6 header provides more information. The Version field indicates that this is an IPv6 packet. The Next Header field has the value 58, which is the value for ICMPv6. We can also see source and destination IP address. The prefix fe80: indicates that these two addresses are link-local addresses.

Note the first three fields of the ICMPv6 header. They are the fields that are common for every ICMPv6 message: Type, Code, and Checksum field. The Type field contains the value 128, which is the value for an Echo Request.

The Identifier and Sequence Number fields are unique to the Echo Request and Echo Reply message. The Identifier is not used in this case and the sender has set the sequence to 38. It has to be identical in the matching reply that is shown in the following screenshot. The Data field contains arbitrary data that doesn't need to make sense to anyone.

Oh, I almost forgot: I promised to show vendor stack related data in the Echo Request message. What you see here—the alphabet up to the letter w—is what Microsoft uses. Whenever you see this in a trace file, it is a Microsoft stack sending the request. Figure 4-9 shows the Echo Reply in detail.

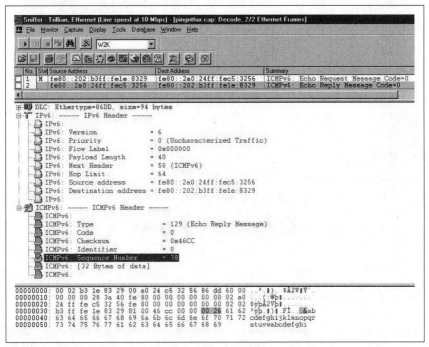

Figure 4-9. Echo Reply in a trace file

Again, the IPv6 header shows a value of 6 for the IP version and a Next Header value of 58 for ICMPv6. The destination address of the previous frame is now the source address, and the previous source address is now the destination address. The Type field in the ICMPv6 header shows a value of 129, which is the value for an Echo Reply. The Identifier and Sequence Number fields, as well as the Data field, match the ones in the Echo Request.

Neighbor Discovery

Neighbor discovery (ND) is specified in RFC 2461 (obsoletes RFC 1970). The specifications in this RFC relate to different protocols and processes known from IPv4 that have been modified and improved. New functionality has also been added. It combines Address Resolution Protocol (ARP) and ICMP router discovery and Redirect. With IPv4, we have no means to detect whether or not a neighbor is reachable. With the neighbor discovery protocol, a neighbor unreachability detection mechanism has been defined. Duplicate IP address detection has been implemented, too. IPv6 nodes use neighbor discovery for the following purposes:

- To determine layer 2 addresses of nodes on the same link
- To find neighboring routers that can forward their packets
- To keep track of which neighbors are reachable and which are not, and detect changed link-layer addresses

The following improvements over the IPv4 set of protocols can be noted:

- Router discovery is now part of the base protocol set. With IPv4, the mechanism needs to get the information from the routing table.
- Router advertisement packets contain link-layer addresses for the router. There is no need for the node receiving a Router Advertisement to send out an additional ARP request (as an IPv4 node would have to do) to get the link-layer address for the router interface. The same is true for ICMPv6 redirect messages; they contain the link-layer address of the new next-hop router interface.
- Router advertisement packets contain the prefix for a link (subnet information). There is no need to configure subnet masks anymore. They can be learned from the Router Advertisement.
- Neighbor discovery provides mechanisms to renumber networks easily. New prefixes and addresses can be introduced and old ones can be deprecated and removed.
- Router advertisements enable stateless address autoconfiguration and can notify hosts when to use stateful address configuration (e.g., DHCP).
- Routers can advertise an MTU to be used on a link.
- Multiple prefixes can be assigned to one link. By default, hosts learn all prefixes from the router, but the router can be configured not to advertise some or all of the prefixes. In that case, hosts assume that a non-advertised prefix destination is remote and send the packets to the router. The router can then issue ICMP redirect messages as needed.

- Neighbor unreachability detection is part of the base protocol. It substantially improves packet delivery in case of failed routers or link interfaces that changed their link-layer address. It solves the issues with outdated ARP caches. ND detects failed connectivity and traffic is not sent to neighbors that are unreachable. The neighbor unreachability detection also detects failed routers and switches to live ones.

- Router advertisements and ICMP redirects use link-local addresses to identify routers. This allows hosts to maintain their router associations even in the case of renumbering or use of new global prefixes.

- Neighbor discovery messages have a hop limit value of 255, and requests with a lower hop limit are not answered. This makes Neighbor discovery immune to remote hosts that try to sneak into your link because their packets have decremented hop limit and are thus ignored.

- The neighbor discovery protocol is used to detect duplicate IP addresses on a link.

- Standard IP authentication and security mechanisms can be applied to neighbor discovery.

This summary gives an idea of what can be expected from this part of the specification. Now let's discuss the different processes in detail. The neighbor discovery protocol consists of five ICMP messages: a pair of Router Solicitation/Router Advertisement messages, a pair of Neighbor Solicitation/ Neighbor Advertisement messages, and an ICMP redirect message (refer to Table 4-2, earlier in this chapter, for a summary of ICMP informational message types).

Router Solicitation and Router Advertisement

Routers send out Router Advertisement messages in regular intervals. Hosts can request Router Advertisements by issuing a Router Solicitation message. This will trigger routers to issue Router Advertisements immediately, outside of the regular interval. The format is shown in Figure 4-10.

In the IP header of a Router Solicitation message, you will usually see the all-routers multicast address of FF02::2 as a destination address. The hop limit is set to 255. The ICMP Type field is set to 133, which is the value for the Router Solicitation message. The Code field is unused and set to 0. The following two Bytes are used for the Checksum. The next four Bytes are unused and reserved for future use. The sender sets them to 0 and the receiver ignores those fields. For a Router Solicitation message, valid

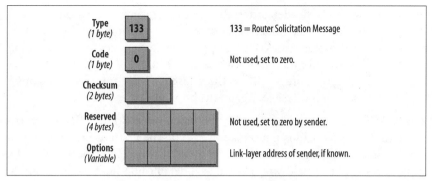

Figure 4-10. Router Solicitation message

Options are the link-layer address of the sending host, if known. If the source address on the IP layer is the unspecified (all-zeros) address, this field is not used.

Routers that receive this Solicitation message reply with a Router Advertisement message. Routers also issue those messages periodically. The format of the Router Advertisement message is shown in Figure 4-11.

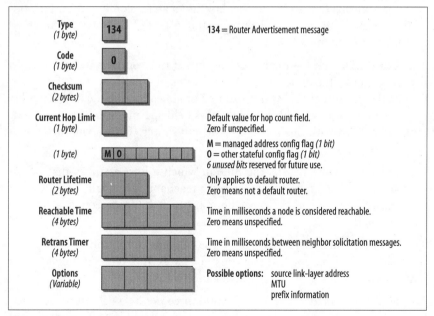

Figure 4-11. Router Advertisement message

By inspecting the IP header of the Router Advertisement message, you can determine whether this Router Advertisement is periodic or was sent in reply to a Solicitation message. A periodic advertisement's destination address will be the all-nodes multicast address FF02::1. A solicited advertisement's destination address will be the address of the interface that originated the solicitation message. Again, the hop limit is set to 255.

The ICMP Type field is set to 134, the value for a Router Advertisement message; the Code field is unused and set to 0. The Current Hop Limit field can be used to configure all nodes on a link for a default hop limit. The value entered in this field will be used as a default hop limit value in outgoing packets by all nodes on the link. A value of 0 in this field means that this option is unspecified by this router—in which case, the default hop limit values of the source hosts are used.

The next 1-bit field, the M flag, specifies whether stateful configuration is to be used. Stateful configuration refers to what we know as DHCP with IPv4. If this bit is 0, the nodes on this link use autoconfiguration. If the bit is set to 1, it specifies stateful configuration. The O flag configures whether nodes on this link use stateful configuration for other than IP address information. A value of 1 means the nodes on this link use stateful configuration for non-address-related information. The remaining 6 bits of this byte are reserved for future use and must be 0.

The Router Lifetime field is important only if this router is to be used as a default router by the nodes on the link. A value of 0 indicates that this router is not a default router and will therefore not appear on the default router list of receiving nodes. Any other value in this field specifies the lifetime, in seconds, associated with this router as a default router. The maximum value is 18.2 hours.

The Reachable Time field is the time in which a host assumes that neighbors are reachable after having received a reachability confirmation. A value of 0 means unspecified. The neighbor unreachability detection algorithm uses this field.

The Retrans Timer field is used by the address resolution and neighbor unreachability detection mechanisms; it states the time in milliseconds between retransmitted Neighbor Solicitation messages.

For the Options field, there are currently three possible values: source link-layer address, MTU size to be used on links with variable MTU sizes (Token Ring, for example), and prefix information. This field is important for auto-configuration. The router inserts all its prefixes for the link that the nodes on the link need to know.

Neighbor Solicitation and Neighbor Advertisement

This pair of messages fulfills two functions: the link-layer address resolution that is handled by ARP in IPv4 and the neighbor unreachability detection mechanism. If the destination address is a multicast address, the source is resolving a link-layer address. If the source is verifying the reachability of a neighbor, the destination address is a unicast address. This message type is also used for duplicate IP address detection (DAD). The format of the Neighbor Solicitation message is shown in Figure 4-12.

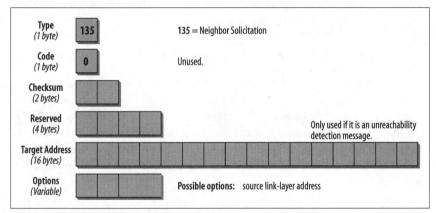

Figure 4-12. Format of the Neighbor Solicitation message

In the IP header of this message type, the source address can be either the interface address of the originating host or, in the case of DAD, the unspecified (all-zeros) address. The hop limit is set to 255. The Type field in the ICMP header is set to 135, and the Code field is unused and set to 0. After the two checksum bytes, four unused bytes are reserved and must be set to 0. The target address is used only in messages that are used for unreachability detection and DAD. It must not be a multicast address.

The Options field can contain the link-layer source address. It contains a link-layer address only if it is not a DAD message. In a DAD message that uses the unspecified address as a source address, the options field is set to 0. The link-layer option must be used in multicast solicitations (neighbor discovery and ARP functionality) and should be used in unicast solicitations (unreachability detection).

Neighbor Advertisement messages are sent as a reply to Neighbor Solicitation messages or to propagate new information quickly. The format of the message is shown in Figure 4-13.

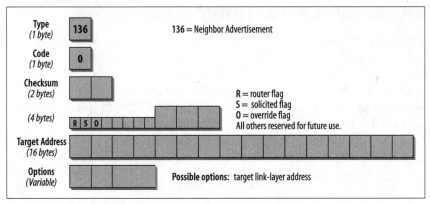

Figure 4-13. Format of the Neighbor Advertisement message

The type of address in the IP header indicates whether the message is the answer to a solicitation or an unsolicited message. In case of a solicited advertisement, the destination IP address is the source address of the interface that sent the solicitation. If the message is the reply to a DAD message that originated from an unspecified source address, the reply will go to the all-nodes multicast address of FF02::1. The same is true for all unsolicited periodic advertisements.

The Type field in the ICMP header is set to 136, the value for Neighbor Advertisement messages. The Code field is unused and set to 0. When the Router flag is set, the sender is a router.

When the Solicited flag is set, the message is sent in response to a Neighbor Solicitation. For instance, if a host confirms its reachability in answer to a unreachability detection message, the S bit is set. The S bit is not set in multicast advertisements. The Override flag indicates that the information in the Advertisement message should override existing neighbor cache entries and update any cached link-layer addresses. If the O bit is not set, the advertisement will not update a cached link-layer address, but it will update an existing neighbor cache entry for which no link-layer address exists. The O bit should not be set in an advertisement for an anycast address. The cache entries are discussed later in this chapter. The remaining 29 bits are reserved for future use and set to 0.

In solicited advertisements, the Target Address contains the address of the interface that sent the solicitation. In unsolicited advertisements, this field contains the address of the interface whose link-layer address has changed. A possible option for the Options field is the target link-layer address.

The ICMP Redirect Message

Routers issue ICMP Redirect messages to inform a node of a better first-hop node on the path to a given destination. A Redirect message can also inform a node that the destination used is in fact a neighbor on the same link and not a node on a remote subnet. The format of the ICMPv6 Redirect message is shown in Figure 4-14.

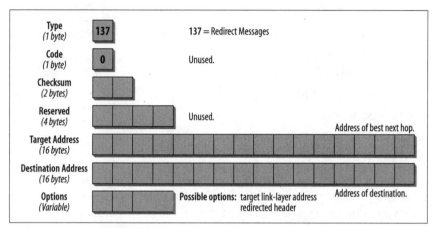

Type (1 byte)	137	137 = Redirect Messages
Code (1 byte)	0	Unused.
Checksum (2 bytes)		
Reserved (4 bytes)		Unused.
Target Address (16 bytes)		Address of best next hop.
Destination Address (16 bytes)		
Options (Variable)		Possible options: target link-layer address redirected header Address of destination.

Figure 4-14. Format of the ICMP Redirect message

The source address in the IP header must be the link-local address of the interface from which the message is sent. The destination address in the IP header is the source address from the packet that triggered the redirect message. The hop limit is set to 255.

The Target Address field contains the link-local address of the interface that is a better next-hop to use for the given destination address. The Destination Address field contains the address of the destination that is redirected, which should be used to get to the destination address. If the address in the Target Address field is the same as the address in the Destination Address field, the destination is a neighbor and not a remote node. The Option field contains the link-layer address for the target (the best next-hop router). This is an improvement on the IPv4 version, in which the host needed to issue a separate ARP request to determine the link-layer address of the next-hop router.

Neighbor Discovery Options

Neighbor discovery messages contain a variable-size Options field that has the format shown in Figure 4-15.

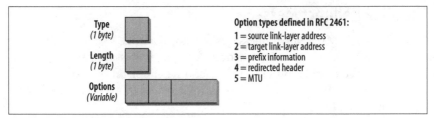

Figure 4-15. Format of the Option field

The Type field indicates what type of option follows. The following types are defined in RFC 2461:

- Type 1: source link-layer address
- Type 2: target link-layer address
- Type 3: prefix information
- Type 4: redirected header
- Type 5: MTU

The Length field indicates the length of the option. Value 0 is invalid for this field, and packets with this value must be discarded. The calculation of the length includes the Type and Length fields.

The screenshot in Figure 4-16 shows the details of a Router Advertisement with two Option fields. This trace file was taken when we had just set up our router. Besides initializing the IPv6 stack and configuring it for the prefix, we have not changed any of the configuration parameters. The options used in this case are option 1 (source link-layer address) and option 3 (prefix information). Note the format of the Option fields.

The Type field is set to 134, the value for a Router Advertisement. The Current Hop Limit has a value of 64. All nodes on this link will use this value for their Hop Count field. The M and O flags are not set by default. The Router Lifetime is set to 1800, which also indicates that this is a default router. The first Option listed is type 1. The link-layer address in the detail screen shows a lot of question marks, but don't worry about them. The link-layer address of the router can be seen in the hex part of the window (not shown in the screenshot); it is just not decoded in the detail window. The second Option is of type 3 for prefix information. Note all the additional information that can be given with a prefix. The Prefix Length field specifies the number of bits valid for the prefix (i.e., the length of the subnet mask). The L bit is the on-link flag. If set, it indicates that this prefix can be used for on-link determination. If it is not set, the advertisement does not make a statement and the prefix can be used for on-link and off-link configuration. The A-bit is the autonomous address configuration flag. If set, it indicates that the prefix can

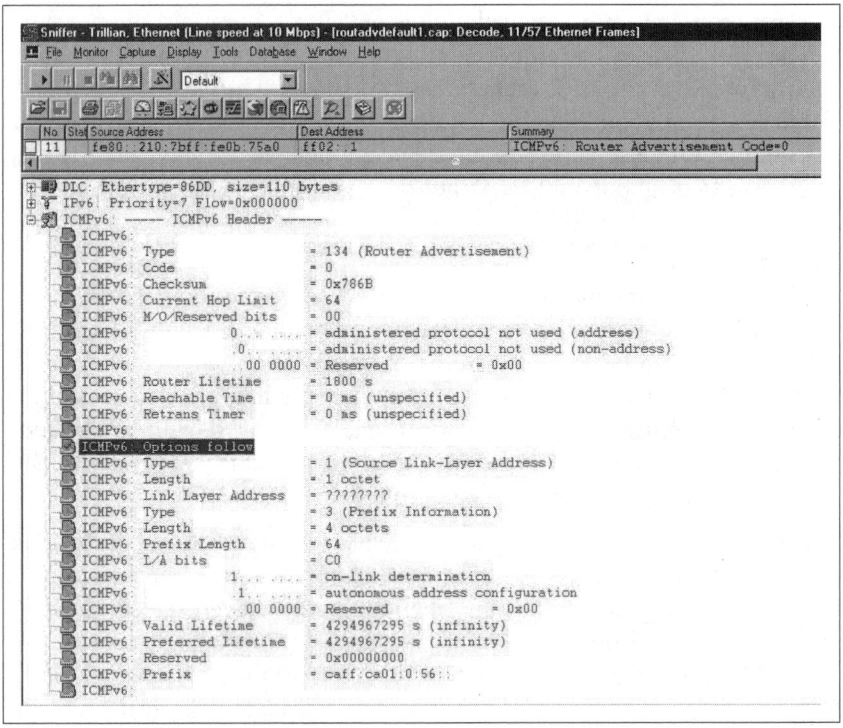

Figure 4-16. The router advertisement in a trace file

be used for autonomous address configuration. In this case, the host will generate an address by adding the interface identifier to the prefix or, if the privacy options are used, by adding a random number. The Valid Lifetime field specifies how long this prefix is valid. A value of all F means infinity. The Preferred Lifetime specifies how long the address being configured with this prefix can remain in the preferred state. Again, a value of all F means infinity.

Neighbor Cache and Destination Cache

IPv6 nodes need to maintain different tables of information. Among these tables, the neighbor cache and destination cache are particularly important. Depending on the IPv6 stack you are working with, the implementation and the troubleshooting utilities will be different. But the information must be available on every IPv6 node.

Neighbor cache

The neighbor cache maintains a list of neighbors to which traffic has been sent recently. They are listed by their unicast IP address, and each entry contains information about the neighbor's link-layer address and a flag that indicates whether the neighbor is a router or host. This can be compared to the ARP cache in an IPv4 node. The entry also contains information about whether there are packets queued to be sent to that destination, information about the neighbor's reachability, and the time the next neighbor unreachability detection event is scheduled to take place.

Destination cache

This table maintains information about destinations to which traffic has been sent recently, including local and remote destinations. The neighbor cache can be seen as a subset of destination cache information. In case of remote destinations, the entry lists the link-layer address of the next-hop router. The destination cache is updated with information received by ICMP Redirect messages. It can also contain additional information about MTU sizes and roundtrip timers.

The neighbor cache and destination cache have been mentioned in regard to the Override flag that can be set in a Neighbor Advertisement message. If the Override flag is set, the information in the Advertisement message should override existing neighbor cache entries and update any cached link-layer addresses in the cache of the host that receives the advertisement. If the O bit is not set, the advertisement will not update a cached link-layer address, but will update an existing neighbor cache entry for which no link-layer address exists.

The screenshot in Figure 4-17 shows the neighbor cache entries of our Cisco router. There were two hosts on the link at the time the screenshot was taken.

```
client#show ipv6 neighbors
IPv6 Address                          Age Link-layer Addr State Interface
FE80::202:B3FF:FE1E:8329                5 0002.b31e.8329  DELAY Ethernet0/0
CAFF:CA01:0:56:202:B3FF:FE1E:8329       0 0002.b31e.8329  REACH Ethernet0/0
FE80::A00:20FF:FE20:ADC2                4 0800.2020.adc2  STALE Ethernet0/0
CAFF:CA01:0:56:A00:20FF:FE20:ADC2       4 0800.2020.adc2  STALE Ethernet0/0
```

Figure 4-17. Neighbor cache entries on a router

A neighbor cache entry can be in one of five states, according to RFC 2461. The five states are explained in Table 4-6.

Table 4-6. States of neighbor cache entries

State	Description
Incomplete	Address resolution is currently being performed and awaiting either a response or a timeout. Specifically, a Neighbor Solicitation has been sent to the solicited-node multicast address of the target, but the corresponding Neighbor Advertisement has not yet been received.
Reachable	This neighbor is currently reachable, which means positive confirmation was received within the last ReachableTime milliseconds that the neighbor was functioning properly.
Stale	More than ReachableTime milliseconds have elapsed since the last positive confirmation that the forward path was functioning properly was received. No action will take place regarding this neighbor until a packet is sent
Delay	This neighbor's Reachable Time has expired, and a packet was sent within the last DelayFirst-ProbeTime seconds. If no confirmation is received within the DelayFirstProbeTime seconds, then send a Neighbor Solicitation and change the neighbor state to Probe state.
	The use of Delay allows upper-layer protocols additional time to provide reachability confirmation. Without this extra time, possible redundant traffic would be generated.
Probe	A reachability confirmation is being actively attempted by sending Neighbor Solicitations every RetransTimer milliseconds until reachability is confirmed.

Autoconfiguration

The autoconfiguration capability of IPv6 saves network administrators a lot of work. It has been designed to ensure that manually configuring hosts before connecting them to the network is not required. Even larger sites with multiple networks and routers should not need a DHCP server to configure hosts. The autoconfiguration features of IPv6 will be a key feature of the protocol when all sorts of devices, such as TVs, refrigerators, DVD players, and mobile phones, use IP addresses. You don't want to depend on a DHCP server to use your home devices.

IPv6 knows both stateless and stateful autoconfiguration. Stateful autoconfiguration is what we call DHCP in the IPv4 world; it is discussed in Chapter 9. What's really new with IPv6 is that hosts can autoconfigure their IPv6 address without any manual configuration of the host. Some configuration might be done on the routers, but no DHCP servers are required for this configuration mechanism. To generate their IP address, hosts use a combination of local information, such as their MAC address, and information received from routers. Routers can advertise multiple prefixes, and hosts determine prefix information from these advertisements. This allows for simple renumbering of a site: only the prefix information on the router has to be changed. For instance, if you change your ISP and the new ISP assigns a new IPv6 prefix, you can configure your routers to advertise this new prefix, keeping the SLA that you used with the old prefix. All hosts attached to those routers will renumber themselves through the autoconfiguration mechanism. If there is no router present, a host can generate a link-local address only with the prefix FE80. But this address is sufficient for communication of nodes attached with the same link.

Stateless and stateful autoconfiguration can also be combined. For instance, a host can use stateless autoconfiguration to generate an IPv6 address but then use stateful autoconfiguration for additional parameters.

An IPv6 address is leased to a node for a certain lifetime. When the lifetime expires, the address becomes invalid. To make sure an address is unique on a link, a node runs the DAD process. The DAD algorithm is defined in RFC 2462. An IPv6 address can have different states:

Tentative address
> This is an address that has not yet been assigned. It is the state prior to the assignment, when uniqueness is being verified.

Preferred address
> This is the address that has been assigned to an interface and that can be used without any restrictions.

Deprecated address
> The use of this address is discouraged but not forbidden. A deprecated address might be one whose lifetime is about to expire. It can still be used to continue a communication that would disrupt a service if the address changed. It is no longer used as a source address for newly established communications.

When a node is autoconfigured, the following steps are performed:

1. A link-local address is generated by using the link-local prefix of FE80 and appending the interface identifier. This address is a tentative address.

2. The node joins the following multicast groups: the all-nodes multicast group (FF02::1) and the solicited-node multicast group for the tentative address (from step 1).

3. A Neighbor Solicitation message is sent out with the tentative address as the target address. The IP source address of this message is the all-zeros address; the IP destination address is the solicited-node multicast address. This detects if another node on the link already uses this address; i.e., this is DAD. If there is such a node, it replies with a Neighbor Advertisement message and the autoconfiguration mechanism stops. In this case, manual configuration of the host is required. If there

is no answer to the Neighbor Solicitation, it is safe to use the address; the address is assigned to the interface and the state of the address changes to "preferred." IP connectivity on the local link is now established. So far, the process is the same for hosts and routers. Only hosts perform the next step.

4. In order to determine what routers are out there and what the prefix is, the host sends a Router Solicitation message to the all-routers multicast group of FF02::2.

5. All routers on the link reply with a Router Advertisement. For each prefix in Router Advertisements with the autonomous flag set, an address is generated, combining the prefix with the interface identifier. These addresses are added to the list of assigned addresses for the interface.

All addresses, before they are assigned, must be verified with a Neighbor Solicitation message (DAD). If the link-local address was generated through the autoconfiguration mechanism using the interface identifier, uniqueness has been verified in step 3 and may not need to be repeated for additional addresses that use the interface identifier. All other addresses configured manually or through stateful configuration need to be verified individually. Multihomed hosts perform autoconfiguration for each interface.

The trace shown in the screenshots in Figures 4-18 to 4-20 was taken during the autoconfiguration process of *Marvin*, our Windows 2000 host. Figure 4-18 shows some of the processes and message types discussed earlier, and the discussion of the trace summarizes the concepts in this section.

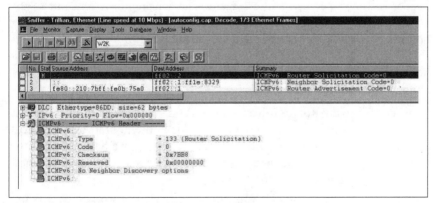

Figure 4-18. Autoconfiguration in the trace file

The first two packets are sent out by the unspecified address because this host is just booting and does not yet have an IP address. The first packet is a Router Solicitation message and therefore sent out the the all-routers multicast address FF02::2. According to the autoconfiguration specification, we would expect to see the duplicate address detection described in Figure 4-19 first. It seems that this implementation is trying to expedite the learning of the prefix information. The detail window shows the ICMPv6 header with the type number 133 for Router Solicitation. There are no neighbor discovery options specified. The option could be the link-layer address of the sender, but in the case of a message sent from the unspecified address, this option is not used. Figure 4-19 shows the details of the second packet, the Neighbor Solicitation.

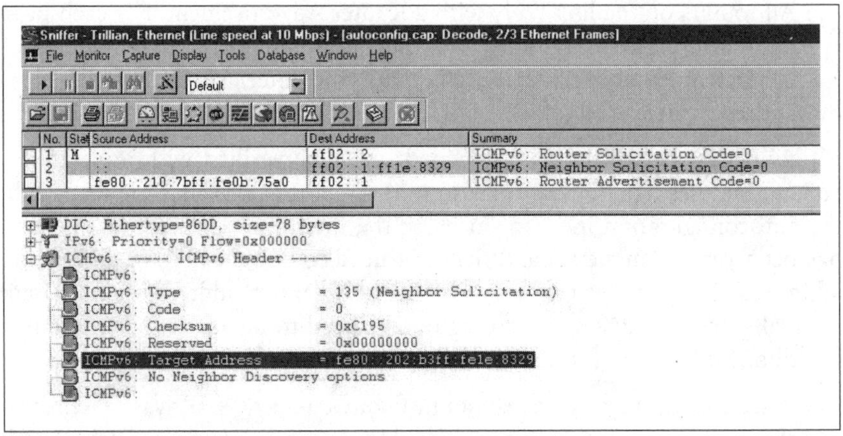

Figure 4-19. Neighbor Solicitation

The address is still in the tentative state, so the source address in the IPv6 header is the unspecified address again. The solicitation is sent out to the solicited-node multicast address. The important field here is the target address in the ICMPv6 header, which is highlighted. If a node already uses this address, it will already be a member of this solicited-node multicast address group and will reply with a Neighbor Advertisement. Then the auto-configuration process will stop.

Now let's get to the Router Advertisement. You saw a trace file earlier in this chapter, when we discussed the Options fields in the Router Advertisement message. To make this topic a little more interesting, we have changed the router configuration in the meantime. The new Router Advertisement message can be seen in Figure 4-20.

The message type for a Router Advertisement is 134. The first field that has changed is the current hop limit. It now has the value 32, the value we have configured on our router. All hosts configured with this Router Advertisement will now use a hop limit of 32 for their communication. (And yes, we have verified it; even *Marvin* now uses the new hop limit.) The next thing we changed is the O flag. Our router now configures all hosts on this link to use a

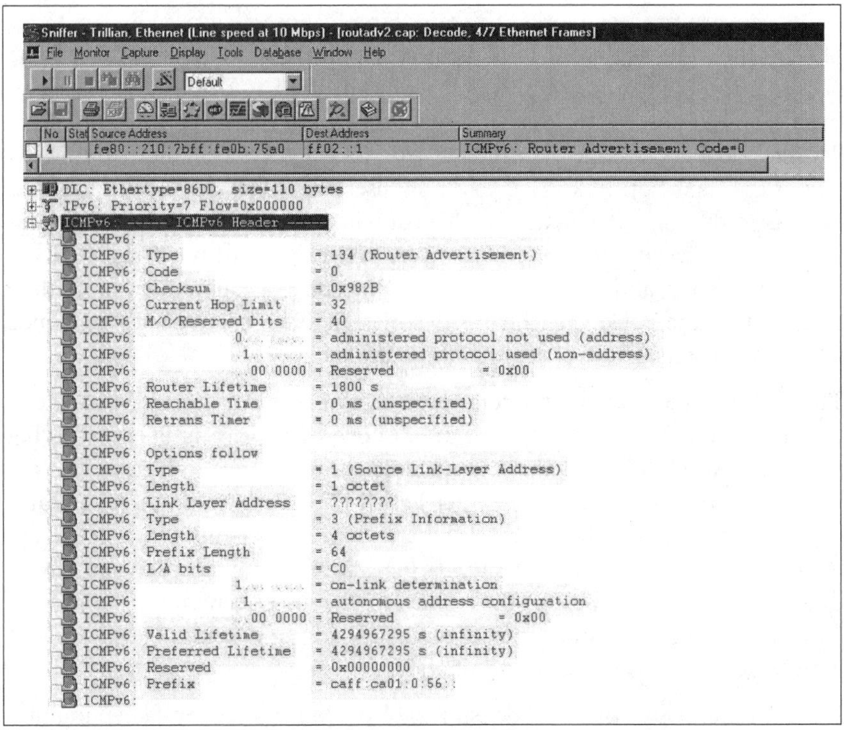

Figure 4-20. Router Advertisement

stateful configuration server for non-address-related information. The remaining fields are the same as in Figure 4-16, shown earlier in the chapter. If the router were configured for more than one prefix, the additional prefixes would be listed consecutively with the same fields.

Path MTU Discovery

With IPv4, every router can fragment packets, if needed. If a router cannot forward a packet because the MTU of the next link is smaller than the packet it has to send, the router fragments the packet. It cuts it into slices that fit the smaller MTU and sends it out as a set of fragments. The packet is then reassembled at the final destination. Depending on the network design, an IPv4 packet may be fragmented more than once during its travel through the network.

With IPv6, routers do not fragment packets anymore; the sender takes care of it. Path MTU discovery tries to ensure that a packet is sent using the largest possible size that is supported on a certain route. The Path MTU is the smallest link MTU of all links from a source to a destination. The discovery of the Path MTU is described in RFC 1981.

The discovery process works like this. First, a host assumes that the Path MTU is the same as the MTU of the first hop link and it uses that size. If the packet is too big for a certain router along the path to deliver the packet to the next link, the router discards the packet and sends back an ICMPv6 Packet Too Big message. Recall that this message type includes the MTU size of the next hop link. The host now uses this MTU for sending further packets to the same destination. The host will never go below the IPv6 minimum MTU size of 1280 bytes, however. The process of receiving a Packet Too Big message and reducing the size of the packets can happen more than once, before the packet reaches its destination. The discovery process ends when the packets arrive at the final destination.

The path from a given source to a given destination can change, and so can the Path MTU. Smaller MTU sizes are discovered by getting Packet Too Big messages. An IPv6 host will try to increase the MTU size from time to time in order to be able to detect a larger Path MTU. Path MTU discovery also supports multicast destinations. If the destination is multicast, there are many paths that copies of the packets may travel, and each path can have a different Path MTU. Packet Too Big messages will be generated just as with a unicast destination, and the packet size used by the sender is the smallest Path MTU of the whole set of destinations.

If you wonder why your host doesn't use Path MTU discovery, keep in mind that IPv6 nodes are not required to implement Path MTU discovery and that the implementation is vendor-specific. Nodes that do not implement Path MTU discovery watch Packet Too Big messages and react appropriately, but they do not actively challenge the packet MTU size and store it in a database.

Multicast Group Management

In Chapter 3, we discussed the use and format of multicast addresses. Multicast group addresses are used as an identifier for a group of nodes. They are identified by a high-order byte of FF. A protocol is required to manage the efficient routing of packets with multicast group addresses as a destination.

Multicast group management in IPv4 is done through Internet Group Management Protocol (IGMP). Version 2 of IGMP is defined in RFC 2236. IPv6 uses ICMPv6 messages for the same functionality; development was based on IGMPv2 specifications. It is now called *Multicast Listener Discovery (MLD)*, and is defined in RFC 2710.

All MLD messages are sent with a link-local IPv6 source address and a hop limit of one to make sure they remain in the local network. If the packet has a Hop-by-Hop Options header, it has the Router Alert flag set. Thus, routers will not ignore the packet, even if they are not listening to the multicast group address in question.

All three message types have the same format, which is shown in Figure 4-21.

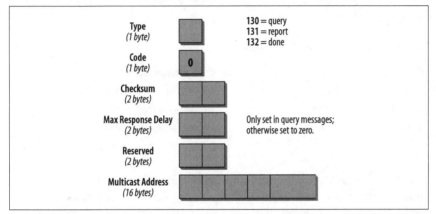

Figure 4-21. MLD message format

The Type field is 130 for Multicast Listener Queries, 131 for Multicast Listener Reports, or 132 for Multicast Listener Done messages. There are two types of query messages. One is a general query that is used to determine which multicast group addresses have listeners on a link. The other is an address-specific query that is used to determine whether there are listeners for a specific address on a link. The Maximum Response Delay field is used only in query messages. This is the maximum allowed delay (in milliseconds) in which a node has to send a report if it has a listener. In all other messages, this field is set to 0. The Multicast Address field is set to 0 in a general query. In an address-specific query, it contains the multicast group address to be queried. In report and done messages, this field contains the multicast group to which a member listens or the group it is leaving.

Routers use MLD to discover which multicast addresses have listeners on each of their links. For each attached link, the router keeps a list of listener addresses.

General queries are sent to the link-local scope all-nodes multicast address FF02::1. Any station that wants to send a report in answer to a query starts a timer when it receives the query and is supposed to wait some random delay before sending the report. The maximum delay is the one specified in the Maximum Response Delay field in the query. If within that delay, the station sees another station sending a report, it stops the process. Thus, multiple reports for the same address can be avoided. Group membership join reports and terminations are sent to the address in question.

The link-local scope all-nodes address (FF02::1) is a special address. It never sends a membership report or a done message. If an address has a scope of 1 (node-local), MLD messages are never sent. Table 4-7 summarizes the message types and their destination address.

Table 4-7. Message types and their destination

Message type	IPv6 destination address
General Query	link-local scope all-nodes (FF02::1)
Multicast-Address-Specific Query	The multicast address being queried
Report	The multicast address being reported
Done	link-local scope all-routers (FF02::2)

RFC 2710 contains a lot of interesting and detailed information. It discusses various states that nodes can go through and includes state transition diagrams. There is also much detailed information on timers: how they are used, their default values, and how they can be configured.

MLD Version 2 is already in the works as a draft and is based on IGMPv3. There are already implementations available based on the drafts. The current draft is *http://www.ietf.org/internet-drafts/draft-vida-mld-v2-03.txt*. For more information about the implementations, go to *http://mldv2.lip6.fr*.

CHAPTER 5

Security in IPv6

Originally designed for sharing information among researchers, the Internet is now being used for a growing number of business-to-business and business-to-consumer interactions. These interactions require a sufficient level of security, ranging from the correct identification of participants to secure, encrypted payment methods and nonrepudiation interactions. The Internet grew out of the academic community, so security mechanisms that applications could build on were not part of the original protocol and service design. Instead, different and incompatible mechanisms were attached to some individual applications (e.g., passwords for telnet and FTP), while other services (most routing protocols, SMTP, etc.) were not secured at all, or were secured only by limited or proprietary mechanisms.

It is astounding that the Internet has functioned properly for more than 20 years despite these security flaws, which are compounded by security defects in the operating systems, middleware, and application software that is used on systems connected to the Internet. During the discussion on the redesign of the current Internet Protocol Suite, it became clear that a redesign should also incorporate some basic security features that could be used "as is" on every Internet-enabled platform. The intent was for these features to provide some minimum level of security against many Internet-based attacks and form well-known and tested building blocks for applications and middleware using the Internet.

Types of Threats

A large number of attacks have been documented on Internet systems, and several observations have been made.

- Hackers could have caused much more damage than they have so far; perhaps it is too boring for true hackers to attack such easy targets.

- Most of these attacks can be traced back to a few archetypal attacks that can be used individually or combined for various purposes, as shown in Figure 5-1.

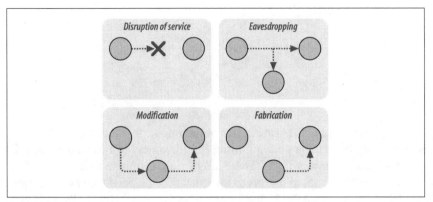

Figure 5-1. Classification of IT security threats

The four archetypical attacks can be described as follows:

- A *disruption or denial of service* is usually easy to recognize (access to information or business processes is no longer possible), but it can be hard to determine and remove the real cause of the problem. In a brute-force attack (i.e., physical destruction through fire or violent acts), significant resources must be spent on repair or replacement of damaged equipment. A subtle variation of service disruption is the (hidden) degradation of service quality, such as by introducing artificial communication delays, which may disturb the proper execution of a business process but not be perceived as an attack.

- The *fabrication, modification, or deletion of information* is much harder to detect or defend against than service disruption, unless specific protection mechanisms are in place. A broad spectrum of attack possibilities exists, ranging from the modification of individual data elements (such as the sending time of an email message) to the insertion of falsified payment orders through masquerading, the distribution of a virus, or the complete deletion of database or log files.

- *Electronic eavesdropping*, or picking up and evaluating of information, may be carried out in a variety of ways, from "classic" wiretapping to the usage of Trojan horses on systems under the attacker's control or the gathering of electronic radiation emanating from devices such as screens, printers, telephones, encryption devices, or video cards. Such passive attacks are usually impossible to detect directly (unless the wiretap or antenna is detected by chance or through exhaustive physical and electronic searches). Indirect detection (e.g., by "leaking" specific data whose distribution is intended to locate the path by which the information was picked up by an unauthorized party) is possible, but it is expensive and inherently dangerous. Besides attacks on the actual data content, indirect information, such as a traffic or addressing analysis (i.e., who is "talking" to whom, how often, etc.), can also be of interest to an attacker.

Basic Security Requirements and Techniques

Just as the threats outlined above can be traced back to a few archetypal forms of attack, basic security properties can also be classified into a few fundamental building blocks. These properties can be combined to satisfy more complex security requirements:

Confidentiality
Stored or transmitted information cannot be read or altered by an unauthorized party.

Integrity
Any alteration of transmitted or stored information can be detected.

Authenticity
The identity of the provider of information (in some cases, the identity of the intended receiver as well) can be proven.

Obligation
A specified action such as sending, receiving, or deleting of information cannot be denied by any of the parties involved.

These security requirements need to be provided by two basic security elements: encryption (to provide confidentiality) and secure checksums (to provide integrity). Suitable combinations of these two elements may then be used to provide more complex services, such as authenticity and obligation.

The oldest form of encryption is usually termed *symmetric encryption*, which requires the sender and recipient to agree on a shared secret (i.e., a key or password), which is then used to encrypt and decrypt the information exchanged (see Figure 5-2). A large number of symmetric cryptosystems have been devised over the centuries, but despite their growing strength against cryptanalysis, they share two substantial operational shortcomings. The first is the problem of secure, reliable, and economically practical key distribution. The other is the problem of missing obligation: because both parties hold the same key, it therefore cannot be proved which of the parties possessing the shared key actually generated the encrypted information.

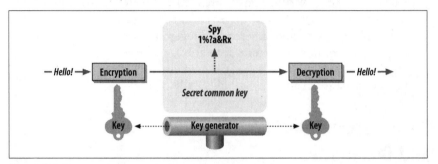

Figure 5-2. Symmetric cryptography

These unresolved problems triggered research into mathematical "one-way" functions, which are easy to calculate in one direction, but difficult or impossible to reverse. As an analogy, mixing paint is a one-way function: mixing two colors to obtain a new color is easy, but reversing the process and ending up with the two original colors is practically impossible. Some mathematical functions display similar characteristics, particularly when carried out in modular arithmetic, which operates differently than a "plain" arithmetic system. (Our 12-hour clocks, for instance, work in modular arithmetic: if it is 10 a.m. at the moment, and we have an appointment 6 hours from now, the meeting time is 4 p.m., not 16 p.m., so we have mentally calculated $10 + 6 = 4$ modulo 12).

Using appropriate functions and dependencies between numeric values, the problem of negotiating a shared key over an insecure channel was finally overcome independently by American and British researchers. Because the British research took place within the intelligence community and was therefore classified, the American researchers Diffie, Hellman, and Merkle have been credited with overcoming the key distribution problem.

Based on the idea of one-way functions operating in modular arithmetic, the next step was to devise a scheme of *asymmetric encryption*: instead of a shared key, a pair of mathematically related keys is used, based on the one-way function arithmetic described above and using multiplication of prime numbers (another process that is easy to do, but hard to reverse). One key is termed the "public key" and is widely published. The other key is termed the "secret key" and is not revealed to any third party. The whole mechanism, which was first put in practice by researchers Rivest, Shamir, and Adleman as the "RSA" algorithm, is often termed "public key cryptography."

Sending an encrypted message to any recipient now involves retrieving the public key and encrypting the message with it, as shown in Figure 5-3. Thus, everyone can encrypt information for the intended recipient with his public key, while only the intended recipient possesses the secret key necessary for correct decryption.

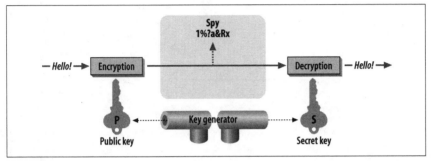

Figure 5-3. Asymmetric cryptography

The same mechanism can be used for authentication of information. A sender can calculate a cryptographically secure checksum or hash value for the information to be transmitted, thus creating an integrity code, or electronic signature. The sender then encrypts the resulting integrity code with a private key and transmits it together with the original information (see Figure 5-4).

Any recipient of the information and the integrity code can retrieve the sender's public key, use it to decrypt the sender's integrity code, and compare the result to his own checksum calculation. If the results match, the recipient can be sure that the information comes from the intended sender and has not been modified in transit.

In practice, information is often both encrypted and authenticated, thus fulfilling all basic security requirements, namely confidentiality, integrity, authenticity, and obligation.

Another technique is often used to combine the benefits of asymmetric encryption with the increased performance of traditional, symmetric encryption. In a first step, a symmetric session key is generated to efficiently encrypt the information to be transmitted. Then the encrypted message, the session key asymmetrically encrypted with the public key of the recipient,

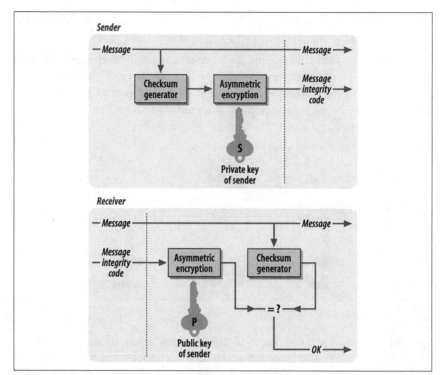

Figure 5-4. Digital signature

and a digital checksum over both elements are transmitted to the recipient, as shown in Figure 5-5. The recipient is able to verify the authenticity and integrity of the message using the sender's public key, retrieve the session key using the private key, and efficiently decrypt the message using the decrypted symmetric session key.

While these definitions appear relatively straightforward at first sight, and while sufficient implementations exist for strong encryption (in particular, public key encryption) and high-quality digital signatures (refer to *The Code-Breakers* by David Kahn [Scribner]), a large number of conceptual and technical problems make it difficult and sometimes unfeasible to introduce and maintain such protection mechanisms in real-world network environments. This is true particularly when these environments do not operate in isolation, but are required to interoperate in a worldwide context, such as the current Internet.

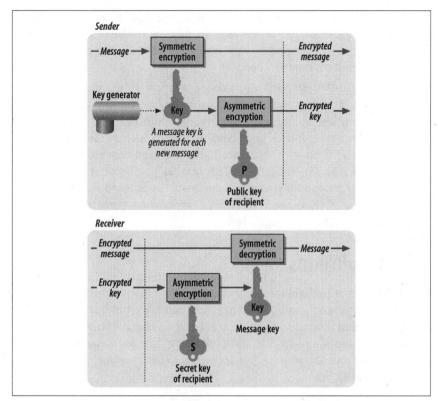

Figure 5-5. Combination of symmetric and asymmetric cryptography

Security in the Current Internet Environment

The original designers of the current IP protocol (IPv4) did not have to worry too much about security because the Internet was a trusted network for "the happy few." In addition, the design that is still in use today was considered a prototype that would be redesigned and extended over time. This historical development leads to two fundamental observations concerning security in today's Internet:

- Many protocols base their security on the assumed authenticity of IP addresses and port numbers. Based on the assumption that there are networks connected to the Internet that are entirely controlled by their respective user groups, we must not anticipate that any element in an IP packet is secure or cannot be read or modified. This implies that we must not trust an IP sender address or port number (nor any other element in the IP or transport header).

- Most protocols (application protocols, in most cases) that use a user identification and password authentication mechanism transmit the password in clear text or in a form that can easily decoded, such as Base 64. One-time password mechanisms or challenge/reply mechanisms are seldom used, although some standards have been developed to protect password/credential exchanges. This implies that security flaws in one of the lower protocol layers, which enable an attacker to read the data in transmission, can be used to attack application programs and user accounts (i.e., the application layer).

Current Solutions

As the Internet grew larger and more business-critical applications were designed and operated, ad hoc security solutions were provided; these offer semi-trusted and semi-secure Internet access. These security solutions mostly fight symptoms instead of addressing the fundamental security issues, but are still the only choice to provide at least some security in an insecure environment.

Packet Filters and Firewalls

The basic idea of such hardware and/or software security solutions is to filter traffic based on predefined rules (from IP addresses to virus patterns in files) and possibly also to determine "unusual" behavior. (This determination is made by intrusion-detection mechanisms that may also be able to catch nontrivial attacks, such as the slow and seemingly arbitrary scanning of systems for weak spots, or the use of covert channels for leaking information to the outside.) Such filtering takes place either on the network/transport layer (i.e., header fields of protocols such as IP, ICMP, UDP, and TCP are examined) or on the application layer (i.e., application protocols such as HTTP or FTP, as well as the actual information content, are examined, unless they are encrypted and thus unavailable for analysis). Many commercial systems allow filtering on both the network/transport and application layers and distinguish the direction of the data flow (inbound/outbound).

Corresponding security devices may also provide additional services, such as semi-trusted zones for different types of services via separate interfaces, strong authentication (using a variety of mechanisms from transaction code numbers to SecurID cards or smart cards), rewriting of IP addresses to disassociate the internal use of IP addresses from the official numbering schemes in the Internet, etc.

 There are a multitude of packet-filtering and firewalling strategies and a correspondingly large number of vendors and products. As there is no catch-all design to cover every conceivable network and application structure with their corresponding security requirements, the interested reader is referred to *Building Internet Firewalls* by D. Brent Chapman and Elizabeth D. Zwicky (O'Reilly), for a detailed discussion of firewall design and implementation.

Transport Layer Protection

The predominant security service on these lower protocol layers is Secure Sockets Layer (SSL). Originally designed by Netscape for securing HTTP sessions between web servers and web clients, almost all vendors of web software and providers of other client/server software, such as telnet and FTP, have incorporated SSL into their products. Meanwhile, the IETF has started formal standardization of SSL as one possible solution for the Transport Layer Security (TLS) standard (see RFC 2246).

SSL is located above the reliable transport service TCP in the Internet Protocol Suite. During the setup of a secure communication channel between client and server, each involved party may authenticate the other party using X.509-based digital certificates. In most cases, this authentication process takes place only on the client (i.e., the client starts the authentication process and investigates a certificate transmitted by the server to make sure it is talking to the authentic server). To prevent "man in the middle" attacks, in which an intruder places itself between the client and server and masquerades as the counterparty on both sides of the connection, client authentication (i.e., the server makes sure that it is talking to the authentic client) would be a necessary prerequisite. However, this part of the authentication process is hampered by the lack of a ubiquitous certificate generation, distribution, and administration system on the Internet (see "Open Issues in IPv6 Security" later in this chapter). After the (optional) authentication step, both parties agree on a session key. The actual handshake sequence differs, depending on the key exchange system used (in most cases, either RSA or the Diffie-Hellman key exchange is used; see RFC 2246). This common session key (mostly based on the RC-4 algorithm using a key length between 40 and 128 bits) is then used to encrypt all data exchanged during the session.

Application Security

In addition to the "standard" applications using username/password combinations that are transmitted unencrypted, many newer Internet applications have devised and implemented their own security mechanisms. In most cases, these mechanisms cover authentication (i.e., some proof that data is received from or sent to the "right" counterparty and that the data has not been changed during transit) and encryption (i.e., protection against the data being read or altered) during transit. Corresponding products such as Secure Shell (SSH) are frequently used as a replacement for telnet and as an encrypted tunnel for services such as FTP and XWindows. Other application frameworks, such as MIT's Kerberos, provide elaborate authentication services for the programming of networked applications.

The most notable advances in security for end users have been made in the area of electronic mail. Despite efforts to promote Privacy Enhanced Mail (PEM) as an Internet standard for secure (i.e., encrypted and authenticated) email, and despite the growing support for the S/MIME standard, security for today's email community is largely based on Pretty Good Privacy (PGP). PGP is intended to be used with the most commonly used mail clients, such as Netscape Messenger, Microsoft Outlook, Eudora, Elm, etc., and is available both commercially and free of charge. PGP, as well as PEM, offers the capability to digitally sign and/or encrypt email messages, based on cryptographic algorithms as described above, and an embedded key generation, distribution, and management system. Since a worldwide repository for public keys or digital certificates does not yet exist, PGP—in contrast to PEM—relies on a "web of trust" scheme, which requires each individual PGP user to cross-certify (i.e., digitally sign) public keys received from other PGP users. In such a scheme, if user A trusts user B and user B trusts user C, then user A may also place sufficient trust in user C (the common credential being user B) and accept user C's public key into her key repository as genuine. PGP has been extended to work with X.509 certificates, which may be managed by key servers on the Internet, and to offer additional security services—e.g., for the encryption and authentication of voice communication over the Internet.

Open Security Issues in the Current Internet

A vast number of problems surround these ad hoc solutions—in particular, when these services need to interwork in a complex environment:

- There are too many noninteroperable encryption/authentication systems and products, with more to come. It is almost impossible for an organization with a deployed, heterogeneous operating system and network infrastructure to provide one standard over all platforms or to obtain sufficient interworking between a range of (unharmonized) products.

- A generally available public key infrastructure (PKI) is still missing. While corresponding standards have been available for some time, a common PKI is not yet been provided on the Internet, and many of the regulations concerning digital certificates are still pending. In addition, interoperability problems have plagued the deployment of PKIs and corresponding directories, as well as "PKI-ready" products provided by different vendors.

- There is an open debate as to which security services should be provided by which functional layer (network, operating system, middleware, application, or presentation). While some have championed IPv6 and its security elements as the end of all security problems on the Internet, it is still unknown (and consequently not reflected in the deployed IT base) which security service elements will be provided and accepted by the market as part of the networking base, the operating system, or application services.

- The interworking of a large number of components and the corresponding dependencies create an additional level of complexity, which has so far substantially hampered deployment of common security platforms. A subtle change in one operating system covered by a security framework, for instance, may imply the upgrade of the security framework (or parts of it), may in turn imply upgrades in other deployed platforms, upgrades of middleware components, and/or upgrades of applications on these platforms.

- Externally supplied frameworks (such as SAP) utilize their own "embedded" security modules and methods, which may not be compatible with the security model and systems already installed. In some cases, it is almost impossible to obtain enough information about the inner workings of these systems to assess whether the embedded security is up to the standards required from all other systems and applications in the organization.

- The complexity and openness of interfaces between the organization and entities in the outside (i.e., untrusted) world poses another problem for a coherent security environment. One financial information vendor, for instance, may give customers the choice to separate a financial data stream from an email channel (i.e., allow them to block unwanted email gatewaying between the organization and the Internet through the financial service provider). At the same time, another provider may opt to code all these functions into one proprietary data stream, thus making it virtually impossible to selectively block email gatewaying.

- Many organizations suffer from severe integration problems when it comes to deploying "just one" security framework. Although it has become popular in the IT community (especially in the sales force) to term all systems sold and paid for as "legacy" in order to boost next year's sales, a large number of business-critical systems in the mainframe and midrange area have their own, well-built but incompatible security environments, while they are still perfectly suited to run the organization's business applications. No head of IT would be able to justify the replacement of these investments "just because of IT security."

- As in every software area, bugs and deficiencies also exist in IT security software, as well as in particular configurations. While the IT industry as a whole has learned a lesson with respect to covering up security holes (also thanks to the self-organization of the Internet community into Computer Emergency Response Teams [CERTs] and other security communities), such security holes still exist and will continue to exist as the corresponding software becomes even more complex.

In addition to technical and organizational shortcomings, legal and regulatory issues add another layer of complexity to the provision of a coherent IT security environment.

Therefore, a redesign of security within the scope of IPv6 had to "go back to the roots" and determine the few important key elements of security that need to be provided by IPv6. These elements are to be used within IPv6 itself or by applications on top of IP without imposing organizational or legal settings that may render these basic services unusable for the world-wide Internet.

The IPSEC Framework

The security framework for the IP protocol layer has been formally defined and standardized by the IETF IP Security Protocol Working Group (IPSEC) in RFC 2401. The framework currently consists of six distinct elements, as shown in Figure 5-6:

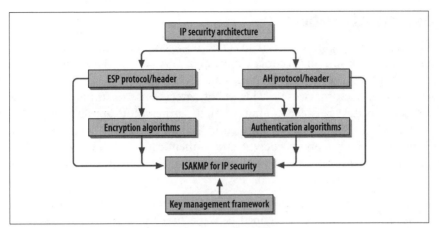

Figure 5-6. Relationship between IPSEC components (RFC 2411)

- A general description of security requirements and mechanisms on the network layer
- A specific security element for encryption (Encrypted Security Payload [ESP]; see RFC 2406)
- A specific security element for authentication (Authentication Header [AH]; see RFC 2402)
- Definitions for using concrete cryptographic algorithms for encryption and authentication
- The definition of security policies and Security Associations between communicating partners
- IPSEC key management, which is based on key management on a more general framework.

It must be noted that these mechanisms are considered generic; they could be used in both IPv4 and IPv6 contexts. They would have to be retrofitted into existing IPv4 software, but they are an integrated, mandatory part of the basic IPv6 protocol suite.

The work of the IPSEC Working Group is closely related to work in other Working Groups in the Security Area, such as IP Security Policy (IPSP) and X.509 Public-Key Infrastructure (PKIX).

IPv6 Security Elements

The following section introduces the individual security elements of the IPv6 security framework and discusses how they work together.

Security Associations

Communicating partners need to agree on a common set of information before they can use the security elements of IPv6: a key, the authentication or encryption algorithm to be used, and some additional parameters specific to the algorithms used. This set of agreements constitutes a Security Association (SA) between communication partners. SAs are unidirectional, and one SA is required for each security service; thus, two communication partners wishing to both encrypt and authenticate a two-way connection require a total of four SAs (one for each of the two required security features, in each of two directions).

Two types of SA are differentiated: transport mode and tunnel mode. In transport mode, the SA is defined between two end systems and describes either encryption or authentication for the payload contained in all IP packets related to that particular connection. In tunnel mode, the SA is defined between two security gateways, which surround the IP packet and payload with an outer IP packet "wrapper", thus being able to apply either encryption or authentication to the whole inner packet, including the inner IP header. Based on these two modes of operation, individual SAs may be bundled either through transport adjacency (i.e., the use of both encryption and authentication services in the same IP packet) or iterated tunneling (i.e., nested use of the encryption and/or authentication services within the same IP packet). This allows mapping of more complex security environments into a security policy, as described by the SA.

Although the local implementation is outside the scope of IPv6 standardization, SAs are supposed to be administered in two nominal databases, namely the Security Association Database (SAD) and the Security Policy Database (SPD), which are required to be present for each security-enabled interface on the system. In reality, the SAD and SPD may be realized as one database with corresponding internal organization.

The SPD specifies the policies that determine the handling of *all* IP traffic inbound or outbound from the system, not just traffic carrying encryption or authentication elements. To this end, the SPD relies on an ordered rule base, as well as a selector element that consists of IP and upper layer protocol header fields (such as IP addresses, or the type of transport protocol or port numbers) and a wildcard matching mechanism to map inbound or outbound traffic to a policy—i.e., to a SA or SA bundle (for example, to express ranges of IP addresses to be filtered). Based on the SPD settings, for each IP packet passing through the system, a decision is made: to discard the packet, to apply security rules for encryption and/or authentication, or to bypass security rules and pass on the packet "as is."

Usually, a (correspondingly privileged) system or security administrator defined rules in the SPD. The Internet Security Architecture, however, does not explicitly rule out the possibility for applications to request specific security settings in the SPD—provided that such requests are within the limits determined by the security administrator and that the requests can be secured against misuse.

All defined SAs are held in a SAD and are uniquely identified by a value triple consisting of a Security Parameter Index (SPI), an IP destination address, and a security protocol (AH or ESP) identifier (although both security elements are optional, one of them must be present). The IP destination address may be a unicast, multicast, or IP broadcast address, but only SA management mechanisms for unicast addresses are defined so far. In a unicast communication, the SPI is chosen by each recipient of a packet and negotiated during connection setup. Each system needs to remember the SPI of each communication partner (i.e., the SPI becomes part of the local SA for that communication type). In a multicast environment, the SPI is the same for all members of the multicast group.

Conversely, packets are related to an SA by the SPI in each encryption or authentication Extension header. Thus, an SA in the SAD determines the result of the concrete negotiation results during the connection setup phase (e.g., concerning the use of a specific encryption or authentication algorithm, key length, etc.). When a system checks individual IP packets against the definitions in a SA, it may then use all fields defined in the respective security extension headers (such as sequence numbers, checksums, etc.), as well as locally defined parameters such as SA lifetime, mode of operation, or Path MTU). Management of SA is assumed to be handled either manually or through an automated SA/key-management protocol.

Authentication in IPv6

Authentication alone does not provide all the security features outlined above, but in turn, not all applications require all those features. Routing or neighbor discovery information, for instance, is usually not considered a secret, but as a multitude of attacks on the routing system have demonstrated, integrity and authenticity of IP packets carrying routing information would be highly desirable. Likewise, authentication of individual IP packets would provide sufficient prevention against popular Internet-based attacks, such as IP address spoofing and session hijacking. This is because the associated SA may instruct the IP protocol implementation to drop or reject all IP packets whose cryptographically secure checksum cannot be correctly verified.

To this end, the Authentication Extension header (Next Header type 51) provides integrity and authentication for all end-to-end data transported in an IP packet. In other words, in the sequence of Extension headers, the AH is located in front of the end-to-end Extension header (if present), the Encrypted Security Payload (ESP) Extension header (if present), and the following transport (e.g., TCP or UDP), network control (e.g., ICMP), or routing (e.g., OSPF) protocol header.

Each Authentication Extension header contains a fixed sequence of protocol elements:

Next Header (1 byte)
> The Next Header field identifies the type of header that follows the Destination Options header. It uses the values listed in Table 2-1.

Length of Payload (1 byte)
> Describes the number of 32-bit values following the SPI field. This length indication is necessary because the authentication data in the AH may differ in length, depending on the algorithm used.

Reserved (2 bytes)
> Not used; set to zero.

Security Parameter Index (SPI) (4 bytes)
> Indicates which checksum algorithm has been used.

Sequence Number (4 bytes)
> Prevents replay attacks, with the known limit that connections using more than 2^{32} packets may become vulnerable to replay attacks. The receiver must also be aware that, as in IPv4, the correct transmission order of packets is also not guaranteed in IPv6.

Authentication Data (variable length)
> A cryptographically secure checksum over the payload, as well as some fields of the IP and extension headers, concatenated with a shared secret negotiated between the communication partners during the setup of the SA and indexed by the SPI value.

For the computation of the cryptographically secure checksum (also termed message digest or hash) from the payload, as well as from selected fields of the IP and extension headers, the following rules apply:

- In the IP header, the Version, Class, and Flow Label are excluded from the computation and the Hop Count field is assumed to contain a zero.

- All Extension headers with a change-en-route-bit set within the Option Type are computed as a sequence of zero bytes.

- If a Routing Extension header is present (which requires swapping the IPv6 destination address and the next address listed in the Routing Header and incrementing the Next Address field value), the value of the IPv6 destination field is set to the address of the final destination.

The result of this computation is a relatively short checksum (for instance, the MD-5 checksum consists of 128 bits; for SHA-1, the checksum is 160 bits long). The checksum may then be truncated slightly to allow alignment of the complete Authentication Header to a multiple of 64 bits, thus allowing optimization of memory usage in routers.

The IPv6 specification contains two cryptographically secure checksum algorithms that must be supported by every implementation by default: Keyed Message Digest No. 5 (MD-5, which was originally proposed as the only default but is currently considered theoretically breakable) and Secure Hash Algorithm No. 1 (SHA-1). As the name suggests, Keyed MD-5 requires a secret key (negotiated using the SPI during setup of the SA) to be prepended and appended to the payload to be authenticated. Computing the secure checksum then authenticates the concatenation pattern key-payload-key.

Other, potentially stronger or less computation-intense algorithms may be negotiated using corresponding SAs and SPIs. In contrast to ongoing debates on the strength of encryption allowed by governments or other regulatory bodies, strong authentication for IP packets and their payload is not debated (ironically, even a very restrictive government is assumed to be interested in strong authentication, in order to be able to verify the origin of a message or data stream).

Payload authentication

There are two modes of operation for IP authentication. The straightforward mode is the transport mode, which authenticates all end-to-end payload and selected header fields, as described above and depicted in Figure 5-7.

Header and payload authentication

In transport mode authentication, some values in the IP header are not protected. Some application contexts, however, may require protection of exactly these values. In addition, rewriting IP addresses during Network Address Translation (NAT)—e.g., as part of a VPN environment or through the use of unofficially assigned IP addresses—will not work with transport

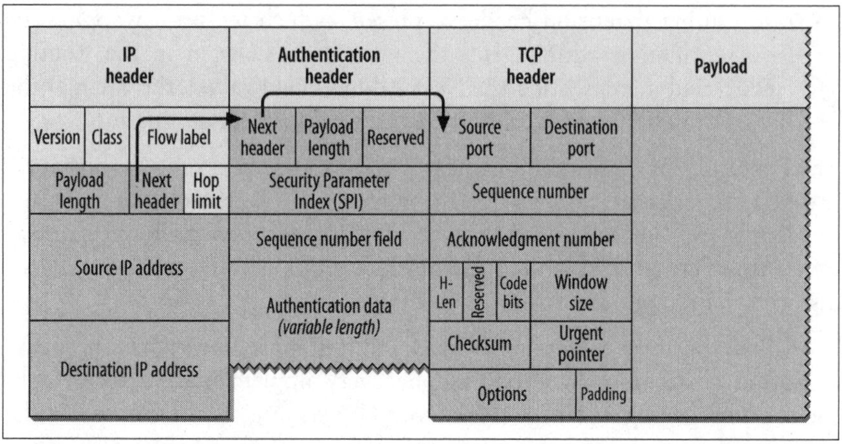

IP header			Authentication header			TCP header		Payload
Version	Class	Flow label	Next header	Payload length	Reserved	Source port	Destination port	
Payload length	Next header	Hop limit	Security Parameter Index (SPI)			Sequence number		
Source IP address			Sequence number field			Acknowledgment number		
			Authentication data *(variable length)*			H-Len	Reserved	Code bits	Window size	
Destination IP address						Checksum	Urgent pointer	
						Options	Padding	

Figure 5-7. Transport mode authentication header (dark gray = authenticated)

mode authentication because the IP addresses are covered by the checksum; recent work on NAT is addressing this issue. In addition, the Next Header value, which is also protected by the secure checksum, may change while the IP packet is in transit—for example, through the insertion of a Fragmentation Extension header (despite MTU path discovery, fragmentation may still occur due to dynamic route changes) or the insertion of a Hop-By-Hop Extension header.

In these cases, a tunnel (e.g., between two VPN security gateways) must be created by wrapping the original, fully protected IP packet in an outer IP packet, whose content is only partially protected by the authentication checksum. This is shown in Figure 5-8. The sending security gateway wraps the IP packet and content, while the receiving security gateway checks the checksum of the outer IP packet, unwraps the IP packet, and retrieves the inner IP packet, whose checksum can then be verified by the receiving end system holding the end-to-end SA.

Encryption in IPv6

Whenever protection against modification or even publication of information is required, some sort of encryption is necessary. Typical applications of encryption on the level of individual IP packets may be protection of telnet, FTP, mail transfer, or web sessions. Such sessions could also be protected by encryption on the transport layer (e.g., through SSL) or on the application layer (e.g., through S/MIME for email).

IP header	Authentication header	Inner IP header	TCP header	Payload
Version / Class / Flow label	Next header / Payload length / Reserved	Version / Class / Flow label	Source port / Destination port	
Payload length / Next header / Hop limit	Security Parameter Index (SPI)	Payload length / Next header / Hop limit	Sequence number	
Source IP address	Sequence number field	Source IP address	Acknowledgment number	
	Authentication data (variable length)		H-Len / Reserved / Code bits / Window size	
Destination IP address		Destination IP address	Checksum / Urgent pointer	
			Options / Padding	

Figure 5-8. Tunnel mode authentication header (dark gray = authenticated)

In IPv6, the Encrypted Security Payload Extension header (ESP, Next Header value 50) provides integrity and confidentiality for all end-to-end data transported in an IP packet. In other words, in the sequence of Extension headers, the ESP is located in front of the following transport (e.g., TCP or UDP), network control (e.g., ICMP), or routing (e.g., OSPF) protocol header.

Each ESP Extension header contains a fixed sequence of protocol elements:

Security Parameter Index (4 bytes)
Indicates which encryption algorithm has been used.

Sequence Number (4 bytes)
Prevents replay attacks, with the limit that connections using more than 2^{32} packets may be vulnerable to a replay attack. The receiver also must have some reordering capabilities because IPv6 does not guarantee the correct transmission order of packets.

Payload Data (variable length)
Contains encrypted data described by the Next Header field (see below), as well as the encryption initialization vector, if required by the encryption mechanism.

Note that there is no specific Next Header field in an ESP header. To allow proper processing of the payload, however, ESP carries the identification of the payload type (e.g., TCP, UDP, ICMP, or a routing protocol) in a separate trailer. The ESP is the only Extension header that is actually split into two parts: a header carrying the essential information for proper processing and checking of the encrypted SA by the receiver, and a trailer carrying additional information:

- Padding for 64-bit alignment, along with an indication of the actual padding length in bytes
- Indication of the Next Header type (e.g., TCP) to allow further processing by the receiver
- Authentication data (as in the AH, described earlier) to protect the encrypted data and the sequence number in the ESP header from modification by an attacker

The IPv6 specification contains one cryptographic algorithm that must be supported by every implementation by default: Data Encryption Standard in Cypher Block Chaining mode (DES-CBC). In this mode of operation, the ESP Encryption Parameters field contains a variable-length random initialization vector necessary for the operation of DES; the vector is specified in the corresponding SA identified by the SPI.

DES is a seasoned, well-known symmetric encryption algorithm endorsed by the US government for export, but is currently replaced by the AES variant of the stronger Rijndael algorithm. DES operates on a key length of 56 bits, out of which 8 bits are used for parity checking. The CBC mode indicates that during encryption of each data block, some checksum property from the preceding data block is fed into the encryption process, thus preventing the arbitrary swapping of encrypted data blocks by an attacker.

Other, stronger algorithms may be negotiated using corresponding SAs and SPIs. Keeping in mind the then-current debate on export and free use of strong cryptography, the designers of ESP chose DES as the default algorithm to enforce interworking of different implementations of IPv6. Negotiation capabilities as in AH were foreseen, however, to allow selection of a stronger algorithm (e.g., Triple-DES or IDEA) and key length, provided that the vendor of the IP software is able to offer stronger cryptography and the user is allowed to use strong cryptographic products.

Payload encryption

There are two modes of operation for IP encryption. As is the case for authentication, the simple mode is the transport mode, which encrypts all end-to-end payload, including the transport protocol header, as shown in Figure 5-9.

Header and payload encryption

In transport mode encryption, the IP header and all Extension headers following it, up to the actual ESP header, are not encrypted and therefore not protected. Encrypting these headers would render the whole mechanism

---

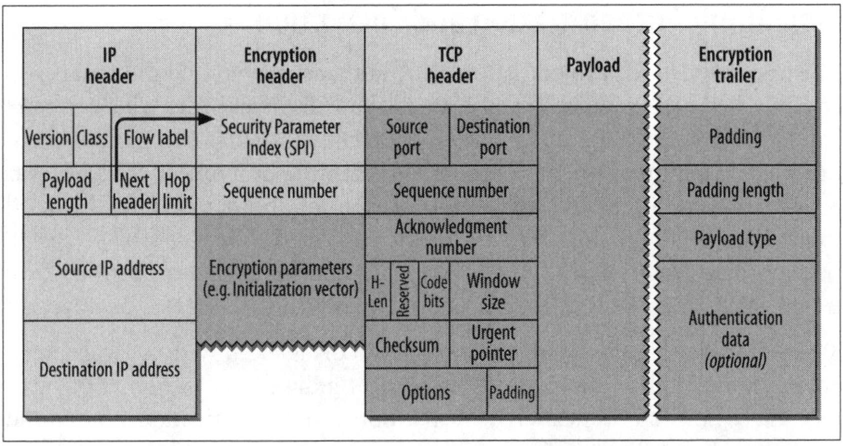

Figure 5-9. Transport mode encrypted security payload header (dark gray = encrypted)

useless because all routers and similar devices need to view, process, and even modify these headers while the IP packet is in transit.

Thus, if encryption of the whole IP packet is required, a tunnel (like that between two VPN security gateways, for example) must be created by wrapping the original, fully encrypted IP packet in an outer IP packet, whose content is unprotected by the encryption. The sending security gateway encrypts the IP packet and its content and wraps it in an outer IP packet, while the receiving security gateway decrypts the payload of the outer IP packet and retrieves the inner IP packet, which can then be passed on to the receiving end system (see Figure 5-10).

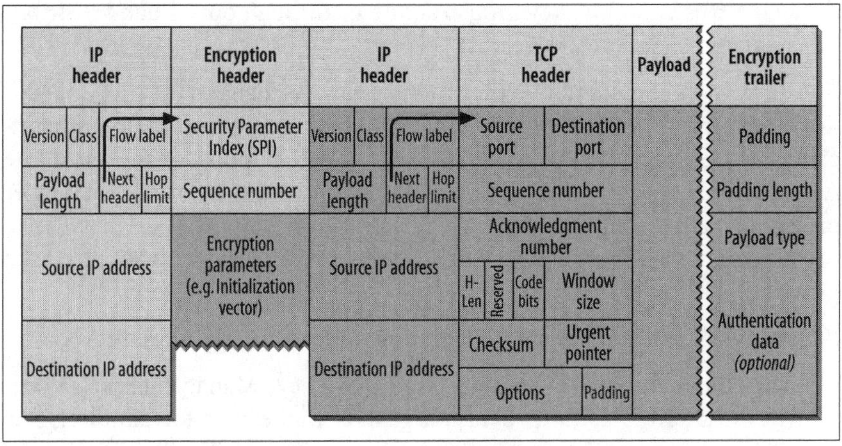

Figure 5-10. Tunnel mode encrypted security payload header (dark gray = encrypted)

Combining Authentication and Encryption

The original idea for providing integrity, authenticity, and confidentiality to an IP packet was to use both the AH and the ESP (in an order where the AH would precede the ESP, thus allowing the recipient to first check the authenticity and integrity of the packet before attempting decryption). Since it was envisaged that, in many cases, both Extension headers would be used together and would thus lead to an increase in the overall size of the IP packet, the authentication function was additionally embedded into the ESP trailer, protecting the ESP sequence number as well as the actual payload.

Thus, the programmer of higher-level protocols is faced with a choice here, either to use both the AH and ESP headers individually in sequence or to rely solely on the ESP header, with the optional authentication function in the ESP trailer. In any case, the choice between transport mode and tunnel mode is available regardless of the combination of AH and ESP used.

Security Association Negotiation and Key Management

To establish a SA between communicating entities, the entities must first agree on a common security policy and a compatible set of cryptographic algorithms. To facilitate the secure exchange of corresponding information, they must also agree on a shared key or secret, which must be negotiated over a potentially insecure communication path (shared secret) or which must be based on previously defined and authenticated certificates (either through a trusted public key infrastructure or through out-of-band distribution and verification of certificates).

The corresponding standard, the Internet Key Exchange (IKE, RFC 2409) describes a protocol that allows communicating entities to obtain authenticated keying material and to manage Security Associations for the use of the AH and ESP services within IPSEC. IKE is considered an application-layer protocol from an IPSEC point of view, and it runs on port 500/UDP. Thus, other key management frameworks besides the default IKE could be provided.

IKE is a collection and selective adaptation of three more general protocols:

- The Internet Security Association and Key Management Protocol (ISAKMP, RFC 2408) provides a general framework for handling SAs and key exchange, but does not define them specifically. To suit the

IPSEC requirements, the Internet IP Security Domain of Interpretation (DOI, RFC 2407) describes the tailoring and parameterization of ISAKMP to be used in IPSEC. In particular, the DOI describes the naming convention for protocol IDs, the Situation field (allowing the selection of an identity, secrecy, or integrity mode of operation), advice concerning the correct implementation of a security policy, the syntax to be used for SA descriptions and IKE payload formats, and any additional key exchange and notification message types. However, ISAKMP is designed to be independent of key exchange, so additional key exchange protocols are required.

- The Oakley key-determination protocol (see RFC 2412) is based on the Diffie/Hellman key exchange discussed earlier. It describes a series of key exchanges, called modes, and specifies the services provided by each type of key exchange (e.g., identity protection, authentication, and perfect forward secrecy for keys, such that even if a key is compromised, later keys or encrypted material are not endangered). IKE does not require the entire Oakley protocol, however—only a subset necessary to satisfy its specific goals.

- The Versatile Secure Key Exchange Mechanism for Internet (SKEME; see "A Versatile Secure Key Exchange Mechanism for Internet," by H. Krawczyk, in *IEEE Proceedings of the 1996 Symposium on Network and Distributed Systems Security*) describes a fast key-exchange technique that provides anonymity, repudiability, and quick key refreshment. Again, as with Oakley, IKE does not require the entire SKEME protocol, just the method of public key encryption for authentication and the concept of fast rekeying using an exchange of special tokens termed *nonces*. Nonces are large (64- to 2048-bit) random numbers used to add entropy to the key negotiation process and provide limited protection against replay attacks.

Thus, IKE can be roughly described as a negotiation protocol that utilizes data formats defined in ISAKMP to exchange key and SA information based on the Oakley and SKEME key-exchange mechanisms. It should be noted that two other proposals, Photuris and SKIP, exist. Photuris corresponds roughly to the "main mode" of ISAKMP (see below). SKIP was eventually dropped by the IETF Working Group due to the additional overhead (each protected IP packet also has to carry a SKIP header, in addition to AH and/ or ESP) and the directory-based, fixed key exchange protocol, despite advantages such as simplicity and stateless mode of operation. Future extensions may, however, reintroduce ideas and methods employed by SKIP.

Figure 5-11 indictes the individual elements of association and key management standards and their relation.

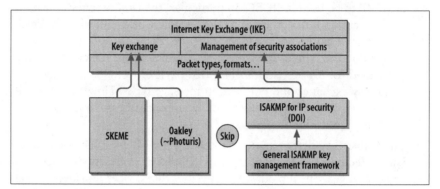

Figure 5-11. Relationship of association and key management standards

IKE operates in two phases.

In phase 1, ISAKMP peers negotiate a secure, authenticated channel (e.g., encryption with DES and authentication with MD-5, or encryption with IDEA and authentication with SHA-1), based on their SPD, over which all further communication takes place. This channel is set up based on the exponential Diffie/Hellman key exchange with 64-bit cookies (not to be confused with web cookies) to prevent flooding or clogging attacks on the recipient (since the response is computationally intense) and to demultiplex several IKE negotiations in parallel on port 500. It is also set up with encrypted identification tokens (containing a chosen identity ranging from an IP address to a domain name, certificate, or email address) to prevent man-in-the-middle attacks, in which the attacker masquerades itself as the corresponding communication partner to each peer. This channel forms the ISAKMP SA.

Two different modes of operation can be used for a phase 1 exchange: Main Mode, the normal exchange, using six messages and providing identity protection; and Aggressive Mode, using only three messages, but at the cost of slightly less security, since identity protection is not available.

Authentication of the communication partners may use different methods, such as sharing a secret prior to ISAKMP SA setup (e.g., on a chip card), securing the negotiation data with an RSA (or DSA) checksum encrypted with the sender's private key, or securing the negotiation data by encrypting it with the receiver's public key. The keys resulting from the original Diffie/Hellman key exchange are finally used to derive further keys for encryption, authentication, and refreshing the keying material, if required, to hinder cryptanalysis on the cyphertext.

In phase 2, further SAs are negotiated over the secure channel on behalf of services such as IPSEC or any other service using Quick Mode with only three messages exchanged. Also, SAs requiring new key material may negotiate the corresponding data by employing the New Group Mode, using only two messages. An ISAKMP SA is always considered bidirectional after connection setup, so each of the communicating peers may initiate Quick Mode or New Group Mode exchanges at any time. Because multiple Quick Mode negotiations may take place in parallel, they must be differentiated by a unique identifier (the cookie exchanged in phase 1 of IKE is the same for all SAs between the same communication partners). ISAKMP SA negotiation is shown in Figure 5-12.

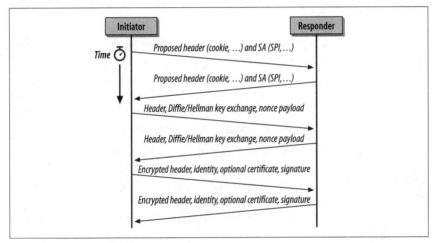

Figure 5-12. ISAKMP SA negotiation

Because the setup of a secure application connection (e.g., between a web client and a web server) requires the negotiation and setup of a whole SA, including the necessary computations, performance has been an issue with the design of IKE. Using the different ISAKMP phases, however, an implementation may, when necessary, employ very fast keying by reuse. A phase 1 exchange may be viewed as a generic IKE "control channel" and may be used for more than one phase 2 negotiation. Additionally, multiple SAs can be based on one individual phase 2 negotiation. The IKE specification therefore mentions, "With these optimizations, an implementation can see less than one message exchange per SA, as well as less than one Diffie/Hellman exponentiation per SA."

As described above, much of IKE's functionality around authentication of communication peers is based either on preshared secrets or on some knowledge of the other party's public key or digital certificate. There is sufficient flexibility in the IKE protocol for eventual support of more complex infrastructure elements, such as Key Distribution Centers (KDC), the Kerberos framework and key distribution in multicast groups, or a PKI providing authentic certificates of persons or software processes. However, a common PKI or KDC infrastructure is still missing in the Internet, and there is no indication when and by whom such a service—which is also subject to substantial technical, organizational, and political debate on privacy versus control issues—will be provided.

Interworking of IPv6 Security with Other Services

The provision of IPSEC in IPv6 is a giant step forward with respect to providing security on the Internet. There are a variety of different uses of IPSEC within the basic Internet Protocol Suite, such as general confidentiality of transmission, authentication of peer entities (e.g., for routing updates, server lookups for DNS, DHCP-based autoconfiguration, etc.) and prevention (or at least reduction) of denial-of-service and man-in-the-middle attacks.

However, the provision of IPSEC service also influences the security elements used in application-layer protocols. Simple services such as telnet, FTP, DNS, and SNMP-based network management may now rely solely on IPSEC for obtaining sufficient security (the operating system environment is considered outside the scope of IPSEC, although some recommendations exist concerning the handling of keying material within the software). Other, more complex applications, such as electronic mail, require more complex security elements, however, such as nonrepudiation of receipt, proof of origin, or specific encryption of information on the application or even user level; these elements are not directly obtainable from IPSEC operating solely on the network layer. Although these application-level security elements may profit from the provision of IPSEC services (i.e., they may rely on completely secure, authentic, and reliable end-to-end transport of content), they still need to provide their own security elements, which are not necessarily compatible with the SAs and key exchanges used by IPSEC. In some areas, such as the identity authentication in phase 1 of the IKE negotiation protocol, the use of application-level elements such as certificates is specifically required, and corresponding standardization and deployment activities must be well coordinated.

Unfortunately, there are some areas in which the IPSEC security elements do not fit in well with other relevant IPv6 service elements:

- Tunneling, which is an important architectural element both of IPSEC and of phased IPv6 deployment, creates problems when passing through existing border-level security gateways or firewalls; this is because an IPSEC tunnel that has been defined end-to-end will deny the firewall any possibility to check for dangerous or unauthorized content (such as viruses). Thus, end-to-end SAs must be replaced by "end-to-security-gateway" SAs. However, this process has not yet been designed, let alone standardized. In addition, there are subtle security problems with tunneling because the inner IP packet may contain routing or network control messages that can be harmful to the receiving network or system (such as source routing in IP, ICMP routing redirects, etc.).

- A similar problem exists with NAT, which has been widely deployed on the Internet to save IP address space and limit administrative address change overhead when switching between Internet service providers. NAT gateways rewrite IP headers to masquerade systems on the internal network when they communicate on the Internet. In many scenarios, NAT gateways also rewrite transport-layer port numbers (e.g., when more than one internal system uses the same officially assigned address on the Internet and the port number is used to demultiplex traffic). NAT gateways even have to rewrite application-layer data, such as ICMP error messages that contain the first bits of a faulty IP header, or passive mode FTP requests that carry IP addresses. With IP packets protected by authentication and/or encryption, NAT becomes problematic. Currently, a proposal on realm-specific IP is being discussed; it allows an IPSEC client to negotiate shared addressing and security parameters with its local gateway. A solution or standard does not yet exist, however.

- Quality of Service, as defined in IPv6, allows routers to drop packets, depending on priority and service class as specified in the corresponding Class and Flow Label IPv6 header elements. With IPSEC employed, dropping packets would be considered a security violation that could deny the requested service (e.g., an IKE exchange) in which the handling of time-outs, duplicates, and retransmissions has not yet been defined). Additionally, all receivers of IPSEC-protected traffic must employ a heuristic to deal with nonsequential arrival of IP packets (e.g., they must memorize the highest sequence number received so far and accept packets with a lower sequence number, up to a defined backward window size—usually 64 sequence numbers).

- Finally, mobility (roaming and remote access) must be considered carefully in an IPSEC environment because corresponding protocols often assign dynamic IP addresses. When dynamic IP addresses are used for identity checks (e.g., in an IKE phase 1 negotiation), the key exchange will fail, or the SAs and security policies governing the SA setup must be so relaxed that security can be easily compromised by an intruder. Corresponding modifications to IKE have been proposed, but they have not yet been standardized. They would also introduce a further layer of complexity to the already complex IKE protocol. Furthermore, providers of network services will have to carefully administer admission policies to their networks, despite flexible and easy-to-use autoconfiguration mechanisms being deployed with IPv6.

Open Issues in IPv6 Security

Although security was one of the foremost concerns after address-space enlargement when IPv6 was designed, it appears that some ad hoc solutions, such as NAT and CIDR, as well as the availability of security elements such as SSL (standardized by IETF as TLS), SSH, and secure email (S/MIME, PGP) in IPv4 networks, have delayed the deployment of IPv6. While this delay leaves the Internet open for attacks for a longer period of time and leads to additional complexity and management overhead, it has given protocol designers more time to improve their plans.

While the base standards for IPSEC are considered stable and will be extended mostly in the area of allowing additional encryption or authentication algorithms, more work remains to be done in the IKE area and in improving protection mechanisms against traffic analysis and denial-of-service/flooding attacks. The full deployment of IPSEC will also largely depend on the availability of a technically, organizationally, and politically acceptable and workable PKI capable of handling a large number of user or software process certificates.

A final issue for IPSEC is the management of its complexity. Many IPSEC mechanisms and their consequences are no longer easy to understand and are thus error-prone in implementation and operation, even though "intuitive" user interfaces for end-system configuration (e.g., for applying ESP or AH security to connections specified by port numbers, IP addresses, etc.) are available. Adding further functionality, such as various styles of tunneling, will also add complexity and thus endanger the original idea of providing simple, ubiquitous security in IPv6.

CHAPTER 6

Quality of Service in IPv6

The basic Internet design handles traffic in a manner close to George Orwell's *Animal Farm* paradigm in which all animals are alike. Like the pigs in Orwell's gloomy vision, only a very few packet types, under special circumstances, are treated differently—in most cases only by end systems, not by intermediate routers during transport. This flat paradigm was well suited for uniform, best-effort services as provided by the original Internet. Today's applications are more differentiated and require different classes of service for real- or near-time traffic, e.g., for multimedia data that needs to be captured, transmitted, and played back with sufficient, homogeneous, consistent quality regarding throughput, delay, or jitter. As the Internet grows into the consumer market, expectation levels are high with respect to these services because users are already experiencing such real-time services from telephony and cable television services.

Changing the Internet to handle real-time as well as traditional traffic requires changes at the very root of the Internet: the IP packet design and the routing and forwarding functions. Routes in IP are determined by the IP destination address and the state of routing tables in each router on the path to the destination. Thus, all IP packets follow the same route until the route changes due to congestion, topology updates, etc.; thus, there is no implicit route per service possible. An attempt in IPv4 to classify traffic according to a Type of Service (TOS) byte in the IP header did not succeed Internet-wide because the TOS byte was based on fair self-classification of applications with respect to other application traffic. Multimedia applications were scarce at the time, so no real efforts were made to address this problem in the early stages of the Internet and the TOS byte was never used uniformly.

In addition, it is debated whether merely indicating the required type of service is sufficient to solve the problem. For true real-time support, users or programs must be able to specify acceptable upper and/or lower service limits, and to enforce different routing for specific services. This, in turn, requires information about which routes in the network are suited for real-time traffic and at what time, as well as information in each router about traffic streams or flows with specific quality requirements. This touches another basic Internet paradigm: so far, IP networks deal with individual IP packets and do not store global state information. This keeps the complexity at the edges of the network and the routing and forwarding as simple (and fast) as possible.

The redesign of IP provided an opportunity to address the QoS issue along with other functional additions. However, QoS is still a topic of research and controversy, and corresponding services and protocols employ very complex, often heuristic, mechanisms, which will most likely coexist in the "new" Internet, but that must not disturb the overall operation of the Internet. Design and experimentation continue and designers know that there will be surprises and pitfalls along the route because results from simulation environments and research networks may not be the same as those in the "big" Internet.

Thus, this chapter will provide the reader with the basic ideas, approaches, and protocols known so far, without being able to conclusively outline a unique QoS architecture for the Internet.

QoS Paradigms

There are already different schools of thought on the issue of identifying the right location for providing QoS. Again, no clear winner is likely to emerge soon and parallel deployment is likely. To complicate things further, limited combinations of these different paradigms are possible.

End System–Based QoS

The purely end system–based approach argues that a quarter century of experience with IP networks shows that the network is quick and stupid: it has no knowledge about traffic characteristics at all and transmits all packets on a best-effort basis. As there is no basis for intelligent traffic handling in the network, the end systems must be able to compensate for delay, jitter, etc., by themselves. Corresponding mechanisms exist that use extrapolation of missing data, intelligent playback buffers that can compensate for variances in interarrival times (like a car CD player that reads ahead and buffers enough music data to be able to reposition itself after shaking without stopping to play). These mechanisms have been proven to work even over long Internet routes and moderately busy lines. While this type of QoS has its merits (e.g., simplicity), it does not scale well for true multimedia support.

Service-Based QoS

In IPv6, different service classes could also be implemented by different multicast groups, so one could define, for example, four different classes of the same audio traffic—each encoded with different quality (such as 5.5, 11, 22, and 44 KHz). In this paradigm, not even an explicit priority indication is required because it is implicitly bound to the respective multicast group (which must be handled accordingly through different queuing and processing by the routers and end systems). The existing IPv6 ICMP multicast feedback control message mechanism can be used to shape the traffic characteristics at the sender and intermediate routers (e.g., the highest quality to be generated by the sender, which links need to carry this multicast group because of a multicast member downstream, how to enter/leave an multicast group, etc.).

On the downside, the sender will have to provide basically the same data (but of different quality) multiple times, and the receiver needs to know which group to subscribe to in order to match the specific transmission and end-system capabilities. Intelligent local decisions using this paradigm could also include supervision of traffic characteristics and dynamic switching between multicast channels with different quality.

Class/Priority-Based QoS

Another paradigm proposes that, to handle multimedia traffic requirements, routers need explicit information on how to deal with packets with different service requirements. To provide this information to routers, IP packets have to contain corresponding information, as well as signaling information concerning route changes. Fortunately, no new signaling protocol is required because the IPv6 Routing Extension header can be used for special route setup and the Hop-By-Hop Extension header can transmit control messages to inform all routers on the path.

Using this paradigm, the network basically still transmits in best-effort mode, but it may implement a feedback loop to the sender so that the sender can adapt its multimedia coding, if necessary, or it may drop packets according to priority, while senders code and label packets with proper priority. For example, to transmit high-quality (44 KHz) audio, hierarchical coding may be used in which data is encoded as a base audio packet containing the data for 5.5 KHz quality, a second packet containing the difference between 5.5 and 11 KHz, a third packet containing the difference between 11 and 22 KHz, and a fourth packet containing the difference between 22 and 44 KHz. Routers are then allowed to drop packets in case of congestion, in the order fourth, third, second, and finally first. The audio quality may differ, but the audio packet is completely lost only if all four packets are dropped. The negative effect of class/priority-based QoS is the additional overhead for the sender (e.g., for IP header management and hierarchical coding) and variable, unguaranteed service quality on the receiver side.

Resource Reservation–Based QoS

The most complex QoS paradigm is based on the assumption that routers must have full knowledge of connections and their QoS requirements to reserve sufficient resources (such as queues and buffer space, computing time, specific algorithms, etc.) to guarantee processing of packets within their specified QoS limits. With proper resource reservation setup negotiations and signaling, QoS can be guaranteed end-to-end between sender and receiver(s), either in a unicast model or using multicast, receiver-driven group management mechanisms. In other words, the receiver decides on the quality versus cost ratio and signals requirements upstream toward the sender, while routers are multicast-aware and forward traffic according to current group membership.

While this model relies on traditional IP packet forwarding as the default case, it requires sources and destinations to exchange extensive signaling and control messages using, for example, the Resource Reservation Protocol (RSVP). RSVP establishes packet classification and forwarding status information in each router along the path, thus introducing state information in a previously stateless datagram-forwarding network.

Main points of criticism include the substantial complexity of the protocol and the introduction of state information into a stateless network paradigm (the amount of state on each router scales in proportion to the number of concurrent reservations). There are also fears that the current Internet "for everyone" will be separated into a "rich" and "poor" Internet by means of chargeable reservations. Finally, the application support required to handle the RSVP signaling protocol is also a concern.

Quality of Service in IPv6 Protocols

Given the different QoS paradigms, the designers of IPv6 had to be careful not to impose a specific mechanism, but to provide enough flexibility to support multiple QoS mechanisms. Thus, after much debate and many redesigns, the IPv6 protocols carry a small number of QoS-specific service elements in the IP Base and Extension headers, which can be used in different ways and in several combinations.

IPv6 Base Header

The following section describes the QoS-specific service elements in the IP Base header, namely flows and corresponding flow labels.

Flows

A flow is a sequence of packets sent from a particular source to a particular (unicast or multicast) destination(s), for which the source requires special handling by the intermediate routers. The nature of that special handling can be communicated to the routers by a corresponding control protocol, such as RSVP, or by information within the flow's packets themselves—e.g., in an IP Base header or a Hop-By-Hop Extension header. There may be multiple active flows from a sender to a receiver, as well as traffic that is not associated with any flow at all. A flow in the IP protocol is uniquely identified by the combination of a source IP address and a non-zero identification, the flow label. Packets that do not belong to a flow carry a flow label of all zeros.

All packets belonging to the same flow must be sent with the same IP source address, IP destination address, and non-zero flow label. If any of these packets includes a Hop-By-Hop Extension header, they all must be originated with the same Hop-By-Hop Extension header contents (excluding the Next Header field of the Hop-By-Hop Extension header, which is allowed to differ). If any packet includes a Routing Extension header, they all must be created with the same contents in all Extension headers up to and including the Routing Extension header (again excluding the Next Header field in the Routing Extension header). The routers or receivers are allowed to verify that these conditions are satisfied. If a violation of these consistency rules is detected, a corresponding error message is returned, indicating the exact location of the rule violation.

Flow Labels

The 20-bit Flow Label field in the IPv6 header may be used by a source to label packets for which it requests special handling by the IPv6 routers, such as nondefault QoS or real-time service.

A flow label is assigned to a flow by the flow's source node. New flow labels must be chosen randomly from the range 00001 to FFFFF. The purpose of the random allocation is to make any combination of bits within the Flow Label field suitable for use as a hash key by routers, for looking up the state associated with the flow.

Hosts or routers that do not support the functions of the Flow Label field (most of today's applications, which will not be changed to require or set a flow, or which do not need QoS handling) are required to set the field to all zeros when sending a packet, to pass the field on unchanged when forwarding a packet, and to ignore the field content when receiving a packet.

Priority/Class

In the original 1996 IPv6 proposal, a 4-bit Priority field in the IPv6 header was intended to let a source identify the desired priority of its packets, relative to other packets from the same source. Priorities were divided into two ranges: 0–7 for *fixed priority*, and 8–15 for *real-time traffic drop priorities*. The first range was to be used to specify the priority of traffic for which the source provides congestion control—traffic that limits its bandwidth requirements in response to congestion (e.g., TCP traffic); digits 0 to 7 indicated traffic classes, such as interactive traffic, attended transfers, unattended transfers, filler traffic, etc. The second range was intended to specify the priority of traffic that does not back off in response to congestion—e.g., real-time packets that are sent at a constant transmission rate. For this type of traffic, the lowest priority (8) was to be used for packets that the sender was willing to have dropped first in a congestion situation (e.g., high-quality video traffic), while the highest value (15) was for those packets that the sender was least willing to have dropped (e.g., low-quality audio traffic). No relation exists between the congestion-controlled priorities and the non-congestion-controlled priorities.

After substantial discussions within the IETF, it was agreed that the original proposal's open loop transmission model was suboptimal in terms of bandwidth consumption and would increase the potential for congestions. Thus, the IPv6 header was redesigned to contain an 8-bit Class field (at the expense of the flow label, which was shortened from 24 to 20 bits). The underlying idea for using the QoS header fields changed from an isolated "how important are my flows relative to each other" view to a "network global" view, preferably accompanied by hierarchical coding. This allows some packets to be dropped at the router level while retaining real-time service at a lower quality, without the need for retransmissions or data extrapolation. The Class field proposal of 1997 thus contained a "D" bit for marking delay-sensitive traffic and three bits for network-wide priorities (allowing eight different traffic classes); the remaining four bits were reserved for possible use within a congestion-control protocol.

A further redesign in 1998 (RFC 2474) finally defined a complete replacement of the Class Header field: the Differentiated Services field, which is intended to supersede both the existing definitions of the IPv4 TOS byte and the IPv6 Traffic Class byte. In short, the differentiated service (DS) paradigm enables scalable service differentiation in the Internet without the need to define and administer status information per flow at every end system or router. Instead, each router offering differentiated service support contains a small, well-defined set of routines to deal with DS requests for performance (such as peak bandwidth) or for relative performance (e.g., differentiation of service classes), based on the signaling contained in the DS field in an IP packet requesting DS. The DS may be defined and used either end-to-end, when an IP packet is crossing a network boundary, or just within an Internet domain.

The initial six bits of the DS field are used as a *DS codepoint* (DSCP) to select the per-hop behavior (PHB) that a packet requires at each router. The remaining two bits are currently unused and are ignored by DS-compliant systems when determining the PHB for a received IP packet, as shown in Figure 6-1.

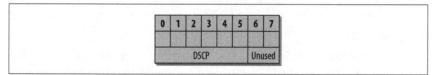

Figure 6-1. Format of the DS field

The DSCP field within the DS field can distinguish 64 codepoints. The codepoint space has been divided into three pools to allow controlled codepoint assignment. A pool of 32 recommended codepoints (pool 1) is assigned through formal standardization, a pool of 16 more codepoints (pool 2) is reserved for experimental or local use, and the final pool of 16 codepoints (pool 3) is initially available for experimental or local use, but should be used as an overflow pool if pool 1 is used up (Table 6-1).

Table 6-1. The codepoint pools

Pool	Codepoint space	Assignment policy
1	xxxxx0	Standard use
2	xxxx11	Experimental/local use
3	xxxx01	Experimental/local use, potential standard use in the future

A default PHB, denominated by an all-zeros DS codepoint, must be provided by any DS router. The default PHB describes the common, best-effort forwarding behavior available in existing routers. Such packets are forwarded without adhering to any priority policy; in other words, the network will deliver as many of these packets as possible as soon as possible, based on existing resources, such as memory or processing capacity. Packets received with an undefined codepoint should also be forwarded as if they were marked for the default behavior.

The RFC 2474 standard assigns eight recommended class selector codepoints (xxx000), which are drawn from pool 1. The DSCP field within the DS field is capable of differentiating 64 different codepoints. PHBs that are referred to by these codepoints must satisfy the class selector PHB requirements, in addition to preserving the default PHB requirement as described by the codepoint 000000. A class selector codepoint with a larger numerical value than another class selector codepoint has a higher relative order and will receive correspondingly better treatment by routers; a numerically smaller class selector codepoint has a lower relative order. The set of PHBs that the eight possible class selector codepoints map to must provide at least two independently forwarded classes of traffic in a router. PHBs selected by a class selector codepoint should give packets a probability of timely forwarding that is not lower than the forwarding probability given to packets marked with a lower class selector codepoint (given reasonable operating conditions and traffic loads).

To preserve some limited backward compatibility with existing uses of the TOS byte in IPv4, where IP precedence values 110 and 111 denominate routing traffic, PHBs selected by codepoints 11x000 must give packets a preferential forwarding in comparison to the PHB selected by the default codepoint 000000.

Class selector-compliant PHBs can be realized by a variety of mechanisms within a router, including strict priority queuing, weighted fair queuing, or class-based queuing, depending on the implementation strategy chosen by the vendor of the particular routing equipment.

IPv6 Extension Headers

As already outlined, two IPv6 Extension headers can be used to signal QoS requirements:

- The Routing Extension header can be used to request a specific route by indicating a sequence of IP addresses of nodes to be used (a loose source route, in IPv4 terminology). However, use of this Extension header requires the requester to have knowledge about the preferred route (i.e., the network topology and QoS-sensitive parameters, such as possible throughput, etc.). To discourage attacks on the routing system, a packet sent in response to a received packet that included a routing header must not include a routing header that was automatically generated by "reversing" the received routing header (as is often done in IPv4), unless the integrity and authenticity of the received source IP address and routing header can be verified (e.g., via an Authentication Extension header in the received packet).

- The Hop-By-Hop Extension header can be used to transport a maximum of one router alert signaling message per IP packet (RFC 2711) to every router on the path of QoS-sensitive traffic, indicating that each router should specifically process the IP packet. The use of the Hop-By-Hop Extension header allows fast processing by the router because no analysis of higher-level protocol headers is required. Routers that are unable to recognize the router alert option type are required to ignore this option and continue processing the header. Also, routers are not allowed to change the option while the packet is in transit. Router alert types that have been defined so far are shown in Table 6-2.

Table 6-2. Currently defined router types

Value	Description
0	IP packet contains a Multicast Listener Discovery message.
1	IP packet contains an RSVP message.
2	IP packet contains an Active Networks message—the sender is attempting to load a program into the router for executing customized functions.
3-65535	Reserved to IANA for future use.

RSVP

Although the Resource Reservation Protocol (RFC 2205) is not considered part of the core IPv6 standardization efforts, but instead an internal application on top of IPv6 (similar to ICMP or routing protocols), it is closely related to the "new Internet" design. It utilizes some IPv6 protocol elements—in particular, the flow label. Although the transport header could also characterize traffic, the flow label is used because the transport header is too far away from the IP header in the chain of Extension headers for efficient processing by a router, and it also may be encrypted by an ESP Extension header.

The RSVP protocol is used by an application running on an end system to request specific, unidirectional QoS for its unicast or multicast flows from the network. Routers also use RSVP to send QoS requests to all other routers along the path of a flow and to establish and maintain status information (soft state with refresh and expiration mechanisms) in each router to provide the QoS requested. Routers along the data path processing RSVP requests will usually reserve resources for specified flows. The direction for QoS is usually from the receiver to the sender; this allows each individual receiver full control over the quality/cost ratio and it remains in line with the receiver-based paradigm of IPv6 multicasting.

RSVP implements QoS for a particular data flow by executing traffic control. The traffic control, in turn, contains the following subsystems:

- A packet classifier, to determine the QoS class and derived route for an IP packet
- An admission control entity, to decide whether the system can dedicate sufficient resources to the requested QoS
- A policy control entity, to decide whether the requester is permitted to obtain a specific QoS
- A packet scheduler, to ensure timely forwarding of IP packets to the next hop

RSVP uses a flow descriptor to describe the QoS requirements per flow. A flow descriptor contains a flow specification (the desired QoS, including the service class and numeric parameters) as input for the packet scheduler and a filter specification (the identification of the flow to receive the QoS specified) as input for the packet classifier. Different reservation styles (options) govern whether senders are identified explicitly or per wildcard, and whether reservations for the same flow but from different senders in the same session can be shared within a router or must be distinct per recipient.

Although RSVP has been designed to provide QoS for applications, identified by TCP- or UDP-style port numbers in the flow descriptor, there is also limited support for providing QoS to lower-layer protocols. In particular, QoS support for IPSEC is provided with service granularity similar to port number-based applications (RFC 2207).

The main RSVP protocol elements are reservation requests and path messages. Each receiver sends RSVP reservation requests upstream toward the sender(s) on the reverse path of the flow received. These packets create and maintain state information (reservations) in each router passed and inform the sender, who may then adapt his traffic control, if necessary. In the opposite direction, each sender transmits "path" messages downstream along the same path as the data flow, informing all RSVP routers about the paths used for flows. (Note that routers on the path may not understand RSVP, but they are still able to forward IP packets with RSVP content to the next router capable of processing the RSVP protocol.) Tear-down messages are used to explicitly get rid of paths or reservations (although deletion of unused paths or reservations also happens through a timeout mechanism).

A number of router and software vendors have implemented RSVP mechanisms in their products, although with limitations in functionality (note that RSVP does not rely on IPv6, but can also be retrofitted into IPv4 installations). However, the complexity of RSVP in terms of implementation, operation, and processing, as well as architectural considerations as outlined in the following section, have so far limited the deployment of RSVP.

QoS Architectures

The bottom-up mechanisms described so far can be considered building blocks in a larger architecture that describes how the Internet may deal with real-time traffic requirements. Two different architectures exist: Integrated Service and Differentiated Service. Both are based on common traffic policing strategies and can be combined in order to allow QoS optimizations both in local and wide area network environments.

Traffic Policing

Traffic policing describes the general concept of allowing traffic to enter the network only when certain conditions (such as sufficient resources to handle QoS requirements) can be met, as well as supervising traffic behavior. This is done to adapt the network to traffic requirements or to impose restrictions in cases of unfair resource usage.

There are different methods for traffic policing, ranging from fair queuing algorithms based on the QoS requirements within routers to the use of network-wide priority classes (which determine the handling of QoS-sensitive traffic within the routing/forwarding system) and adaptive mechanisms, such as random early detection by routers to probe traffic behavior and its sensitivity to artificially and randomly caused packet loss or delay.

Traffic policing (and its corresponding administrative and technical overhead) is used not only because of the QoS requirements imposed by real-time, multimedia traffic. There may be economic reasons, as well—for instance, to exercise cost control, such as when different tariffs are used by network providers at different weekdays or times of day.

Integrated Services Architecture

The Integrated Services Architecture (IntServ) is based on the general paradigm that bandwidth and all corresponding resources are reserved per flow on an end-to-end basis This is similar to the original telephony service, where a circuit was reserved exclusively for the communication partners and could not be used by any other party while the connection was active.

Although the model uses traditional IP packet forwarding in the default case, it allows senders and receivers to exchange explicit signaling messages that make resource reservations, establish paths through the network, and manage packet classification and forwarding status information on each router along the path. It also requires application support for the RSVP signaling protocol because applications need to be able to register their QoS requirements with the underlying network environment.

The Resource Reservation Protocol was designed specifically to support IntServ. A corresponding standard defines the use of RSVP within this architecture (RFC 2210).

Although IntServ was the predominant school of thought in the early QoS debate, its general applicability has been questioned in comparison to the Differentiated Services Architecture. In addition, the complexity of RSVP has led to further resistance against IntServ as the general Internet QoS model.

Differentiated Services Architecture

The Differentiated Services Architecture (DiffServ, RFC 2475) is based on the general paradigm stating that relative priority and type-of-service markings within the codepoints of the DS byte in each QoS-sensitive IP packet are sufficient to derive QoS-specific treatment of packets at each router, without the need for explicit path setup and reservation signaling. DiffServ is not considered an end-to-end service, but is based on the determination of the PHB in each router. Within the network, the scope of DiffServ may be restricted to DiffServ domains, which can in turn be connected via a non-QoS-aware routing network.

An IP packet's DS field is used to indicate the packet's QoS requirements and is then used by each DiffServ router to determine the forwarding treatment for the packet; dynamic elements such as classifiers and traffic conditioners can therefore be used to select which packets are to be added to QoS classes (or aggregates). These aggregates receive differentiated treatment in a DS domain, and traffic conditioners change the temporal characteristics of the aggregate to be able to conform to traffic policing requirements.

In addition to being a contender to the IntServ paradigm, DiffServ mechanisms may also work with IntServ—in particular, to aggregate IntServ/RSVP QoS state. This is used on local area networks with integrated management and service quality, in the core of the wide area transmission network, and consists of a sequence of subnetworks that are not uniquely managed and therefore cannot provide end-to-end QoS. In such a scenario, RSVP would be used only inside the LAN environments and between routers at the edges between providers (Figure 6-2).

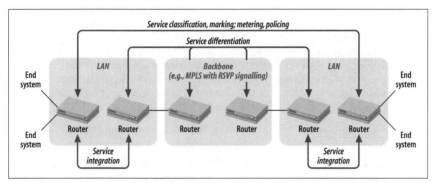

Figure 6-2. Possible common service architecture

Mapping IP QoS to Underlying Transmission Networks

IP is traditionally able to run over almost any network transmission layer. While this approach has a clear advantage in terms of connectivity and interoperability on the network layer, it also means that only common-denominator functionality is required from the transmission layer. Even if the underlying transmission protocols offer advanced services, such as fragmenting or reassembly of packets and QoS-handling capabilities, IP standardization has a tendency to be self-sustained and either ignores these capabilities or redesigns them within the network or transport layer.

Along these lines, IP QoS elements have been designed as standalone mechanisms. Any mapping onto lower-layer QoS elements, such as ATM traffic classes or Multi-Protocol Label Switching (MPLS) traffic engineering attributes, are either not foreseen or are in the early stages of design and implementation (often driven by interested vendors).

While mapping IP QoS elements to fixed-quality transmission services such as ATM traffic classes may seem straightforward, the dynamic mapping of IP QoS to MPLS attributes is a much more difficult task. For this mapping, path-forwarding state and traffic management or QoS state is defined for traffic streams on each router along the path. According to the general model in RFC 2475:

"...traffic aggregates of varying granularity are associated with a label switched path at the ingress point, and packets/cells within each label switched path are marked with a forwarding label that is used to lookup the next-hop node, the per-hop forwarding behaviour, and the replacement label at each node. This model permits finer granularity resource allocation to traffic streams, since label values are not globally significant but are only significant on a single link; therefore resources can be reserved for the aggregate of packets/cells received on a link with a particular label, and the label switching semantics govern the next-hop selection, allowing a traffic stream to follow a specially engineered path through the network. This improved granularity comes at the cost of additional management and configuration requirements to establish and maintain the label switched paths..."

Both MPLS and IP QoS are still areas of research, simultaneously being standardized by the IETF and implemented and improved by vendors. Substantial changes and extensions can be expected in this area, which in turn keeps many customers from introducing corresponding services within their networks.

Further Issues in IP QoS

Besides the issue of having to harmonize the competing IntServ and DiffServ architectures, a number of other open issues drive the further development of QoS on the Internet:

- Some QoS services will be based on complex multicast mechanisms; thus, full interoperability with the Internet-wide multicasting will have to be maintained, while not disturbing the operation of the non-QoS Internet.

- QoS mechanisms need to operate properly in tunneling and IPSEC environments, which may require a mapping function of QoS requirements between "inner" and "outer" IP packets. In some topologies, QoS determination may not be possible at all—in particular, when the "inner" IP packet is protected by encryption.

- QoS for mobile IP networks is still a topic of research. As a mobile system uses different access points in the Internet, the path to the mobile system also changes, which in turn leads to varying QoS behavior. A recent IETF working draft proposes a new IPv6 option (QoS object) carried by a destination, of Hop-by-Hop Extension header and signaling QoS requirements.

- Finally, the main issue with Internet QoS is the inherent complexity of the problem and of possible solutions. This complexity affects designers, vendors, managers, and users of QoS services alike, and it can only be compensated for by careful design, standardization, implementation, and deployment.

Despite all the open issues, QoS provisioning on the Internet will eventually become a reality. It will most likely grow from the inside out, with QoS islands being connected by non-QoS-aware Internet trunks. QoS will also need more time for large-scale experimentation, but commercial pressure is mounting—not only by end users requiring multimedia support, but also by Internet service and content providers striving to better utilize their bandwidth and commercially distribute multimedia information.

CHAPTER 7
Networking Aspects

IP sits between the Data Link layer and the Transport layer. One of the goals in the development of IPv6 was that it be able to support as many different physical networks as possible and require no changes in the Transport layer. This approach is called "IP over Everything." In order to make IP as independent as possible from the Data Link layer, it needs an interface to this layer, which can be Ethernet, ATM, Token Ring, or any other media. The interface needs to be flexible and able to adapt to different requirements. For this purpose, features such as Path MTU discovery and fragmentation have been optimized. For UDP and TCP, it should not matter whether IPv4 or IPv6 is used. Obviously, changes are needed whenever IP addresses are used, because of the difference in the address format. All these requirements lead to changes built into the IP layer itself. Multicast has been enhanced and broadcast will not be used with IPv6. This chapter discusses the interface to the Data Link layer and IP features such as multicasting and mobility, and it also shows some sample network design scenarios that can be deployed.

Layer 2 Support for IPv6

Different terms are used when the Data Link layer is discussed. The TCP/IP model has four layers, the first of which is called the Link layer. The OSI model has seven layers. It subdivides the Link layer of the TCP/IP model into two layers, called the Physical layer and the Data Link layer. Thus, when the term Layer 2 is used, it refers to the second layer of the OSI model.

IPv6's independency of the physical network media is important. When a packet is sent from one network to another, we do not usually know in advance the kind of physical networks the packet will travel through. IP cares only about the destination address and needs to find a way to get there, regardless of the network hardware used. Then IP passes the packet to the Data Link layer. In 802 networks, the interface driver on the Data Link layer applies a Media Access Control (MAC) header to the datagram and sends it out to the physical network. The interface driver needs to be aware of the physical requirements for transmission. Each network hardware technology defines a specific addressing mechanism. Neighbor discovery, as described in Chapter 4, is used to map between IPv6 addresses and MAC addresses.

The rules and packet sizes for the transport of IPv6 datagrams differ depending on the topology. There is an RFC covering each topology in detail. This chapter summarizes the main points to consider; a complete list of the RFCs can be found in the Appendix.

Ethernet (RFC 2464)

Ethernet is a widely used LAN technology, developed in the early 1970s at Xerox. There are many different variants used these days: Twisted Pair Ethernet, also known as 10Base-T and operating at 10 Mbps; Fast Ethernet, also known as 100Base-T and operating at 100 Mbps; Gigabit Ethernet also known as 1000Base-T and operating at 1 Gbps; and now even 10 Gigabit Ethernet, also known as 10GE and operating at 10 Gbps. The Institute of Electrical and Electronic Engineers (IEEE), together with a number of IT and telecom companies, is working on a new proposal called Ethernet for the First Mile (EFM) or Long Reach Ethernet (LRE). They are investigating ways in which the Ethernet standard could be used for first-mile connections to homes and companies. For information about 10GE, refer to *http://www. 10gea.org*; for information about EFM, refer to *http://grouper.ieee.org/ groups/802/3/efm/public/index.html*.

RFC 2464 describes the format of IPv6 datagrams transmitted over Ethernet. It also describes how link-local and stateless autoconfigured addresses are formed. It obsoletes RFC 1972. All Ethernet variants are supported, as well as VLAN technologies such as 802.1Q and Cisco's Inter-Switch Link (ISL).

Ethernet hardware addresses use a 48-bit addressing scheme. Ethernet hardware manufacturers are assigned blocks of Ethernet addresses, known as OUI or company ID. No two Ethernet hardware interfaces have the same address because each vendor assigns the addresses within its block in sequence. An Ethernet frame can be of variable size, but it can be no smaller than 64 bytes and no larger than 1518 bytes (header, data, and CRC). Packets over Ethernet have a default MTU of 1500 bytes. A smaller MTU can be configured through Router Advertisements containing an MTU option or through manual configuration of each device. If a Router Advertisement contains an MTU larger than 1500 bytes or larger than a manually configured MTU, the Router Advertisement must be ignored.

The Ethernet header contains the source and destination Ethernet addresses and the Ethernet type code. The Ethernet type code for IPv6 is 0x86DD. Figure 7-1 shows the Ethernet header for an IPv6 datagram.

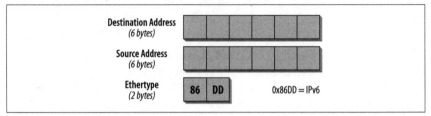

Figure 7-1. The Ethernet header for an IPv6 datagram

The fields for Destination and Source address each have six bytes, and the Ethernet Type field takes two bytes, containing the value 86DD for Ethernet.

For stateless autoconfiguration, the MAC address is used to build the IPv6 address. Chapter 3 explains how this process works. If the destination address is a multicast address, the first two bytes of the MAC address are set to 3333 and the last four bytes are the last four bytes of the IPv6 destination multicast address. If the destination address is the solicited-node multicast address (described in Chapter 3), the first two bytes in the MAC header contain the multicast prefix 3333, the third byte contains the value FF, and the last three bytes contain the last three bytes of the IPv6 solicited-node multicast address. Figure 7-2 shows the format.

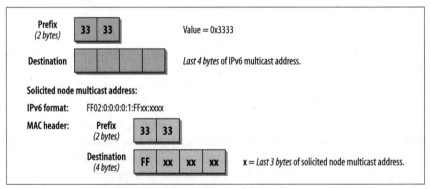

Figure 7-2. Relation of the IPv6 multicast address to Ethernet MAC address

In a trace file, this looks like Figure 7-3.

In the summary line at the top of the figure, you can see the IPv6 source address, which is the address of my Cisco router. The destination address is the all-nodes multicast address. The Ethernet destination prefix shows 3333,

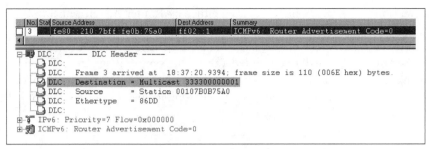

Figure 7-3. MAC header for an IPv6 multicast destination address

which identifies this MAC address as a multicast address, and the remaining four bytes contain the last four bytes of the IPv6 destination address—in this case 00-00-00-01. The Ethernet source address contains the MAC address of the Cisco router, and the *Ethertype* has the value for IPv6, which is 0x86DD.

> For useful information about Ethernet refer to Charles E. Spurgeon's site: *http://www.ethermanage.com/ethernet/ether-net.html*. He is also the author of *Ethernet: The Definitive Guide* (O'Reilly & Associates).

FDDI (RFC 2467)

Fiber Distributed Data Interconnect (FDDI) is a LAN technology operating at 100Mbps over optical fiber using light pulses. FDDI is a Token Ring protocol, using a token to control transmission. A station that wants to transmit waits for the token circulating the ring, sends the packet, and passes the token to the next station in the ring. Just like Token Ring, FDDI has a lot of built-in self-healing mechanisms. An FDDI frame has fields measured in 4-bit units called symbols.

RFC 2467 describes the format of IPv6 datagrams transmitted over FDDI. It also describes how link-local and stateless autoconfigured addresses are formed and specifies the content of the Source/Target Link-layer Address option that is used in Router Solicitation, Router Advertisement, Neighbor Solicitation, Neighbor Advertisement, and Redirect messages when transmitted over an FDDI network. It obsoletes RFC 2019.

An FDDI hardware address can be 4 or 12 symbols long. The maximum packet size for FDDI is 4500 bytes (9000 symbols). 22 bytes are used for Data Link encapsulation when long-format addresses are used, and another 8 bytes are used for the LLC/SNAP header. This leaves a maximum size of 4470 bytes for the IPv6 packet. The default MTU size for IPv6 packets on FDDI networks has been set to 4352 bytes in order to allow possible future extensions. This size can be reduced either by Router Advertisements containing an MTU option or by manual configuration of each device. If a Router Advertisement contains an MTU value higher than 4352 bytes or higher than a manually configured value, this option is ignored. The IPv6 datagrams are transmitted in asynchronous frames using unrestricted tokens and with a LLC/SNAP frame using 48-bit long-format addresses. Figure 7-4 shows the format of the FDDI header.

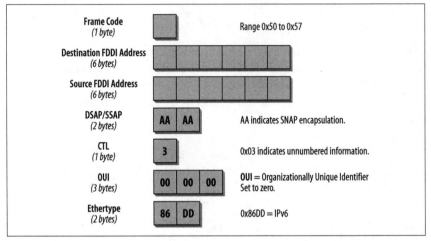

Figure 7-4. The FDDI header for an IPv6 datagram

The Frame Code field (FC) has a size of 1 byte and contains a value in the range 0x50 to 0x57. The 3 low order bits indicate the frame priority. Both the Destination Service Access Point (DSAP) and the Source Service Access Point (SSAP) fields contain the value AA, which indicates SNAP encapsulation. The Control field (CTL) is set to 0x03, indicating Unnumbered Information. The Organizationally Unique Identifier (OUI) is set to zero. The Ethertype field contains the value 0x86DD, for IPv6.

The rules that govern how a stateless autoconfigured IPv6 address is built from the MAC address and the rules that govern how IPv6 multicast destination addresses are converted to MAC addresses are the same as those used and described in the paragraph on Ethernet.

For tutorials and resources on FDDI, refer to *http://www.iol.unh.edu/training/fddi/htmls*.

Token Ring (RFC 2470)

Token Ring is a well-known LAN technology developed by IBM. It is a token-ring protocol using a token for transmission control, as described for

FDDI. It operates at either 4 or 16 Mbps. The frame size of a Token Ring packet varies, depending on the time a node can hold the token.

RFC 2470 describes the format of IPv6 datagrams transmitted over Token Ring. It also describes how link-local and stateless autoconfigured addresses are formed and specifies the content of the Source/Target Link-layer Address option that is used in Router Solicitation, Router Advertisement, Neighbor Solicitation, Neighbor Advertisement, and Redirect messages when transmitted over a Token Ring network.

A Token Ring hardware address uses a 48-bit format. Because the frame size is variable, it should be configured through Router Advertisements or manually. In the absence of information, a default size of 1500 bytes should be used. As is always the case when working with Token Ring, we have to consider that Token Ring adapters read the address in noncanonical rather than canonical form, meaning they read the bits in reverse order (last bit first). Thus, when analyzing and troubleshooting Token Ring in mixed environments, we need to make sure that implementations process the addresses correctly.

The Token Ring header is shown in Figure 7-5.

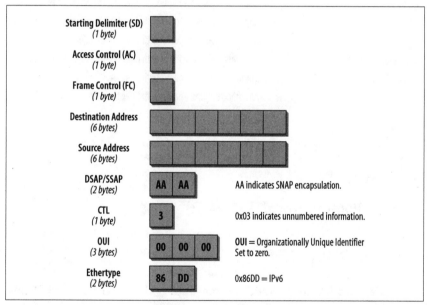

Figure 7-5. The Token Ring header for an IPv6 datagram

The first three fields for Starting Delimiter (SD), Access Control (AC), and Frame Control (FC) each have a size of 1 byte. The fields for Source and Destination Address each have 6 bytes. The DSAP and SSAP fields are set to the value AA, which indicates SNAP encapsulation. The Control field (CTL) is set to the value 0x03, indicating Unnumbered Information. The OUI is set to zero. And the *Ethertype* field contains the value for IPv6 0x86DD.

The rule governing how a stateless autoconfigured IPv6 address is built from the MAC address is the same as that used and described in the paragraph on Ethernet. Multicast addresses are treated differently with Token Ring, as described in RFC 2470. Packets with multicast destination addresses are sent to Token Ring Functional Addresses. The RFC states ten different functional addresses, and multiple IPv6 multicast addresses are mapped to each. Table 7-1 lists the mappings that have been defined.

Table 7-1. Mapping IPv6 multicast addresses to Token Ring Functional Addresses

MAC Functional Address (canonical)	Multicast addresses
03-00-80-00-00-00	All-nodes (FF01::1 and FF02::1)
	Solicited-node (FF02:0:0:0:0.1:FFxx:xxxx)
03-00-40-00-00-00	All-routers (FF0X::2)
03-00-00-80-00-00	Any other multicast address with three least significant bits = 000
03-00-00-40-00-00	Any other multicast address with three least significant bits = 001
03-00-00-20-00-00	Any other multicast address with three least significant bits = 010
03-00-00-10-00-00	Any other multicast address with three least significant bits = 011
03-00-00-08-00-00	Any other multicast address with three least significant bits = 100
03-00-00-04-00-00	Any other multicast address with three least significant bits = 101
03-00-00-02-00-00	Any other multicast address with three least significant bits = 110
03-00-00-01-00-00	Any other multicast address with three least significant bits = 111

 For a great Token Ring resource, refer to *Novell's Guide to LAN/WAN Analysis* by Laura A. Chappell (John Wiley & Sons).

Point-to-Point Protocol (RFC 2472)

Point-to-Point Protocol (PPP) is a mechanism for running IP and other network protocols over a serial link. It supports synchronous and asynchronous lines.

RFC 2472 describes the method for transmitting IPv6 packets over PPP and how IPv6 link-local addresses are formed on PPP links.

PPP's control protocol for IPv6, IPV6CP, is responsible for establishing and configuring IPv6 communication over PPP. One IPv6 packet can be encapsulated in a PPP Data Link layer frame, and the protocol field is set to 0x0057 for IPv6. If the PPP link is to support IPv6, the MTU size must be configured to IPv6's minimum MTU size of IPv6, which is 1280 bytes. A higher value (1500 bytes) is recommended.

IPV6CP has a distinct set of options for the negotiation of IPv6 parameters. The Options field has the same format as that defined for the standard Link Control Protocol (LCP). The only currently defined options for IPV6CP are Interface-Identifier and IPv6-Compression Protocol. A PPP interface does not have a MAC address. The Interface-Identifier option provides a way to negotiate a 64-bit interface identifier, which must be unique within the PPP link. The IPv6-Compression option is used to negotiate a specific packet compression protocol, which applies only to IPv6 packets transmitted over the PPP link. The option is not enabled by default.

IPv6 address negotiation is different from IPv4. It is done through ICMPv6 neighbor discovery and not through PPP, as with IPv4. For ISPs, PPP in combination with IPv6 offers many advantages. For instance, it is no longer a problem to assign static addresses to customers because the IPv6 address space is large enough. With IPv4, due to the shortage of addresses, dynamic addresses often had to be used. The IPv6 functionality for address autoconfiguration supports easy administration and customer configuration with minimal cost. Prefix assignment to the customer site can be done through router discovery or through a process called ICMPv6 prefix assignment protocol, currently in development. To get IPv6 to work over ADSL, ISPs need to choose an encapsulation that meets their needs, such as PPP over ATM (PPPoA) or PPP over Ethernet (PPPoE). IPv6 also has an impact on the Authentication, Authorization, Accounting (AAA) process. With IPV6CP, the address assignment occurs after the authentication. ISPs should note that Radius must support IPv6 attributes.

ATM (RFC 2492)

Asynchronous Transfer Mode (ATM) is a connection-oriented, high-speed network technology that is used in both LANs and WANs. It works over optical fiber and operates up to gigabit speed. It uses special hardware and software mechanisms to achieve this speed.

An ATM network uses fixed-size frames called cells. Each cell is exactly 53 bytes long, and because it always has the same size, processing is very fast. An ATM cell has a header length of 5 bytes and 48 bytes of data. The ATM Adaptation Layer (AAL5, RFC 2684) is the mechanism responsible for dividing a big packet, such as an IP packet, into small cells. This can be compared to the way fragmentation works. The sender divides the packet into a set of 53 byte cells, and the receiver verifies that the packet has been received intact without errors and puts it back together again. If one cell is lost in transit, the whole set has to be resent. Because ATM does not support hardware broadcast and multicast, another mechanism that emulates it has been defined. All hosts in an ATM network register with the ATMARP server. If a host on the subnet sends a broadcast or multicast, the packet is sent to the ATMARP server, which distributes the packet to all registered hosts on the subnet/link. ATMARP is a variant of ARP and is defined in RFC 2225.

RFC 2492 describes the transmission of IPv6 packets over an ATM network. It is a companion document to RFC 2491, "IPv6 over non-broadcast multiple access (NBMA) Networks."

When the ATM network is used as a Permanent Virtual Circuit (PVC), each PVC connects two nodes, and the use of neighbor discovery is limited. IPv6 ATM interfaces have only one neighbor on each link. Multicast and broadcast are transmitted as a unicast on the ATM level. PVCs do not have link-layer addresses, so the link-layer address option is not used in neighbor discovery messages. IPv6 unicast and multicast packets sent over ATM are encapsulated using the LLC/SNAP encapsulation. Just as with FDDI and Token Ring, the DSAP and SSAP fields contain the value AA, and the CT field contains the value 0x03. The OUI field is set to zero and the *Ethertype* field contains the value for IPv6, 0x86DD (see Figures 7-4 and 7-5). The default MTU size for an ATM PVC link is 9180 bytes.

If the ATM network is used as a Switched Virtual Circuit (SVC), unicast packets are transmitted using LLC/SNAP encapsulation, as described for PVC. For the transmission of multicast packets over SVC, the OUI field is set to 0x00005E, and the Ethertype field to 0x0001.

A good place for information about ATM is the ATM Forum at *http://www. atmforum.com*. Another great resource site can be found at *http://cell-relay. indiana.edu/cell-relay*.

There were a lot of discussions going on about whether IP was necessary on ATM networks: why not write applications to run natively on ATM? Finally, "IP over Everything" was developed. With the growing popularity of Fast Ethernet and Gigabit Ethernet, application designers have decided not to port their applications for transport over ATM directly. By writing their applications for IP, they needed to write only one interface and use the layer 2 functionality to run on all physical networks.

Frame Relay (RFC 2590)

Frame Relay is a connection-oriented, high-speed network technology used in WANs. It was developed in the Bell Labs in the late 1980s as part of the

ISDN specification. The standard was refined in the early 1990s. By using a short, 2-byte header, Frame Relay is very efficient in forwarding packets.

RFC 2590 specifies how IPv6 packets are transmitted over Frame Relay links, how IPv6 link-local addresses are formed, and how IPv6 addresses are mapped to Frame Relay addresses. It applies to Frame Relay devices that act as end stations (Data Terminal Equipment [DTEs]) on public or private Frame Relay networks. The Frame Relay Virtual Circuits can be PVCs or SVCs, and they can be point-to-point or point-to-multipoint. The default IPv6 MTU size for a Frame Relay interface is 1592 bytes.

Figure 7-6 shows the header of an IPv6 packet transmitted over Frame Relay.

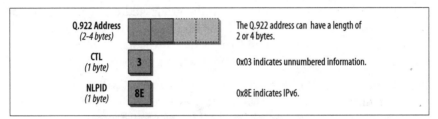

Q.922 Address (2-4 bytes)		The Q.922 address can have a length of 2 or 4 bytes.
CTL (1 byte)	3	0x03 indicates unnumbered information.
NLPID (1 byte)	8E	0x8E indicates IPv6.

Figure 7-6. The Frame Relay header for an IPv6 datagram

The field for the Q.922 Address can be 2 or 4 bytes, depending on the address. The Control field (CTL) is set to 0x03, indicating Unnumbered Information. The Next Level Protocol ID (NLPID) contains the value 0x8E, indicating IPv6. The mapping of IPv6 addresses follows the specification for neighbor discovery, as described in Chapter 3. The details regarding addressing mechanisms and formats of Frame Relay addresses are discussed in RFC 2590.

A good resource for Frame Relay information can be found at *http://www.frforum.com*.

 If you are looking for a detailed discussion of TCP/IP internetworking issues on all layers, refer to Douglas E. Comers's book *TCP/IP: Principles, Protocols, and Architectures* (Prentice Hall).

Multicasting

Multicast has been available in IPv4 since 1988 and is used to address a certain group of hosts at the same time. Instead of sending out a broadcast, which is not routable and has to be processed by every node on the subnet, the multicast packet is addressed to a multicast group address out of the

Class D address range. Only the hosts that are members of that multicast group will process the packet. Internet Group Management Protocol (IGMP) manages group memberships and routing of IPv4 multicast packets. The deployment of IPv4 multicast capabilities was supported by the MBONE project, started in 1992. The MBONE is a virtual network layered on top of portions of the physical Internet to support routing of IP multicast packets; it was created because that function had not yet been integrated into many production routers. The network is composed of islands that can directly support IP multicast, such as multicast LANs (like Ethernet) linked by virtual point-to-point links (tunnels).

In IPv6, multicast is an integral part of the protocol and available on all IPv6 nodes. A new multicast address format has been defined with added functionality by using scopes in addition to the group address. For example, a multicast group address can be in a link-local scope (FF02), in a site-local scope (FF05), or in a global scope (FF0E). For an explanation of the multicast address format and a list of scope identifiers, refer to Chapter 3.

The functionality of IGMP has been incorporated in ICMPv6 and is called Multicast Listener Discovery (MLD). It uses three different ICMPv6 message types. For a detailed discussion of MLD, refer to Chapter 4.

 A list of assigned IPv6 multicast group addresses can be found at *http://www.iana.org/assignments/ipv6-multicast-addresses* or in the Appendix.

Multicast routing is still a topic of research and development. A number of multicast routing protocols have already been standardized for IPv4. Distance Vector Multicast Routing Protocol (DVMRP) was the first multicast routing protocol deployed on the Internet. It maintains topological knowledge via a distance-vector routing protocol, similar to RIP, and it implements a multicast-forwarding algorithm called Truncated Reverse Path Broadcasting. Just like any distance-vector routing protocol, DVMRP suffers from scaling problems. Multicast Extension to OSPF (MOSPF) provides routing capabilities for OSPF. Protocol Independent Multicast (PIM) is the most popular multicast routing protocol used on the Internet. It has been designed specifically to support multicast routing where multicast group members are spread sparsely across a WAN. A newer protocol, Border Gateway Multicast Protocol (BGMP), operates more efficiently. It is based on BGP and was designed to manage interoperability between multicast routing protocols in different domains.

IPv6 multicast routing is similar to IPv4 multicast routing. The multicast extensions for OSPF have been carried over in OSPFv3 (discussed in

Chapter 8). PIM can be implemented with minimal changes. IPv6's extended address space provides a large number of multicast group addresses, and the addition of the multicast scope field makes multicast more flexible and scalable. PIM Version 2 is widely deployed and is defined in RFC 2362. The specification in this RFC is insufficient, however, and the working group is rewriting the RFC and has added information about IPv6. This is currently a draft but is intended to obsolete RFC 2362. The current draft is *http://www.ietf.org/internet-drafts/draft-ietf-pim-sm-v2-new-05.txt* (the number of the draft may have increased by one or more). We can expect the multicast routing issue to be taken a step further with the advent of IPv6.

Mobile IP

In the past, we were used to making phone calls from home or from the office. Public phones allowed us to make phone calls while on the road. Today, the use of mobile phones is common and we make phone calls from almost anywhere and in any life situation. The use of notebook computers, wireless networks, and portable devices is expanding, and we can imagine having mobile phones or PDAs with IP addresses and using them from wherever we are. If these devices are to use IP as a transport protocol, we need Mobile IP to make this work. We expect our network communication to reconnect automatically and without interaction when we move around and change our point of attachment to the network, just as we are used to roaming from one cell to the next with our mobile phones today. For example, suppose you have a PDA with an 802.11 (wireless) interface and a General Packet Radio Service (GPRS) interface. In your hotel room, you are connected to the network through your wireless interface; when you leave your room and go out to the street, you switch automatically to GPRS without losing your connection. All the applications running on your PDA stay up. Isn't this cool? This section about Mobile IP explores the mechanisms needed and shows how IPv6 is ready for this challenge.

With IPv4 and IPv6, the subnet address or prefix address changes depending on the network we are attached to. When a mobile node changes its point of access to the network, it will most likely need to get a new IP address, which disrupts its TCP or UDP connection. RFC 2002, "IP Mobility Support," describes protocol enhancements that allow transparent routing of IP datagrams to mobile nodes in the Internet. RFC 2002 describes Mobile IP concepts and specifications for IPv4. Mobile IP has a lot of advantages with IPv6. This is currently described in a draft at *http://www.ietf.org/internet-drafts/draft-ietf-mobileip-ipv6-15.txt*. (Note that the draft number may have increased by one or more.)

Most Internet traffic uses TCP connections. A TCP connection is defined by the combination of IP address and port number of both end-points of the communication. If one of these four numbers changes, the communication is disrupted and has to be reestablished. If a mobile node connects to a different access point to the network, it needs a new IP address. Mobile IP addresses the challenge of moving a node to a different connection point without changing its IP address by assigning the mobile node two different IP addresses. One is the home address; it is static and does not change. It is therefore used to identify the TCP connection. The second IP address is called the care-of address. It changes depending on the network to which the node is currently attached. To make this work, Mobile IP requires a Home Agent. When the mobile node is not attached to its home network, the Home Agent collects all the packets directed to the mobile node's home address and forwards them to the mobile node's care-of address. Whenever the mobile node moves to a different network, it has to register its new care-of address with its Home Agent. In Mobile IPv4, the foreign network has a Foreign Agent assisting the mobile node in receiving the datagrams. A node sending packets to a mobile node is called a correspondent node. Figure 7-7 shows the interaction between the mobile node and the agents.

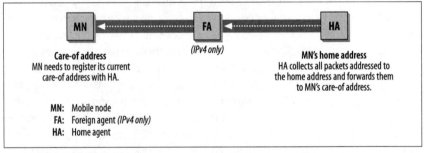

Figure 7-7. The Mobile IP agents

Figure 7-7 shows the Home Agent (HA) receiving the packets addressed to the mobile node's (MN) home address and forwarding them to the care-of address. The Home Agent knows the care-of address because the mobile node has to register it whenever it moves to a different network.

The Home Agent, when redirecting a packet addressed to the mobile node's home address, has to change the destination IP address to the care-of address of the mobile node. When the mobile node receives the datagram, the IP address is changed again so that it appears to have the home address of the mobile node as a destination IP address. The Home Agent does this by applying a new IP header with the care-of address in the destination address field and encapsulating the original packet in this new IP header.

When the mobile node receives the packet, it removes the additional IP header, and the original packet is processed as usual. So what the Home Agent actually does is tunneling. The Mobile IP discovery process uses Router Advertisements (as defined in RFC 1256 and RFC 2461) and extends them to add mobility information such as the care-of address. These extended Router Advertisements are called Agent Advertisements. Agents advertise at regular intervals, and mobile nodes can solicit advertisements if they do not want to wait for the next advertising. These solicitation messages are called Agent Solicitation messages.

A mobile node sends a registration request to its Home Agent containing the care-of address. The Home Agent accepts the request and sends a registration reply back. Registration requests contain parameters and flags regarding this specific tunnel, including a registration lifetime. The combination of Home address, care-of address, and registration lifetime is called a binding. When the mobile node moves to a different network, it issues a binding update registering the new care-of address. It is evident that this mechanism poses a potential security hole. The mobile node and the Home Agent need an authentication mechanism so the Home Agent can determine that the binding update is received from the mobile node. The mobile node and the Home Agent must be able to use Message Digest 5 (MD5, RFC 1321) with 128-bit keys to create unforgeable digital signatures for registration requests. The signature is computed by performing MD5's one-way hash algorithm over all the data within the registration message header and the extensions that precede the signature.

The concepts discussed so far apply to both IPv4 and IPv6. The advanced features of IPv6 make Mobile IP easier to implement. Mobile IPv6 does not need a Foreign Agent because stateless autoconfiguration and neighbor discovery offer the needed functionality and are built into IPv6. Tunneling of IPv6 within IPv6, which is what the Home Agent does when forwarding a packet to the care-of address of the mobile node, is specified in RFC 2473. With Mobile IPv4, all packets sent to the mobile node always go through the Home Agent. This undesirable behavior is called triangular routing. With Mobile IPv6, Extension headers are used to allow the sending of packets to the mobile node's care-of address directly by caching the binding of a mobile node's home address with its care-of address. The mobile node attached to a foreign network now uses its care-of address as a source address when sending packets. The mobile node's home address is carried in a Destination Options header, which means the session control information is piggybacked onto the same packet. In Mobile IPv4, those control messages had to be sent in separate UDP packets. The use of the care-of address as the source address also simplifies multicast routing. With Mobile IPv4, multicast packets had to be tunneled to the Home Agent in order to use the home address as source address of the multicast packet. In IPv6, this information is included in the Destination Options header and can be processed by every receiving node. With Mobile IPv4, all packets sent to the home address while the mobile node is connected to a foreign network must be encapsulated. With IPv6, packets sent to the mobile nodes home address must still be encapsulated, but packets exchanged directly once the binding update has happened can be sent using a Routing header, which is more efficient and creates less overhead. With Mobile IPv4, a mobile node detects a Home Agent by sending out a broadcast request and therefore receives separate answers from all Home Agents on its segment. With IPv6, the request is sent using an anycast address, which results in one reply only.

 Great reference sites about Mobile IP on the Internet include: *http://computer.org/internet/v2n1/perkins.htm* and *http://www.computer.org/internet/v2n1/mobile.htm*.

There is still development work to be done to make Mobile IP a reality, but the specification has a lot of potential. Much care must be taken to make it secure. Mobile IP is a solution for wireless networks and the demand for wireless networks has been growing considerably in recent months. Mobile IP has been studied in a number of wireless communication research projects at the University of California at Berkeley and other universities. The links mentioned in the note contain more detailed information.

Network Designs

When we start using IPv6, different approaches are possible. I'll give some sample scenarios here. It is important to understand that getting started with IPv6 does not mean you have to tear down your IPv4 infrastructure or switch everything at one time. The specific mechanisms for coexistence of IPv4 and IPv6, such as 6to4 operations, tunneling, and protocol translation, are explained in Chapter 10.

The simplest way to start using IPv6 is to implement single IPv6 hosts in an IPv4 network. They will autoconfigure for a link-local IPv6 address and be able to communicate with one another over IPv6. They use ICMPv6 neighbor discovery messages to locate one another. If they also have an IPv4 stack, they can communicate with the IPv4 world. Using ISATAP, a large number of hosts within a site with no IPv6 router can communicate. If one of the IPv6 nodes is configured as a 6to4 gateway and is connected to the

Internet, other IPv6 sites on the Internet can be reached through the use of a 6to4 relay router.

The next expansion step is to add an IPv6 router to the scenario. As discussed in Chapter 4, router discovery and Router Advertisement messages can be used for configuration of IPv6 hosts on the subnet. For instance, the router can be configured to advertise a subnet prefix and hop limit. Thus, all IPv6 hosts on the subnet can be configured for their address without the need for static configuration or even a DHCP server. This is all done by the autoconfiguration mechanisms, including the subnet prefix advertisement of the router. Within a corporate network, multiple combinations are possible. There can be segments with mixed IPv6 and IPv4 hosts and dual-stack hosts. There can also be segments with IPv6-only hosts. The IPv6-only segment can communicate with IPv6 hosts on the mixed segment by going through a router that has an IPv6 interface to the IPv6-only segment and a dual-stack interface to the mixed segment.

As soon as two IPv6 routers are added to the subnet, a routing protocol must be used—RIPv6, for instance. The router can also be configured as 6to4 gateways connecting the internal IPv6 network to other IPv6 sites on the Internet. At this point, DNS and DHCP servers can be added to the scenario. The DNS server has to run BIND 9 because that is the version that supports IPv6. If it is a third-party DNS server, it must be based on BIND 9 and support IPv6 functionality.

The sample design in Figure 7-8 combines different scenarios and should help explain the scope of configurations that are possible.

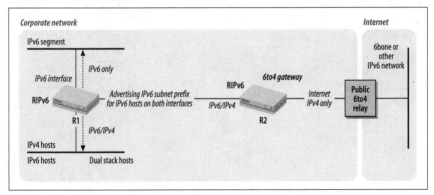

Figure 7-8. Example of a corporate network design

The corporate network has different segments. Some segments are IPv6-only, some are IPv4-only, and some have a mixture of IPv6-only, IPv4-only, and dual-stack hosts. To simplify the picture, I show just one IPv6 segment and an IPv6/IPv4 segment. Router R1 has one interface connected to the IPv6-only segment, running IPv6 and RIPv6 and advertising the subnet prefix for the IPv6-only segment to the hosts out on the network. R1's other interface is connected to the mixed segment and has both protocol versions bound. Some hosts on that segment are IPv4-only, some hosts are IPv6-only, and some hosts run in dual-stack mode. Router R1 advertises the subnet prefix to that subnet and runs RIPv6. R1 is connected to router R2. R2's internal interface is dual-stack. It is also configured as a 6to4 gateway and connected to the public Internet with its other interface. The other interface is IPv4-only and has a public IPv4 address. In the configuration of the 6to4 gateway, the address of a public 6to4 relay agent can be specified, or it can use the 6to4 anycast address to find the nearest 6to4 relay router. In that case, any of the IPv6 hosts within the corporate network can reach any other IPv6 host connected to the 6to4 relay router, such as another corporate site connected to the Internet. That site could also have mixed IPv6/IPv4 segments and IPv6-only segments. Alternatively, the IPv6 hosts on our site can connect to any of the hosts in the 6Bone or the growing community of public IPv6 hosts with production addresses.

 For more detailed scenarios, go to Cisco's web site at *http:// www.cisco.com* and search for "IPv6 Deployment Strategies." It guides you through the planning and deployment tasks step by step.

Allocation of production IPv6 addresses has started all over the world, and Chapter 1 includes some information about the first IPv6 production networks.

CHAPTER 8

Routing Protocols

Forwarding an IPv6 datagram beyond local media requires a router. Routers look at the datagram's destination IPv6 address and search for a matching prefix in their local routing table. (A routing table is a list of IPv6 destinations, each in the form of an IPv6 address prefix and its length.) Once the router has found a matching destination entry, the datagram is forwarded according to the next-hop information associated with this entry in the routing table. If no match is found in the routing table, the datagram is dropped, so it is very important for the router to have all relevant destinations in its routing table. But how do they get there? The routing table could be entered manually on all routers, but this is not very economical. Routing protocols define exchange procedures to synchronize the routing table between routers dynamically. Routing information needs to be distributed either within an autonomous system (AS) or between autonomous systems. An AS is defined as a set of networks governed by a single authority. Routing protocols that distribute information within an AS are called Interior Gateway Protocols (IGP). RIPng and OSPF for IPv6 belong to this category. Protocols that distribute information between ASes are called Exterior Gateway Protocols (EGP). BGP-4 and its extension for IPv6 represent such a protocol. This chapter explains RIPng, OSPF for IPv6, and BGP-4. The last section of this chapter focuses on additional and upcoming protocols for IPv6.

 There is no distinction between network, subnet, and host routes in the routing table because an IPv6 address prefix is unambiguous. Throughout this document, IPv6 destinations will be referred to as IPv6 routes.

RIPng

RIPng is a routing protocol based on a distance-vector algorithm known as the Bellman-Ford algorithm. The theory and math behind this algorithm will be outlined briefly in this section. Most of the concepts for RIPng have been taken from RIPv1 and RIPv2. Please consult RFC 1058 (RIPv1) and RFC 2453 (RIPv2) for detailed explanations regarding the distance-vector algorithm. RIPng was defined in RFC 2080 in January 1997.

Distance-Vector Algorithm for RIPng

Each router keeps a routing table listing the best path to each IPv6 route. Figure 8-1 shows an example of such a routing table.

For each route, the router keeps the following entries in the routing table:

IPv6 route
> The IPv6 address prefix and prefix length of the destination address.

Next Hop address
> The IPv6 address (normally link-local) of the first router along the path to the IPv6 route. If the route is directly connected to the router, there is no need for a Next Hop Address.

Next Hop interface
> The physical interface used to reach the next hop.

Metric
> A number indicating the total distance to the destination. In RIP, a very simple metric counts the number of hops to the destination. Directly connected routes are usually assigned a metric of 0. RIPng advertises directly connected routes with the configured outgoing metric of the link, normally 1.

Timer
> The amount of time since the information about the route was last updated.

Route Change flag
> Indicates that information about this entry has recently been changed. This flag is needed to control triggered routing updates.

Route Source
> The entity that provided the information about the route. For example, this may be a static entry or directly connected, or the source may be RIP, OSPF, etc.

```
                                                   Next Hop
                Prefix                  Protocol   Intf.
-------------------------------------   ----------  -------
FEC0::0008:0000/112                       DIRECT    3
   RIPv6 Metric: 3, Prefix on a directly attached link
   Last updated 3865 seconds ago

FEC0::0080:0000:0000:0000:0000/64         DIRECT    2
   RIPv6 Metric: 1, Prefix on a directly attached link
   Last updated 4703 seconds ago

FEC0::0004:0000:0000:0000:0000/64         DIRECT    1
   RIPv6 Metric: 1, Prefix on a directly attached link
   Last updated 4745 seconds ago

FEC0::0000/112                            RIPv6     3
   RIPv6 Metric: 5, Nexthop: FE80::0002
   Last updated 17 seconds ago

FEC0::0004:0000/112                       RIPv6     2
   RIPv6 Metric: 2, Nexthop: FE80::0003:A209:A348
   Last updated 2 seconds ago

FEC0::0001:0000:0000:0000:0000/64         RIPv6     2
   RIPv6 Metric: 2, Nexthop: FE80::0003:A209:A348
   Last updated 2 seconds ago

FEC0::0002:0000:0000:0000:0000/64         RIPv6     2
   RIPv6 Metric: 2, Nexthop: FE80::0003:A2E0:BEF2
   Last updated 9 seconds ago

FEC0::0003:0000:0000:0000:0000/64         RIPv6     3
   RIPv6 Metric: 4, Nexthop: FE80::0002
   Last updated 17 seconds ago

FEC0::0005:0000:0000:0000:0000/64         RIPv6     1
   RIPv6 Metric: 2, Nexthop: FE80::0280:2DFF:FE41:C90B
   Last updated 10 seconds ago
```

Figure 8-1. An IPv6 routing table

The router periodically distributes information about its routes to its directly connected neighbors using RIPng update messages. Upon receiving RIPng update messages from its neighbor, the router adds the distance between the neighbor and itself (usually 1) to the metric of each route received. The router then processes the newly received route entry using the Bellman-Ford algorithm.

Figure 8-2 provides a closer look at this algorithm.

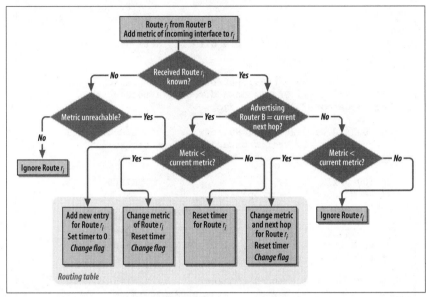

Figure 8-2. The Bellman-Ford algorithm

Router A receives a routing update from router B and has already added the distance of 1 to each route *ri* advertised by B. For each route *ri*, the router steps through the algorithm depicted in Figure 8-2. According to Figure 8-2, the routing table will be updated if the following criteria are true; otherwise, route *ri* is discarded:

Route ri is new and the metric is reachable
> The route, metric, and next hop are added as a new entry to the routing table. The timer is set to zero and the Route Change flag is raised.

Route ri is already known and the next hop is the same as the one in the routing table
> If the metric has changed, it is updated and the Route Change flag is raised. The timer is reset to zero in any case.

Route ri is already known, but the next hop is different and the metric is smaller than the entry in the routing table
> The metric and next hop are updated. The timer is set to zero and the Route Change flag is raised.

Route ri is already known, but the next hop is different and the metric is equal to the one in the routing table
> If the routing process allows for multiple equal-cost paths to the same destination in the routing table, the route is treated as a new entry (see above). If the routing process does not provide for multiple equal-cost

paths, route *ri* is discarded. Multiple equal-cost paths allow for load sharing of IPv6 traffic among multiple paths. The algorithm for distributing traffic among these paths is at the discretion of the routing process itself, normally based on the source and destination IPv6 addresses.

The next hop of *ri* is taken either from the information within the routing update message or from the source IPv6 address of the RIPng packet. See the later section "Next Hop" for more information.

When the routers are first initialized, they know only their directly connected routes. This information is passed to all neighbors, processed, and then distributed to the neighbors of the neighbors. Eventually, all IPv6 routes are known by all routers. The routers keep sending update messages periodically to prevent valid routes from expiring.

Limitations of the Protocol

RIPng, like the earlier versions of RIP, is primarily designed for use as an IGP in networks of moderate size. The limitations specified for RIP Versions 1 and 2 apply to RIPng, as well. They are described in the following list:

The RIPng diameter is limited
> The longest path to any IPv6 route is limited to a metric of 15 when propagated with RIPng. Normally, the metric is equal to the hop count, assuming the cost of 1 is used for each link crossed. The protocol allows for larger costs to be assigned to any link, thereby limiting the number of hops even further.

Routing loops can cause high convergence time
> When IPv6 routes that are no longer valid are being propagated in a looped environment, RIPng depends on "counting to infinity" to eliminate these routes eventually. Counting to infinity is explained in the next section.

The metric does not reflect line speed
> RIPng uses a fixed metric normally set to 1 for each link crossed. A route cannot be chosen based on bandwidth or real-time parameters such as measured delay, load, or reliability.

Changes in Topology and Preventing Instability

A change in topology means a newly added route or a route that has gone down. Newly added routes are advertised with the next update message sent by the router with the direct connection to that route. Its neighbors process the route and pass it on to their neighbors. Eventually, all routers know about the newly added route.

What happens if a route goes down or a router crashes? These routes will time out, as they are no longer being advertised. The question is how long this will take and whether this time is acceptable for the network? The time it takes for all routers to learn the changed topology is called convergence time. To keep the convergence time to a minimum, several measures can be introduced.

Route poisoning and the hold-down timer

If an interface goes down on a router, the router does not remove the route(s) associated with that interface immediately. Instead, the router keeps the route in the routing table and raises the metric to 16 (unreachable). A garbage-collection timer, also known as a hold-down timer, determines how long the router keeps this unreachable route in the routing table. The route is now advertised to the neighbors with a metric of 16. The neighbors are running a hold timer as well, so they keep the route in the routing table to inform their respective neighbors of the invalidity of the route. This process is called route poisoning.

Split horizon, with or without poison reverse

Let's assume route *r1* is directly connected to router A, as shown in Figure 8-3.

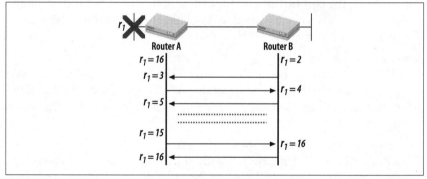

Figure 8-3. Convergence of route r1 without split horizon

Router A advertises *r1* to its neighbor, router B, with a cost of 1. Router B adds 1 to the cost and lists *r1* in its routing table using router A as the next hop. Now *r1* goes down. Router A poisons *r1* and waits for the update timer to expire before advertising *r1* to B with a cost of 16. In the meantime, however, router B advertises *r1* back to A with a cost of 2. According to Bellman-Ford, router A changes the entry for *r1*, using B as the next hop with a metric of 3. Now router A advertises *r1* with a cost of 3 (not 16) to router B.

Router B adds 1 to the cost and lists *r1* in its routing table with a cost of 4. The routers send *r1* back and forth, each time raising the cost by 1 until counting to infinity strikes and both reach a cost of 16, declaring *r1* invalid. This will take quite some time, however. The core problem lies in the fact that router B advertises routes learned from A back to A. Split horizon prevents this from happening. With split horizon, a router never advertises a route back over its next hop interface. An additional option is split horizon with poison reverse. With this option, a router always advertises a route back over its next hop interface with a metric of 16. In the very unlikely situation that both router A and B have the same route pointing to each other, the routers don't have to wait for a timeout to eliminate this route because reverse poisoning invalidates each of them immediately. Poison reverse can, however, have the disadvantage of increasing the size of routing messages, especially if many destinations have to be advertised back as poisoned.

There are very few situations in which split horizon (with or without poison reverse) cannot be used at all. If there is a point-to-multipoint (also called hub-and-spoke) topology using a single common IPv6 network, split horizon prevents the spoke routers from learning routes advertised by other spoke routers. Split horizon must be turned off at the central router (the hub router).

Triggered updates

Any changes in the routing table have to wait to be advertised until the update timer has expired. Triggered updates speed up the process by allowing the changed route entry to be advertised almost immediately. A very small hold timer is introduced before sending the update. Because only the changes are advertised, regular periodic updates need to stay in place.

All these measures speed up convergence, but the world is not perfect. Erroneous information may always come back over larger loops, especially within a large network with a topology containing many loops. The process of counting to infinity will, however, always prevail to eliminate the erroneous information.

Message Format

RIPng is a UDP-based protocol using UDP port number 521; let's call it the RIPng port. The RIPng routing process always listens to messages arriving on this port. With the exception of specific requests, all RIPng messages set the source and destination port to the RIPng port. Specific queries are discussed later in this chapter.

The RIPng message format is shown in Figure 8-4.

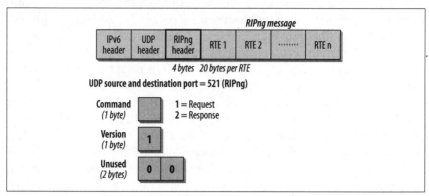

Figure 8-4. RIPng message format

The fields of the RIPng message are explained in the following list:

Command (1 byte)

A value of 1 specifies a request message asking the responding system to send all or part of its routing table.

A value of 2 sends an update message containing all or part of the sender's routing table. It may be sent as a response to a previous request or as an unsolicited update used in periodic or triggered routing updates.

Version (1 byte)

The version field is set to a value of 1.

Route Table Entry (RTE) (20 bytes each)

The RIPng header is followed by one or more Route Table Entries, using the format depicted in Figure 8-5.

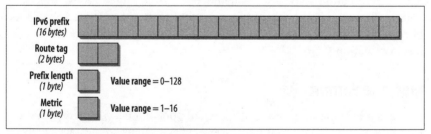

Figure 8-5. Format of a Route Table Entry

Each RTE describes the route to be advertised by using the IPv6 Prefix (16 bytes) and its Prefix Length (1 byte). The metric field (1 byte) contains the metric used by the sender for this route. A valid metric has a value between 1 and 15. A metric of 16 describes the route as unreachable by the sending router.

Each RTE contains a Route Tag field, as well. It may be used to carry additional information about a route learned from another routing protocol—e.g., BGP. A router importing external routes into RIPng may set this tag. RIPng will preserve and redistribute this tag within its routing domain. Information within this tag can be used to redistribute the route out of the RIP domain. RIPng itself makes no use of this tag.

The number of RTEs within single updates depends on the MTU of the medium between two neighboring routers. The formula is:

number of RTEs = Int ((MTU – length of IPv6 headers – UDP_hdrlen – RIPng_hdrlen)/RTE_size)

Next Hop

If you are familiar with RIPv2, you probably miss the field for the next hop address. Not to worry: RIPng provides this feature, too. With RIPv2, each entry has a designated field specifying the next-hop address. This would not be very economical for RIPng because it would nearly double the size of each RTE. As shown in Figure 8-6, a specially constructed RTE, the next hop RTE, is introduced to indicate the next hop's IPv6 address. All subsequent RTEs use this next hop IPv6 address until the end of the message has been reached or another next hop RTE is encountered.

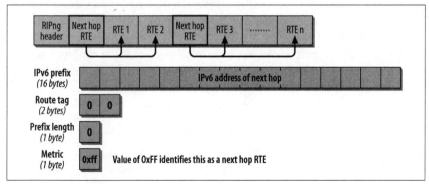

Figure 8-6. The next hop RTE

The next hop RTE is identified by a value of 0xFF in the metric field of the RTE. The IPv6 address within the RTE is now identified as the next hop IPv6 address to be used by the subsequent RTE. The route tag and the prefix length are set to zero on sending and ignored on reception.

Specifying a value of 0:0:0:0:0:0:0:0 in the prefix field of the next hop RTE indicates that the next hop IPv6 address should be set to the source IPv6 address of the RIPng message. The purpose of naming a specific next hop is to eliminate unnecessary routing hops. For example, routers A, B, and C are directly connected on a common subnet. Router C does not run RIPng. Assume that router A somehow knows a route *ri* using router C as its next hop. Router A could advertise *ri* to B with the next hop address of Router C. Router B can now forward traffic for *ri* directly to Router C, therefore avoiding the unnecessary hop through Router A.

The next hop IPv6 address must always be a link-local address (starting with a prefix of FE80). If there is no next hop RTE, or if the received next hop address is not link-local, it should be considered 0:0:0:0:0:0:0:0.

Addressing Considerations and the Default Route

Any prefix with a length of zero is considered to be a default route, but normally, a prefix of 0:0:0:0:0:0:0:0 with a prefix length of zero is used. A default route is used if the route to the destination is not explicitly listed in the routing table. The next hop router for the default route is called the default router. Sending traffic to the default router assumes that the default router knows all the routes or has a default router itself. It is at the discretion of the implementer to determine if and how such a path of default routers should be implemented. The mechanism of default routers is usually used to lead the way out of the autonomous system or to lead traffic from remote sites to central sites. The advantage of distributing the default route is to reduce the number of routing updates to be distributed throughout the system. Default routes should not be propagated further than intended—that is, they should not leave the autonomous system. A metric is assigned to the default route at its origin to establish precedence among multiple default routers. RIPng handles a default route in exactly the same way as any other destination.

Timers

RIPng implements different timers to control updates of the routing information. The name and purpose of these timers are specified in the following list:

Update timer
>By default, every 30 seconds the RIPng process wakes up on each interface to send an unsolicited routing response to the neighboring routers.

This response contains the entire routing table except routes that follow the split horizon rule.

Timeout timer
Each time a route entry is updated, the timeout time for this route entry is reset to zero. If the route entry reaches 180 seconds (default value) without another update, it is considered to have expired. The metric is set to 16 and the garbage collection process begins. In addition, the Route Change flag is raised to indicate a change. The output process uses this flag to trigger an update.

Garbage collection timer (sometimes referred to as hold-down timer)
This timer is set for 120 seconds for each route entry that has timed out (see timeout timer) or been received with a metric of 16. Only upon expiration of this timer will the route entry finally be removed from the routing table. If a new update to this route arrives before the garbage collection timer expires, the route is replaced and the garbage collection timer is cleared.

Packet Processing

Let's have a look at how the router processes incoming and outgoing RIPng messages.

Request message

A request message asks a router to respond with all or part of its routing table by specifying the requested RTE. The incoming request is processed as follows.

If there is exactly one RTE with a prefix of zero, a prefix length of zero, and a metric of 16, the request is for the entire routing table, and the router responds by sending the entire routing table. Figure 8-7 shows a trace of such a request message.

Otherwise, the request message is processed one RTE at a time. If the RTE's coresponding prefix is found in the routing table, the RTE's metric is placed into the metric field of the RTE; otherwise, a metric of 16 is placed into the metric field, indicating that the route is unknown. Once all RTEs have been processed, the command field in the RIPng header is changed to response and the newly formed response message is sent back to the requestor.

There are two types of request messages, General and Specific, which are handled differently by the receiving router.

A General Request is sent by a router that has just come up and wants to fill its routing table quickly. The router sends out a General Request message,

```
Sniffer - Local, Ethernet (Line speed at 10 Mbps) - [rip6book.cap: Decode, 1/3 Ethernet Frames]
  File   Monitor   Capture   Display   Tools   Database   Window   Help

  ▶ ‖ ■ ‖ ▲  Default  ▼

  No.   Status   Source Address      Dest Address       Summary
   1    M        fe80::280:2dff:    ff02::9            RIPng: Request Version=1
   2             fe80::200:a2ff:    fe80::280:2dff:    RIPng: Response Version=1
   3             fe80::280:2dff:    ff02::9            RIPng: Response Version=1

⊟ DLC:  ----- DLC Header -----
   DLC:
   DLC:   Frame 1 arrived at   19:36:12.4960; frame size is 86 (0056 hex) bytes.
   DLC:   Destination = Multicast 333300000009
   DLC:   Source      = Station Xylogi41C90B
   DLC:   Ethertype   = 86DD
   DLC:
⊟ IPv6: ----- IPv6 Header -----
   IPv6:
   IPv6: Version             = 6
   IPv6: Priority            = 7 (Internet Control Traffic)
   IPv6: Flow Label          = 0x000000
   IPv6: Payload Length      = 32
   IPv6: Next Header         = 17 (UDP)
   IPv6: Hop Limit           = 255
   IPv6: Source address      = fe80::280:2dff:fe41:c90b
   IPv6: Destination address = ff02::9
   IPv6:
⊟ UDP: ----- UDP Header -----
   UDP:
   UDP: Source port      = 521 (RIPng)
   UDP: Destination port = 521 (RIPng)
   UDP: Length           = 32
   UDP: Checksum         = 0532
   UDP: [24 byte(s) of data]
   UDP:
⊟ RIPng: ----- RIPng -----
   RIPng:
   RIPng: Command         = 1 (Request)
   RIPng: Version         = 1
   RIPng: Reserved        = 0::0000
   RIPng: IPv6 Prefix     = ::
   RIPng: Route tag       = 0
   RIPng: Prefix length   = 0
   RIPng: Metric          = 16 (infinity: destination unreachable)
```

Figure 8-7. RIPng request message asking for the entire routing table

asking all directly connected neighbors to send their entire routing table.
The neighbors each reply with a response message containing the entire
routing table, using the split horizon rule.

A Specific Request message is sent by a monitoring station asking for all or
part of the routing table. The queried router replies to the requestor by sending the requested information from its routing table. Split horizon is not
used because it is assumed that the requestor is using the requested information for diagnostic purposes only.

Table 8-1 summarizes the characteristics of the two types of requests.

Table 8-1. RIPng request messages

Request type	IPv6 source address	IPv6 destination address	Source UDP port	Destination UDP port	Use split horizon in response?
General	Link-local address of the requestor's sending interface	ff02::9 (multicast)	*RIPng* port (521)	*RIPng* port (521)	Yes
Specific	Global or site-local unicast address of the requestor	Global or site-local unicast address of the queried router	Any except the *RIPng* port	*RIPng* port (521)	No

Response message

A response message carries routing information to be processed by the receiving router by using the Bellman-Ford Algorithm (see the earlier section "Distance-Vector Algorithm for RIPng"). A response message is accepted by a router only if the IPv6 source address is a link-local address of a directly connected neighbor and the UDP source and destination ports are set to the RIPng port. In addition, the hop count must be set to 255 to guarantee that the response has not traveled over any intermediate node.

Once the response message is accepted, each RTE must be checked for its validity. The test includes the prefix itself (not a multicast or link-local address), the prefix length (between 0 and 128), and the metric (between 1 and 16). If the RTE is accepted, the metric of the incoming interface is added to the metric of the RTE. The RTE is now passed to the Bellman-Ford process as described in the earlier section "Distance-Vector Algorithm for RIPng." Figure 8-8 shows a trace of a response message.

The above rules for receiving and validating a response message do not apply for a response to a specific query. The hop count may be less than 255, and the source IPv6 address is not a link-local address. The diagnostic station uses the received RTE not for routing, but to provide input into its diagnostic software. It is entirely up to the implementer of such software to determine the validity of a response message.

There are two types of response messages: Unsolicited and Solicited. An Unsolicited Response message is sent by a periodic or triggered update process. The periodic update process examines the entire routing table upon expiration of the Update Timer on any given interface. The triggered update process wakes up as soon as the Route Change flag is raised and examines only routes with the Route Change flag set. Both processes then proceed

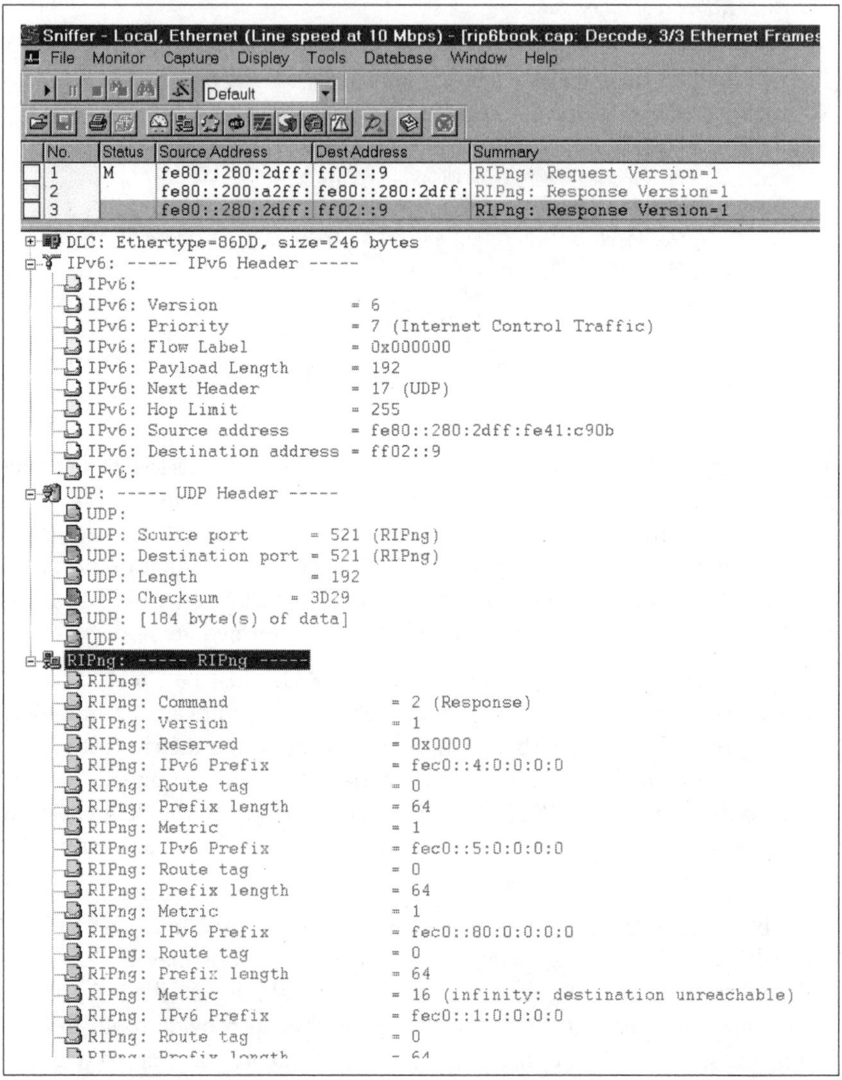

```
Sniffer - Local, Ethernet (Line speed at 10 Mbps) - [rip6book.cap: Decode, 3/3 Ethernet Frames
 File   Monitor   Capture   Display   Tools   Database   Window   Help

 ▶  ‖  ■  ▚  ⏴  ⎙  Default      ▾

 ⬚  ⬚  ⬚  ⬚   ⬚  ⬚  ⬚  ⬚  ⬚  ⬚  ⬚  ⬚  ⬚  ⬚

 No.  Status   Source Address      Dest Address       Summary
 ☐ 1   M       fe80::280:2dff:   ff02::9            RIPng: Request Version=1
 ☐ 2           fe80::200:a2ff:   fe80::280:2dff:   RIPng: Response Version=1
 ☐ 3           fe80::280:2dff:   ff02::9            RIPng: Response Version=1
```

⊞▓ DLC: Ethertype=86DD, size=246 bytes
⊟▼ IPv6: ----- IPv6 Header -----
　▢ IPv6:
　▢ IPv6: Version   = 6
　▢ IPv6: Priority   = 7 (Internet Control Traffic)
　▢ IPv6: Flow Label   = 0x000000
　▢ IPv6: Payload Length   = 192
　▢ IPv6: Next Header   = 17 (UDP)
　▢ IPv6: Hop Limit   = 255
　▢ IPv6: Source address   = fe80::280:2dff:fe41:c90b
　▢ IPv6: Destination address = ff02::9
　▢ IPv6:
⊟▓ UDP: ----- UDP Header -----
　▢ UDP:
　▢ UDP: Source port   = 521 (RIPng)
　▢ UDP: Destination port = 521 (RIPng)
　▢ UDP: Length   = 192
　▢ UDP: Checksum   = 3D29
　▢ UDP: [184 byte(s) of data]
　▢ UDP:
⊟▓ RIPng: ----- RIPng -----
　▢ RIPng:
　▢ RIPng: Command   = 2 (Response)
　▢ RIPng: Version   = 1
　▢ RIPng: Reserved   = 0x0000
　▢ RIPng: IPv6 Prefix   = fec0::4:0:0:0:0
　▢ RIPng: Route tag   = 0
　▢ RIPng: Prefix length = 64
　▢ RIPng: Metric   = 1
　▢ RIPng: IPv6 Prefix   = fec0::5:0:0:0:0
　▢ RIPng: Route tag   = 0
　▢ RIPng: Prefix length = 64
　▢ RIPng: Metric   = 1
　▢ RIPng: IPv6 Prefix   = fec0::80:0:0:0:0
　▢ RIPng: Route tag   = 0
　▢ RIPng: Prefix length = 64
　▢ RIPng: Metric   = 16 (infinity: destination unreachable)
　▢ RIPng: IPv6 Prefix   = fec0::1:0:0:0:0
　▢ RIPng: Route tag   = 0
　▢ RIPng: Prefix length = 64

Figure 8-8. RIPng response message

with the following: if the examined route entry has a link-local address or
should not be used because of split horizon processing, skip it. Otherwise,
put the prefix, prefix length, and metric into the RTE, and put the RTE into
the response message. If the maximum MTU has been reached, send the
packet and build a new packet.

A Solicited Response message is sent as a response to a request message. See
the earlier section "Request message" for more detail.

Table 8-2 summarizes the characteristics of the two types of responses.

Table 8-2. RIPng response messages

Request type	IPv6 source address	IPv6 destination address	Source UDP port	Destination UDP port
Unsolicited (periodic update or triggered update)	Link-local address of the sending interface	ff02::9 (multicast)	*RIPng* port (521)	*RIPng* port (521)
Solicited (answer a request)	Link-local address (general request), global or site-local unicast address (specific request)	Source IPv6 address of the request message	*RIPng* port (521)	Source UDP port of the request message

Sending the Unsolicited Response message to the multicast address ensures that the response message reaches all neighbors on any particular directly connected network. There are cases in which this may not work—e.g., on a non-broadcast-capable network. A static list of all neighbors on such a network may be provided to send the messages directly to each neighbor. It is up to the implementer to determine how this should be done.

Control Functions and Security

RIPng does not provide specifications for administrative control. However, experience with existing RIP implementations suggests that such controls may be important. Administrative controls are filters, which allow or disallow certain routes to be advertised or received. In addition, a list of valid neighbors could be specified, and a router would accept or announce routes only to neighbors on this list. These filters can be used to change the update behavior to comply with routing policies set within an autonomous system. Again, RIPng does not need such controls to function, but it is strongly recommended that the implementer provide such controls. Cisco Systems, for example, implements RIPng distribution lists, and Nortel implements RIPng Announce and Accept Policies.

Because RIPng runs over IPv6, it relies on the IP Authentication Header and the IP Encapsulating Security Payload to insure integrity and authentication of routing exchanges.

OSPF for IPv6 (OSPFv3)

OSPF for IPv6 modifies the existing OSPF for IPv4 to support IPv6. The fundamentals of OSPF for IPv4 remain unchanged. Some changes have been necessary to accommodate the increased address size of IPv6 and the changes in protocol semantics between IPv4 and IPv6. OSPF for IPv6 is defined in RFC 2740, which emphasizes the differences between OSPF for IPv4 and OSPF for IPv6. It contains a large number of references to the documentation of OSPF for IPv4, which makes it hard to read. This chapter tries to concatenate the two worlds to make the reading a little bit more comfortable. It starts with an overview of OSPF, including the area structure and external routes. After the overview, it opens up the protocol to get down to the implementation details: it starts with the OSPF message format, proceeds to the neighbor relationship, and finishes with the actual link state database and the calculation of the routing table.

Overview of OSPF for IPv6

OSPF for IPv4 (OSPFv2) is standardized in RFC 2328. In addition to this document, several extensions to OSPF have been defined. RFC 1584 describes IPv4 multicast extensions to OSPF. RFC 1587 adds not-so-stubby areas (NSSAs) to OSPF. RFC 2740 modifies OSPF to support the exchange of routing information for IPv6. OSPF for IPv6 has a new version number: version 3.

OSPF is classified as an IGP, which are used within autonomous systems. It was designed to overcome some of the limitations introduced by RIP, such as the small diameter, long convergence time, and a metric that does not reflect the characteristics of the network. In addition, OSPF handles a much larger routing table to accommodate large number of routes.

Differences between OSPF for IPv4 and OSPF for IPv6

Most of the concepts of OSPF for IPv4 have been retained; the following is a brief overview of the changes:

Protocol processing per-link, not per-subnet
> IPv6 connects interfaces to links. Multiple IP subnets can be assigned to a single link and two nodes can talk directly over a single link, even if they do not share a common IP subnet. OSPF for IPv6 runs per-link instead of per-subnet. The terms "network" and "subnet" used in OSPF for IPv4 should be replaced with the term "link"; i.e., an OSPF interface now connects to a link instead of an IP subnet.

Removal of addressing semantics
> IPv6 addresses are no longer present in OSPF packet headers. They are only allowed as payload information.
>
> Router-LSA and Network-LSA (yes, they still exist) do not contain IPv6 addresses.OSPF Router ID, Area ID, and Link State ID remain at 32 bits, so they can no longer take the value of an IPv6 address. Desig-

nated Routers (DRs) and Backup Designated Routers (BDRs) are now always identified by their Router ID and no longer by their IP address.

Flooding scope

Each LSA type contains an explicit code to specify its flooding scope. This code is embedded in the LS type field. Three flooding scopes have been introduced: link-local, area, and AS.

Explicit support for multiple instances per-link

Multiple OSPF protocol instances can now run over a single link. This allows for separate ASes, each running OSPF, to use a common link. Another use of this feature is to have a single link belong to multiple areas.

Use of link-local addresses

OSPF assumes that each interface has been assigned a link-local unicast address. All OSPF packets use the link-local address as the source address. The routers learn the link-local addresses of all their neighbors and use these addresses as the next hop address. Packets sent on virtual links, however, must use either the global or site-local IP address as the source for OSPF packets.

Authentication

Authentication has been removed from OSPF for IPv6 because it relies on the authentication of IPv6.

OSPF packet format changes

See the section "Message Format of OSPF for IPv6."

LSA format changes

Type 3 (Summary Link) has been renamed Inter-Area-Prefix-LSA.

Type 4 (AS Summary Link) has been renamed Inter-Area-Router-LSA.

Two new LSAs carry IPv6 prefix information in their payload. Link-LSA (Type 8) carries the IPv6 address information of the local links, and Intra-Area-Prefix-LSA (Type 9) carries the IPv6 prefixes of the router and network links.

For other changes, such as Link State ID and the Options field, see the section "LSAs."

Handling unknown LSA types

Instead of simply discarding them, OSPF for IPv6 introduces a more flexible way of handling unknown LSA types. A new LSA handling bit has been added to the LS Type field to allow flooding of unknown LSA types.

Stub area support

The concept of stub areas has been retained in OSPF for IPv6. An additional rule specifies the flooding of unknown LSAs within the stub area.

Link state-based protocol

Each router maintains a database describing the link states within the autonomous system. This database is being built by exchanging Link State Advertisements (LSAs) between neighboring routers. Depending on its contents, an LSA is flooded to all routers in the autonomous system (AS flooding scope), all routers within the same area (area flooding scope), or simply to its neighbors. The flooding always occurs along a path of neighboring routers, so a stable neighbor relationship is extremely important for OSPF to work properly. The neighbor relationship is called adjacency. The exact process of forming an adjacency is described in the later section "Forming Adjacencies."

Each router originates router LSAs advertising the local state of its interfaces to all routers within the same area. Additional LSAs are originated to identify links with multiple routers (multiaccess networks), IPv6 routes from other areas, or IPv6 routes external to the OSPF autonomous system. All LSA types and the flooding mechanism are described in the sections "LSAs" and "LSA Flooding," respectively. Each router puts the received LSA into its LSA database, called the Link-State Database (LSDB).

Using the LSDB as the input, each router runs the same algorithm to build a tree of least-cost paths (shortest-path-first tree [SPF tree]) to each route. The LSDB is like having a map of the network used to plot the shortest paths to each destination. The cost is described by a single dimensionless metric, which is configurable on each interface of the router. The metric assigned to the interface is usually inversely proportional to its line speed, i.e., higher bandwidth means lower cost. A common formula, according to the RFC, is to divide 10^8 by the line speed in bits per second. You can, however, choose your own formula according to corporate standards.

OSPF can put multiple equal-cost paths to the same route into the routing table. The algorithm for distributing traffic among these paths is at the discretion of the routing process itself, normally based on the source and destination IPv6 addresses. The process of building the SPF and its routing table will be discussed in detail in the later section "The Link State Database."

OSPF areas and external routes

The LSDB can become quite large, and processing such a large database can be CPU- and memory-intensive because changes to the database affect every router in the AS. OSPF allows the AS to be partitioned into areas to reduce processing overhead. In addition, OSPF can import routes derived from external sources (e.g., RIP, BGP, and static routes) into OSPF. Areas and external routes are discussed in detail in the section "OSPF Areas and External Routes."

Authentication and security

Because OSPF for IPv6 runs over IPv6, it relies on the IP Authentication Header and the IP Encapsulating Security Payload to insure integrity and authentication of routing exchanges. The authentication of OSPF for IPv4 has been removed. One integrity check remains, which comes in the form of the checksum that is calculated over the entire OSPF packet.

OSPF Areas and External Routes

Within an autonomous system, routers can be grouped together to form areas. Each area is assigned a unique Area ID, a 32-bit integer typically noted as a dotted decimal number. It has no addressing significance other than uniquely identifying the area. An LSA with area flooding scope will never be flooded outside the area. Together, they form the area data structure, also known as the area LSDB. The Router-LSA and Network-LSA belong to this category. Routers and networks from one area are hidden in other areas. It is like splitting the map of the network into multiple maps, each of which represents the topology of one area. Each router within one area calculates the SPF tree to all routes within the same area. These routes are called intra-area routes. Routers with all interfaces belonging to a single area are called internal routers. To find paths to routes outside the area, "exit points" are provided in the form of area border routers (ABR). Each area must always be attached to a single common area called backbone area. This is achieved by the ABR having at least one interface in the backbone area and one interface in the local area. The ABR advertises all routes of the local area to the backbone area. In return, it advertises all the routes of the backbone area to the local area. This ensures that all routes are distributed within the AS.

Routing within the AS takes place at two levels. If the source and destination IP address of a packet belong to the same area, the packet is forwarded solely on information obtained from the area LSDB. This is called intra-area routing. If the destination address is outside the area, the packet will have to be forwarded along the path to the ABR of the local area. The ABR knows all destinations and forwards the packet either across the backbone to the ABR of the destination area or to the backbone area. This is called inter-area routing.

The advantage of having areas is the reduction of processing overhead. Because the topology of each area is smaller than the entire AS, the calculation of the SPF tree takes less time. In addition, changes in the topology stay local, and only the routers in the local area need to recalculate the SPF tree. Routers in other areas are less affected because their area topology was not changed. Internal routers profit the most from splitting the AS into areas because their LSDB is much smaller.

The backbone area

The backbone area is a special area using Area ID 0.0.0.0 (area 0). The backbone area contains all ABRs of the autonomous system. If the AS is not split into areas, the backbone area is usually the one configured area. If the AS is split into areas, the backbone area is the collection of all routes from all non-backbone areas. The backbone area must be contiguous: each router within the same area has at least one direct link to another router in the same area, and that link belongs to the area. However, with the introduction of virtual links, a backbone area doesn't have to be physically contiguous. A transit area can be used to create a tunnel (a virtual link) belonging to the backbone area. This will be further discussed in the later section "Virtual links."

Non-backbone areas

Non-backbone areas receive a unique Area ID other than 0.0.0.0. They must be physically contiguous. Each non-backbone area must have an ABR connected to the backbone, using either a physical link or a virtual link. An ABR advertises all routes of the non-backbone into the backbone area. In reverse, an ABR advertises all the routes known to the backbone area into the non-backbone area. Normally, the ABR uses one LSA (called the Inter-Area-Prefix-LSA) for each route advertised. The ABR can be configured to summarize routes using a shorter IPv6 prefix representing some or all of the routes to be advertised. This reduces the number of advertisements and memory and processing requirements. It is very important to plan the assignment of IPv6 prefixes within the area to achieve the most benefit from the summary.

A non-backbone area can have multiple ABRs. Figure 8-9 explains ABRs advertising Inter-Area-Prefix-LSAs.

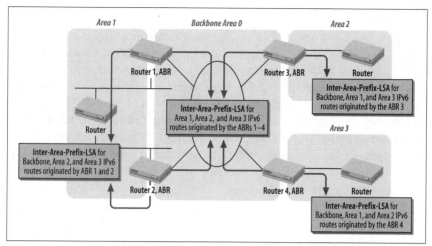

Figure 8-9. OSPF areas and its routing updates

Virtual links

A virtual link is a logical link that tunnels backbone traffic through a non-backbone area. It can be configured between two ABRs by using a common non-backbone area called a transit area. A virtual link belongs to the backbone and can only cross a single transit area. The transit area must not be a stub area. A remote area without a physical interface to the backbone area can be connected to the backbone by using virtual links. Virtual links can also be used to create redundant connections to the backbone. OSPF considers a virtual link a point-to-point link. The shortest path between the ABRs through the transit area determines the actual endpoint addresses of the tunnel. These addresses must be global or site-local unicast IPv6 addresses. Figure 8-10 shows an example of virtual links.

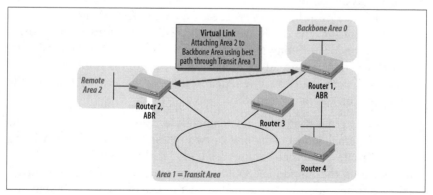

Figure 8-10. Virtual link connecting a remote area

External routes

A router can learn about IPv6 routes from different sources, such as RIP, static entries, BGP, IS-IS, etc. Every route from a non-OSPF source is considered to be an OSPF external route and can be imported into OSPF. To import external routes into OSPF, a router must have at least one interface configured with OSPF and know about at least one non-OSPF network. This router is called an autonomous system border router (ASBR). External routes are imported using a single AS-External-LSA for each external route. Depending on the implementation, an ASBR can summarize a range of external routes to a single external LSA. Figure 8-11 explains how external routes are imported into OSPF.

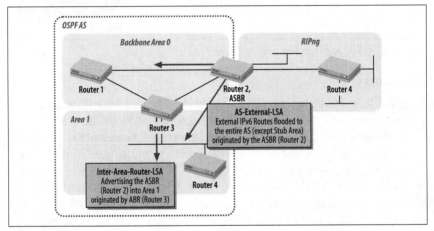

Figure 8-11. External routes imported into OSPF

AS-External-LSAs must be flooded throughout the autonomous system. Any router within the AS forwards packets to external networks to the ASBR or to an optional forwarding address specified by the ASBR. Therefore, there must be an entry to the ASBR in the Area-LSDB, or the forwarding address must be in the local routing table. If the ASBR is not within the local area, the ABR is responsible for advertising the existence of the ASBR to the local area. This is done using an Inter-Area-Router-LSA. Figure 8-11 shows the usage of the Inter-Area-Router-LSA.

Metrics of external routes are not compatible with OSPF metrics. ASBRs advertise external routes using one of two types of metrics, external-1 and external-2 routes. External-1 routes are considered to be close to the ASBR. Routers within the AS add the OSPF cost to reach the ASBR or the advertised forwarding address to the metric of the external-1 route. External-2 routes are assumed to be further away from the ASBR. A metric larger than the cost of any intra-AS path will therefore be added to the metric of the external-2 route.

If the same route is advertised as an OSPF internal route as well as an external route, the path to the OSPF internal route is always chosen over the path to the external route. This can happen if there are multiple ASBRs connected to the same external network. One ASBR advertises an OSPF route to the external routing protocol, and the other ASBR imports the same route back to OSPF.

Stub areas

In short, a stub area is a zone free of AS-External-LSAs. These LSAs would normally be flooded throughout the entire AS, which could result in quite a large LSDB consisting of many external advertisements. To reduce the size of the LSDB, an ABR can block AS-External-LSAs into the local area. As the ABR deprives the area of knowledge about external routes, it must make up for it by advertising a replacement route in the form of the default route. It uses the Inter-Area-Prefix-LSA, advertising the prefix 0:0:0:0:0:0:0:0 with a prefix length of 0. The metric associated with the default route is called the stub metric. If there are multiple ABRs for that area, each ABR blocks AS-External-LSAs and replaces them with a default route. Routers internal to the area calculate the best path of the default route by adding the metric to get to the ABR (according to the SPF) to the stub metric. Because there are no external routes within a stub area, there is no need for the ABR to advertise the presence of the ASBR into a stub area. The ABR therefore does not originate Inter-Area-Router-LSAs into a stub area. All routers within the stub area must be configured to be in a stub area by turning off the external-capability option. This external-capability option is crucial to forming adjacencies (see the section "Forming Adjacencies"), as all routers within an area have to agree on the same external-capability option.

There are some restrictions for stub areas. They cannot be configured as transit areas for virtual links. In addition, no ASBR can be placed in a stub area because the routers in a stub area cannot import external information. The backbone area can never be a stub area. To prevent unknown LSA types from being flooded into a stub area, certain measures must be taken. An unknown LSA can be flooded only if the LSA has link-local or area flooding scope and the handling bit (called the U-bit) for flooding unknown LSAs is set to 0. Refer to the section "LSA Flooding" for details.

As the ABR advertises a default route into the stub area, it could optionally stop originating routes to other areas as well. This can be useful if it is not crucial for the internal routers of a stub area to know the details of all routes to other areas. As long as they have the default route, they are happy. Such an area is sometimes called a totally stubby area. Figure 8-12 gives an example of stub areas.

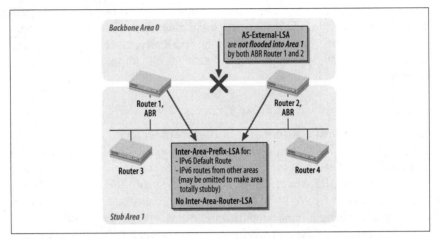

Figure 8-12. Stub area

Not-so-stubby areas

There are cases when stub areas need to connect to routers that have non-OSPF routes. The implementer does not want to revert the area to a normal area to allow these external routes to be imported. Because no AS-External-LSAs are allowed in a stub area, the OSPF designers came up with a new type of LSA called Type-7-LSA. Type-7-LSAs are exactly like AS-External-LSAs, but they can exist in a stub area. Stub areas in which Type-7-LSAs exist are humorously referred to as Not-So-Stubby Areas, or NSSAs. Type-7-LSAs are flooded only within the NSSA. An NSSA ASBR issues one Type-7-LSA per external route. ABRs of the NSSA can translate Type-7-LSAs into AS-External-LSAs to advertise them to the rest of the AS. In addition, these ABRs still behave like ABRs in a stub area and they advertise a default route by using a Type-7-LSA in this case. All routers within the NSSA must be configured to be in an NSSA by turning the NSSA capability option on. This option must be set on all routers to form adjacencies (see the section "Forming Adjacencies"). In addition, the external-capability option still must be turned off on all routers within the NSSA. The NSSA has the same restrictions as the stub area. In addition, it cannot be a totally stubby area.

Message Format of OSPF for IPv6

Let's have a closer look now at the protocol implementation. We will start with the actual OSPF packet encapsulation. The routers use OSPF packets to exchange LSA information and to establish and maintain neighbor relations.

 When explaining packet fields, the term "this router" or "this interface" always refers to the originator of the packet or the interface over which the packet is sent.

Encapsulation in IP datagrams

OSPF packets are directly encapsulated in IPv6 specified by protocol number 89. This number should be inserted in the Next Header field of the encapsulating IPv6 header.

OSPF doesn't use fragmentation, therefore relying entirely on IP fragmentation when sending packets larger than the MTU. Fragmentation should be avoided whenever possible. Potentially large OSPF packets like Database Description packets or Link State Update packets can easily be split into multiple packets by OSPF itself.

OSPF messages normally use the link-local IPv6 address of the outgoing interface as their source address. The exception is messages sent on a virtual link. They use the link-local or global unicast address of the virtual link as their source. Depending on the situation, OSPF messages can be sent as a unicast to a specific neighbor or as a multicast to multiple neighbors. The following two multicast addresses are set aside for this purpose:

AllSPFRouters (FF02::5)
> All routers running OSPF must listen to this multicast address. Hello packets are always sent to this address, with the exception of non-broadcast-capable networks. This address is also used for some packets during LSA flooding.

AllDRouters (FF02::6)
> Both the DR and the BDR on a multiaccess medium must listen to this multicast address. This address is used for some packets during LSA flooding.

OSPF packets sent to the multicast address have link-local scope and their IPv6 hop limit set to 1. They will never be sent over multiple hops.

OSPF header

There are five different packet types used by OSPF. All OSPF packets begin with a standard 16-byte header, shown in Figure 8-13.

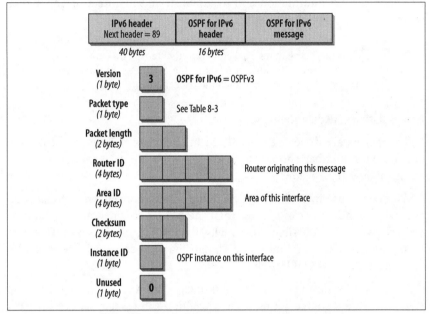

Figure 8-13. The OSPF for IPv6 packet header

 OSPF uses the word *type* in many instances. Carefully distinguish between OSPF packet type, LSA types, and Link type. This book uses the name of a particular type rather than the type number.

The fields of the OSPF header are explained in detail in the following list:

Version (1 byte)
    OSPF for IPv6 uses version number 3.

Type (1 byte)
    This field represents the type of OSPF messages from this router. Table 8-3 lists all possible types.

Table 8-3. OSPF for IPv3 packet types

Packet type	Name	Description
1	Hello	Initializes and maintains adjacencies. Elect DR and BDR.
		See the section "Forming Adjacencies."
2	Database Description	Exchanges database description during the formation of adjacencies.
		See the section "Forming Adjacencies."
3	Link State Request	Requests missing or outdated LSAs.
		See the section "Forming Adjacencies."
4	Link State Update	Exchanges LSAs either responding to requests when forming adjacencies or during LSA flooding.
		See the sections "Forming Adjacencies" and "LSA Flooding."
5	Link State Acknowledgment	Acknowledges the reception of an LSA. Every LSA must be acknowledged.
		See the sections "Forming Adjacencies" and "LSA Flooding."

Packet length (2 bytes)

This is the length of the OSPF protocol packet in bytes, including the OSPF header.

Router ID (4 bytes)

This is the Router ID of the router originating this packet. Each router must have a unique Router ID, a 32-bit number normally represented in dotted decimal notation. The Router ID must be unique within the entire AS.

Area ID (4 bytes)

This is the Area ID of the interface where this OSPF packet originated. This identifies the area this packet belongs to. All OSPF packets are associated with a single area. The Area ID is a 32-bit integer, normally represented in dotted decimal notation. Area 0 represents the backbone area.

Checksum (2 bytes)

OSPF uses the standard checksum calculation for IPv6 applications: the 16-bit one's complement of the one's complement sum of the entire contents of the packet, starting with the OSPF packet header and prepending a "pseudoheader" of IPv6 header fields (as specified in Chapter 9). The Upper-Layer Packet Length in the pseudoheader is set to the value of the OSPF packet header's length field. The Next Header value used in the pseudoheader is 89. If the packet's length is not an integral number of 16-bit words, the packet is padded with a byte of zero before checksumming. Before computing the checksum, the checksum field in the OSPF packet header is set to 0.

Instance ID (1 byte)

This identifies the OSPF instance to which this packet belongs. The Instance ID is an 8-bit number assigned to each interface of the router. The default value is 0. The Instance ID enables multiple OSPF protocol instances to run on a single link. If the receiving router does not recognize the Instance ID, it discards the packet. For example, routers A, B, C, and D are using a common multiaccess link n. A and B belong to an AS different from the one C and D belong to. To exchange OSPF packets, A and B will use a different Instance ID from the one C and D use. This prevents routers from accepting wrong OSPF packets. In OSPF for IPv4, this was done using the Authentication field, which no longer exists in OSPF for IPv6.

Processing OSPF packets

When a router sends an OSPF protocol packet, it fills in the header fields as described above. The Area ID and Instance ID are taken from the outgoing interface data structure. If authentication is required, it is the responsibility of IPv6 to add the necessary headers.

When a router receives an OSPF protocol packet, IPv6 validates it first by checking the IPv6 headers (IPv6 addresses, protocol field, and authentication). The packet is then given to the OSPF process. OSPF checks the version number (which must be 3), the checksum, the Area ID, and the Instance ID. The Area ID must match the Area ID configured on the incoming interface. If there is no match, but the Area ID is 0, the incoming interface must be the endpoint of a virtual link. The Instance ID must match the interface's Instance ID. If the packet's destination IPv6 address is the All-DRouters multicast address, the router must be either a DR or a BDR on this link. (DR and BDR will be explained in the next section.) If the packet passes all the above tests, it is passed to the appropriate OSPF process for further processing. Otherwise it must be dropped.

Forming Adjacencies

In order to exchange LSAs, the routers must create reliable channels, called adjacencies, to its neighbors. These channels allow the routers to synchronize the LSDB upon initialization and to flood the LSA in case of a change.

The neighbors need to be discovered first. This is done using the Hello protocol. Each interface on an OSPF router is assigned one of four link types: point-to-point, transit, stub, or virtual. On point-to-point or virtual links, only one neighbor can be discovered. On multiaccess networks, multiple neighbors can be discovered. OSPF calls these networks transit links. Forming adjacencies with all routers on transit links is not necessary. Each transit link elects a DR to form adjacencies with all routers on the transit link. This guarantees that all routers on this link have a synchronized LSDB. To ensure uninterrupted operation, a BDR is elected as well; it forms adjacencies with all routers on the transit link, too. Figure 8-14 shows adjacencies on point-to-point links and transit links. If no neighbor is discovered on any given link, the link is declared to be a stub link, and obviously no adjacencies are being formed on such a link.

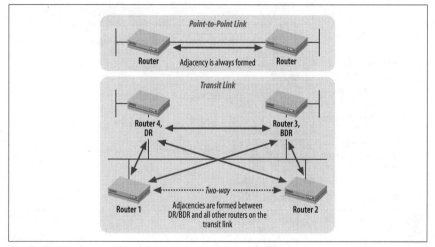

Figure 8-14. Adjacencies on point-to-point and transit links

The Hello packet

The Hello Protocol is responsible for initializing and maintaining adjacencies, as well as electing a DR/BDR. It ensures that communication between two routers is bidirectional. Hello packets are sent out through each interface at regular intervals. On point-to-point or broadcast-capable transit networks, OSPF Hello packets are sent to the multicast address AllSPFRouters. The neighbors are discovered dynamically. Multiaccess networks not capable of transmitting broadcast or multicast packets (e.g., X.25 and Frame Relay) are called non-broadcast-multi-access networks (NBMA). NBMA networks can be configured either as point-to-multipoint links or transit links. On point-to-multipoint links, logical point-to-point links are created to each neighbor. As in point-to-point links, no DR or BDR is needed. NBMA networks configured as transit links have static IPv6 address entries for each neighbor. A DR and BDR are elected. OSPF messages are sent as unicast to these statically configured neighbors.

Figure 8-15 shows the Hello packet format. It is an OSPF packet type 1, as explained earlier in Table 8-3.

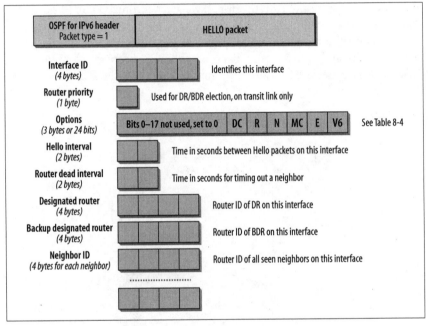

Figure 8-15. The Hello packet

The following list explains all the fields of the Hello packet in detail.

Interface ID (4 bytes)
Identifies the interface over which this Hello packet was sent by this router. Each interface of an OSPF router is assigned an Interface ID. The Interface ID must be unique within the same router. Some implementations use the MIB-II Interface Index, as specified in RFC 2233.

Router priority (1 byte)
Identifies the priority number assigned to this interface by this router. It is used for the election of the DR or BDR. This field is meaningful only on transit links. The router with the highest priority becomes the DR or BDR, but only if a DR or BDR has not already been elected. If this field is set to zero, the router on this interface can never be a DR or BDR.

Options (3 bytes)

Describes this router's optional capabilities. This field is set in OSPF Hello packets, Database Description packets and the following LSAs: Router-LSA, Network-LSA, Inter-Area-Router-LSA, and Link-LSA. Table 8-4 explains the bits used in the Options field. Only 6 bits are currently used.

Table 8-4. The Options field

Bit	Name	Description
0–17	Not used	Reserved for future use.
18	DC	Handling of Demand Circuits, as described in RFC 1793.
19	E	External-routes capability of this router. All members of an area must agree on the external capability. In a stub area, all routers must set this bit to 0 to achieve adjacency. The E-bit is meaningful only in Hello packets (similar to the N-bit).
20	MC	Multicast capability, as defined in RFC 1584.
21	N	All routers within an NSSA must set this bit. In addition, the E-bit must be set to 0 (see RFC 1587).
22	R	Indicates that the originator of the Hello packet is an active router. If this bit is set to 0, the originator will not forward packets: for example, a multihomed host that wants to build an OSPF routing table without actually routing packets.
23	V6	Indicates that this router supports OSPF for IPv6. If set to 0, this router/link should be excluded from IPv6 routing calculation.

Hello interval (2 bytes)

Specifies the number of seconds between Hello packets sent by this router on this interface. The default is 10 seconds.

Router Dead Interval (2 bytes)

Specifies the number of seconds before this router declares a silent router on this link to be down. (A silent router is no longer sending Hello packets.) The default is 40 seconds. If this interface is a transit link, the Router Dead Interval also determines the waiting timer during the election of the DR or BDR. Upon initialization of a transit link, the interface enters a waiting state to determine whether a DR or BDR has already been elected.

Designated Router ID (4 bytes)

Specifies the Router ID of the DR as seen from this router on this link. This field is set only on transit links. It is set to 0.0.0.0 when no DR has yet been elected, or on point-to-point links.

Backup Designated Router ID (4 bytes)
Specifies the Router ID of the BDR as seen from this router. This field is set only on transit links. It is set to 0.0.0.0 when no BDR has yet been elected, or on point-to-point links.

Neighbor ID (4 bytes)
Specifies the Router ID of each router from which the router received valid Hello packets on this link during the last Router Dead Interval.

Election of DR/BDR

As soon as the IPv6 on an OSPF interface is operational, the link is up, and the processing of Hello packets begin. A point-to-point link changes its state to point-to-point. A transit link enters the waiting state to discover the DR/BDR.

Each transit link needs a DR and a BDR, which form adjacencies with all routers on that particular transit link. During the waiting period, the router listens to Hello packets to determine if a DR/BDR already exits. It also sends Hello packets with the DR/BDR field set to zero to indicate that it is in discovery mode. If a router already claims to be the DR, no election of a DR takes place. If no router declares itself as the DR (all Hello packets contain zero in their DR field), the router with the highest router priority declares itself the DR. If the priorities are equal, the router with the highest Router ID wins the election. The BDR is elected in exactly the same way. Routers that were not elected as DR/BDR are called DR-Other. Routers with a priority of zero never become DR/BDR. Their interfaces change immediately to DR-Other without entering the waiting state.

If the DR goes silent (not sending Hellos for Router Dead Interval), the BDR becomes the DR and a new BDR is elected. Because the BDR has already formed all adjacencies, there is no disruption of the synchronized LSDB on that transit link. If the original DR comes back online, it recognizes that there is already a DR and a BDR and it enters the DR-Other state. If the BDR goes silent, a new BDR is elected. The OSPF interface is now up and in the state of point-to-point, DR, BDR, or DR-Other.

Processing of Hello packets

Before a Hello packet is accepted, a number of criteria must be met. Figure 8-16 shows the decision process to accept a Hello packet.

The OSPF input process has already accepted the packet, as described in the section "Processing OSPF packets." Now the Hello Interval and Router Dead Interval are checked. They must match the values set on the receiving interface. Next the E-bit and N-bit in the Options field are examined. The setting of these bits must match the value set on the receiving interface.

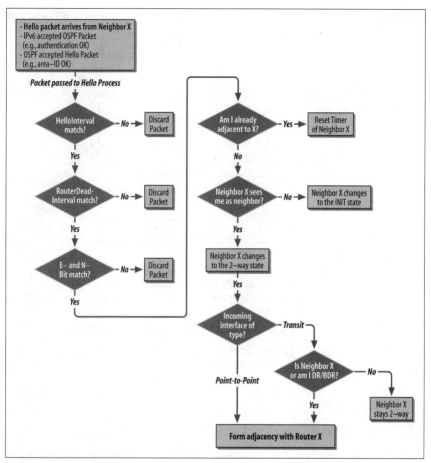

Figure 8-16. Processing a Hello packet

At this point, if all the criteria matched, the packet is accepted and the neighbor is identified by its Router ID. For each neighbor on each interface, the router keeps a neighbor state machine. If there is already a full adjacency with this neighbor, the Hello timer is simply reset. Otherwise, state of this neighbor changes to initialize (Init). The router examines the list of neighbors proclaimed in the received Hello packet. If the router identifies its own Router ID in that list, bidirectional communication has been established and the neighbor's state changes to two-way. The router decides whether to form an adjacency with this neighbor. If the interface is a point-to-point state, an adjacency is formed with this neighbor. On a transit link, if the router itself or this neighbor is the DR/BDR, an adjacency is formed. If the router decides not to form an adjacency, this neighbor stays in a two-way state.

Figure 8-17 explains the different phases of forming an adjacency and the corresponding neighbor states.

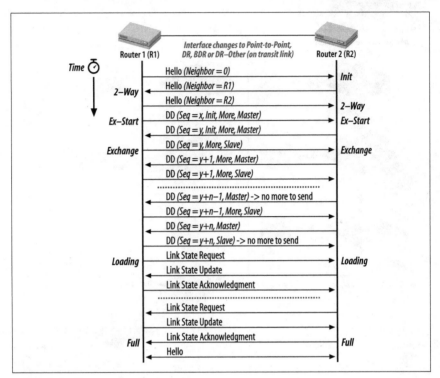

Figure 8-17. Forming an adjacency

The two routers forming an adjacency start communicating the contents of their LSDB. This phase is called the database description exchange. Once the routers know the contents of each other's databases, they request the missing or outdated information. This is the loading phase. After completing the loading phase, the routers are fully adjacent. Continuous sending of Hello packets prevents the adjacency from timing out.

Database description exchange

The routers change their neighbor state to exchange-start and send an initial Database Description packet without data. They establish a master-slave relationship to achieve an orderly exchange. Each router declares itself as the master in the initial Database Description packet. The only relevant information within the initial Database Description packet is the database description (DD) sequence number issued by each side. The router with the higher Router ID stays master during the entire DD exchange phase.

The neighbors now enter the Exchange state. Starting with the slave, a series of packets describing the contents of their LSDB are exchanged. The master always increments the sequence number and the slave always uses the master's sequence number in its packet. Each router indicates that is has more data to send by setting the more bit (see Figure 8-17). If one router has sent its entire database description, but the other hasn't yet, the first router is obliged to send empty packets to keep the sequence numbers matched. To describe the LSDB, the router only sends the database headers (LSA headers), as described in Figure 8-18. (The LSA header is discussed in the section "LSAs".) All Database Description packets are sent as unicast to the neighbor. The unicast addresses are discovered by looking at the source IPv6 address of the Hello packet sent by the neighbor. As soon as both routers have nothing more to send, the routers enter the loading phase.

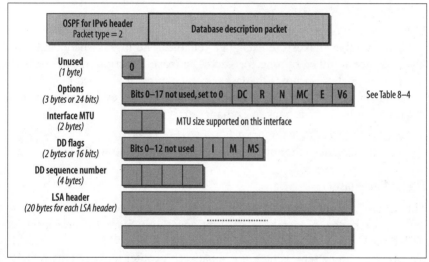

Figure 8-18. Database Description packet

The following list explains all the fields of the Database Description packet in detail.

Options (3 bytes)
> The optional capabilities supported by this router, according to Table 8-4. They should be the same options advertised in the Hello packet. Changes in the Options field during DD exchange will stop the exchange and the routers revert back to exchange-Start.

Interface MTU (2 bytes)
> The largest frame size that can be sent through this interface without fragmentation. On virtual links, this should be set to zero. The MTU of

common Internet link types can be found in RFC 1191. If this router receives a DD packet stating an MTU larger than it can handle on this interface, the packet is rejected.

Init bit (I bit)
When set to 1, this bit indicates the first Database Description packet sent by this router. This packet contains no data and starts the exchange process. The M/S bit is set as well.

More bit (M bit)
When set to 1, this bit indicates that there are more Database Description packets to follow. When set to zero, it indicates that all database descriptions have been delivered.

Master/slave bit (M/S bit)
When set to 1, this bit indicates this router to be the master; otherwise, the slave.

DD sequence number (4 bytes)
This number makes the exchange reliable. The master increments the sequence number by one for each Database Description packet sent. The slave always quotes the last sequence number received by the master. A mismatch in sequence number causes the DD exchange to fail and the routers to revert back to exchange-start.

List of LSA headers (20 bytes for each header)
This list describes the entry in the LSDB. See the section "LSAs."

The loading phase

The routers are now requesting the missing or outdated LSAs learned during the exchange of database descriptions. Link State Request packets (OSPF packet type 3) identify the requesting LSA by its LSA header. Multiple requests can be sent using a single packet. A router replies to the request by sending the corresponding LSA from its database. The LSA is sent using Link State Update packets (OSPF packet type 4). Multiple LSAs can be sent in a single packet. Each Link State Update must be acknowledged by using a Link State Acknowledgment packet (OSPF packet type 5). The Link State Acknowledgment packet contains the LSA header of the LSA to be acknowledged. Multiple LSAs can be acknowledged in a single packet. The Link State Request and Acknowledgment packets simply contain a list of requested or acknowledged LSA headers, so I won't discuss them in more detail. Like Database Description packets, all the packets just mentioned are sent to the unicast address of the neighbor. The neighbors now enter the full state. Hello packets keep the adjacency alive. Adjacencies must stay alive, as they are used for flooding changed LSA. Refer to the section "LSA Flooding."

The Link State Database

The link state database is the most important component of OSPF. Figure 8-19 illustrates the components of the LSDB.

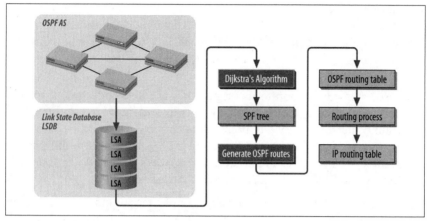

Figure 8-19. Components of the LSDB

The LSDB is a data structure consisting of LSAs exchanged in the AS. The link state information is structured to allow the building of a tree whose branches and leaves represent the shortest paths to all routes within the AS. Each router builds such a tree from its point of view. Most commonly, the routers use the algorithm developed by Dijkstra to build this tree of shortest paths (SPF tree). First, the router builds the intra-area tree to all destinations within its own area. Inter-area and external routes are then attached to the branch representing an ABR or ASBR. At the end, each route within the tree is added to one of four sections of the OSPF routing table: the intra-area routes, inter-area routes, external-1 routes, and finally, external-2 routes. The next hop is always the link-local address of first router in the shortest path to the route. The following sections describe each of these components, starting with the contents of the LSDB. Then I'll discuss how Dijkstra calculates the SPF tree and puts the routes into the routing table.

Contents of the LSDB

RFC 2328 describes the SPF as a system of directed graphs using vertices to build a tree. This basically describes the network topology as set of pointers building a tree. There are four basic pointers within the tree:

Router to router

Describes a router's point-to-point interface identifying the Router ID of the neighboring router on a point-to-point link. In LSDB terminology, it points from a Router-LSA to another Router-LSA.

Router to transit link

Describes a router's interface to a transit link by identifying the Interface ID of the DR for this transit link. In LSDB terminology, it points from a Router-LSA to a Network-LSA.

Transit link to routers

Describes a transit link and points to all its attached routers. In LSDB terminology, it points from a Network-LSA to one or many Router-LSAs.

Informational

Associates information to its originator (e.g., IPv6 addresses, IPv6 prefixes, etc.). Using tree terminology, it is like adding leaves to branches. Unlike the three previous pointers, which build the actual tree, this pointer just adds information to the tree. LSAs belonging to this kind of pointer are Inter-Area-Prefix-LSA, Inter-Area-Router-LSA, AS-External-LSA, Type-7-LSA, Link-LSA, and Intra-Area-Prefix-LSA.

Figure 8-20 shows the basic pointers in a sample tree structure.

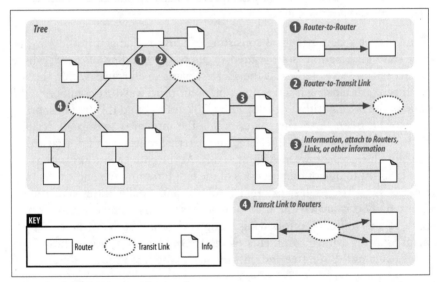

Figure 8-20. LSDB structural pointers

LSAs

Each LSA within the LSDB incorporates one or more of the previously mentioned pointers. It consists of an LSA header and an LSA body. The LSA header identifies each LSA uniquely.

LSA header

Each LSA starts with a common 20-byte header. Figure 8-21 shows the details of this header. The Link State (LS) type, the LS ID, and the Advertising Router together uniquely identify the LSA.

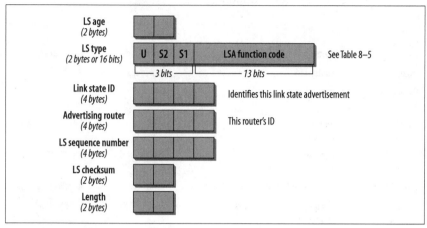

Figure 8-21. LSA header

The LSA header fields are fully detailed in the following list:

LS Age (2 bytes)
  LS Age is the time in seconds since the LSA was originated. If it has reached *MaxAge* (3,600 seconds), the LSA is no longer considered for the SPF tree calculation. The originating router of this LSA must renew the LSA and increment the sequence number before *MaxAge* is reached to prevent the LSA from ageing out. It is recommended to renew an LSA after *MaxAge/2*.

LS type (2 bytes)
  This is the type of this advertised LSA. The first three bits of the LSA type field indicate special properties of the LSA.

  U-bit (handling of unknown LS Type)
    Identifies the handling of unknown LSA types by the routers. If the bit is set, the LSA must be stored and flooded as if the type were understood. Otherwise, if the bit is 0, the LSA has to be treated as if it had link-local flooding scope.

  S2 and S1 bit (flooding scope)
    Define the flooding scope of the LSA. The four values are:

    00 = Link-local, flooded only on the link on which it originated.
    01 = Area, flooded to all routers in the originating area.

10 = AS, flooded to all routers in the AS.

11 = Reserved.

The last 13 bits represent the actual LSA Function Code. See Table 8-5 for details on link state types. The LS Type is represented in hexadecimal notation to reflect the flooding scope.

Table 8-5. Link state types

LS Type	Name	Flooding scope	Advertised by	Link State ID
0x2001	Router-LSA	Area	Each router	Router ID
0x2002	Network-LSA	Area	DR	DR's Interface ID of the transit link
0x2003	Inter-Area-Prefix-LSA	Area	ABR	Any ID set by ABR
0x2004	Inter-Area-Router-LSA	Area	ABR	Any ID set by ABR
0x4005	AS-External-LSA	AS	ASBR	Any ID set by ASBR
0x2006	Group-Membership-LSA	Area	See RFC 1584	See RFC 1584
0x2007	Type-7-LSA	Area	See RFC 1587	See RFC 1587
0x0008	Link-LSA	Link	Each router for each link	Interface ID
0x2009	Intra-Area-Prefix-LSA	Area	Each router	Any ID set by router

Link State ID (4 bytes)

The Link State ID is part of the link state identification. With Router-LSA and Network-LSA, the Link State ID serves as a value for a pointer in the tree to identify this router or network. For all other LSA, the originating router uses a locally unique ID.

Advertising Router (4 bytes)

The Advertising Router is the Router ID of the router originating this LSA.

LS Sequence Number (4 bytes)

The LS Sequence Number identifies the instance of this LSA. It is used to determine which LSA is newer in case of multiple occurrences of the same LSA. The higher the sequence number, the newer the LSA is. The starting sequence number is always 0x80000000. The highest sequence number possible is 0x7FFFFFFF. If this number has been reached, the LSA is aged out (LS Age equals *MaxAge*) and flooded before a new instance of the LSA (now using 0x80000000) is issued.

Checksum (2 bytes)

This is the Fletcher checksum of the complete contents of the LSA, including the LSA header but excluding the LS Age field.

Length (2 bytes)

This is the length of the entire LSA in bytes.

The following paragraphs explain all types of LSA in detail, with the exception of Group-Membership-LSAs and Type-7-LSAs. Group-Membership-LSAs are defined in RFC 1584, which has not yet been updated for IPv6. Type-7-LSAs are explained in RFC 1587, which introduces the concept of NSSA; it also has not been updated to IPv6.

Router-LSA (Type 0x2001)

Router links describe the router's point-to-point, virtual, or transit links. Basically, it includes all links having at least one neighbor. Unlike OSPF for IPv4, stub links are no longer advertised within a router link. An ABR must originate separate router links for each attached area, containing only links belonging to that particular area. Virtual links always belong to area 0 and are only advertised by ABR. Figure 8-22 outlines a Router-LSA.

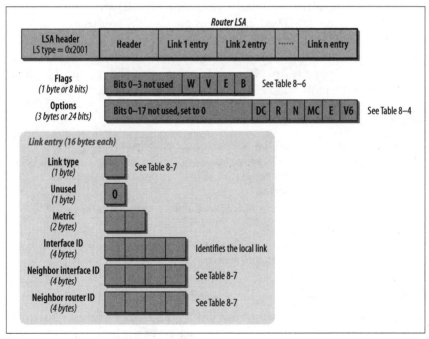

Figure 8-22. Router-LSA

The fields of the Router-LSA are fully detailed in the following list:

Flags (1 byte)

The Flags field indicates the special function of this router. Table 8-6 shows the possible values and their corresponding functions.

Table 8-6. Flags in Router-LSA

Bit	Name
W bit	This router is a wildcard multicast receiver. See RFC 1584 for more information.
V bit	This router is the endpoint of a virtual link using this area as a transit area.
E bit	This router is an ASBR.
B bit	This router is an ABR.

Options (3 bytes)

This field describes the optional capabilities supported by this router, as outlined in Table 8-4.

Link Entry (16 bytes per link)

Table 8-7 explains the possible link types and their corresponding fields. Each link has a metric assigned to it based on the characteristics of the interface. The Neighbor Interface ID and Router ID are learned through the Hello Protocol. The Link Entries are used as pointers to build the intra-area tree. Interface types 1 and 4 point to the Router-LSA specified in the Neighbor Router ID (LS-ID and Advertised Router). Interface type 2 points to Network-LSA, as specified in the Neighbor Interface ID (LS-ID) and Neighbor Router ID (Advertised Router).

Table 8-7. Link Type supported in a Router-LSA

Link type	Name	Neighbor Interface ID	Neighbor Router ID
1	Point-to-point	Interface ID of the neighbor on the other end of the point-to-point link	Router-ID of the neighbor on the other end of the point-to-point link
2	Transit	Interface ID of the DR on this link	Router ID of the DR on this link.
3	Reserved		
4	Virtual	Interface ID of the neighbor on the other end of the virtual link	Router ID of the neighbor on the other end of the virtual link

Network-LSA (Type 0x2002)

The designated router of each transit link in the area originates a Network-LSA. The Link State ID is set to the Interface ID of the DR's interface to the transit link. Figure 8-23 outlines the Network-LSA. It simply contains the

Options field (see Table 8-4, earlier in this chapter), followed by a list of Router IDs identifying all routers attached to this particular transit link. This represents a pointer to all routers attached to this transit link.

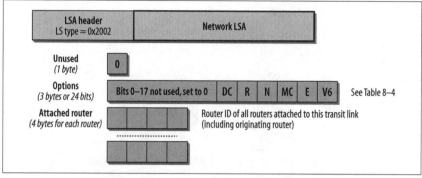

Figure 8-23. Network-LSA

The Options field is set to the logical OR of the Options field received from the Link-LSA of all the routers attached to this transit link. (See the section "Link-LSA.") This provides the common optional capabilities supported by all routers on this link.

Inter-Area-Prefix-LSA (Type 0x2003)

Inter-Area-Prefix-LSAs are originated by the ABR to advertise IPv6 prefixes from other areas into the area of this LSA. A separate Inter-Area-Prefix-LSA is originated for each route. An ABR could summarize a contiguous range of IPv6 prefixes into a single advertisement. For a stub area, the ABR advertises the default route using this LSA. Inter-Area-Prefix-LSA is the equivalent of OSPF for IPv4's Summary-LSA and is outlined in Figure 8-24.

In the tree-building process, this LSA represents an informational pointer associated with the ABR for attaching inter-area routes to the SPF tree. The Inter-Area-Prefix-LSA fields are detailed in the following list:

Metric (20 bits)
Defines the cost from the ABR to the IPv6 address prefix advertised with this Inter-Area-Prefix-LSA. If this route represents a summary, the metric should be taken from the highest metric of the member prefixes.

IPv6 Prefix Representation (0 to 20 bytes, in multiples of 4)
Defines the actual IPv6 prefix advertised. It consists of four fields: the Prefix Length, the Prefix Options, an unused field (set to zero), and the actual IPv6 Address Prefix. The Prefix Length defines the length of the address prefix. The default route is represented by a prefix length of 0.

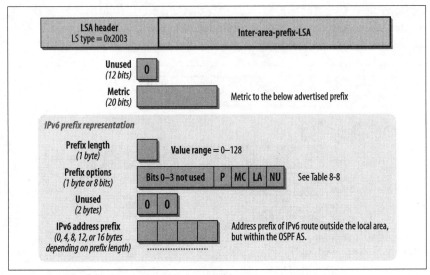

Figure 8-24. Inter-Area-Prefix-LSA

Table 8-8 explains the prefix options. The address prefix represents the IPv6 address. If necessary, it is padded with zero bits to the next full 32-bit word.

Table 8-8. Prefix options starting with the leftmost bit

Bit	Name	Description
0-3	Reserved	
4	P bit	Propagate bit: if set, the NSSA ABR readvertises the prefix into the backbone. Only used in Type-7-LSA.
5	MC bit	Multicast bit: if set, the prefix should be included in IPv6 multicast routing calculations.
6	LA bit	Local address bit: if set, the prefix is actually a local IPv6 address of the originating router.
7	NU bit	No unicast bit: if set, the prefix should be excluded from IPv6 unicast calculation.

Inter-Area-Router-LSA (Type 0x2004)

Inter-Area-Router-LSAs are originated by ABRs to advertise ASBRs from other areas into this area. A separate Inter-Area-Router-LSA is originated for each ASBR. This is necessary to inform all routers in this area of the existence of an outside ASBR. Inter-Area-Router-LSA is the equivalent of OSPF for IPv4's AS-Summary-LSA. As shown in Figure 8-25, the Inter-Area-Router-LSA contains the Options field (refer back to Table 8-4), the Metric field, and the Router ID of the ASBR. The Metric field represents the cost from the ABR to the ASBR.

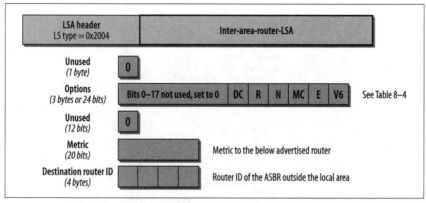

Figure 8-25. Inter-Area-Router-LSA

In the tree-building process, this LSA represents an informational pointer associated with the ABR for attaching an ASBR to the SPF tree.

AS-External-LSA (Type 0x4005)

AS-External-LSAs are advertised by ASBRs to import external IPv6 prefixes into the AS. Each AS-External-LSA represents one IPv6 prefix external to OSPF—i.e., learned from RIP, BGP, static, etc. They are flooded throughout the entire AS and are therefore known to every router except the routers in a stub area. Figure 8-26 explains the AS-External-LSA.

In the tree-building process, this LSA represents an informational pointer associated with the ASBR for attaching external routes to the SPF tree. The AS-External-LSA fields are described in the following list.

E bit

If set, the specified metric is a Type 2 external metric as explained in the section "OSPF areas and external routes." The metric is considered larger than any path to any route within the AS. If set to zero, the metric is a Type 1 external metric. It is expressed using the same units as the metric used in Router-LSA, Inter-Area-Prefix-LSA, and Intra-Area-Prefix-LSA.

F bit

If set, a forwarding address has been included in this LSA.

T bit

If set, an external router tag has been included in the LSA.

Metric (3 bytes)

Defines the cost from the ASBR to the external IPv6 prefix. The interpretation of the metric value depends on the E bit.

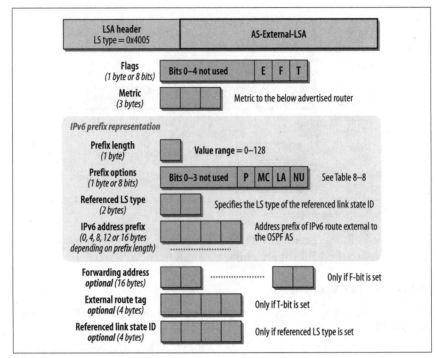

Figure 8-26. AS-External-LSA

IPv6 Prefix Representation (0 to 20 bytes, in multiples of 4)

> Defines the actual IPv6 prefix advertised. It consists of four fields: the Prefix Length, the Prefix Options, the Referenced LS Type, and the actual IPv6 Address Prefix. The Prefix Length defines the length of the address prefix. The default route is represented by a 0 length prefix. Table 8-8 explains the prefix options. The Address Prefix represents the IPv6 address. If necessary, it is padded with zero bits to the next full 32-bit word.

Referenced LS Type (part of the IPv6 Prefix Representation)

> If set to a value other than zero, an additional LSA is associated with this external route. This LSA is specified in the Referenced Link State ID field.

Forwarding address (4 bytes)

> If the F bit is set, any router in the AS forwards data traffic (to the external IPv6 prefix specified with this LSA) to this forwarding address. If the F bit is not set, data traffic is forwarded to the ASBR originating this LSA. This field must never be set to the IPv6 unspecified address (0:0:0: 0:0:0:0:0). If any router within the AS cannot reach the forwarding address or the ASBR, the IPv6 prefix of the external route is not added to the routing table.

External Route Tag (4 bytes)

    If the T bit is set, this field contains additional information about the external route. This information, however, will never be used within the OSPF AS. See RFC 1745 for more details.

Referenced Link State ID (4 bytes)

    If and only if the Referenced LS Type is set to a value other than zero, the Referenced LS Type, Referenced Link State ID (this field), and the advertising router of this LSA represent an existing LSA in the LSDB, providing additional information for this external IPv6 prefix. This information, however, is not used by the OSPF protocol itself. The precise nature of such information is not part of the OSPF specifications.

Link-LSA (0x0008)

Link-LSAs are originated by each router, one for each link of the router. They are never flooded beyond this link. The Link State ID is set to the Interface ID of this link. The Link-LSA serves three purposes:

- It provides the router's link-local address to all other routers attached to this link.
- It provides a list of IPv6 prefixes associated with this link.
- It provides a list of options to be used by the designated router for this link.

Figure 8-27 outlines the Link-LSA.

In the tree-building process, this LSA represents an informational pointer associated with each link from or to a Router-LSA. It attaches the link-local address of the link to the SPF tree. The Link-LSA fields are described in the following list:

Router Priority (1 byte)

    The priority number given to this router on this interface.

Options (3 bytes)

    This router would like to use the options specified here (see Table 8-4). This is an indication (to the DR on this transit link) of which options it should use. See the section "Network-LSA".

Link-local address (16 bytes)

    The link-local address of the originating router's interface for this link.

Number of prefixes (4 bytes)

    The number of prefixes to be advertised with this LSA.

IPv6 Prefix Representation (4 to 20 bytes, in multiples of 4)

    All IPv6 prefixes will be listed here according to the number of prefixes. It consists of four fields: the Prefix Length, the Prefix Options, an

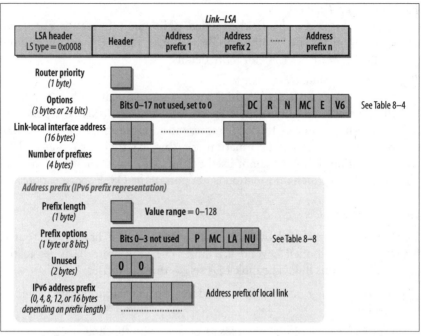

Figure 8-27. Link-LSA

unused field (set to zero), and the actual IPv6 Address Prefix. The Prefix Length defines the length of the address prefix. Table 8-8 explains the prefix options. The Address Prefix represents the IPv6 address. If necessary, it is padded with zero bits to the next full 32-bit word.

Intra-Area-Prefix-LSA (Type 0x2009)

A router uses the Intra-Area-Prefix-LSA to advertise one or more IPv6 prefixes associated with either this router or a Network-LSA. As OSPF for IPv6 has removed all addressing semantics from the Router-LSAs and Network-LSAs, the Intra-Area-Prefix-LSA provides this information. Each address prefix advertised is associated with a Router-LSA or a Network-LSA. Figure 8-28 shows the contents of an Intra-Area-Prefix-LSA. Particular attention should be paid to the Referenced LS Type, Link State ID, and Advertising Router fields, as explained below.

In the tree-building process, this LSA represents an informational pointer associated with a router, attaching IPv6 prefixes of its local interfaces to the SPF tree. It can also be associated with a transit link, attaching its IPv6 prefixes to the SPF tree. The Intra-Area-Prefix-LSA fields are detailed in the following list:

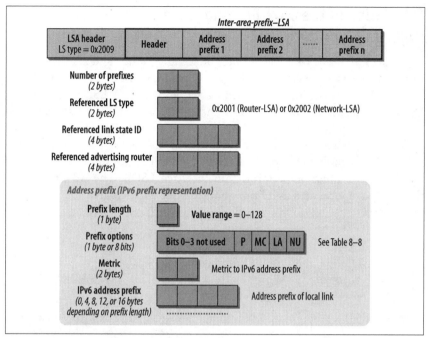

Figure 8-28. Intra-Area-Prefix-LSA

Number of prefixes (2 bytes)

The number of prefixes to be advertised with this LSA.

Referenced LS Type, Link State ID, Advertising Router (10 bytes)

If the Referenced LS Type is set to 1, the address prefixes are associated with this router. The Referenced Link State ID is set to 0, and the Referenced Advertising Router is set to the Router ID of the router originating this LSA. If the Referenced LS Type is set to 2, the address prefixes are associated with the Network-LSA. The Referenced Link State ID is set to the Interface ID of the link's DR, and the Referenced Advertising Router is the Router ID of the DR.

IPv6 Prefix Representation (4 to 20 bytes, in multiples of 4)

All IPv6 Prefixes are listed here according to the length of prefixes. It consists of four fields: the Prefix Length, the Prefix Options, the Metric, and the actual IPv6 Address Prefix. The Prefix Length defines the length of the address prefix. Table 8-8, earlier in this chapter, explained the prefix options. The Address Prefix represents the IPv6 address. If necessary, it is padded with zero bits to the next full 32-bit word. The Metric field defines the cost of this prefix.

Calculation of the OSPF Routing Table (Dijkstra Algorithm)

Using the LSDB as a base, each router builds an SPF tree and adds the routes to the routing table. Each router keeps multiple LSDBs. The Link LSDB contains all LSAs with link-local flooding scope, the Area LSDB contains all LSAs with area flooding scope, and finally, the AS LSDB contains all LSAs with AS flooding scope. The ABR has one Area LSDB for each locally attached area. The tree-building involves the three-step process described below. The sample network depicted in Figure 8-29 illustrates the process. Steps 1 and 2 must be performed on the Area LSDB. The ABR has to do them for each local area as it builds one SPF tree for each area.

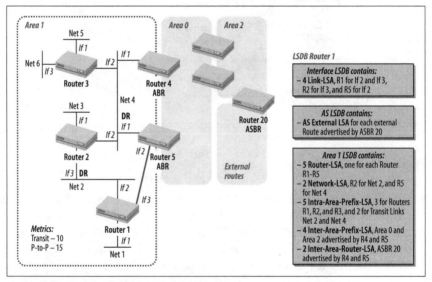

Figure 8-29. Sample network and its LSDB

Step 1: Intra-area routes

In Step 1, the router builds the core tree using the Router-LSA and Network-LSA for this area. Remember that these two LSAs contain actual pointers. Each router places its own Router-LSA at the root of the tree. Each link entry in the Router-LSA represents a pointer to another Router-LSA (link type 1 or 4) or to a Network-LSA (link type 2). The Neighbor ID and, on link type 2, the Interface ID identify the respective LSA. Each adjacent LSA is placed temporarily in the tree as a branch, along with its metric, and the least-cost branch is made permanent because it represents the shortest path. Its LSA is examined next. If it is a Router-LSA, each link entry provides a new set of LSAs as candidates for the tree. If it is a Network-LSA, each attached router identifies a new set of LSAs as candidates, this time without a metric, because the metric to this transit link has already been determined. The candidates are added to the tree temporarily unless the candidate is already permanently in the tree and can therefore be ignored. Again, the LSA with the smallest metric (accumulated metric from the root) is made a permanent branch and its contents are examined. If this particular LSA exists as a temporary branch anywhere else in the tree, the temporary branch(es) can be eliminated. This process continues until there are no more Network-LSAs or Router-LSAs to be added. In case of two or more branches having the same least costs, each branch is made permanent.

The SPF core tree is now built. The tree, however, contains no addressing information. This address information is provided by the Intra-Area-Prefix-LSA. The router simply adds the Intra-Area-Prefix-LSA to the Router-LSA or Network-LSA according to the referenced LSA. The last step is to find the next hop information. Next hop addresses are the link-local addresses of directly connected routers. This information is provided by the Link-LSA originated by the directly connected routers. The router has now found all routes within the area and adds them to the OSPF routing table as Intra-area routes. Figure 8-30 explains the building of the SPF tree of area 1 for Router R1.

Step 2: Inter-area routes

The router identifies all Inter-Area-Link-LSAs of this area. Its ABR must exist in the previously constructed tree. These LSAs are now associated with the ABR and added to the tree with the advertised metric. This attaches IPv6 prefixes of inter-area routes to the tree. The total cost to these routes consists of the cost to the ABR added to the cost advertised in the Inter-Area-Link-LSA. If the same prefix appears more than once, the one with the best total cost is considered. If the costs are equal, all equal-cost prefixes must be accepted into the inter-area routing table. The next hop is determined as the directly connected router on the shortest intra-area path to the ABR. Figure 8-31 illustrates this process for router R1.

If the router itself is an ABR, only Inter-Area-Link-LSAs originated by other ABRs are considered. All Inter-Area-Link-LSAs that represent routes for directly attached areas are ignored, because there is always an intra-area path to that destination, and intra-area paths are always preferred.

Step 3: External routes

The router first identifies all Inter-Area-Router-LSAs and associates them with the ABRs as described in step 2. This ensures that all ASBRs have been

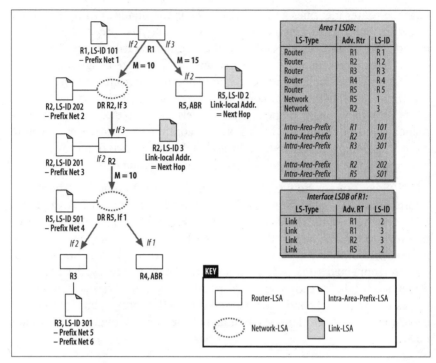

Figure 8-30. Intra-area tree for router R1 in area 1

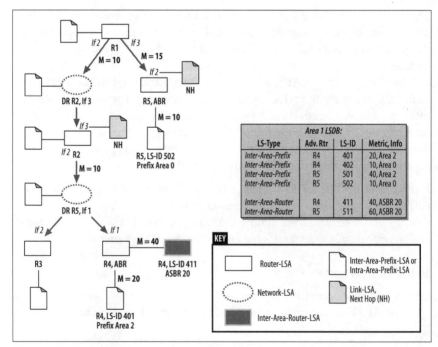

Figure 8-31. Inter-area routes for router R1

identified. Next, the router associates all AS-External-LSAs with their corresponding ASBR and adds them to the SPF tree. The IPv6 prefixes of all newly added LSAs form the external routes. Depending on the metric type, the router now enters these routes into the external-1 or external-2 routing table. If the same prefix appears more than once, external-1 routes are preferred over external-2 routes. If the same prefix still appears more than once, the one with the best total cost is considered. If the costs are equal, all equal-cost prefixes must be accepted. The next hop is determined as the directly connected router on the shortest intra-area path to the ASBR or to the forwarding address, if the F bit has been set within the LSA. Figure 8-32 illustrates this process for router R1.

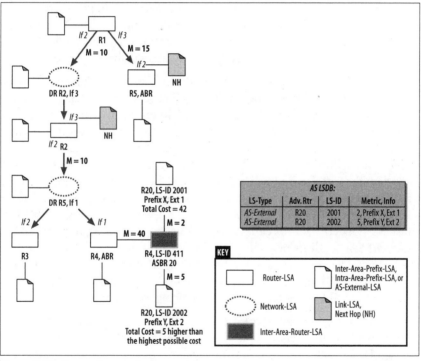

Figure 8-32. External routes for router R1

The calculation of the OSPF routing table is now finished, and its content is handed to the internal routing process of the router.

LSA Flooding

Any change in the network causes certain link state information to change. Examples of such changes include the following:

- The state of a router's interface changes.
- A neighbor transitions from or to full state.
- The DR changes.
- A new prefix is added or deleted on any given interface.
- An area's summary information changes.
- An external route is added or withdrawn at the ASBR.

The router detecting the change rewrites the LSA accordingly, increases the sequence number, and gives the LSA to the flooding process. According to Table 8-5, the LSA is then flooded to a neighbor only (link scope), to all neighbors in the same area (area scope), or to all neighbors (AS scope).

Flooding means that the LSA is passed from the advertising router to its adjacent neighbors. Depending on the flooding scope of the LSA, the neighbors then pass it on to their neighbors, and so on. Each router receiving an LSA first evaluates whether the LSA is new or has a higher sequence number than the one already installed in the LSDB. If either of these two conditions is true, the LSA is added or replaced in the LSDB. Now the router considers the interfaces to be used for further flooding. It will not flood the LSA out the incoming interface, with one exception: if the router is a DR for the incoming interface of the LSA and the LSA was not sent by the BDR, it must be flooded back out the same interface. The DR is responsible for sending LSAs to all its neighbors. Another reason not to flood the LSA is if the LSA is older than or the same age as the one already installed. This prevents LSAs from looping in the network. LSAs are normally sent to the multicast address AllSPFRouters, with the following exceptions:

- On transit networks, routers in the DR-Other state send LSAs to the address AllDRouters. The update reaches the DR/BDR, which in turn sends it back to all other routers on this transit link using the AllSPFRouter address.
- If a router requests a link state update sending a Link State Request packet, the LSA uses the unicast address of the requesting router.
- On NBMA, all LSAs are sent unicast to the statically configured neighbors.

Figure 8-33 shows the process of a DR receiving new or changed LSAs and flooding them to all routers.

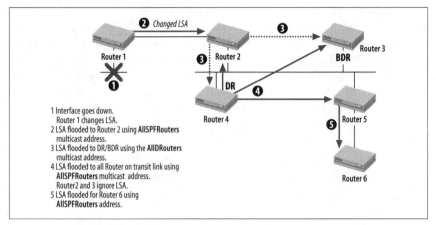

Figure 8-33. LSA flooding

Each router receiving a new or changed LSA has to acknowledge this LSA. Sending a Link State Acknowledgment packet usually accomplishes this. It could also be acknowledged by sending back the LSA if the received LSA is older or the same age as the one already installed in the LSDB. In that case, the sequence number is set to the one already installed. Unacknowledged LSAs have to be retransmitted. Each router keeps track of which neighbor has acknowledged which LSA. Retransmissions are always sent to the unicast address of the neighboring router.

A sequence number is assigned to the LSA by the advertising router to keep track of the most recent instance of this particular LSA. The sequence number is incremented by the advertising router each time the LSA is changed. When a new or changed Router-LSA or Network-LSA is received and accepted, the router installs it in the LSDB. It then recalculates the SPF tree. If a new or changed LSA of another type is received, it is not necessary to recalculate the SPF tree because these LSAs represent informational pointers only. They replace or remove the existing information. The new information is used to reevaluate the best path for the intra-area, inter-area, or external routers.

Aging an LSA

In addition to the sequence number, each LSA maintains an Age field. The age is expressed in seconds. Each router increments the Age field of its LSA continuously. If an LSA is transmitted to the neighbor router, a transmit delay must be added to the Age field. An LSA can never age beyond a Maximum Age (*MaxAge*), which is an architectural constant set to 3,600 seconds. Usually a router is flooding a new instance (increment sequence number) of its own LSA when it has reached *MaxAge*/2. LSAs that have reached *MaxAge* are not considered for the SPF tree and are eventually deleted from the LSDB. The advertising router can prematurely age an LSA to flush it from the OSPF area or AS. This would be done if, for example, an external route was withdrawn. Another reason to prematurely age an LSA might occur if the LSA has reached the biggest sequence number possible. Before wrapping the sequence number (starting again), the LSA has to be flushed.

Self-originating LSAs

A router may receive an LSA that it has issued itself. This could happen if there are redundant links within the area, forming a loop. Self-originated LSAs are normally discarded, unless the self-originated LSA is newer. Obviously, this should not happen because only the advertising router can increment the sequence number of the LSA. If, however, the router has been rebooted, previously issued LSA are still held in the other router's LSDB. If a newer, self-originated LSA is received, the router prematurely ages that LSA, thereby flushing it from the area or AS.

Handling of unknown LSAs

OSPF for IPv6 has added the capability to handle unknown LSAs. Each LSA header contains the U bit in its LSA Type field. If the U bit is set, the unknown LSA is flooded according to the encoded flooding scope. A U bit set to zero indicates link-local flooding scope. The exception to the above rule is flooding into a stub area. AS-External-LSAs are never flooded into a stub area. To prevent unnecessary flooding of LSAs into a stub area, the following rule applies: if the LSA is unknown and either its flooding scope is set to AS or its U bit is set, the LSA is discarded and not flooded into a stub area.

BGP Extensions for IPv6

There is no actual BGP for IPv6. The IPv6 support derives from the capability of BGP-4 to exchange information about network layer protocols other than IPv4. These multiprotocol extensions of BGP-4 are defined in RFC 2858, which obsoletes RFC 2283. RFC 2283 is mentioned here because it is the base document for RFC 2545, which defines the IPv6 extensions of BGP-4. It is important to understand BGP-4 fully before looking at its multiprotocol extensions. The following sections start with a short overview of BGP-4 and its operations as defined in RFC 1771. BGP message types are then discussed. The last part covers the implementation of IPv6 information carried within BGP-4.

BGP-4 Overview

Each AS runs its interior routing protocol (RIP, OSPF, etc.) to distribute all routing information within the AS. The BGP is an exterior routing protocol whose primary function is to exchange information about the reachability of networks between ASes. Each AS receives a unique AS number assigned by the numbering authority. Figure 8-34 shows the different types of ASes that can be interconnected using BGP-4.

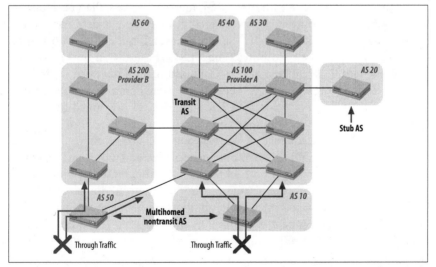

Figure 8-34. BGP traffic and AS types

The AS types are further explained in the following list:

Transit AS
> A transit AS has multiple connections to other AS. Routing updates from any AS arriving at the transit AS may be passed through the AS and distributed out to other neighboring ASes. A transit AS can forward traffic to any other ASes based on the routing information received. The ASes of larger ISPs are usually of this type.

Stub AS
> A stub has a single connection to another AS. All traffic to or from the stub AS passes through this link. Smaller ISPs and campus or corporate networks use this kind of AS.

Multihomed nontransit AS
> A multihomed nontransit AS has multiple connections to one or more other AS. It does not pass routing updates through. Traffic not belonging to this AS is therefore never forwarded. A multihomed nontransit AS allows multiple entry/exit points to be used for load sharing of inbound and outbound traffic.

Two routers exchanging routing information with BGP are called BGP Peers or BGP speakers. They establish a TCP session first because TCP guarantees a reliable connection. The peers then open a BGP connection to exchange BGP messages. The most important BGP message is the UPDATE message, which contains the routes to be exchanged. A BGP route is defined as a unit of information consisting of the Network Layer Reachability Information (NLRI) and a set of path attributes. The NLRI is basically an IPv4 prefix and its prefix length. Any concept of IPv4 class information has been eliminated. The NLRI may represent a single network or, more commonly, an aggregate (summary) of a range of addresses. Each NLRI is accompanied by a set of path attributes that add additional information to the BGP route, i.e., the next hop address, a sequence of ASes through which the route has passed during its update, or its origin. Routing decisions and traffic management are often based on these path attributes. One attribute must be emphasized here, as it plays a very important role in loop detection:it is called AS_PATH, and it carries a sequence of AS numbers through which the route has passed. If the receiving peer recognizes its own AS number within the AS_PATH, it rejects the corresponding route.

BGP routing updates are exchanged between two peers. They are governed by a set of rules called policies. Outbound policies specify which NLRIs are advertised to a particular peer. A router can advertise only the NLRI it uses itself. Inbound policies specify which NLRIs are accepted from a particular peer. Policies may also be used to modify an NLRI and its attributes to change the characteristics of a route.

Establishing a BGP connection

In order to exchange routing updates, two peers first have to establish a BGP connection. Figure 8-35 illustrates the steps needed to establish a BGP connection, including the different BGP messages exchanged and the peer state. The entire state machine is explained in detail in RFC 1771. Each message and its fields are explained in the section "BGP Message Header."

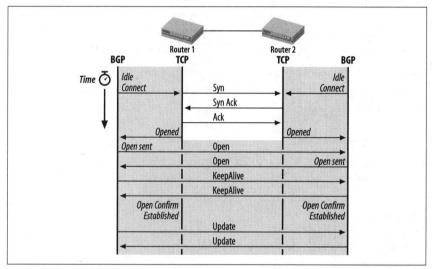

Figure 8-35. Establishing a BGP connection

If both routers simultaneously try to establish a BGP connection to each other, two parallel connections might well be formed. To avoid this connection collision, one router has to back down. The connection initiated by the router with the higher BGP Identifier prevails. The BGP Identifier is uniquely assigned to each BGP router and is exchanged during the OPEN message. Once the open is confirmed, the routers exchange the entire routing table based on their policies. Only changes in the routing table are exchanged from now on. KEEPALIVE messages prevent the connection from timing out. The TCP session guarantees reliable delivery of each packet.

BGP distinguishes between the following peer connections:

IBGP connection
> The peers are in the same AS and are called internal peers. BGP routes learned from internal peers must not be sent back to other internal peers; they can only be sent to external peers. Each internal peer must have a connection to all other internal peers. Internal peers are fully

meshed. The introduction of AS confederation for BGP (RFC 3065) or BGP route reflection (RFC 2796) relaxes the above rule. The AS_PATH and NEXT_HOP attributes must not be modified when passing updates to internal peers.

EBGP connection

The peers are in different ASes and are called external peers. BGP routes learned from external peers can be updated to all other peers. When sending an update to an external peer, the AS_PATH and NEXT_HOP attributes are modified. The sending router adds the local AS number to the AS_PATH and sets the NEXT_HOP field to its local IPv4 address.

NOTIFICATION messages inform the peers of any errors during the open or update process. The connection can be shut down gracefully using a cease NOTIFICATION message.

Route storage and policies

BGP routes are stored in a Routing Information Base (RIB). Figure 8-36 shows the three different RIBs and their interaction.

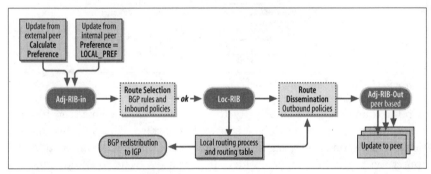

Figure 8-36. BGP RIBs and its interactions

Incoming messages could contain new feasible routes, replacement routes of earlier updates, or routes that have been withdrawn by the advertising peer. All these routes are placed into the Adj-RIB-In. For each new or changed route, a degree of preference is calculated based on the inbound policy. This preference is placed into the attribute LOCAL_PREF. If the route arrives from a internal peer, the LOCAL_PREF is already carried in the update and should not be recalculated. Each route in the Adj-RIB-In is now processed by the route selection process and entered into the Loc-RIB. The selection process first looks at the NEXT_HOP and AS_PATH attributes of the route. The IP address specified by the NEXT_HOP must be reachable through an entry in the local routing table. The AS_PATH must not contain the local AS number. If the two attributes comply, the route is accepted or ignored based on the inbound policy; otherwise, the route is ignored. In case of multiple routes to the same destination, the route with the highest preference is accepted. In case of the same preference, a complex tie-breaking rule ensures that only one of the routes to the same destination is accepted. See RFC 1771 for more details on this tie-breaking rule.

Routes in the Loc-RIB are now placed into the local routing table. The true next hop address is taken from the local route entry to the IPv4 address specified in the NEXT_HOP attribute.

All routes in the Loc-RIB and all routes in the local routing table are eligible to be advertised to external peers of this router. Only routes in the Loc-RIB learned from external peers are eligible to be advertised to all internal peers of this router unless route reflection is enabled (see RFC 2796). The outbound policy disseminates the routes to a peer-specific Adj-RIB-Out. The outbound policy may perform route aggregation or path attribute modification. Changes in the Adj-RIB-Out cause the update process to send an update to the peer.

BGP Message Header

BGP messages are carried on top of TCP connections, which can be established either over IPv4 or IPv6. The source and destination IP addresses of the datagram depend on the peer configuration. They are always unicast. BGP connections use the well-known TCP port 179. Remember that only one TCP connection is established between two peering routes. Figure 8-37 shows the BGP message header format. The header has a fixed size of 19 bytes.

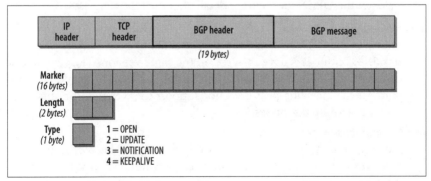

Figure 8-37. BGP message header format

The fields of the BGP header are explained in detail in the following list:

Marker (16 bytes)
> Contains authentication data if authentication was negotiated between the peers. All bits are set to one if no authentication is used or in the OPEN message.

Length (2 bytes)
> The total length of the BGP message, including headers. The value must be between 19 and 4096. The maximum message size of any BGP message is 4096 bytes.

Type (1 byte)
> Indicates the BGP message types, as listed in Table 8-9.

Table 8-9. BGP message types

Type	Name	Description
1	OPEN	Initializes BGP connection and negotiates session parameters
2	UPDATE	Exchanges feasible and withdrawn BGP routes
3	NOTIFICATION	Reports errors or terminates BGP connections
4	KEEPALIVE	Keeps the BGP connection from expiring

OPEN Message

As soon as the TCP connection between two BGP peers has been established, the routers send OPEN messages to initialize the BGP connection. This message verifies the validity of the peer and negotiates parameters used for the session using the fields illustrated in Figure 8-38. To verify the validity of a peer, each side of the connection must configure the IP address and the AS number of the peer.

The fields of the OPEN message are detailed in the following list:

Version (1 byte)
> Indicates the BGP version used by the sending peer. The current version is 4. Both peers have to agree on the same version. The version can be negotiated. Each peer usually indicates the highest version it supports. If the receiving peer does not support this version, it notifies the peer and terminates the session.

My Autonomous System (2 bytes)
> Indicates the AS number of the sending router. The receiving router must verify this number to be the peer's AS number. If it is incorrect, the peer is notified and the session is terminated. If the AS number is the same as the receiving router's AS number, the peer is internal (IBGP); otherwise, the peer is external (EBGP).

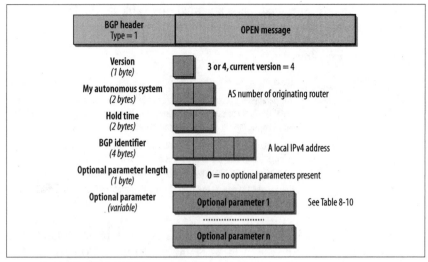

Figure 8-38. The BGP OPEN message

Hold time (2 bytes)

Proposes a maximum time in seconds that may elapse before any BGP message must arrive on this interface. The hold timer is negotiated to the smaller value advertised by either peer. To keep a BGP connection from expiring, the peers send KEEPALIVE messages once every *HoldTime*/3 second. A hold time of zero indicates that no KEEPALIVE messages need to be sent. The value of the hold time is 0 or greater than 2.

BGP Identifier (4 bytes)

Each router must be identified by a unique, globally assigned BGP identifier. At startup, the BGP Identifier is set to an IPv4 address of a local interface. This means the router must a have at least one IPv4 address configured locally, even in an IPv6-only environment. The message is rejected if the BGP Identifier equals the BGP Identifier of the receiver or if the BGP Identifier is illegal. During route selection, the BGP Identifier may be used to break a tie.

Optional Parameter Length (1 byte)

Indicates the length of optional parameters to be negotiated. A length of zero indicates that there are no optional parameters.

Optional Parameters

Each Optional Parameter consists of a <Type, Length, Value> (TLV) triplet. Both routers must know and agree on the optional parameter; otherwise, the peer is notified of the rejection of the parameter. This could lead to the termination of the session. At the moment, two parameters are specified, as explained in Table 8-10. The optional parameter BGP Capability is very important for IPv6 support.

Table 8-10. Optional parameters

Type	Name	Description
1	Authentication	The parameter consists of two fields: Authentication Code and Authentication Data. The Authentication Code defines the authentication mechanism used and how the marker and authentication data field are to be computed.
2	BGP Capability	The parameter consists of one or more <Code, Length, Value> triplets identifying different BGP Capabilities. It is defined in RFC 2842. The capability parameter may appear more than once in the OPEN message.
		The Capability Code set to 1 indicates the Multiprotocol Extension Capability, as defined in RFC 2858.

The Multiprotocol Extension Capability has a 4-byte value field. The first 2 bytes identify the Address Family Identifier (AFI), byte 3 is reserved, and byte 4 defines the Subsequent Address Family Identifier (SAFI). AFI defines the network layer protocol used in the multiprotocol extension. SAFI defines additional information about the protocol, such as whether the protocol uses unicast forwarding (SAFI=1), multicast forwarding (SAFI=2), or both (SAFI=3). To support IPv6, the Multiprotocol Extension Capability is set to <Code=1, Length=4, Value=hexadecimal 0x0002 0001).

UPDATE Message

An UPDATE message carries BGP route(s) advertised by the originating peer. It is divided into three sections, as outlined in Figure 8-39. The first section specifies the IPv4 NLRI that the sending peer is withdrawing. The second section defines all path attributes associated with the feasible IPv4 NLRI followed in section three. Multiple NLRI with the same exact same set of path attributes can be placed in a single UPDATE message.

The fields of the UPDATE message are detailed in the following list:

Unfeasible Routes length (2 bytes)
Defines the length of the Withdrawn Routes field. Set to zero, it indicates that the originating peer has no route to withdraw with this message.

Withdrawn Routes
A list of IPv4 NLRIs that are no longer valid. Each NLRI is encoded as <length, prefix> and represents an IPv4 prefix. The 1-byte Length field

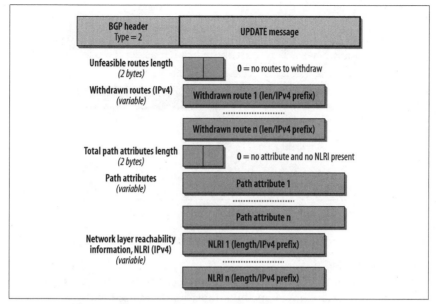

Figure 8-39. The BGP UPDATE message

defines the length of the corresponding Prefix field. The Prefix field is padded to the full octet with zero bits. Because the NLRIs are IPv4 prefixes, this field can never be used to withdraw IPv6 routes. See the section "BGP Extension for IPv6" for further details.

Total Path Attribute length (2 bytes)
Defines the length of the Path Attributes field.

Path attributes
Contains a list of path attributes that belong the feasible NLRI advertised. Attributes are further explained in the section "BGP Attributes."

Network Layer Reachability Information
A list of IPv4 NLRIs that are advertised with this update. Each NLRI is encoded as <length, prefix> and represents an IPv4 prefix. The 1-byte Length field defines the length of the corresponding Prefix field. The Prefix field is padded to the full octet with zero bits. The total length of this field is calculated as follows:

    UPDATE message length-23-Unfeasible Routes Length-Total Path Attribute Length

Because the NLRIs are IPv4 prefixes, this field can never be used to advertise IPv6 routes. See the section "BGP Extension for IPv6" for further details.

BGP Attributes

Path attributes provide additional information about the advertised NLRI. Each path attribute has a 2-byte attribute header, as depicted in Figure 8-40.

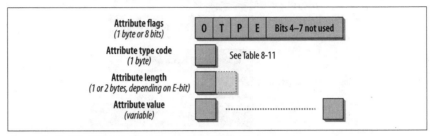

Figure 8-40. The BGP path attributes

The Path Attribute header is explained in detail in the following list.

O bit (Optional bit)
> Defines whether the attribute is optional (set to one) or well known (set to zero). A well-known attribute must be recognized and supported by each BGP router. Optional attributes may not be recognized by some routers.

T bit (Transitive bit)
> Defines whether the attribute is transitive (set to one) or nontransitive (set to zero). Transitive attributes must always be passed on when the NLRI is advertised to another peer. Well-known attributes must always be transitive.

P bit (Partial bit)
> Applies to optional transitive attributes only. If any router along the update path does not recognize the optional transitive attribute, it must set the P bit to one. This indicates that at least one router in the path to the route does not recognize this attribute. This bit must always be set to zero for optional nontransitive or well-known attributes.

E bit (Extended length bit)
> Defines whether the attribute length field is 1 byte (set to zero) or 2 bytes (set to one). Extended length may be used if the attribute's data is longer than 255 bytes.

Attribute code (1 byte)
> Defines the type of attribute. Table 8-11 lists and explains some of the most common attributes. Detailed explanations should be taken directly from RFC 1771 or any RFC extending BGP (e.g., BGP Route Reflection defines attribute types 9 and 10).

Table 8-11. BGP attributes

Type	Name/Flags	Description
1	ORIGIN (well known)	Defines the original source of this route.
		0=IGP, 1=EGP, 2=Incomplete
2	AS_PATH (well known)	A sequence of AS numbers that this route has crossed during its update. The rightmost AS number defines the originating AS. Each AS crossed is prepended. Prevents loops and can be used for policies.
3	NEXT_HOP (well known)	Specifies the next hop's IPv4 address. Cannot be used for IPv6.
4	MED (optional nontransitive)	The MULTI_EXIT_DISC (MED) indicates a desired preference (4-byte) of this route to the peer. The lower the better. Designed for multiple EBGP connections between two ASes to load-share inbound traffic.
5	LOCAL_PREF (well known)	Defines a local preference (4 byte) of this route. The higher the better. It is usually calculated on routes arriving from external peers and preserved to internal peers. Designed to load-share outbound traffic.
6	ATOMIC_AGGREGATE (well known)	Specifies that one of the routers has selected this less-specific route over a more-specific route.
7	AGGREGATOR (optional transitive)	The BGP Identifier of the router that aggregated routes into this route.
8	COMMUNITY (optional transitive)	Carries a 4-byte informational tag. Can be used by the route selection process. Defined in RFC 1997.
14	MP_REACH_NLRI (optional nontransitive)	Advertises multiprotocol NLRI. Used for IPv6 prefixes. See the section "BGP Extension for IPv6."
15	MP_UNREACH_NLRI (optional nontransitive)	Withdraws multiprotocol NLRI. Used for IPv6 prefixes. See the section "BGP Extension for IPv6."

NOTIFICATION and KEEPALIVE Messages

NOTIFICATION messages are used to report errors. A 1-byte Error Code field specifies the main category of the error. A Subcode field providing the actual error follows the Error Code field. For troubleshooting reasons, additional data about the error is placed in the Data field. See RFC 1771 section 4.5 for all error codes. Additional documents extending BGP add error subcodes. Error messages for the BGP Extension for IPv6 are specified in RFC 2858.

KEEPALIVE messages contain no data whatsoever, just the BGP message header with the message type 4. They are used to prevent a BGP connection from timing out.

BGP Extension for IPv6

BGP-4 carries only three pieces of information that are truly IPv4-specific:

- NLRI (feasible and withdrawn) in the UPDATE message contains an IPv4 prefix.
- NEXT_HOP path attribute in the UPDATE message contains an IPv4 address.
- BGP Identifier is in the OPEN message and in the AGGREGATOR attribute.

To make BGP-4 available for other network layer protocol, the multiprotocol NLRI and its next hop information must be added. RFC 2858 extends BGP to support multiple network layer protocols. IPv6 is one of the protocols supported, as emphasized in a separate document (RFC 2545). To accommodate the new requirement for multiprotocol support, BGP-4 adds two new attributes to advertise and withdraw multiprotocol NLRI. The BGP Identifier stays unchanged. BGP-4 routers with IPv6 extensions therefore still need a local IPv4 address. To establish a BGP connection exchanging IPv6 prefixes, the peering routers need to advertise the optional parameter BGP capability to indicate IPv6 support. BGP connections and route selection remain unchanged. Each implementer needs to extend the RIB to accommodate IPv6 routes. Policies need to take IPv6 NLRI and next hop information into consideration for route selection.

An UPDATE message advertising only IPv6 NLRI sets the unfeasible route length field to zero and carries no IPv4 NLRI. All advertised or withdrawn IPv6 routes are carried within the MP_REACH_NLRI and MP_UNREACH_ NLRI. The UPDATE must carry the path attributes ORIGIN and AS_PATH; in IBGP connections; it must also carry LOCAL_PREF. The NEXT_HOP attribute should not be carried. If the UPDATE message contains the NEXT_HOP attribute, the receiving peer must ignore it. All other attributes can be carried and are recognized.

An UPDATE message could advertise IPv6 NLRI and IPv4 NLRI with the same path attributes. In this case, all fields can be used. For IPv6 NLRI, the NEXT_HOP attribute should, however, be ignored. IPv4 and IPv6 NLRI are separated in the corresponding RIB.

MP_REACH_NLRI path attribute

This optional nontransitive attribute allows the exchange of feasible IPv6 NLRI to a peer, along with its next hop IPv6 address. The NLRI and the next hop are delivered in one attribute, as depicted in Figure 8-41.

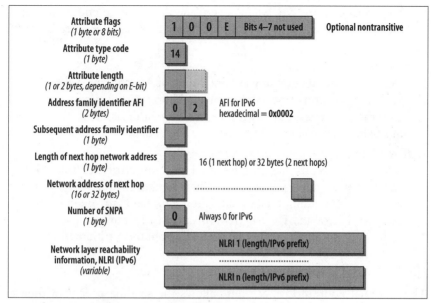

Figure 8-41. The MP_REACH_NLRI path attribute for IPv6

The fields comprising the MP_REACH_NLRI path attribute are detailed in the following list:

Address Family Identifier (AFI) (2 bytes)
Defines the network layer protocol. IPv6 uses the value 0x0002 (hexadecimal) as specified in RFC 1700.

Subsequent Address Family Identifier (SAFI) (1 byte)
Defines if the protocol uses unicast forwarding (SAFI=1), multicast forwarding (SAFI=2), or both (SAFI=3).

Length of the next hop network address (1 byte)
Defines the number of bytes used for the Next Hop Address field. IPv6 sets this field to 16 or 32, depending on the number of the next hop address provided.

Network address of next hop
Contains the next hop IPv6 address of this IPv6 route. This field is updated when advertising this route to an external peer. The router chooses its own IPv6 global/site-local address of the link to the external peer. This field is generally not updated when advertising this route to an internal peer. If the next hop IPv6 address and the peer IPv6 address share a common link—e.g., a link between two external peers—the link-local address of the common link should be added as a second next

hop address. In return, when advertising this route to an internal peer, the link-local address received from an external peer needs to be removed.

Number of SNPA (1 byte)

Defines the number of Subnetwork Points of Attachment (SNPA) to follow right after this field. SNPA carry additional information associated with the router associated with the next hop address. IPv6 does not use this field and sets it to 0. Therefore, no SNPA data field will follow.

Network Layer Reachability Information

A list of IPv6 NLRI that are advertised with this attribute. Each NLRI is encoded as <length, prefix>. The 1-byte Length field defines the length of the corresponding Prefix field. The Prefix field is padded to the full octet with zero bits. The length of this field is the remaining length after deducting the length of all previous fields from the attribute length.

MP_UNREACH_NLRI path attribute

This optional nontransitive attribute allows the sending peer to withdraw multiple, no longer valid IPv6 routes. As illustrated in Figure 8-42, it basically contains a list of IPv6 prefixes that the peer should remove from its RIB.

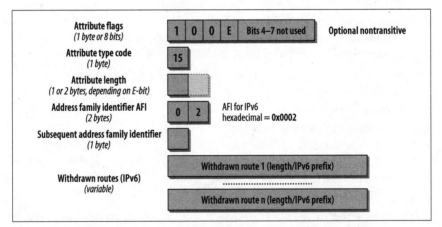

Figure 8-42. The MP_UNREACH_NLRI path attribute for IPv6

The fields comprising the MP_UNREACH_NLRI path attribute are detailed in the following list.

Address Family Identifier (AFI) (2 bytes)
Defines the network layer protocol. IPv6 uses the value 0x0002 (hexadecimal).

Subsequent Address Family Identifier (SAFI) (1 byte)
Defines whether the protocol uses unicast forwarding (SAFI=1), multicast forwarding (SAFI=2), or both (SAFI=3).

Withdrawn routes
A list of IPv6 NLRI that are withdrawn from service. Each NLRI is encoded as <length, prefix>. The 1-byte Length field defines the length of the corresponding Prefix field. The Prefix field is padded to the full octet with zero bits. The length of this field is the remaining length after deducting the length of all previous fields from the attribute length.

Other Routing Protocols for IPv6

The final section of this chapter is focused on upcoming routing protocols that are still in draft stage. The two protocols discussed are Routing IPv6 with IS-IS and EIGRPv6.

Routing IPv6 with IS-IS

IPv6 support with IS-IS defined in the draft document *http://www.ietf.org/internet-drafts/draft-ietf-isis-ipv6-02.txt*. This document is based on the specifications for integrated IS-IS as defined in RFC 1195. Without in-depth knowledge of integrated IS-IS, the IPv6 extension cannot be understood. Note that the draft number may have increased by one or more when you try to find it.

Integrated IS-IS

Unlike the previous routing protocol discussions, this section gives only a very brief overview of integrated IS-IS. IS-IS originally defines the exchange of routing information between Intermediate Systems (ISes, otherwise known as routers) for the OSI network layer protocols CLNP and CONS. Other protocols use other routing protocols. Having separate routing protocols for each network layer is sometimes referred to as "ships in the night." Each routing protocol uses (or maybe wastes) its own resources, such as CPU and memory. A misbehaving routing protocol can destabilize another routing protocol.

An integrated routing protocol uses resources efficiently and is more stable. That is the idea behind integrated IS-IS (i/IS-IS), in which the routing protocol has been adapted to carry concurrently routing information for the OSI network protocols and for IPv4. This is achieved by introducing variable-length data fields in the form <Type, Length, Value> (TLVs). Each network layer protocol can use the TLVs according to its addressing syntax. Each supported network layer protocol is specified by its Network Layer Protocol Identifier (NLPID), assigned by ISO.

Integrated IS-IS is an interior routing protocol based on link state updates. OSPF and IS-IS have many similarities: if you know one, the other is easy to grasp. We have already explained OSPF in detail, so we can briefly compare OSPF features with i/IS-IS. OSPF runs within an AS, and i/IS-IS runs within a routing domain. An i/IS-IS routing domain can be further split into multiple areas with a common central area. Routers within the central area are called Level 2 intermediate systems or L2 routers. Routers in all other areas are called Level 1 intermediate systems or L1 routers. L2 routers are, in most cases, L1 routers as well, like ABR in OSPF. Each area is identified by the first 13 bytes of the ISO NSAP address assigned to the router. Routers keep adjacencies with each other, initiated and maintained by IS-IS Hello packets. Routers can become adjacent only if they are on the same level. Once they have become adjacent, they advertise level 1 or level 2 Link State PDU (L1-LSP or L2-LSP). L1 routers originate L1-LSP advertising their local addresses. L2 routers originate L2-LSP advertising their local address, routes learned from directly attached areas, and external routes. Only L2 routers can advertise routes external to the routing domain, called ASBR in OSPF. To synchronize and acknowledge the most recent LSA, the routers use Sequence Number PDU (SNP), again for level 1 and level 2. A L1 router knows L1 routes in its area only by calculating a SPF tree to all destinations. L1 routers have no knowledge about any route outside their own area. Anything outside the area is reached via the closest L2 router. L2 routers, however, know all the routes internal and external to the routing domain. In addition, transit links are handled in i/IS-IS by implementing pseudonodes. The designated router of a transit link originates LSP on behalf of the pseudonode.

Routing IPv6 with IS-IS

Integrated IS-IS provides for the inclusion of variable-length fields (TLVs) in all IS-IS packets (Hello, LSP, and SNP). Relevant addressing information makes use of this field. Hello packets and LSP packets carry a field specifying the network layer protocols. Each supported network layer protocol is specified by its NLPID, assigned by ISO. The value of the IPv6 NLPID is 142 (0x8E).

The Internet draft proposes two new TLVs for IPv6. They are described in the following list. Remember that this is only a draft document; some of this information may change, or additional information may be added.

The IPv6 Reachability TLV (Type 236)
> Defines the IPv6 prefix advertised within L1-LSP and L2-LSP. Within a L2-LSP, it can also be used to advertise an IPv6 prefix external to the routing domain by setting the external bit in the Control field. The following fields make up this TLV: Prefix Length, IPv6 Prefix, Metric (4 bytes), and the Control field.

IPv6 Interface Address TLV (Type 232)
> Defines the IPv6 addresses of one or more interfaces of this router. It is advertised in Hello packets, L1-LSP, and L2-LSP. For Hello packets, it must contain the link-local IPv6 address assigned to the interface that is sending the Hello packet. In LSP, it must contain the global/site-local addresses assigned to the router.

EIGRPv6

Enhanced IGRP is a routing protocol developed by Cisco Systems, Inc. Cisco Systems has announced plans to enhance EIGRP for IPv6. At the moment, there are no draft documents available.

CHAPTER 9

Upper-Layer Protocols

The impact of IPv6 on upper-layer protocols is minimal because the datagram service has not changed substantially. This chapter discusses UDP and TCP over IPv6 and describes changes for upper-layer protocols, such as DNS, DHCP, SLP, FTP, Telnet, and HTTP, when used over IPv6. The most important changes are always needed where an IP address is used. Any process or application that uses an IP address needs to be updated to be able to handle the extended 128-bit address format. Applications that use a hard-coded 32-bit IPv4 address should be updated to use a DNS name instead so DNS can return either an IPv4 or an IPv6 address to make the IP protocol fully transparent.

UDP/TCP

Checksumming is done on different layers. Remember, the IPv6 header does not have a checksum. But a checksum is important on the transport layer to determine misdelivery of packets. Other upper-layer protocols may use a checksum, too. All checksum calculations that include the IP address in the calculation must be modified for IPv6 to accommodate the new 128-bit address.

Transport protocols like UDP and TCP attach checksums to their packets. A checksum is generated using a pseudoheader. The TCP and UDP pseudo-header for IPv6 contains fields for source and destination address, payload length, and next header value (RFC 2460). If the IPv6 packet contains a routing header, the destination address used in the pseudoheader is the address of the final destination. If the source or destination address was changed in transit, the value of the pseudoheader at the destination will not match the value of the initial packet, which causes checksum calculation failure and an error report.

Because the IPv6 address is so much longer than the IPv4 address, the IPv6 specification includes a new version of the pseudoheader. The IPv6 pseudo-header specification takes into account that an unknown number of extension headers can be present before the UDP or TCP layer, which is essential when calculating the payload length for the pseudoheader. With IPv4, a checksum in the UDP header was optional. With IPv6, the computation of a checksum is mandatory for UDP. IPv6 nodes that receive a UDP packet with a value of zero in the checksum field should discard the packet and log the error.

The source node calculates and stores the checksum and the destination node verifies it. Figure 9-1 shows the format of the pseudoheader that is built and used to calculate TCP and UDP checksums.

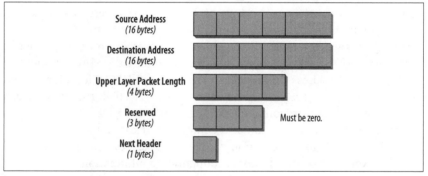

Figure 9-1. Format of the pseudoheader

The following list describes each of the fields:

Source Address (16 bytes)
    The source address of the IPv6 packet.

Destination Address (16 bytes)
    The destination address of the IPv6 packet. If there is a routing header in the packet, the address of the final destination is used for the checksum calculation. On the first node, this address is the last address in the list of the routing header. At the final destination, this is the destination address in the IPv6 header.

Upper Layer Packet Length (4 bytes)
    This field contains the length of the Upper-Layer Protocol header plus data.

Next Header (1 byte)
    The Next Header field identifies the type of the header, using the values listed in Table 2-1.

The same algorithm is used to calculate the checksum with IPv6 as is used with IPv4. The 16-bit checksum is computed over the entire pseudoheader. By including the source and destination addresses in the checksum calculation, any alteration of the addresses en route would be detected.

DHCP

DHCP is widely used to configure hosts with their IPv4 addresses and additional information. If you have an IPv6 network, you do not need DHCP to configure your hosts with address information. The stateless autoconfiguration mechanism will configure your hosts for their IPv6 addresses without the need to set up a DHCP server. All you need to do is configure your IPv6-enabled routers with the prefix information for the links to which they are attached. But you might still choose to have DHCP servers in some cases. Host configuration using DHCP with IPv6 is called stateful configuration. Maybe you have a specific IPv6 addressing scheme, you need dynamic assignment of DNS servers, or you choose not to have the MAC address as a part of the IPv6 address. In these cases, you can use DHCP for address configuration. Or you have IPv6 hosts on links with no IPv6 router, in which case you would need to configure the IPv6 hosts using DHCP to distribute the prefix information. You can also combine stateless and stateful configuration by using autoconfiguration for the IPv6 address configuration and DHCP servers to provide additional configuration information.

Note that DHCPv4 can also be used to configure hosts for IPv4-compatible IPv6 addresses (see RFC 2893). The IPv4 address that is embedded in the four lowest order bytes of the IPv4-compatible IPv6 address can be obtained through DHCP and then mapped into the IPv4-compatible IPv6 address by prepending the well-known 96-bit prefix 0:0:0:0:0:0.

Draft of DHCPv6

The information in this section is based on draft *http://www.ietf.org/internet-drafts/draft-ietf-dhc-dhcpv6-23.txt*, dated February, 2002. Although there will be changes to the final standard, it is interesting to look at parts of it to get a glance at where we are going with DHCP. If you are interested in following the development process, refer to the drafts at *http://www.ietf.org*. All references to DHCP in this chapter refer to DHCPv6.

DHCP uses the following multicast addresses:

All_DHCP_Agents address (FF02::1:2)
> All DHCP agents (servers and relays) are members of this multicast group. DHCP clients use this link-scoped multicast address to reach DHCP agents on their link when they do not know the agents' link-local address.

All_DHCP_Servers address (FF05::1:3)
> All DHCP servers within a site are members of this multicast group. This site-scoped address is used by DHCP clients or relays to reach all DHCP servers within a site. They either do not know the server's unicast address or they want to reach all DHCP servers within the site.

The following UDP ports are used with DHCPv6:

UDP port 546 (Client port)
> Used by DHCP servers as the destination port to reach DHCP relays or DHCP clients. Used by DHCP relay agents as the destination port to reach DHCP clients.

UDP port 547: Agent port
> DHCP clients use this port as the destination port to reach DHCP agents. DHCP relays use this port as the destination port to reach DHCP servers.

The current draft defines 12 DHCP message types. Seeing how the set has been extended gives some information about the new functionality that we can expect. Table 9-1 summarizes the message types.

Table 9-1. DHCPv6 message types

Message type	Description
SOLICIT (1)	Used by clients to locate DHCP servers.
ADVERTISE (2)	Used by servers as a response to SOLICIT.
REQUEST (3)	Used by clients to get information from servers.
CONFIRM (4)	Used by clients to verify that their address and configuration parameters are still valid.
RENEW (5)	Used by clients to renew their configuration parameters with their original DHCP server when their lease is about to expire.
REBIND (6)	Used by clients to extend the lifetime of their address(es) and renew their configuration parameters with any DHCP server when their lease is about to expire.
REPLY (7)	Used by DHCP servers responding to Request, Confirm, Renew, Rebind, Release, and Decline messages.
RELEASE (8)	Used by clients to release their IP address
DECLINE (9)	Used by clients to indicate that one or more addresses assigned to them are already in use on the link.

Table 9-1. DHCPv6 message types (continued)

Message type	Description
RECONFIG-INIT (10)	Used by DHCP servers to inform clients that the server has new or updated configuration information. The clients then must initiate a request in order to obtain the updated information.
INFORM (11)	Sent by clients to request configuration parameters without the assignment of any IP addresses to the client.
RELAY-FORW (12)	Used by DHCP relays to forward client messages to servers. The relay encapsulates the client message in an option in the relay-forward message.
RELAY-REPL (13)	Used by DHCP servers to send messages to clients through a relay. The client message is encapsulated as an option in the relay-reply message. The relay decapsulates the message and forwards it to the client.

The DHCP server-initiated configuration exchange is a great new feature. It can be used, for example, when links in the DHCP domain have to be renumbered or when new services or applications have been added and need to be configured on the clients. When services or applications need to be configured on the client, the DHCP server sends out a RECONFIGURE-INIT message (type 10). The client that receives this message must initiate a REQUEST/REPLY message exchange to get the updated information. Haven't we been waiting for this?

Authentication of DHCP messages is possible and can be accomplished through the use of the Authentication option. The authentication information carried in the Authentication option can be used to reliably identify the source of a DHCP message and to confirm that the contents of the DHCP message have not been changed. Multiple authentication protocols can be used with the Authentication option. Two such protocols are defined in this draft.

According to this draft, DHCPv6 will support the following new features:

- Configuration of dynamic updates to DNS
- Dynamic renumbering
- Relays can be preconfigured with server addresses or can use multicast addresses
- Authentication
- Requests by clients for multiple IP addresses
- Reclamation of addresses using the RECONFIGURE-INIT message
- Integration of stateless and stateful address autoconfiguration
- Dynamic location of off-link servers by relays and clients

IANA is the authority for managing multicast addresses, message types, options, and status codes. You can refer to their site for updated information.

Other interesting drafts are out there. For example, *http://www.ietf.org/ internet-drafts/draft-ietf-dhc-failover-10.txt* defines a protocol that allows synchronization of DHCP data between DHCP servers to provide redundancy in the case of server failure. Another, *http://www.ietf.org/internet-drafts/draft-ietf-dhc-ldap-schema-00.txt*, defines a schema for representing DHCP information in an LDAP directory, which allows for central administration of multiple DHCP servers in an enterprise. And the draft at *http:// www.ietf.org/internet-drafts/draft-ietf-dhc-dhcproam-00.txt* defines authentication mechanisms for the configuration of roaming users. Other memos define options for DHCP configuration in VPN environments or for clients with wireless cards. Note that when you want to find those drafts, the draft number may have increased by one or more.

Dynamic Updates to DNS

With the widespread use of DHCP and autoconfiguration for dynamic IP address configuration, the need for a dynamic update of DNS for addition and deletion of records arose. RFC 2136 introduced the mechanism called Dynamic DNS (DDNS). It is supported by BIND Versions 8 and 9. The update functionality is usually used by applications like DHCP, but it can be implemented on hosts, too. With IPv6, dynamic addresses are often assigned using stateless autoconfiguration. A DNS update mechanism is necessary on each host to update its DNS records. There are important security aspects to consider when DDNS updates are made. It is important that you can control which nodes are authorized to make changes to your DNS records. Update policies must be implemented and Transaction Signatures (TSIG) or Domain Name System Security Extensions (DNSSEC) mechanisms should be used.

DNS

DNS is used in the IPv6 world to do name-to-address mappings and vice versa. Mixed IPv4/IPv6 environments need multiple host entries in DNS. A host communicating with both versions of TCP/IP needs at least two entries in DNS—one with its IPv4 address and the other with its IPv6 address. Two new DNS record types have been defined for IPv6 hosts. RFC 1886 defines the AAAA type record (called quad-A), and RFC 2874 defines the A6 type record, which is designed to make renumbering of networks and TLA changes easier to administer.

For information about using DNS in combination with NAT-PT (the "PT" stands for Protocol Translation), which is described in Chapter 10, refer to RFC 2766.

AAAA Records (RFC 1886)

RFC 1886 describes DNS extensions for IPv6 implementations based on AAAA records. This record type can store a 128-bit IPv6 address, and the DNS value for this type of record is 28 (decimal). A host that has more than one IPv6 address has an AAAA record for each address. The corresponding reverse lookup domain is IP6.INT. The reverse lookup records are PTR records of type 12.

An AAAA type record can look like this (RFC 1886):

```
moon.universe.com    IN    AAAA    4321:0:1:2:3:4:567:89ab
```

For reverse lookups, each subdomain level under IP6.INT represents 4 bits of the 128-bit address. The least significant bit appears at the far left of the domain name. Omitting leading zeros is not allowed in this case. So the PTR record for the previous example looks like this:

```
b.a.9.8.7.6.5.0.4.0.0.0.3.0.0.0.2.0.0.0.1.0.0.0.0.0.0.0.1.2.3.4.IP6.INT.IN
PTR    moon.universe.com
```

Note that there are several ways to represent reverse IPv6 addresses in DNS. It depends on the implementation, so refer to your vendor's documentation to find out what format is expected.

DNAME and A6 Records (RFC 2672, RFC 2874)

RFC 2672 describes DNAME records and RFC 2874 defines A6 records. These new record types support renumerable and aggregatable IPv6 addressing. The combination of DNAME and A6 records allows the maintenance of name-to-address mappings in a situation in which a network is renumbered or an organizational unit is renamed. For instance, if a company changes the NLA, all the AAAA records in DNS need to be changed. With the new A6 type, this is much easier. An A6 record can include a complete IPv6 address or just a contiguous portion of an address, such as the last 64 bits (the interface ID), and then refer to the rest of the address by a symbolic domain name. The resolver or name server must then follow the chain of A6 records from the host's domain name to the TLA ID. The delegation of the address space with IPv6 is not accomplished through zone partitions and NS records, but rather through DNAME records. Similar to the CNAME record, which provides an alias to a single host, the DNAME record provides an alias to an entire subtree of the name space.

For example, a resolver looks up a qualified name of *host.universe.com* and finds a DNAME record of universe.com DNAME venus.universe.com. It resolves *universe.com* to *venus.universe.com* and looks up host.venus. universe.com. RFC 2874 has a detailed example for a multi-homed site connected to two providers. The RFC explains the prefix allocation and what kind of records would be in DNS to make it work. The full impact of nesting A6 chains is not measurable today. It is recommended that a chain go no deeper than 3 levels.

The corresponding reverse lookup domain is rooted at IP6.ARPA. Only the first level of delegation needs to be under that domain. Reverse mapping with A6 records is a little more complex. It includes the use of the DNAME records and introduces bitstring labels defined in RFC 2673. Bitstring labels are a compact way of representing long sequences of binary labels in a domain name. The example in RFC 2874 also details the reverse lookup records for the same multi-homed site.

The following is a summary of record type values in decimal:

- The value for the AAAA record type is 28.
- The value for the A6 record type is 38.
- The value for the DNAME record type is 39.

Most applications on the market support and use the AAAA record type. The A6 and DNAME record types are experimental.

DNS Servers

BIND implements IPv6 DNS in an upgraded version of BIND 8 and completely in BIND Version 9. For BIND 8.2.3, a patch that adds IPv6 support is available.

I installed BIND 9.1.2 on my SuSE Linux 7.2 with Kernel version 2.4.4. The minimum Kernel version required for BIND 9 is 2.4. I downloaded the bind sources from the Internet Software Consortium homepage at *http://www.isc. org/products/BIND*. The same site has a list of vendor implementations based on BIND at *http://www.isc.org/products/BIND/vendorware.html*. There are also links to versions of BIND that run on Windows NT and Windows 2000.

The most important file for configuring a name server on Unix is */etc/named. conf*. The file itself contains detailed information on how to configure it. To make name resolution work over IPv6, you need to add one important entry: listen on ipv6 { any }. This entry tells the name server to listen for IPv6 queries. Then update */var/named* with the entries for all IPv6 hosts.

The entries in our zone record file are shown in Figure 9-2.

```
$TTL 3h
$ORIGIN universe.com.
@       IN      SOA     ford.universe.com. mail.universe.com. (
        20011017        ; Serial
        3h              ; Refresh
        1h              ; Retry
        1w              ; Expire
        1h )            ; Minimum

universe.com.   IN NS   ford.universe.com.

ford    IN A    192.168.0.99
        IN AAAA fe80:0:0:0:2a0:24ff:fec5:3256
        IN A6 0 fe80:0:0:0:2a0:24ff:fec5:3256

arthur      IN A    192.168.0.66
        IN AAAA fe80:0:0:0:a00:20ff:fe20:adc2
        IN A6 0 fe80:0:0:0:a00:20ff:fe20:adc2

marvin      IN A    192.168.0.20
        IN AAAA fe80:0:0:0:202:b3ff:fe1e:8329
        IN A6 0 fe80:0:0:0:202:b3ff:fe1e:8329
```

Figure 9-2. The zone record file

Obviously, you would not usually put link-local addresses into your DNS. I did it in my lab just to show you how DNS replies to my queries. If you need a guide to how to configure your DNS for IPv6, go to Native6Group's web site at *http://www.native6group.com*. They have very good technical documents about IPv6, one of which explains in detail how to configure DNS for IPv6.

For a detailed explanation of BIND and DNS configuration, refer to *DNS and BIND*, by Paul Albitz and Cricket Liu (O'Reilly). It is a masterpiece, and we have nothing to add.

Resolvers

Resolvers must be able to handle all record types: the A record type for IPv4 and the A6 and AAAA record types for IPv6. Resolvers also need a mechanism for choosing the protocol on a dual-stack host. When the DNS server replies with a set of different addresses, resolvers need to implement a feature for a default choice of address, and this should be configurable. If the

DNS reply contains an IPv4 and an IPv6 address, the resolver can either forward both addresses to the requesting application and let the application make the choice or make a choice on behalf of the application. If the resolver forwards the IPv4 address, the application will communicate over IPv4; if it forwards the IPv6 address, the application will communicate over IPv6. Applications written for dual-stack hosts should be able to determine whether they communicate with IPv6 or IPv4 peers.

When people talk about IPv6 DNS, they are usually referring to two different aspects that are sometimes not pointed out clearly. One aspect is whether your DNS server supports IPv6 address records (AAAA or A6 and DNAME records). The other issue is whether your resolver uses IPv4 or IPv6 as a transport when doing a lookup of records on a DNS server. For instance, if you have Windows 2000 or Windows XP with the IPv6 stack running, they both do lookups for IPv6 records, but they use IPv4 as the transport for the query. The support for resolving DNS names over IPv6, in the case of Microsoft, is planned for a future release.

DNS Lookup

For the DNS lookup of IPv6 records, your client needs a resolver that supports the new record types. In my case, I used SuSE Linux host *Ford* with BIND 9 utilities and my Windows 2000 host *Marvin* with the IPv6 stack.

I used *nslookup* to play with my new DNS server. You can also use *dig* and *host* for DNS lookups. They are installed with BIND 9. *nslookup* has many configuration options. It can be run in interactive mode, and you can specify what types of records you want to query. You can set the query mode to either A records for IPv4 or AAAA type records for IPv6, or you can set it to "any," in which case *nslookup* will request all records. The *nslookup* version I used did not support the A6 type. The DNS server still sends the information back, which is why you see the "unrecognized record" type in the answer.

 Hint for using *nslookup*: if you want to do a reverse lookup, you cannot use the abbreviated version for an IPv6 address. You have to type the address as, for example, fe80:0:0:0: a00:20ff:fe20:adc2. You can skip leading zeros, but you cannot replace a sequence of zeros with two colons. Newer implementations may change this. Use *nslookup* in debug mode to get additional information.

Figure 9-3 shows the output of *nslookup* on *Marvin*.

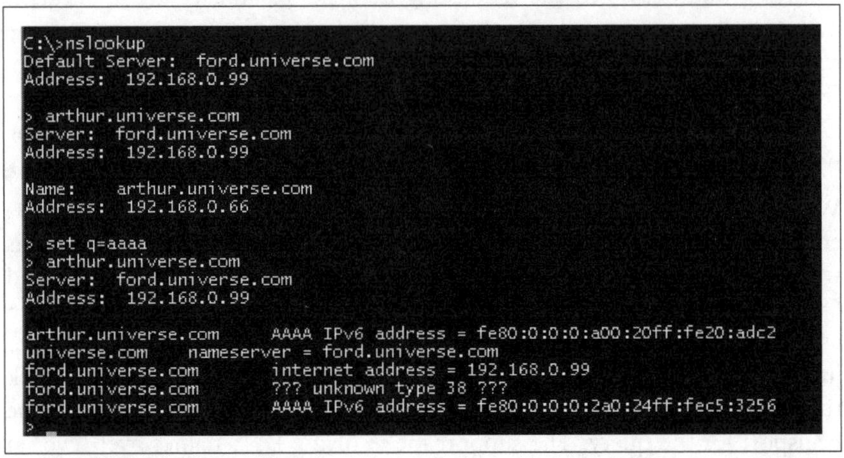

```
C:\>nslookup
Default Server:  ford.universe.com
Address:  192.168.0.99

> arthur.universe.com
Server:  ford.universe.com
Address:  192.168.0.99

Name:     arthur.universe.com
Address:  192.168.0.66

> set q=aaaa
> arthur.universe.com
Server:  ford.universe.com
Address:  192.168.0.99

arthur.universe.com      AAAA IPv6 address = fe80:0:0:0:a00:20ff:fe20:adc2
universe.com    nameserver = ford.universe.com
ford.universe.com        internet address = 192.168.0.99
ford.universe.com        ??? unknown type 38 ???
ford.universe.com        AAAA IPv6 address = fe80:0:0:0:2a0:24ff:fec5:3256
>
```

Figure 9-3. Output of nslookup

We first used *nslookup* in interactive mode with the default options. *nslookup* defaults to query type A. Looking up *arthur.universe.com* with the default gave us the IPv4 address of *arthur* (192.168.0.66). Next, we changed the query type to AAAA. The reply gave us the IPv6 address of *arthur* plus additional information about our name server *Ford*: IPv4 address, AAAA type IPv6 address, and A6 type entry. Because this version of *nslookup* did not support A6 type records, the answer was shown as "unknown type 38."

Being curious by nature, I traced the whole communication with Sniffer. Figure 9-4 shows how the same query looks in the trace file.

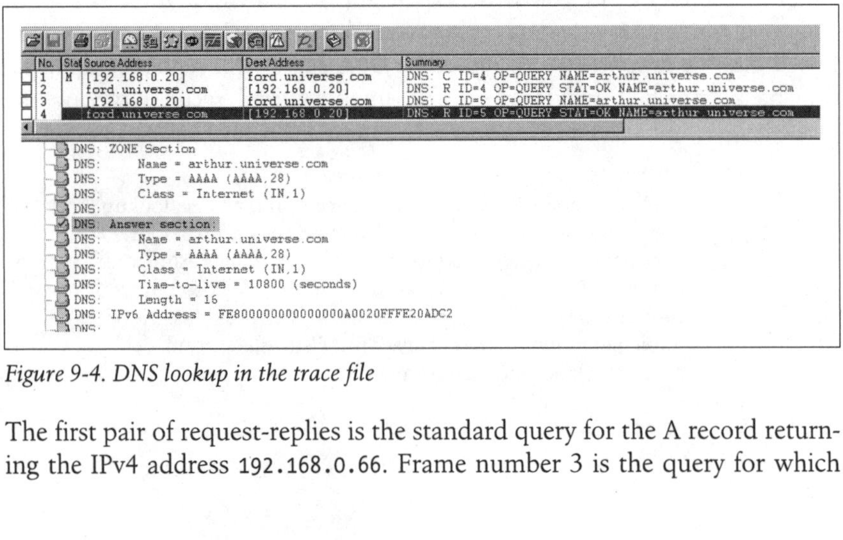

Figure 9-4. DNS lookup in the trace file

The first pair of request-replies is the standard query for the A record returning the IPv4 address 192.168.0.66. Frame number 3 is the query for which we set the query type to AAAA. Figure 9-4 shows the part of the DNS reply that refers to *arthur*'s IPv6 address. In the zone section, you can see what we have been asking for. We did *nslookup* for *arthur.universe.com* with the query type set to AAAA. The answer section provides the IPv6 address of *arthur*. You may be wondering about the "unknown type" message and the question marks in the *nslookup* output in Figure 9-3. Let's see what's actually in the reply coming from the server. Figure 9-5 shows the authority and additional record section in the same frame.

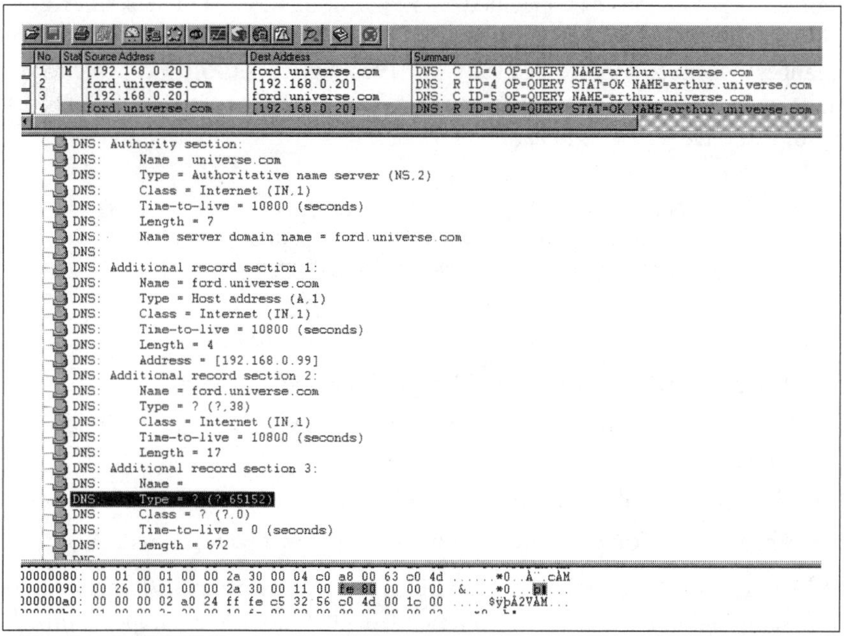

No.	Stat	Source Address	Dest Address	Summary
1	M	[192.168.0.20]	ford.universe.com	DNS: C ID=4 OP=QUERY NAME=arthur.universe.com
2		ford.universe.com	[192.168.0.20]	DNS: R ID=4 OP=QUERY STAT=OK NAME=arthur.universe.com
3		[192.168.0.20]	ford.universe.com	DNS: C ID=5 OP=QUERY NAME=arthur.universe.com
4		ford.universe.com	[192.168.0.20]	DNS: R ID=5 OP=QUERY STAT=OK NAME=arthur.universe.com

```
    DNS: Authority section:
    DNS:     Name = universe.com
    DNS:     Type = Authoritative name server (NS.2)
    DNS:     Class = Internet (IN.1)
    DNS:     Time-to-live = 10800 (seconds)
    DNS:     Length = ?
    DNS:     Name server domain name = ford.universe.com
    DNS:
    DNS: Additional record section 1:
    DNS:     Name = ford.universe.com
    DNS:     Type = Host address (A.1)
    DNS:     Class = Internet (IN.1)
    DNS:     Time-to-live = 10800 (seconds)
    DNS:     Length = 4
    DNS:     Address = [192.168.0.99]
    DNS: Additional record section 2:
    DNS:     Name = ford.universe.com
    DNS:     Type = ? (?.38)
    DNS:     Class = Internet (IN.1)
    DNS:     Time-to-live = 10800 (seconds)
    DNS:     Length = 17
    DNS: Additional record section 3:
    DNS:     Name =
    DNS:     Type = ? (?.65152)
    DNS:     Class = ? (?.0)
    DNS:     Time-to-live = 0 (seconds)
    DNS:     Length = 672
    DNS:
```

```
00000080:  00 01 00 01 00 00 2a 30 00 04 c0 a8 00 63 c0 4d  ......*0..A..cM
00000090:  00 26 00 01 00 00 2a 30 00 11 00 fe 80 00 00 00  .&....*0...b....
000000a0:  00 00 00 02 a0 24 ff fe c5 32 56 c0 4d 00 1c 00  .....$ypA2VM...
```

Figure 9-5. Authority and additional record section

The authority section states that the name server for the domain *universe. com* is *Ford.universe.com*. The content in the authority section can be seen in the *nslookup* screenshot (Figure 9-3), the line just after the IPv6 address for the AAAA record of *arthur* (bottom of screenshot). Next, in the trace file, we see the additional record section 1. It contains the IPv4 address (A record) for the name server *Ford.universe.com*. This refers to the third line in the *nslookup* output in Figure 9-3. The fourth line in the *nslookup* output is the one beginning with the three question marks and the unknown type 38 comment. This can also be seen in the trace file. Look at the additional record section 2. Sniffer doesn't decode type 38 yet, but we know that type 38 is the A6 record type. I checked the hexadecimal part of the reply packet in the trace, and following the A6 type value, the IPv6 address for *Ford.universe*.

com can be seen. The additional record section 3 is not properly decoded either, but if we check the hex part of the trace, we can see that it contains the values seen in the *nslookup* output. It is the AAAA record (type 28 decimal, 1C in hex) for *Ford.universe.com*, containing the IPv6 address for *Ford*.

SLP

The Service Location Protocol (SLP) discovers and selects services in IP networks. SLP Version 2 is specified in RFC 2608. RFC 3111 describes how SLPv2 can be used in IPv6 networks. SLP uses UDP and TCP, so only minor changes are necessary to use SLP on IPv6 networks. SLPv1, which was defined in RFC 2165, does not support IPv6. If you want to use SLP over IPv6, you have to use SLPv2.

 For a detailed discussion of SLP concepts, refer to my book *Guide to Service Location Protocol* (podbooks.com) or to *http://playground.sun.com/srvloc/slp_white_paper.html*.

The changes made for SLPv2 can be summarized as follows:

- The use for broadcasting of SLP requests was eliminated.
- The format of SLP URLs (service entries) must be able to hold IPv6 addresses.
- SLP must be able to use IPv6 multicast addresses and multicast scopes.
- The propagation of Service Advertisements must be restricted.

When SLP is used over IPv4, it can be configured to use broadcasts for service requests, but this is not recommended. IPv6 no longer supports broadcasts, so if SLP is used over IPv6, it has to use multicast addresses to discover service or directory agents.

Table 9-2 shows the multicast addresses that have been defined for SLP over IPv6.

Table 9-2. Multicast addresses for SLP over IPv6

Multicast address	Description
FF0X:0:0:0:0:0:0:116	Service Agent (SA), used for Service Type and Attribute Request Messages.
FF0X:0:0:0:0:0:0:123	Directory Agent (DA), used by User Agents (UA) and SAs to discover DAs. Also used by DA for sending unsolicited DA Advertisement messages.
FF0X:0:0:0:0:0:1:1000 to FF0X:0:0:0:0:0:1:13FF	Service Location, used by SAs to join the groups that correspond to the Service Types of the services they advertise. The Service Type string is used to determine the corresponding value in the 1000 to 13FF range, which has been assigned by IANA for this purpose. For an explanation of the algorithm used to calculate the group ID, refer to RFC 3111.

The X in FF0X is the placeholder for the multicast scope to be used for this group ID. For instance, 2 would be link-local scope and 5 would be site-local scope. For a list of the multicast scopes, refer to Table 3-6.

SLP also uses scopes. All SLP agents (i.e., User Agents, Service Agents and Directory Agents) support scopes, and Service Registration and Service Requests work only if the SLP scope is configured on all agents. Using SLP over IPv6 adds multicast scopes to this scenario. For instance, an SLPv2 agent cannot join a multicast group that has a greater multicast scope. If the SA has only a link-local address, it will join scope FF01 and FF02. If the SA is configured with a site-local or global address, it will join multicast groups in the range FF01 to FF05. An SLPv2 agent issues requests using a source address with a scope no less than the scope of the multicast group it addresses. This prevents, for example, a site-local multicast message being sent from a link-local source address. An SA and a DA must join all multicast scopes to which an SLP agent may send a message. The maximum scope for SLPv2 messages is site-local (FF05). The service URL in an SLP message can contain a hostname instead of an IP address, in which case the agent has to resolve the name to a set of addresses using DNS.

FTP

FTP has been designed to work over IPv4 supporting 32-bit addresses. With RFC 2428, "FTP Extensions for IPv6 and NATs," a specification was made that allows FTP to work over IPv4 and IPv6. During the time in which both protocols coexist (and this will be a long time), it is important that FTP servers have a mechanism to negotiate the network protocol that should be used for a session.

The RFC specifies two new FTP commands to replace the PORT and PASV commands from the earlier FTP specification (RFC 959). The PORT command is used to specify a port different from the default ports used for the data connection. It contains IPv4 address information and therefore cannot be used with IPv6 without modification. The PASV command is used to put the server into passive mode, which means the server listens on a specific data port rather than initiating the transfer. This command includes the host and port address of the FTP server and therefore does not work over IPv6 without modification.

The PORT command is replaced by the EPRT command, which allows the specification of an extended address for the data connection. The extended address specifies the network protocol (IPv4 or IPv6, for instance), as well as the IP address and the port to be used. The EPSV command replaces the

PASV command. The EPSV command has an optional argument that allows it to specify the network protocol, if necessary. The server's reply contains only the port number on which it listens, but the format of the answer is similar to the one used for the EPRT command and has a placeholder for network protocol and address information that might be used in the future. The new commands not only accommodate IPv6; they also provide greater flexibility in using FTP through firewalls and NATs (RFC 2428).

The FTP extensions specified in RFC 2428 work with both IPv4 and IPv6. If your FTP implementation supports the new extensions, you are ready to use FTP over IPv6.

Figure 9-6 shows an FTP login over IPv6.

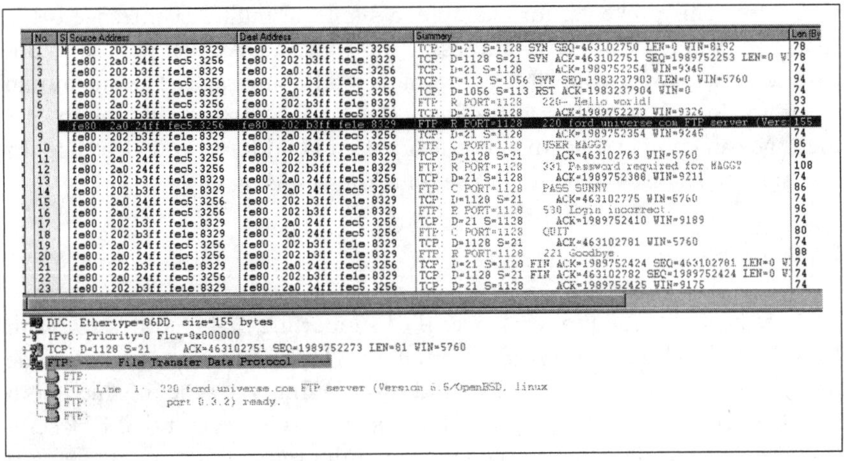

Figure 9-6. FTP session over IPv6

We installed an FTP server on our Linux host *Ford*. We logged in to FTP from our Windows 2000 host *Marvin*. In the detail window, you can see the layers. On the MAC layer, the Ethertype is set to 86DD for IPv6. The IPv6 layer specifies TCP (value 6) in the next header field (not seen in the picture). On the TCP layer, you can see the port number for FTP, 21. Now you know Maggy's password, right? But who is Maggy?

There are other applications like Secure Copy (SCP) that provide encrypted file transfers, thus protecting your passwords. These are also ready for IPv6 and have been working in the IPv4 world.

Telnet

Telnet is a virtual terminal protocol used to log into a computer across the Internet or an intranet. RFC 854 contains the Telnet protocol specification and RFC 855 contains the Telnet options specification. Telnet connects to a remote host by establishing a TCP connection over port 23 and passing keystrokes from the user's keyboard to the remote machine as if they had been entered on a keyboard attached to the remote host. The Telnet protocol uses TCP for transport. No modifications have to be made to Telnet.

I had a Telnet server running on Windows 2000, accessing it from the Linux host *Ford*, and also did the opposite—running an IPv6-enabled Telnet server on the Linux host and accessing it with the Microsoft Telnet client. Both ways are no problem. The Telnet protocol works over TCP over IPv6 with the standard Telnet port number 23. Figure 9-7 shows the Telnet session.

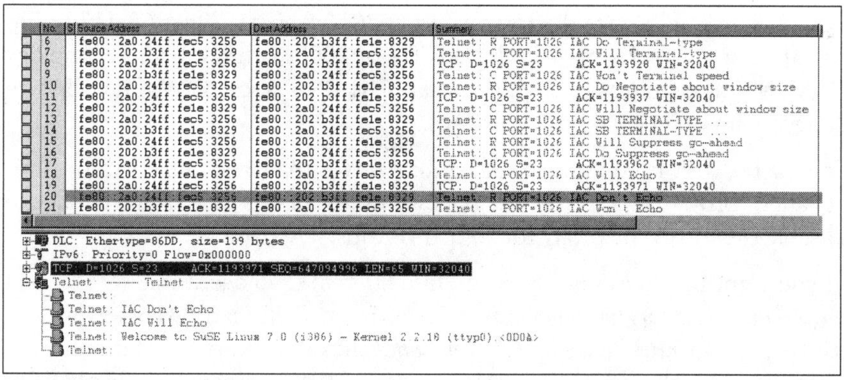

Figure 9-7. A Telnet session over IPv6

The figure shows the negotiation of the Telnet session. In the detail window, you can see the layers: the MAC layer with Ethertype 86DD, the IPv6 layer using TCP value 6 in the Next Header field, the TCP layer using port 23 for Telnet, and the Telnet header. Telnet also sends passwords and all session data in clear text that an intermediary may discover. Software like SSH provides an encrypted terminal for security. SSH is IPv6-ready today and available on many platforms.

Web Servers

If you want to surf the Internet over IPv6, you need web servers and a browser that supports IPv6.

There are different HTTP servers that already support IPv6. Probably the best known is Apache. Whatever HTTP server you use, you must be able to configure it to listen on the HTTP port (usually 80) over IPv6. If you are using proxy servers, you need to make sure that they are enabled for IPv6, too.

If you are looking for references on how to set up Apache 2 on Linux, refer to *http://linuxdoc.org/HOWTO/Linux+IPv6-HOWTO*. There is one chapter that explains configuration of different daemons, including BIND (*named*) and Apache 2 (*httpd2*).

Browser Support

What you need to browse IPv6 sites is to have DNS return an IPv6 address for the name of the web server you are trying to access. In some cases, you can also enter a literal IPv6 address (described in RFC 2732) in your browser. It would have the format *http://[2010:836B:4179::836B:4179]*. For instance, if you are using Windows NT 4 or 2000 with the IPv6 Technology Preview Stack, you can use this format. The IPv6 stack of Windows XP no longer supports literal IPv6 addresses.

If your browser is configured for a proxy server that is not enabled for IPv6, it cannot browse local or remote IPv6 web sites. In this case, you will have to disable the use of the proxy for your IPv6 trips.

If you want to experiment, you can find a list of IPv6-accessible web sites at *http://www.ipv6.org/v6-www.html*. For a list of IPv6-ready web servers and clients, go to *http://www.ipv6forum.com*, click on "Implementations" and then "IPv6 Applications," and scroll down to "Web servers and clients." For Linux people, the best link will probably be *http://www.bieringer.de/linux/ IPv6/status/*.

CHAPTER 10

Interoperability

IPv6 and IPv4 will coexist for many years. A wide range of techniques has therefore been defined that make the coexistence possible and provide an easy transition. There are three main categories:

- Dual-stack techniques allow IPv4 and IPv6 to coexist in the same devices and networks.

- Tunneling techniques allow the transport of IPv6 traffic over the existing IPv4 infrastructure.

- Translation techniques allow IPv6-only nodes to communicate with IPv4-only nodes.

These techniques can and likely will be used in combination with one another. The migration to IPv6 can be done step by step, starting with a single host or subnet. You can migrate your corporate network, or parts of it, while your ISP still runs only IPv4. Or your ISP can upgrade to IPv6 while your corporate network still runs IPv4. This chapter describes the techniques available today for each category mentioned above. RFC 2893, "Transition Mechanisms for IPv6 Hosts and Routers," describes the initial set of transition mechanisms. As IPv6 grows into our networks, new tools and mechanisms will be defined to further ease the transition.

Dual-Stack Techniques

A dual-stack node has complete support for both protocol versions. This type of node is often referred to as an IPv6/IPv4 node. In communication with an IPv6 node, such a node behaves like an IPv6-only node, and in communication with an IPv4 node, it behaves like an IPv4-only node. Implementations probably have a configuration switch to enable or disable one of the stacks. So this node type can have three modes of operation. When the IPv4 stack is enabled and the IPv6 stack is disabled, the node behaves like an IPv4-only node. When the IPv6 stack is enabled and the IPv4 stack disabled, it behaves like an IPv6-only node. When both the IPv4 and IPv6 stacks are enabled, the node can use both protocols. An IPv6/IPv4 node has at least one address for each protocol version. It uses IPv4 mechanisms to be configured for an IPv4 address (static configuration or DHCP) and uses IPv6 mechanisms to be configured for an IPv6 address (static configuration or autoconfiguration).

DNS is used with both protocol versions to resolve names and IP addresses. An IPv6/IPv4 node needs a DNS resolver that is capable of resolving both types of DNS address records. The DNS A record is used to resolve IPv4 addresses and the DNS AAAA or A6 record is used to resolve IPv6 addresses.

 For a detailed discussion of IPv6 DNS record types, refer to Chapter 9.

In some cases, DNS returns only an IPv4 or an IPv6 address. If the host that is to be resolved is a dual-stack host, DNS might return both types of addresses. Hopefully, for this case, both the DNS resolver on the client and an application using DNS will have configuration options that let us specify orders or filters of how to use the addresses (i.e., preferred protocol settings). Generally, applications that are written to run on dual-stack nodes need a mechanism to determine whether it is communicating with an IPv6 peer or an IPv4 peer. Note that the DNS resolver may run over an IPv4 or IPv6 network, but the worldwide DNS tree is mainly reachable through an IPv4 network layer.

A dual-stack network is an infrastructure in which both IPv4 and IPv6 forwarding is enabled on routers. The disadvantage of this technique is that you must perform a full network software upgrade to run the two separate protocol stacks. This means all tables (e.g., routing tables) are kept simultaneously, routing protocols being configured for both protocols. For network management, you have separate commands, depending on the protocol (e.g., *ping.exe* for IPv4 and *ping6.exe* for IPv6 on a host with a Microsoft operating system—both commands with different command options), and it takes more memory and CPU power.

Tunneling Techniques

Tunneling mechanisms can be used to deploy an IPv6 forwarding infrastructure while the overall IPv4 infrastructure is still the basis. Tunneling can be used to carry IPv6 traffic by encapsulating it in IPv4 packets and tunneling it over the IPv4 routing infrastructure. For instance, if your provider still has an IPv4-only infrastructure, tunneling allows you to have a corporate IPv6 network and tunnel through your ISP's IPv4 network to reach other IPv6 hosts or networks. The tunneling techniques and the encapsulation of IPv6 packets in IPv4 packets are defined in several RFCs, such as RFC 2473, 2893, and 3056, which differentiate two types of tunneling:

Manually configured tunneling of IPv6 over IPv4
  IPv6 packets are encapsulated in IPv4 packets to be carried over IPv4 routing infrastructures. These are point-to-point tunnels that need to be configured manually.

Automatic tunneling of IPv6 over IPv4
  IPv6 nodes can use different types of addresses, such as IPv4-compatible IPv6 addresses or 6to4 or ISATAP addresses, to dynamically tunnel IPv6 packets over an IPv4 routing infrastructure. These special IPv6 unicast addresses carry an IPv4 address in some of the IPv6 address fields.

How Tunneling Works

The concepts discussed in this paragraph apply to tunneling in general. The next two paragraphs discuss the difference between configured tunnels and automatic tunneling. Figure 10-1 shows two IPv6 networks connected through an IPv4-only network.

Host *Marvin* is on an IPv6 network and wants to send an IPv6 packet to host *Ford* on another IPv6 network. The network between router R1 and router R2 is an IPv4-only network. Router R1 is the *tunnel entry point. Marvin* sends the IPv6 packet to router R1 (Step 1 in Figure 10-1). When router R1 receives the packet addressed to *Ford*, it encapsulates the packet in an IPv4 header and forwards it to router R2 (Step 2 in Figure 10-1), which is the *tunnel exit point.* Router R2 decapsulates the packet and forwards it to its final destination (Step 3 in Figure 10-1). Between R1 and R2, any number of IPv4 routers are possible.

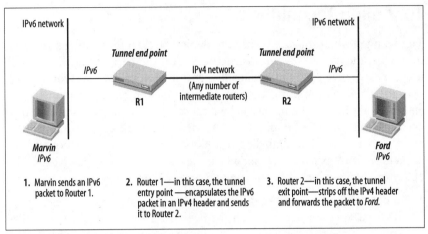

IPv6 network

IPv6 network

Tunnel end point

Tunnel end point

IPv6

IPv4 network
(Any number of
intermediate routers)

IPv6

R1

R2

Marvin
IPv6

Ford
IPv6

1. Marvin sends an IPv6 packet to Router 1.

2. Router 1—in this case, the tunnel entry point —encapsulates the IPv6 packet in an IPv4 header and sends it to Router 2.

3. Router 2—in this case, the tunnel exit point—strips off the IPv4 header and forwards the packet to *Ford*.

Figure 10-1. Encapsulation and tunneling

A tunnel has two endpoints: one is the tunnel entry point, and the other, the tunnel exit point. In the scenario in Figure 10-1, the tunnel end points are two routers. But the tunnel can be implemented in different ways. It can be set up router-to-router, host-to-router, host-to-host or router-to-host. Depending on which scenario is used, the tunnel entry and exit point can be either a host or a router. If the tunnel exit point is a host, the IPv6 destination address of the original packet is identical to the tunnel exit point and can be taken from the IPv6 header in the original packet. If the tunnel exit point is a router, the original packet's IPv6 destination address is not identical to the tunnel exit point address. In this case, the tunnel entry point must provide the address information to the tunnel exit point.

The steps for the encapsulation of the IPv6 packet are the following:

1. The entry point of the tunnel decrements the IPv6 hop limit by one, encapsulates the packet in an IPv4 header, and transmits the encapsulated packet through the tunnel. If necessary, the IPv4 packet is fragmented.

2. The exit point of the tunnel receives the encapsulated packet. If the packet was fragmented, the exit point reassembles it. Then the exit point removes the IPv4 header and processes the IPv6 packet to its original destination.

Figure 10-2 shows the encapsulation of an IPv6 packet in an IPv4 packet.

The following fields in the IPv4 header are interesting to note: the Header Length field contains the length of the IPv4 header, plus the length of the IPv6 header, plus any extension headers and the length of the IPv6 payload. If the encapsulated packet has to be fragmented, there will be correspond-

| IPv6 header | Payload | | Original IPv6 packet sent from source host to tunnel entry point. |

| IPv4 header | IPv6 header | Payload | Encapsulated packet sent to tunnel exit point. |

Fields in IPv4 Header:

Header Length:	Length of IPv4 header plus IPv6 header plus any extension headers and IPv6 payload.
Time to Live (TTL):	Implementation-specific.
Protocol:	Value 41 (assigned for IPv6).
Source Address:	IPv4 address of outgoing interface of tunnel entry point.
Destination Address:	IPv4 address of tunnel exit point.

Figure 10-2. Encapsulation

ing values in the Flags field and the Fragment Offset field. The value of the Time to Live (TTL) field depends on the implementation used. The Protocol Number is set to 41, the value assigned for IPv6. Thus, if you want to analyze your tunneled IPv6 traffic, you can set a filter in your analyzer to display the packets containing the value 41 in the Protocol Number field. The IPv4 Source Address is the address of the outgoing interface of the tunnel entry point and the IPv4 Destination Address is the IPv4 address of the tunnel exit point. The IPv6-over-IPv4 tunnel is considered a single hop. The hop limit field in the IPv6 header is therefore decremented by one. This hides the existence of a tunnel to the end user and is not detectable by common tools such as *traceroute*. Figure 10-3 shows an encapsulated IPv6 packet in the trace file.

This is a *ping* generated on *Marvin*, our Windows 2000 host. We were pinging a host on the 6Bone. The TTL is set to 128. The Protocol field shows value 41 for IPv6, which identifies this packet as an encapsulated packet. The source address 62.2.84.115 is the IPv4 address of *Marvin*, which was configured for this address by a DHCP server. The destination address is the IPv4 address of a 6to4 relay router (6to4 concepts are explained in a separate section in this chapter) in the 6Bone, the tunnel exit point. This router can forward the packet to an IPv6 network, the 6Bone in this case. Compare these IPv4 addresses with the IPv6 source and destination addresses (which can be seen in the highlighted summary line above the detail screen). Use your Windows calculator to find out that the IPv6 source and destination addresses have the 6to4 prefix of 2002 plus the IPv4 address in hexadecimal notation in the low-order 32 bits. This is an example of a host-to-host automatic tunnel because we were actually pinging the 6to4 router.

If an IPv4 router from within the tunnel generates an ICMPv4 error message, the router sends the message to the tunnel entry point because that

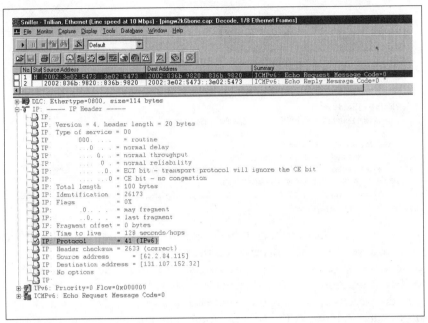

Figure 10-3. Encapsulation in the trace file

host is the source of that packet. If the packet contains enough information about the original, encapsulated IPv6 packet, the tunnel entry point may send an ICMPv6 message back to the original source of the packet.

When the tunnel exit point receives an IPv4 datagram with a protocol value of 41, it knows that this packet has been encapsulated. In case of fragmentation, it reassembles the packets, removes the IPv4 header, and delivers the IPv6 packet to the final destination.

Both tunnel end points need to have a link-local IPv6 address, with the IPv4 address of that same interface being the interface identifier for the IPv6 address. For example, a host with an IPv4 address of 192.168.0.2 has a link-local address of FE80::192.168.0.2/64.

Before forwarding a decapsulated IPv6 packet, the tunnel endpoint must verify that the tunnel source address is acceptable. Thus, unacceptable ingress into the network can be avoided. If the tunnel is a bidirectional configured tunnel, this check is done by comparing the source address of the encapsulated packet with the configured address of the other side of the tunnel. For unidirectional configured tunnels, the tunnel must be configured with a list of source IPv4 address prefixes that are acceptable. By default, this list is empty, which means that the tunnel end point has to be explicitly configured in order to allow forwarding of decapsulated packets.

Automatic Tunneling (RFC 2893)

Automatic tunneling allows IPv6/IPv4 nodes to communicate over an IPv4 infrastructure without the need for tunnel destination preconfiguration. The tunnel endpoint address is determined by the IPv4-compatible destination address. This type of IPv6 address is exclusively assigned to nodes that use automatic tunneling.

Figure 10-4 shows the output of the *ipv6 if* command on my Windows 2000 host *Marvin*.

```
Interface 2 (site 0): Tunnel Pseudo-Interface
  does not use Neighbor Discovery
  link-level address: 0.0.0.0
    preferred address 2002:3e02:5473::3e02:5473, infinite/infinite
    preferred address ::62.2.84.115, infinite/infinite
  link MTU 1280 (true link MTU 65515)
  current hop limit 128
```

Figure 10-4. The IPv4-compatible IPv6 address

The IPv4 address is 62.2.84.115. The IPv4-compatible address is created by taking the IPv4 address for the interface and prepending a 96-bit prefix of all zeroes. The interface to which this address is assigned is commonly called a pseudointerface. In the screenshot, this can be seen as ::62.2.84.115. An automatic tunnel is created by extracting the IPv4 address from the lower portion. As long as the IPv4 address used is not from the private range, the IPv4-compatible address is globally unique.

A special routing table entry can be used to direct packets through the tunnel. The entry would simply be a route to the all-zeros prefix with a 96-bit mask. All packets with an IPv4-compatible IPv6 address as a destination will match this prefix and be sent through the automatic tunnel. The destination IPv4 address is taken from the 32 low-order bits of the IPv6 destination address. The automatic tunnel must not send IPv4 packets to broadcast, multicast, loopback, or the unspecified address.

Configured Tunneling (RFC 2893)

In configured tunneling, the address of the tunnel exit point is configured on the tunnel entry point. When encapsulating the IPv6 packet, the tunnel entry point uses this address as the destination address in the IPv4 header.

IPv6/IPv4 hosts connected to network segments with no IPv6 routers can be configured with a static route to an IPv6 router in the Internet at the other side of an IPv4 tunnel; this enables communication with a remote IPv6 world. In this case, the IPv6 address of an IPv6/IPv4 router at the other end of the tunnel is added into the routing table as a default route. Now all IPv6 destination addresses match the route and can be tunneled through the IPv4 infrastructure. This default route has a mask of zero and is used only if there are no other routes with a more specific matching mask.

Combination of Automatic and Configured Tunneling

In many cases a combination of both tunneling techniques makes sense for IPv6/IPv4 hosts that are connected to segments with no IPv6 router. Such a host can have two routing entries for tunneling. One entry points to the all-zeros 96-bit prefix. All packets with IPv4-compatible IPv6 destination addresses will be sent through this route. The other routing entry points to an IPv6 router that is also configured to perform automatic tunneling. All packets with native IPv6 destination addresses will be routed through the configured tunnel. Reply packets from native IPv6 hosts will be sent to the IPv6 router, which delivers them back to the original host through automatic tunneling.

If a host sending a packet has both an IPv4-compatible IPv6 address and a global native IPv6 address, the host should use the IPv4-compatible address as a source address for packets to IPv4-compatible IPv6 destinations and use the native IPv6 address as a source address for packets to native IPv6 destinations.

To summarize this, let's check the routing table on *Marvin* (Figure 10-5).

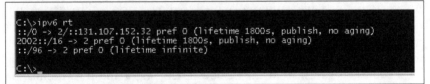

```
C:\>ipv6 rt
::/0 -> 2/::131.107.152.32 pref 0 (lifetime 1800s, publish, no aging)
2002::/16 -> 2 pref 0 (lifetime 1800s, publish, no aging)
::/96 -> 2 pref 0 (lifetime infinite)
C:\>
```

Figure 10-5. Marvin's routing table

The command used to display the routing table is *ipv6 rt*. The first entry is for ::/0. The zero-length prefix specifies this route as a default route. It is going out through interface number 2 with the next hop IPv6 address ::131. 107.152.32. This is the IPv4-compatible IPv6 address of a 6to4 relay router that has been configured on *Marvin*. Thus, any IPv6 traffic that does not match a more specific routing entry is encapsulated in an IPv4 header and routed through this default route. Routing is enabled on *Marvin*; the associated lifetime and the published flag make this a published route. Interface number 2 is the tunnel pseudointerface (refer to Figure 10-4, which shows the interface configuration for the tunnel pseudointerface). All traffic going out through interface 2 is encapsulated in an IPv4 header. The entry for

2002::/16 is the route for the 6to4, also going out through interface 2 and being encapsulated. With these two routes, this host can reach the 6Bone and 6to4 hosts. The third routing entry specifies the route to the all-zeros prefix with a 96-bit mask, as discussed earlier. All IPv4-compatible IPv6 addresses match this prefix and will be routed through interface 2 if they don't match a more specific entry.

Encapsulation with IPv6 (RFC 2473)

RFC 2473 specifies the model and the generic mechanisms for encapsulation with IPv6. Most of the rules discussed in this chapter about tunneling in IPv4 apply to tunneling in IPv6. The main difference is that in tunneling in IPv6, the packets are encapsulated in an IPv6 header and sent through an IPv6 network. The packet being encapsulated can be an IPv6 packet, an IPv4 packet, or any other protocol. The tunnel entry point prepends the IPv6 header and, if needed, one or a set of Extension headers in front of the original packet header. Whatever the tunnel entry point prepends is called the *Tunnel IPv6 headers*. Figure 10-6 shows the Tunnel IPv6 headers from the packet view.

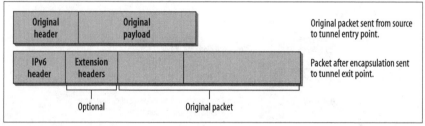

Figure 10-6. Tunnel IPv6 headers from the packet view

In the IPv6 header applied by the tunnel entry point, the source address is the address of the tunnel entry point node and the destination address is the address of the tunnel exit point node. The source node of the original packet can be the same node as the tunnel entry point. The original packet, including its header, becomes the payload of the encapsulated packet. The header of the original packet is treated according to standard forwarding rules. If the header is an IPv4 header, the TTL field is decremented by one. If it is an IPv6 header, the Hop Limit field is decremented by one. The network between the tunnel entry point and the tunnel exit point is thus virtually just one hop, no matter how many actual hops there are in between.

The Tunnel IPv6 header is processed according to the IPv6 protocol rules. Extension headers, if present, are processed as though the packet was a standard IPv6 packet. For example, a Hop-by-Hop Extension header would be processed by every node listed in the Hop-by-Hop Options field. A Destination Options header would be processed by the destination host—i.e., the tunnel exit point. All these options are configured on the tunnel entry point. An example of the use of a Destination Options header is the configuration of a Tunnel Encapsulation Limit Option (RFC 2473). This option may be used when tunnels are nested. One hop of a tunnel can be the entry point of another tunnel. In this case, we have *nested tunnels*. The first tunnel is called the *outer tunnel* and the second tunnel is called the *inner tunnel*. The inner tunnel entry point treats the whole packet received from the outer tunnel as the original packet and applies the same rules as shown in Figure 10-6. The only natural limit to the number of nested tunnels is the maximum IPv6 packet size. Every encapsulation adds the size of the tunnel IPv6 headers. This would allow for something around 1600 nested tunnels, which is not realistic. Also, consider the case in which the packet has to be fragmented. If it has to be fragmented again because the additional tunnel IPv6 headers have increased the packet size, the number of fragments is doubled. So a mechanism was needed to limit the number of nested tunnels. It is specified in RFC 2473 and is called the Tunnel Encapsulation Limit Option. This option is carried in a Destination Option header and has the format shown in Figure 10-7.

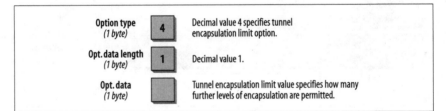

Figure 10-7. Format of the tunnel encapsulation limit option

The Option Type field has 1 byte and the decimal value 4, specifying the Tunnel Encapsulation Limit Option. The Option Data Length field has the decimal value 1, specifying the length of the following Option field. In this case, the Option field has a size of 1 byte and contains the actual value for the Tunnel Encapsulation Limit Option. The value in this field specifies how many further levels of encapsulation are permitted. If the value is zero, the packet is discarded and an ICMP Parameter Problem message is sent back to the source (the tunnel entry point of the previous tunnel). If the value is non-zero, the packet is encapsulated and forwarded. In this case, a new Tunnel Encapsulation Limit Option has to be applied with a value of one less than the limit received in the packet being encapsulated. If the packet received does not have a tunnel encapsulation limit but this tunnel entry point has one configured, the tunnel entry point must apply a destination options header and include the configured value.

Loopback encapsulation should be avoided. Loopback encapsulation happens when a node encapsulates a packet originating from itself and destined to itself. IPv6 implementations should prevent this by checking and rejecting configurations of tunnels where both the entry point and exit point belong to the same host. Another undesirable situation is a routing-loop nested encapsulation. This happens if a packet from an inner tunnel reenters an outer tunnel from which it has not yet exited. This can only be controlled by a combination of the original packet's hop limit plus the configuration of tunnel encapsulation limits.

Let's have a closer look at a Tunnel IPv6 Header (Figure 10-8).

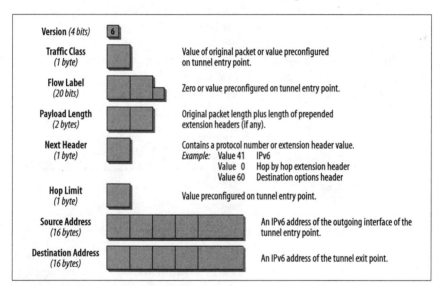

Figure 10-8. The tunnel IPv6 header

The fields of a standard IPv6 header were discussed in Chapter 2. Interesting values here are the following: the values for Traffic Class, Flow Label, and Hop Limit can be preconfigured on the tunnel entry point. The Payload Length has the value for the packet length of the original packet plus the size of any extension headers prepended by the tunnel entry point. The Source and Destination Address of the Tunnel IPv6 header contain the IPv6 addresses of the tunnel entry and exit point, respectively. Note that a host that is configured as a tunnel entry point must support fragmentation of packets that it encapsulates. Packets that are encapsulated may exceed the Path MTU of the tunnel. Because the tunnel entry point is considered the source of the encapsulated packet, it must fragment it if needed. The tunnel exit point node will reassemble the packet. If the original packet is an IPv4 packet with the Don't Fragment bit set, the tunnel entry point discards the packet and sends an ICMP Destination Unreachable message with the code "fragmentation needed and DF set" back to the source of the packet.

6to4 (RFC 3056)

RFC 3056, "Connection of IPv6 Domains via IPv4 Clouds," specifies a mechanism for IPv6 sites to communicate with each other over the IPv4 network without explicit tunnel setup. This is called 6to4. The wide area IPv4 network is treated as a unicast point-to-point link layer, and the native IPv6 domains communicate via 6to4 routers, also referred to as 6to4 gateways. This is intended as a transition mechanism used during the period of co-existence of IPv4 and IPv6. It will not be used as a permanent solution. The IPv6 packets are encapsulated in IPv4 at the 6to4 gateway. At least one globally unique IPv4 unicast address is required for this configuration. The IANA has assigned a special TLA for the 6to4 scheme. The address prefix is 2002::/16. Figure 10-9 shows the format of the 6to4 prefix in detail.

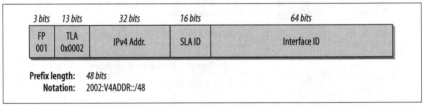

3 bits	13 bits	32 bits	16 bits	64 bits
FP 001	TLA 0x0002	IPv4 Addr.	SLA ID	Interface ID

Prefix length: 48 bits
Notation: 2002:V4ADDR::/48

Figure 10-9. Format of the 6to4 prefix

The 32 bits after the prefix 2002::/16 are the IPv4 address of the gateway in hex representation. If you refer back to Figure 10-4, you can see how the IPv4 address 62.2.84.115 is converted to 2002:3e02:5473::/48. This leaves you with 80 bits of address space for your internal network. If you use, let's say, 16 bits for the local network addressing, you can create 65,536 networks! The remaining 64 bits can be used for the nodes on your network; that is, 2^{64} nodes per network. It looks like getting familiar with the extended address space has some advantages. Now all the hosts on your network can communicate with other 6to4 hosts on the Internet.

If your hosts want to speak to other IPv6 hosts on remote IPv6 networks, such as the 6Bone, you need a *6to4 relay router*. The relay router is a router that is configured for 6to4 and IPv6. It connects your 6to4 network to the native IPv6 network.

 There are a number of public 6to4 relay routers in the Internet that you can use. For a list, go to *http://www.kfu.com/~nsayer/6to4/*.

If you want to manually configure your 6to4 network for a 6to4 relay router, you can choose the best relay router for your site and use it as your IPv6 default route.

RFC 3068 defines a 6to4 relay router anycast address to simplify the configuration of 6to4 gateways that need a default route to find a 6to4 relay router on the Internet. IANA assigned an IPv4 6to4 Relay anycast prefix of 192.88.99.0/24. The assigned anycast address corresponds to the first node in the prefix, e.g., 192.88.99.1. The 6to4 routers have to be configured with a default route pointing to this anycast address. Using this address means that 6to4 packets are routed to the nearest available 6to4 relay router automatically. If one 6to4 relay goes down, you do not need to reconfigure your 6to4 gateway; packets will automatically be rerouted to the next available relay. With the ongoing deployment of IPv6 in commercial networks, the number of public 6to4 relay routers will increase. If a host wishes to communicate with a node on a native IPv6 subnet (i.e., destination address 3ffe:b00:c18:1::10), the IPv4 header destination address will be the reserved anycast address 192.88.99.1 and will be delivered to the nearest 6to4 relay router. In the reverse, a native IPv6 host that wants to send packets to a host that is in a 6to4 cloud will route its packets to the nearest 6to4 relay router advertising the prefix 2002::/16.

When IPv6 packets leave a 6to4 site to the external IPv4 cloud, they are encapsulated in IPv4 packets by the 6to4 gateway. Figure 10-10 shows the IPv4 header and the encapsulated IPv6 header in a trace file.

The TTL field in the IPv4 header and the Hop Limit in the IPv6 header are set to the value 128, which is a common default value for Microsoft. The IPv4 header contains a Protocol Type field of 41, for IPv6. The Source Address in the IPv4 header is the globally unique IPv4 address used for the 6to4 router configuration. The IPv4 destination address is the IPv4 address of the relay router used. When you compare the IPv4 addresses with the IPv6 6to4 addresses used, you can see how the translation is done.

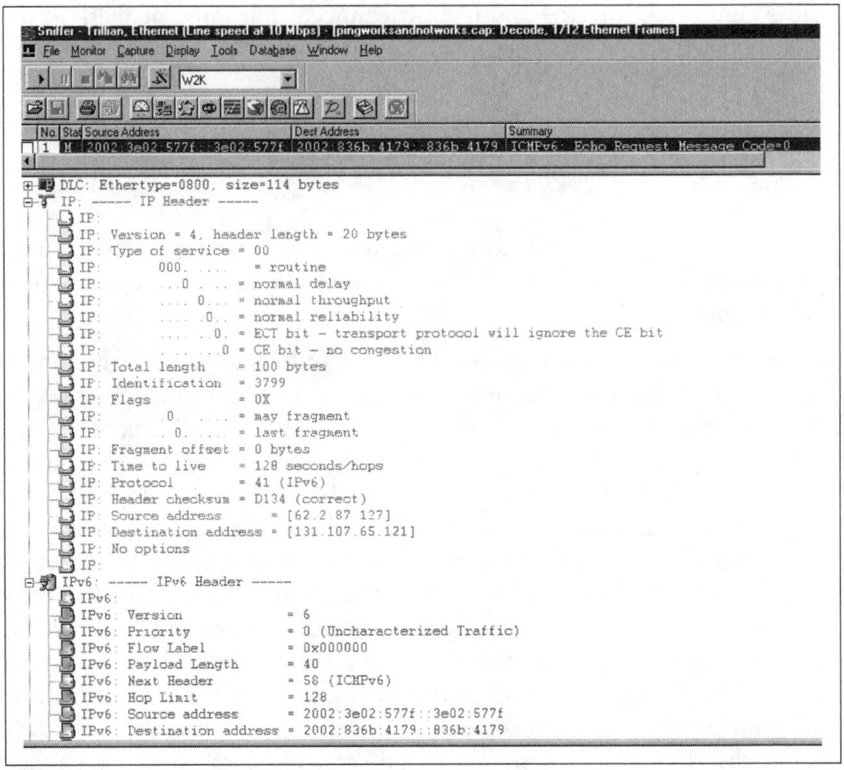

Figure 10-10. The IPv4 and IPv6 headers in the trace file

62.2.87.127 is represented with the prefix 2002:3e02:577f::/48, and 131. 107.65.121 is represented as 2002:836b:4179::/48. Convert the decimal IPv4 address to hex and see how the IPv4 address is used for building the prefix.

If two hosts communicate—one with only a 6to4 address and the other one with a 6to4 address plus a native IPv6 address—the two hosts should both use the 6to4 address for communication. If both hosts have a 6to4 and a native IPv6 address, they should both use either the 6to4 address or the IPv6 address. Which choice is made should be configurable and the default should be IPv6.

Let me show you 6to4 in a simple example. In the public 6to4 relay router list mentioned earlier, I found that Zama Networks offers a public 6to4 relay with the DNS name *6to4.zama6.com*. Note that this router is not there anymore, so don't try to use it. These are historic screenshots! Now let's find the address. The following pings were generated on my Windows 2000 host *Marvin*, which is configured for 6to4 (Figure 10-11).

The first ping is an IPv4 ping (*ping.exe*), which tells us that the 6to4 relay's IPv4 address is 203.142.128.42. The second ping is an IPv6 ping (*ping6.exe*)

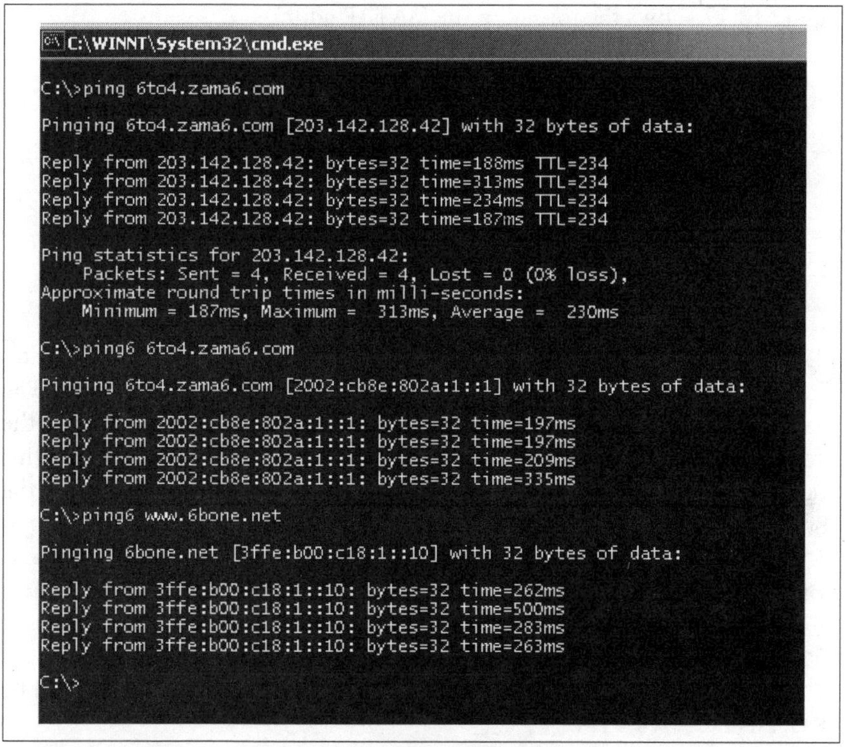

```
C:\WINNT\System32\cmd.exe

C:\>ping 6to4.zama6.com

Pinging 6to4.zama6.com [203.142.128.42] with 32 bytes of data:

Reply from 203.142.128.42: bytes=32 time=188ms TTL=234
Reply from 203.142.128.42: bytes=32 time=313ms TTL=234
Reply from 203.142.128.42: bytes=32 time=234ms TTL=234
Reply from 203.142.128.42: bytes=32 time=187ms TTL=234

Ping statistics for 203.142.128.42:
    Packets: Sent = 4, Received = 4, Lost = 0 (0% loss),
Approximate round trip times in milli-seconds:
    Minimum = 187ms, Maximum = 313ms, Average = 230ms

C:\>ping6 6to4.zama6.com

Pinging 6to4.zama6.com [2002:cb8e:802a:1::1] with 32 bytes of data:

Reply from 2002:cb8e:802a:1::1: bytes=32 time=197ms
Reply from 2002:cb8e:802a:1::1: bytes=32 time=197ms
Reply from 2002:cb8e:802a:1::1: bytes=32 time=209ms
Reply from 2002:cb8e:802a:1::1: bytes=32 time=335ms

C:\>ping6 www.6bone.net

Pinging 6bone.net [3ffe:b00:c18:1::10] with 32 bytes of data:

Reply from 3ffe:b00:c18:1::10: bytes=32 time=262ms
Reply from 3ffe:b00:c18:1::10: bytes=32 time=500ms
Reply from 3ffe:b00:c18:1::10: bytes=32 time=283ms
Reply from 3ffe:b00:c18:1::10: bytes=32 time=263ms

C:\>
```

Figure 10-11. Pinging the 6to4 relay and a 6bone node

and shows that the IPv6 address is 2002:cb8e:802a:1::1. Thus, DNS resolution works for both record types. Again, if you convert the IPv4 address to hexadecimal, you get cb8e:802a. The next IPv6 ping goes to a 6Bone host, to *www.6bone.net*. It has the IPv6 address 3ffe:b00:c18:1::10. Note that the prefix 3ffe is the prefix assigned for 6Bone testing (refer to Chapter 3 for details about reserved prefixes).

ISATAP

The Intra-Site Automatic Tunnel Addressing Protocol (ISATAP) is designed to provide IPv6 connectivity between IPv6 nodes within a mainly IPv4-based intra-network that does not have an IPv6 router in the site. With ISATAP, you can deploy IPv6 in your corporate network, behind your firewall, even if you do not have an IPv6 router. ISATAP even allows you to use an automatic tunneling mechanism if you are using private IPv4 addresses and NAT. ISATAP addresses embed an IPv4 address in the EUI-64 interface identifier. ISATAP is still experimental and currently described in draft at *http://www. ietf.org/internet-drafts/draft-ietf-ngtrans-isatap-04.txt*. It is expected to become very popular.

Figure 10-12 shows the format of the ISATAP address.

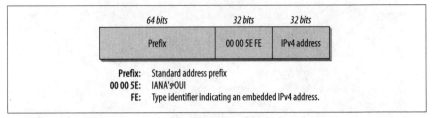

Figure 10-12. The format of the ISATAP address

The ISATAP address has a standard 64-bit prefix that can be link-local, site-local, a 6to4 prefix, or belong to the global aggregatable unicast range. The Interface identifier is built using the IANA OUI 00 00 5E, which follows the prefix. The following byte is a type field, and the value FE indicates that this address contains an embedded IPv4 address. The last four bytes contain the IPv4 address, which can be written in dotted decimal notation. The format of the address can thus be summarized as 64bitPrefix:5EFE:IPv4address. For instance, if you have an assigned prefix of 2001:620:600:200::/64 (guess where that is) and an IPv4 address of 62.2.84.115, your ISATAP address is 2001:620:600:200:0:5EFE:3e02:5473. Alternatively, you can write 2001:620: 600:200:0:5EFE:62.2.84.115. The corresponding link local address would be FE80::5EFE:62.2.84.115.

Using ISATAP, IPv6 hosts within an IPv4 intranet can communicate with each other. There is no need for an IPv6 router. If they want to communicate with IPv6 hosts on the Internet, such as 6Bone hosts, a border router must be configured; it can be an ISATAP router or a 6to4 gateway. The IPv4 addresses of all the hosts within the site do not need to be public. They are embedded in the address with the standard prefix and are therefore unique and routable. Large numbers of ISATAP hosts can be assigned to one ISATAP prefix. If you deploy IPv6 on a segment in your corporate network, you can configure one of the native IPv6 nodes with an ISATAP interface, and it can act as a router between the native IPv6 segment and ISATAP hosts in the IPv4 segments. Because the ISATAP nodes on the IPv4 network do not have an IPv6 router that can send them prefix information for autoconfiguration, they currently need to be configured for the prefix and need a default route pointing to the ISATAP router or 6to4 gateway if connectivity to the Internet is required. The ISATAP draft explains mechanisms that are in development to allow automatic intrasite IPv6 router discovery and stateless address autoconfiguration. An ISATAP router anycast address is in discussion and would work the same way as explained for the 6to4 anycast address described earlier in this chapter.

Teredo

6to4 makes IPv6 available through the IPv4 infrastructure. ISATAP enables deployment of IPv6 hosts within a site without the need for IPv6 routers. Teredo (called Shipworm in earlier drafts) is another mechanism under development. It is designed to make IPv6 available to hosts through one or more layers of NAT, which cannot be upgraded to 6to4, by tunneling packets over UDP. Teredo servers and Teredo relays are needed to make the service work. Teredo is in draft status, and many details still need to be defined. If you are interested in following the process, refer to *http://www. ietf.org/internet-drafts/draft-ietf-ngtrans-shipworm-05.txt*. Note that the draft number may have increased by one or more when you go there.

A Sample Network Design

I will discuss a sample network design to summarize the tunneling concepts and give you a picture of a possible scenario. You will see that you can start to deploy IPv6 step by step on single hosts or subnets and that there is no requirement to change your whole IPv4 infrastructure overnight. If you are familiar with setting up NAT for your IPv4 network, these concepts will not be too difficult to master.

Figure 10-13 shows a 6to4 scenario.

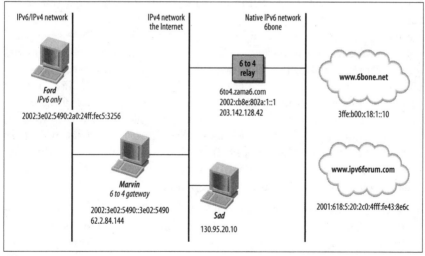

Figure 10-13. A 6to4 design

Marvin is your company's 6to4 gateway. It is connected to the Internet with a routable IPv4 address of 62.2.84.144 and has a logical IPv6 interface into the corporate network advertising the 2002:3e02:5490::/48 prefix for the

6to4 route. It has been configured with the IPv4 address of a 6to4 relay router, in this case *6to4.zama6.com*. This 6to4 gateway (*Marvin*) provides IPv6 transit for all IPv6 machines from within the corporate network. *Ford* is an IPv6-only machine within the network. It has autoconfigured its IP address of 2002:3e02:5490:2a0:24ff:fec5:3256 using the prefix advertised by *Marvin*. The 6to4 relay router used in this example is the public relay offered by Zama Networks (which is not up anymore). As a relay router, it connects 6to4 sites to native IPv6 networks, such as the 6Bone in this example. The relay's DNS name is *6to4.zama6.com*. It is a dual-stack machine, the IPv4 interface with an address of 203.142.128.42 and the IPv6 interface with an address of 2002:cb8e:802a:1::1. It advertises the route 2002::/16 into the 6Bone, so native IPv6 hosts in the 6Bone can reach 6to4 sites. All 6to4-connected sites can get access to native IPv6 networks via this relay router. Figure 10-13 shows two examples for native IPv6 hosts that we can reach from *Ford*: *www.6bone.net*, with an IPv6 address of 3ffe:b00:c18:1::10, and *www.ipv6forum.com*, with the address 2001:618:5:20:2c0:4fff:fe43:8e6c. *Sad* is an IPv4 host connected to the Internet through native IPv4 and has an IP address of 130.95.20.10.

Ford is an IPv6-only node. It can be on either a 6to4 IPv6 network or an IPv4/IPv6 network. If *Ford* wants to talk to other 6to4 sites, it will use *Marvin* as its 6to4 gateway. If it wants to talk to IPv6-only nodes, it will use the 6to4 relay router to get there. So when *Marvin* gets a packet for a 6Bone host, it encapsulates the packet in IPv4 and sends it to the other side of the tunnel to the 6to4 relay. The 6to4 relay strips off the IPv4 header and forwards the native IPv6 packet to the 6Bone. If hosts on the 6Bone send packets to 6to4 sites, these packets will have a destination address beginning with the prefix 2002::/16. This way, the relay router knows that it has to encapsulate the packet in IPv4. The relay router can derive the IPv4 address of the 6to4 gateway from the 6to4 address. The gateway decapsulates the packet and forwards it to *Ford*. If *Ford* wants to talk to other IPv6 hosts on its home segment, it can do so without using *Marvin* as a gateway. If *Ford* wants to talk to *Sad*, which has no IPv6 stack, it can do so only if translation mechanisms are implemented. Without translation techniques, *Sad* is unable to interpret the IPv6 header information.

This design is an example of what can be done with today's tunneling mechanisms. They provide flexible migration order and allow step-by-step upgrades of hosts and routers. Obviously, as known from other tunneling techniques, the tunneling mechanism puts an additional load on the routers and makes troubleshooting more complex. The routers need time and CPU power for encapsulating and decapsulating the packets. Hop count issues, as well as MTU size and fragmentation problems, may occur due to the differences in the specifications for the two protocols.

Network Address and Protocol Translation

Address and protocol translation techniques are described in RFCs 2765 and 2766. They offer transition mechanisms in addition to dual-stack and tunneling techniques. The goal is to provide transparent routing for nodes in IPv6 networks to communicate with nodes in IPv4 networks and vice versa. The NAT gateway uses a pool of globally unique IPv4 addresses and binds them to IPv6 addresses. No changes to the end nodes are necessary.

The following abbreviations are used in RFC 2766 and throughout this section:

Network Address Translation (NAT)
  Translates IP address, IP, TCP, UDP, and ICMP header checksums.

Network Address Port Translation (NAPT)
  In addition to the fields translated by NAT transport, identifiers such as TCP and UDP port numbers and ICMP message types are translated.

Network Address Translation and Protocol Translation (NAT-PT)
  Translates an IPv6 packet into an equivalent IPv4 packet and vice versa.

Network Address Port Translation and Protocol Translation (NAPT-PT)
  Allows IPv6 hosts to communicate with IPv4 hosts using a single IPv4 address.

These concepts are explained in the following sections.

NAT

NAT has widely been used, especially to overcome the limitations of IPv4 address space. Corporate networks use IPv4 addresses from the private range and a NAT router at the border of the corporate network translates the private addresses to a single or a limited number of public addresses. NAT, as described here, provides routing between an IPv6 network and an IPv4 network. With basic NAT, a block of IPv4 addresses is set aside and the fields for IP source addresses, IP, TCP, UDP, and ICMP header checksums are translated. With NAPT, further transport identifiers such as TCP and UDP port numbers and ICMP message types are translated. This allows a set of IPv6 hosts to share a single IPv4 address. NAT can be unidirectional (only IPv6 hosts can initiate a session) or bidirectional (the session can be initiated from both sides). Hosts in the IPv4 network use DNS to resolve names. Therefore, a DNS Application Layer Gateway (ALG) must be capable of translating IPv6 addresses into their IPv4 NAT address bindings and vice versa.

How Packets Translate

To understand how packets are translated, we'll follow a packet being sent from an IPv6 host through a NAPT gateway to an IPv4 host and back. Figure 10-14 illustrates the translation process.

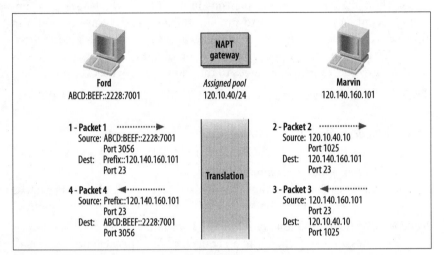

Figure 10-14. Communication flow over NAPT

In this example, *Ford*, the IPv6 host, has an IPv6 address of ABCD:BEEF:: 2228:7001. *Marvin*, on the other side of the NAPT router, has an IPv4 address of 120.140.160.101. The NAPT gateway has been assigned a pool of 120.10.40/24. *Ford* initializes a session with *Marvin* by sending a packet to the destination address prefix::120.140.160.101, port 23. The prefix ::/96 is advertised by NAPT into the IPv6 network, and whenever a packet is sent to that prefix, it will be routed through NAPT. As source address, *Ford* uses its IPv6 address with a port number of 3056 (Step 1). The NAPT gateway now assigns an IPv4 address and a port number out of its pool. Let's say it uses the address 120.10.40.10. The new IPv4 packet going out from NAPT to *Marvin* has a source address of 120.10.40.10, port 1025, and a destination address of 120.140.160.101, port 23 (Step 2). When *Marvin* replies, it sends the packet with a source address of 120.140.160.101, port 23, to destination address 120.10.40.10, port 1025 (Step 3). NAPT translates the packet according to the parameters it has stored in its cache for the duration of the session and sends it from source address prefix::120.140.160.101, port 23, to destination address ABCD:BEEF::2228:7001, port 3056 (Step 4).

Limitations

The translation mechanisms described in RFC 2766 should be used only if no other transition mechanism is possible and dual-stack operation should be avoided for certain reasons. This mechanism has a number of disadvantages. For instance, it does not take full advantage of the advanced capabilities that IPv6 offers. But it is a choice when, for a certain time, access to IPv4-only networks and applications is needed.

The same topology restrictions apply that also apply to IPv4 NATs. The inbound and outbound datagrams pertaining to one session have to traverse the same NAT router. There are applications that use IP addresses in the payload of IP datagrams. NAT is not aware of the application layer and does not look into the payload to detect IP addresses. In this case, NAT would have to be combined with ALG to support such applications in this type of environment. RFC 2766 describes how a DNS ALG or FTP ALG would have to translate to support these applications over NAT. For instance, if a DNS request goes out from the IPv4 network to a DNS server through a NAT-PT device in the IPv6 network or vice versa, a mechanism must be provided that translates IPv4 resource records types (A type) to IPv6 resource record types (AAAA or A6 types). FTP control sessions carry IP address information in the payload, and the format of the command allows only for 32-bit addresses. RFC 2428 defines two new extensions to FTP commands to replace the PORT and PASV commands. The new commands are designed to not only allow long addresses, but also carry additional information about the protocol to be used. These new extensions can also be used for FTP over IPv4. An FTP ALG would have to be able to translate these commands for FTP to work over NAT.

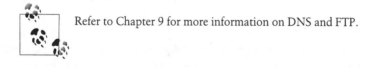 Refer to Chapter 9 for more information on DNS and FTP.

End-to-end security cannot be provided when using any form of NAT. Two end nodes that need IPSEC-level security must use either IPv4 or IPv6 natively. This is a well-known limitation of NAT in general and will be one of the driving reasons to move away from NAT and start to use IPv6 natively. Because the DNS ALG translates DNS requests, the mechanisms of DNSSEC will not work either.

Stateless IP/ICMP Translation

For the case in which IPv4-only hosts want to communicate with IPv6-only hosts or vice versa, RFC 2765 defines how a protocol translator has to translate the IP and ICMP headers for both parties to understand each other. For example, you might have a new network segment and want to roll out native IPv6 hosts. With the implementation of a protocol translator, it is possible to set up the new IPv6-only network internally and have those IPv6-only clients access the standard IPv4 Internet or any other IPv4-only node. For this purpose, a new address type has been introduced: the *IPv4-translatable address*. The format of the address is 0::ffff:0:0:0/96. The host identifier is an IPv4 address that has to be taken from a special pool and assigned to the IPv6 node that wants to communicate with IPv4 nodes.

TCP and UDP headers generally do not need to be modified by the translator. One exception is UDP headers that need a checksum for IPv6 because a pseudoheader checksum is required for IPv6. The same is true for ICMPv4 messages that need a pseudoheader checksum for ICMPv6. In addition to the checksum, ICMP error messages contain the IP header of the original packet in the payload that needs to be modified by the translator; otherwise, the receiving node cannot understand it. IPv4 options and IPv6 Routing headers, Hop-by-Hop Extension headers, and Destination Option headers are not translated. Also, the translation techniques cannot be used for multicast traffic because IPv4 multicast addresses cannot be mapped into IPv6 multicast addresses and vice versa.

Just as with dual-stack nodes, applications running on nodes that use IP/ICMP translation need a mechanism to determine which protocol version to use for communication with their peers.

Translating IPv4 to IPv6

An IPv4-to-IPv6 translator receives an IPv4 datagram. Because it has been configured to know the pool of IPv4 addresses that represent the internal IPv6 nodes, the translator knows that the packet needs translation. It removes the IPv4 header and replaces it with an IPv6 header by translating all the information from the IPv4 header into the IPv6 header.

Path MTU discovery is optional in IPv4 but mandatory in IPv6. If an IPv4 host does Path MTU discovery by setting the Don't Fragment bit in the header, Path MTU discovery works even through the translator. The sender may receive Packet Too Big messages from both IPv4 and IPv6 routers. If the Don't Fragment bit is not set in the IPv4 packet, an IPv6 translator has to ensure that the packet can safely travel through the IPv6 network. It does this by fragmenting the IPv4 packet, if necessary, using the minimum packet size for IPv6, which is 1280 bytes. IPv6 guarantees that 1280-byte packets will be delivered without a need for further fragmentation. In this case, the translator always includes a fragment header to indicate that the sender allows fragmentation. Should this packet travel through an IPv6-to-IPv4 translator, the translator knows it can fragment the packet.

The information that will be translated to the IPv6 header is detailed in Table 10-1.

Table 10-1. Translated IPv6 header fields

Header field	Information
Version	6
Traffic Class	All 8 bits from the Type of Service and Precedence Field are copied.
Flow Label	Zero
Payload Length	The Total Length from the IPv4 header field minus the size of the IPv4 header (including options, if present).
Next Header	Protocol Field copied from the IPv4 header.
Hop Limit	TTL value copied from the IPv4 header. Since the translator is a router, the value has to be decremented by one (either before or after translation) and checked on the value. If zero, an ICMP TTL exceeded message must be generated.
Source Address	Combination of IPv4-mapped address prefix and the IPv4 address in the 32 low-order bits, for example: ::ffff:0:0:192.168.0.1.
Destination Address	Combination of IPv4-translatable address prefix and the IPv4 destination address, for example: 0::ffff:0:0:0:192.168.0.99.
IPv4 Options	If any IPv4 options are present, they are ignored. If a source route option is present, the packet must be discarded and an ICMPv4 "destination unreachable/source route failed" (Type3, Code 5) error message should be returned to the sender.

If a Fragment header needs to be added, the information listed in Table 10-2 is inserted into the IPv6 packet.

Table 10-2. IPv6 header fields with fragmentation

Header field	Information
Header fields	
Payload Length	The Total Length from the IPv4 header field minus the size of the IPv4 header (including options, if present) plus 8 bits for the size of the Fragment header.
Next Header	44 (Fragment Header)
Fragment Header fields	
Next Header	Protocol field copied from IPv4 header.
Fragment Offset	Fragment Offset field copied from IPv4 header.
M-Flag	More Fragments bit copied from the IPv4 header.
Identification	The high-order 16 bits are set to zero; the low-order 16 bits are copied from the Identification field in the IPv4 header.

For a UDP packet with a zero checksum, the translator must calculate a valid checksum for IPv6. If a translator receives the first fragment of a fragmented UDP packet with a zero checksum, it should drop the packet and generate a system message specifying the IP address and the port number. Further fragments should silently be discarded.

Translating ICMPv4 to ICMPv6

For all ICMPv4 messages, the translator has to compute a valid checksum, because it is required with ICMPv6. In addition to this, the type values have to be translated and, for error messages, the included IP header also needs to be translated. Table 10-3 shows the translation in ICMP query messages.

Table 10-3. Translation of ICMPv4 query messages

Message type	Translation
Echo and Echo Reply (types 8 and 0)	Adjust the type to 128 or 129, respectively and adjust the ICMP checksum to take the type change into account and include the ICMPv6 pseudoheader.
Information Request/Reply (types 15 and 16)	Obsoleted in ICMPv6. Silently discard.
Timestamp and Timestamp Reply (types 13 and 14)	Obsoleted in ICMPv6. Silently discard.
Address Mask Request/Reply (types 17 and 18)	Obsoleted in ICMPv6. Silently discard.
Router Advertisement (type 9)	Single hop message. Silently discard.
Router Solicitation (type 10)	Single hop message. Silently discard.
Unknown ICMPv4 types	Silently discard.

IGMP messages are single-hop messages and should not be forwarded over routers. Therefore they do not require translation and are silently discarded.

Table 10-4 shows the translation for ICMP error messages.

Table 10-4. Translation of ICMPv4 error messages

Message type	Translation
Destination Unreachable (type 3)	For all codes not listed here, the type is set to one.
Code 0/1, Network/Host Unreachable	Type 1, Code 0 - No Route to Destination.
Code 2, Protocol Unreachable	Type 4, Code 1 - Port Unreachable. Make the pointer point to the IPv6 Next Header field.
Code 3, Port Unreachable	Type 1, Code 4 - Port Unreachable.
Code 4, Fragmentation needed but DF set	Type 2, Code 0 - Packet Too Big. The MTU field needs to be recalculated to reflect the difference between the IPv4 and the IPv6 header sizes.
Code 5, Source Route Failed	Type 1, Code 0 - No Route to Destination (note that source routes are not translated).

Table 10-4. Translation of ICMPv4 error messages (continued)

Message type	Translation
Code 6, 7, Destination Network/Host Unknown	Type 1, Code 0 - No Route to Destination.
Code 8, Source Route Isolated	Type 1, Code 0 - No Route to Destination.
Code 9, 10, Communication with Destination Administratively Prohibited	Type 1, Code 1 - Communication with Destination Administratively Prohibited.
Code 11, 12, Network/Host Unreachable for TOS	Type 1, Code 0 - No Route to Destination.
Redirect, Type 5	Single hop message. Silently discard.
Source Quench, Type 4	Obsoleted in ICMPv6. Silently discard.
Time Exceeded, Type 11	Type 3 - Time Exceeded. Code field unchanged.
Parameter Problem, Type 12	Type 4 - Parameter Problem. The pointer needs to be updated to point to the corresponding field in the translated and included IP header.

The IP header included in an ICMP error message is translated using the same mechanisms discussed above.

Translating IPv6 to IPv4

This process is not much different from the translation discussed previously. In this case, the translator knows that it has to translate from IPv6 to IPv4 based on the IPv4-mapped destination address. It removes the IPv6 header and replaces it with an IPv4 header. The minimum MTU for IPv4 is 68 bytes; the minimum MTU for IPv6 is 1280 bytes. If a translator receives a packet for an IPv4 network with a smaller MTU, it creates 1280 byte packets and fragments them after translation. Table 10-5 shows the translation for the IPv4 header.

Table 10-5. Translated IPv4 header

Header field	Information
Version	4
Internet Header Length	5 (no options)
TOS and Precedence	All 8 bits from the Traffic Class are copied.
Total Length	Payload Length from the IPv6 header plus length of the IPv4 header.
Identification	Zero
Flags	More Fragments Flag set to zero; Don't Fragment Flag set to one.
Fragment Offset	Zero
Time to Live	Hop Limit value copied from the IPv6 header. Since the translator is a router, the value has to be decremented by one (either before or after translation) and checked on the value. If zero, an ICMP TTL exceeded message has to be generated.
Protocol	Next Header field copied from the IPv6 header.

Table 10-5. Translated IPv4 header (continued)

Header field	Information
Header Checksum	Computed after generation of the IPv4 header.
Source Address	If the IPv6 address is an IPv4-translated address, the low-order 32 bits of the IPv4-translated source address are copied to the IPv4 Source Address field. Otherwise, NAT will assign an IPv4 address out of the configured address pool and copy it into the IPv4 Source Address field.
Destination Address	The low-order 32 bits of the IPv4-mapped destination address are copied to the IPv4 Destination Address field.
Options	If an IPv6 Hop-by-Hop Options header, Destination Options header, or a routing header with the Segments Left field equal to zero are present, they are not translated. In this case, the Total Length field and the Protocol field have to be adjusted accordingly. If a routing header is present with a Segments Left field of non-zero, an ICMPv6 Parameter Problem message (Type 4, Code 0) has to be returned to the sender with the Pointer field pointing to the first byte of the Segment Left field.

If the IPv6 packet contains a Fragment header, the respective fields are translated as shown in Table 10-6.

Table 10-6. Translating the Fragment header

Header field	Information
Total Length	Payload Length from the IPv6 header, minus 8 for the Fragment header, plus the size of the IPv4 header.
Identification	Copied from the low-order 16 bits in the Identification field in the Fragment header.
Flags	More Fragment flag copied from the M flag in the Fragment header. The Don't Fragment flag is set to zero so IPv4 routers can fragment the packet.
Fragment Offset	Fragment Offset field copied from IPv6 header.
Protocol	Next Header value copied from the Fragment header.

Translating ICMPv6 to ICMPv4

Again, similar changes must be done when translating from ICMPv4 to ICMPv6, just in reverse order. Table 10-7 lists the details.

Table 10-7. Translation of ICMPv6 informational messages

Message type	Translation
Echo Request and Echo Reply (types 128 and 129)	Adjust the type to 8 and 0, respectively, and adjust the ICMP checksum to take the type change into account and to exclude the ICMPv6 pseudoheader.
MLD Multicast Listener Query/Report/Done (types 130, 131, 132)	Single-hop message. Silently discard.
Neighbor Discover Messages (types 133 to 137)	Single-hop message. Silently discard.
Unknown Informational Messages	Silently discard.

Table 10-7. Translation of ICMPv6 informational messages (continued)

Message type	Translation
Address Mask Request/Reply (types 17 and 18)	Obsoleted in ICMPv6. Silently discard.
Router Advertisement (type 9)	Single hop message. Silently discard.
Router Solicitation (type 10)	Single hop message. Silently discard.
Unknown ICMPv4 types	Silently discard.

Error messages are treated as shown in Table 10-8.

Table 10-8. Translation of ICMPv6 error messages

Message type	Translation
Destination Unreachable (type 1)	Set the Type field to 3 and the code field as follows:
Type 1, Code 0 - No Route to Destination	Type 3, Code 1 - Host Unreachable.
Type 1, Code 1 - Communication with Destination Administratively Prohibited	Type 3, Code 10 - Communication with Destination Administratively Prohibited.
Type 1, Code 2 - Beyond Scope of Source Address	Type 3, Code 1 - Host Unreachable.
Type 1, Code 3 - Address Unreachable	Type 3, Code 1 - Host Unreachable.
Type 1, Code 4 - Port Unreachable	Type 3, Code 3 - Port Unreachable.
Packet Too Big (type 2)	Type 3, Code 4 - Fragmentation Needed but DF set. The MTU field needs to be adjusted for the difference between the IPv6 and IPv4 headers, including a Fragment header, if present.
Time Exceeded (type 3)	Type 11, Code field unchanged.
Parameter Problem (type 4)	If the Code field is set to 1, translate to a Type 3, Code 2 - Protocol Unreachable, otherwise to Type 12, Code 0 - Parameter Problem. The pointer needs to be updated to point to the corresponding field in the translated and included IP header.
Unknown Error messages	Silently discard.

Again, the IP header included in the ICMP error message is translated following the same rules so the destination host can understand the information.

Comparison

Now that you know the available techniques, I'll summarize them by listing advantages and disadvantages. This summary should help you determine which way to go.

Dual Stack

This technique is easy to use and flexible. Hosts can communicate with IPv4 hosts using IPv4 or communicate with IPv6 hosts using IPv6. As soon as everything has been upgraded to IPv6, the IPv4 stack can simply be disabled or removed. Disadvantages of this technique include the following: you have two separate protocol stacks running, so you need additional CPU power and memory on the host. All the tables are kept twice, one per protocol stack. Also, you need to deal with different commands for each protocol because each command has a different set of command-line options. A DNS resolver running on a dual-stack host must be capable of resolving both IPv4 and IPv6 address types. Generally, all applications running on the dual-stack host must be capable of determining whether this host is communicating with an IPv4 or IPv6 peer. If you are using dual-stack techniques, make sure that you have firewalls in place that protect not only your IPv4 network, but also your IPv6 network.

Tunneling

Tunneling allows you to migrate to IPv6 just the way you want to. There is no specific upgrade order that needs to be followed. You can even upgrade single hosts or single subnets within your corporate network and connect separated IPv6 clouds through tunnels. You don't need your ISP to support IPv6 in order to access remote IPv6 networks because you can tunnel through their IPv4 infrastructure.

The disadvantages are already known from other tunneling techniques used in the past. Additional load is put on the router. The tunnel entry and exit points need time and CPU power for encapsulating and decapsulating packets. They also represent single points of failure. Troubleshooting gets more complex because you might run into hop count or MTU size issues, as well as fragmentation problems.

NAT

This technique should be used only if no other technique is possible and should be viewed as a temporary solution until one of the other techniques can be implemented. The disadvantages are that it does not support the advanced features of IPv6, such as end-to-end security. It poses limitations on the design topology because replies have to come through the same NAT router from which they were sent. The NAT router is a single point of failure, and flexible routing mechanisms cannot be used. All applications that have IP addresses in the payload of the packets will stumble. The advantage of this method is that it allows IPv6 hosts to communicate directly with IPv4 hosts and vice versa.

When to Choose IPv6

A golden rule says never to touch a running system. This also applies to your IPv4 networks. As long as they do what you need them to do, let them run. But when an IPv4 network hits the limits for some reason (if you run out of public address space, if you run into limitations because of using NAT and private addresses and need end-to-end security, or if you need to extend your network by a whole new segment), choose IPv6. IPv6 is mature enough to be used in corporate and commercial networks. Do not make high investments in new setups or complex configurations for IPv4 anymore. When you reach the point where this would be needed, choose the future and invest in IPv6. It is recommended that companies that do business on the Internet today look at the technology as soon as possible. IPv6 is inevitable and it is important that IT staff and engineers get up to speed in time. There are a number of companies that have experience in migrating to IPv6 and offer consulting and training services; one example is Native6Group at *http://www.native6group.com*.

Vendor Support

The techniques described in this chapter do not help if your hardware and applications do not support IPv6. The number of vendors who support IPv6 is growing daily. To give you a list here doesn't make sense. By the time this book hits the shelves, this list would be outdated. In our test lab, we have used the implementations of Microsoft (Windows 2000 research stack and Windows XP built in stack), Suse Linux 7.0, Sun Solaris, and Cisco. These vendors have been helpful in providing information and supporting us. Many other vendors have stacks ready. The following sites can help you get updated information when you need it:

For information on implementations that are updated to IPv6, refer to *http://www.ipv6.org/impl/index.html*. Another good site for this kind of information can be found at *http://playground.sun.com/pub/ipng/html/ipng-implementations.html*. For a list of IPv6-enabled applications, go to *http://www.ipv6.org/v6-apps.html*.

CHAPTER 11

Get Your Hands Dirty

This chapter is your quick-start guide to using different IPv6 stacks. Mastering technology is not done by reading about it, so get your hands dirty and play with it. You have plenty of options.

This chapter offers an overview of some common stacks that can be used. It is not a complete list. I decided to focus on Windows 2000, Sun Solaris, and a Linux implementation in the beginning. During the later stages of the writing process, Windows XP came out, so I added information about Windows XP's IPv6 stack. This chapter describes where to get the stacks, how to install them, and lists the most common utilities for configuring and troubleshooting IPv6. Once you are familiar with one of the stacks, you will have no problems applying your know-how to other stacks.

A good overview of different implementations, with links, can be found at *http://www.ipv6.org/impl/index.html*.

Sun Solaris

IPv6 support is available on Solaris 8. This is the version I used in my test network. The Solaris 8 software is downloadable from Sun Microsystem's homepage, or you can buy a CD.

To find information, whitepapers, FAQs, and the download page for cool utilities for Sun's IPv6 stack, go to *http://www.sun.com/solaris/ipv6*. There is, for instance, a tool called Socket Scrubber, which is written for developers and can identify lines of IPv4 socket code or review IPv6 code in your applications. It is downloadable for free and helps you port your applications to IPv6.

Enable IPv6 and Get Started

If you want to use IPv6 on Sun Solaris, you must enable it during the OS installation. For the configuration of the IPv6 address, a choice between static or automatic address definition is possible. Automatic means that the system will use neighbor discovery to obtain an IPv6 address; static means that the administrator defines the IPv6 address manually. In my tests, I used the automatic address configuration. All IPv6-specific adapter configuration is stored in */etc/hostname6.<interface>*.

Utilities

All utilities described below are available after the Solaris 8 installation and have IPv6 support. The online documentation contains a good description of the command-line utilities and possible parameters.

If you want to display IPv6 related information by default when using the tools *ifconfig* and *netstat*, you need to change the file */etc/default/inet_type* and add the entry DEFAULT_IP=BOTH.

ifconfig
> There are new parameters available to get IPv6-related adapter information. The man pages show all the options.

netstat
> In addition to IPv4 information, it is possible to display IPv6 information. Use the following switch: *netstat –f inet6*. If you changed the default *inet* type, *netstat –p* displays the ARP table for IPv4 and the neighbor cache for IPv6. *netstat –rn* displays the routing table for IPv4 and IPv6.

route
> Route can be used for both routes, IPv4 and IPv6. Use the option *–inet6* to perform operations on IPv6 routes or to change the default *inet* type.

ping, traceroute
> *ping* and *traceroute* used with IPv6 addresses or IPv6 DNS record entries display IPv6-related information.

snoop
> Snoop is a well-known network analysis tool included with Solaris. The latest version has IPv6 support. IPv6 traffic can be viewed by using *snoop ip6*.

A lot of good information about Solaris system administration is available at *http://www.sun.com/bigadmin/*.

Linux

There are a number of different Linux distributions on the market, all based on the same kernel, identified by its version number. The Linux kernel has supported IPv6 since version 2.2.x.

In my test network, I used the SuSE distribution of Linux. I liked the user-friendly installation, and the engineers at SuSE were very supportive in getting me started with the IPv6 issues.

Find more information about the Linux standard and the different available implementations at *http://www.linuxbase. org*. For an IPv6-specific Linux site, refer to *http://www. linux-ipv6.org*.

Where to Get Linux

Most of the common Linux distributions can be downloaded from the Internet, but they can also be purchased from the sales channels of their respective makers, including CDs and manuals. It is usually advisable to buy a distribution because the download files are rather big (100–500 MB).

Installation

I used SuSE Linux Version 7.2. If you do a standard installation of this version, it will be based on the Linux kernel Version 2.4, and the IPv6 protocol stack will automatically be enabled in addition to the IPv4 stack. The current *inet* daemon supports IPv6 and is responsible for all networking tasks, such as FTP, telnet, or finger. The configuration file */etc/inetd.conf* must be changed for IPv6 support. Consult the *inetd* man page for more information.

To find the latest kernel, check with your distributor's support site.

After going through this procedure, I had a Linux host that talks IPv4 and IPv6.

Utilities

There are two packages that you need to download and install to get the cool utilities for Linux. One of them is *net-tools*. This package contains the source code for utilities such as *ifconfig*, *netstat*, *route*, and *hostname*. Another package you'll need is called *iputils* and can usually be found on your distribution CD. It contains *ping6*, *tracepath6*, and *traceroute6*.

> For further information on how to install the utilities and compile the source code, go to *http://www.bieringer.de/linux/ IPv6/*. This is a cool site where you will also find lots of useful information on Linux and protocols. If you need the most current packages for *net-tools*, go to *http://www.freshmeat. net*.

The following is a short description of some of the utilities that can be helpful when working with IPv6. The utilities mentioned here are the ones I have used most when working in my lab. As you probably know, the online help for all Linux utilities is very detailed and there are two ways you can access it:

Man pages
> The man pages can be accessed by entering *man utilityname*, where *utilityname* is the name of the utility. It contains all information about available options and detailed descriptions.

Help screens
> Help screens can be accessed by entering the utility name with the *parameter --help*. For instance, to get the information for *ifconfig*, enter *ifconfig --help*. This screen is like a short version of the man pages.

The following utilities are interesting and new for IPv6:

ifconfig
> This tool is used for general network configuration of the Linux box. If you are using SuSE 7.2, the installed *inetd* supports IPv6. Using the address flag [address family] lets you switch between IPv4 (*inet*) and IPv6 (*inet6*) address families. You can use *ifconfig* to start and stop the interface and to view many different kinds of statistics.

netstat
> The *netstat* version on your Linux box after the installation does support IPv6. However, by installing *net-tools*, you get the most current version. The *netstat* tool provides a lot of useful options and statistics, such as port information, routing table, and interface table. For all IPv6-related information, you need the *--inet6* flag.

route

If you enter *route* without any parameters, it displays the routing table for IPv4. For viewing the IPv6 routing table, add the flag *--inet6*.

ping6, traceroute6, tracepath6, hostname

Most of the utilities for IPv6 are similar to the utilities that we know from IPv4. Instead of using *ping* or *traceroute*, I now use *ping6* or *traceroute6*. Refer to the man pages for details. Instead of using *traceroute6*, try *tracepath6*. It not only displays the path, but also includes MTU information.

 For general Linux resources, go to *http://www.linux.org* and *http://www.kernel.org*.

Microsoft

Microsoft released the first research IPv6 stack in 1998. It runs on Windows NT 4.0 and Windows 2000. It does not work on Windows 95/98. If you have Windows 95/98 or Windows ME or SE, you can use Trumpet's Winsock or consider upgrading to Windows XP, which includes an IPv6 stack. If you have the choice, I strongly recommend that you play with the Windows XP version. It is currently the most developed Microsoft stack and has many features that the research stack for Windows NT and Windows 2000 do not have. Also, when you install Windows XP, you get a great online help with very thorough information about IPv6 and how to use the stack and a guide for setting up a test environment.

Windows NT 4.0 and Windows 2000

The installation is pretty simple—the stack is stable, and it can even be used as a router. This is obviously not its primary use, but it is a nice feature if you want to play with it.

To find information, FAQs, and the download page for the latest versions of Microsoft's IPv6 stack, go to *http://www.microsoft.com/ipv6/*.

Installation

To install the IPv6 stack, run *setup.exe* from the location to which you extracted the IPv6 files. Then go to the Network and Dial-Up Connection window, click on the connection where you want to add the IPv6 protocol and click on Properties. Choose Install → Protocol, click Add, and select the IPv6 Protocol.

The Microsoft IPv6 Protocol is automatically added to all Ethernet interfaces on your computer. The setup program copies the protocol files from the location where you extracted the IPv6 Technology Preview files into the appropriate Windows NT or Windows 2000 directories. It also modifies setup information files so that the Microsoft IPv6 Protocol is in the list of available protocols. The IPv6 protocol driver (*tcpip6.sys*) is installed in the *%systemroot%\system32\drivers* directory. The Winsock helper dynamically linked library for the INET6 address family (*wship6.dll*) and all applications and tools (*ipv6.exe, ping6.exe, tracert6.exe, ttcp.exe,* etc.) are installed in the *%systemroot%\system32* directory.

If you have a Windows 2000 host with SP1 installed, it is no problem to install the IPv6 stack. If you have SP2 already installed on Windows 2000, the IPv6 stack will not install without a modification. You have to unpack the IPv6 files and edit the *hotfix.inf* file so that the line *NtServicePackVersion=256* reads *NtServicePackVersion=512*. Then run *hotfix.exe*.

Utilities

The following is a short description of new or modified command-line utilities available for configuring the stack, displaying statistics, and gathering troubleshooting information.

Net.exe

Net.exe can be used to stop and start the IPv6 protocol. *Net.exe* has many subcommands, each with its own set of arguments and options. Only the following commands are directly relevant to IPv6:

net stop tcpip6

This command stops the IPv6 protocol and unloads it from memory. The command fails if any application has open IPv6 sockets.

net start tcpip6

This command starts the IPv6 protocol if it was stopped. If a new *Tcpip6.sys* driver file is present in the *%systemroot%\System32\ Drivers* directory, it is loaded.

Ipv6.exe

All Microsoft IPv6 protocol configurations in Windows NT and Windows 2000 are done with the *Ipv6.exe* tool, which is primarily used for querying and configuring interfaces, addresses, caches, and routes. *Ipv6. exe* has many subcommands, each with its own set of arguments and options.

You can use *Ipv6.exe* to display interface information, control interface attributes such as forwarding and advertising options, delete interfaces, display or flush cache entries, add or remove unicast or anycast address assignments, display the site prefix table and routing table, add or remove routes in the routing table, and much more. For instance, *ipv6 – nc* displays the neighbor cache, *ipv6 –rc* displays the route cache, and *ipv6 –rt* displays the routing table. For a list of arguments and options, use *ipv6 /?*.

Ping6.exe

The Microsoft IPv6 stack installs the *Ping6.exe* tool, an equivalent to the *Ping.exe* tool supplied with IPv4 in Windows. To ping an IPv6 host, you need to use *ping6.exe*. For example, to ping Host A with the IPv6 address fe80::260:97ff:fe02:6ea5, use the command *ping6 fe80::260: 97ff:fe02:6ea5*.

When pinging a link-local or site-local address, it is recommended that you specify the scope ID to make the destination address unambiguous. The notation to specify the scope ID is *address%scope-ID*. For link-local addresses, the scope ID is equal to the interface number as displayed in the *ipv6 if* command. For site-local addresses, the scope ID is equal to the site number as displayed in the *ipv6 if* command. For example, to send Echo Request messages to Host A with scope ID 4, use the command *ping6 fe80::260:97ff:fe02:6ea5%4*.

tracert6.exe

This is the IPv6 equivalent to *tracert.exe* used for IPv4. It sends ICMPv6 Echo Request messages with increasing values in the Hop Limit field to discover the path traveled by IPv6 packets between a source and a destination.

Ipsec6.exe

Configuration of IPSEC policies and security associations for the Microsoft IPv6 protocol is done with *Ipsec6.exe*. *Ipsec6.exe* has many subcommands, each with its own set of arguments and options. You can use it to display security policies and associations, create files used to configure security policies and associations, and add and delete security policies and associations. Check the online help for details.

6to4cfg.exe

6to4cfg.exe automates 6to4 configuration on Windows NT and Windows 2000 by discovering your globally routable IPv4 address and creating a 6to4 prefix. If you don't specify a relay agent, it will autoconfigure to use Microsoft's relay agent. To learn how 6to4 works, refer to Chapter 10.

checkv4.exe

This tool is used to scan source-code files to identify code that needs to be changed to support IPv6. This is a developer tool and is meant to be used on C/C++ source files. *checkv4.exe* displays the line number and a message recommending how the code should be changed.

checkv4.exe is found in the *bin* folder in the location where the IPv6 Technology Preview files were extracted. *checkv4.exe* is not copied to the *%systemroot%\system32* directory.

Windows XP

The IPv6 stack that comes with Windows XP is more developed than the research stack for Windows NT 4.0 and Windows 2000. It is prerelease code and is intended for developers and test networks. Microsoft encourages developers to port their applications to support IPv6. If you have a choice, use Windows XP to play with IPv6.

The IPv6 protocol for Windows XP in the current version includes the following features:

- 6to4 tunneling
- ISATAP
- 6over4 tunneling
- Anonymous addresses
- Site prefixes in router advertisements
- DNS support
- IPSEC support
- Application support
- RPC support
- Static router support

Installation and configuration

To install IPv6 on Windows XP, simply open a command prompt and enter *ipv6 install*. It does not appear in the list of components in the properties of a LAN connection in Network Connections, if you work with the first release of Windows XP. If you want to verify that IPv6 is installed on an XP host, type *ipv6 if* or *netsh int ipv6 show interface* at the command line. This displays interface information. With SP1 for Windows XP, it will not even be necessary to use the *ipv6 install* command anymore. IPv6 will appear in the list of available protocols to be installed and, after installation, will show in the list of installed protocols.

Utilities

Most utilities described for Windows 2000 are the same with Windows XP. For instance, you can use *ping6* and *tracert6* or use *ipv6 –rc* to display the route cache, *ipv6 –nc* to display the neighbor cache, and *ipv6 –rt* to view the route table. IPv6-specific options have been added to *netstat* for Windows XP. Also new for XP is the IPv6 context in *netsh*, which is a command-line utility that you can use to display or modify the network configuration and display all sorts of statistics. It also provides a scripting feature that allows you to run a group of commands in batch mode. Pretty cool; have a look at it. You must start *netsh* from the command-line prompt and change to the context that contains the command you want to use. The contexts that are available depend on which networking components are installed. Figure 11-1 is a screenshot of *netsh* in action.

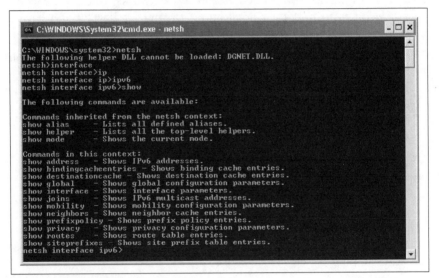

Figure 11-1. The netsh command

From the command prompt, I entered *netsh* to start the utility. Then I started to change to the context where I can work with my IPv6 configuration. First, I changed to the context *interface*, then to the context *ip*, and finally to the context *ipv6*. The command *show* always returns a list of commands that are available in the context where I use it.

Figure 11-2 shows the output of two options that might be helpful when troubleshooting.

The commands I used here are taken from the list shown in Figure 11-1. First, I used *show global* and received some default configuration parame-

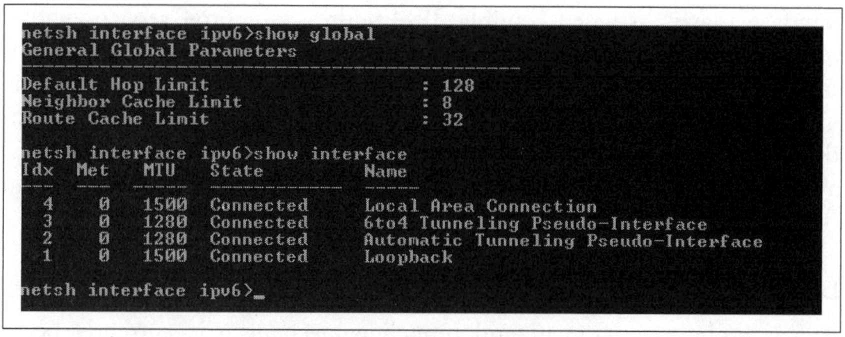

```
netsh interface ipv6>show global
General Global Parameters
-------------------------------------------------
Default Hop Limit                  : 128
Neighbor Cache Limit               : 8
Route Cache Limit                  : 32

netsh interface ipv6>show interface
Idx  Met    MTU  State         Name
---  ---  -----  -----------   --------
  4    0   1500  Connected     Local Area Connection
  3    0   1280  Connected     6to4 Tunneling Pseudo-Interface
  2    0   1280  Connected     Automatic Tunneling Pseudo-Interface
  1    0   1500  Connected     Loopback

netsh interface ipv6>_
```

Figure 11-2. Using netsh for IP and interface information

ters valid on this host. Then I used *show interface* and got an overview of my interfaces, including MTU size, connection state, and name. This host has two pseudointerfaces used for tunneling IPv6 over an IPv4 infrastructure.

Note that the *ipv6* command will eventually be phased out in future releases of the IPv6 stack and completely replaced by *netsh*. To get the information for *ipv6 if*, you have to replace the command with *netsh int ipv6 show interface*, and replace *ipv6 –rt* with *netsh int ipv6 show routes*.

6to4

6to4cfg.exe has been replaced by *netsh*. If you want to configure your XP host for 6to4, do not run *6to4cfg.exe* anymore. Your command is *netsh interface ipv6 6to4*.

Microsoft's 6to4 service currently supports the following functionality:

- It automatically configures 6to4 addresses on an interface named 6to4 Tunneling Pseudointerface (interface ID 3) for all public IPv4 addresses that are assigned to interfaces on the computer.

- It automatically creates a 2002::/16 route that forwards all 6to4 traffic with the 6to4 Tunneling Pseudointerface (interface ID 3). All traffic forwarded by this host to 6to4 destinations is encapsulated in an IPv4 header.

- It automatically performs a DNS query for the name *6to4.ipv6.microsoft.com* to obtain the IPv4 address of the Microsoft 6to4 relay router on the Internet. You can use the *netsh interface ipv6 6to4 set relay* command to specify a different relay router.

If your host has a public IPv4 address, this configures it as a 6to4 host. A 6to4 host can perform its own tunneling to reach 6to4 hosts in other sites or hosts on the 6Bone. If Internet Connection Sharing (ICS) is enabled on an interface that is assigned a public IPv4 address, the 6to4 service enables routing on the private interface and sends Router Advertisements that contain 6to4 address prefixes based on the public IPv4 address of the public interface. The SLA ID in the 6to4 address prefix is set to the interface ID of the interface on which the advertisements are sent. Now this host can act as a 6to4 router that can encapsulate and forward 6to4 traffic to other hosts in the Internet and forward 6Bone traffic to a relay router in the Internet.

ISATAP

A new address assignment and tunneling mechanism is currently being defined that can be used for communication between IPv6/IPv4 nodes on an IPv4 network. The Internet draft on this mechanism is titled "Intra-Site Automatic Tunnel Addressing Protocol (ISATAP)." ISATAP is described in more detail in Chapter 10, and the draft can be found at *http://search.ietf. org/internet-drafts/draft-ietf-ngtrans-isatap-03.txt*. (The number for the draft may have increased by the time you go to get it, so you can search the index or just try increasing the number by one or a higher value.)

ISATAP addresses have the form `64BitPrefix:5EFE:w.x.y.z`. The `64BitPrefix` is any 64-bit prefix that is valid for IPv6 unicast addresses. `5EFE` is the globally unique interface identifier that is formed from the combination of the OUI assigned to the IANA (`00-00-5E`) and the type `FE`, which indicates that an embedded IPv4 address. `w.x.y.z` is a unicast IPv4 address.

The IPv6 protocol for Windows XP automatically configures the ISATAP address `FE80::5EFE:w.x.y.z` on the automatic tunneling pseudointerface for each IPv4 address that is assigned to the node. This link-local ISATAP address allows hosts to communicate over an IPv4 network by using one another's ISATAP addresses.

 The FAQ for IPv6 on Windows XP can be found at *http:// www.microsoft.com/windowsxp/pro/techinfo/administration/ ipv6/default.asp*.

One day a friend came to visit us at our office. He started his notebook to show us a presentation. I realized that the notebook was running Windows XP, one of the beta versions. I asked him if he would mind trying to configure it for IPv6 because I had heard that Windows XP has an IPv6 stack included. He didn't know that, but he was interested. So I went into the help files and immediately found the description of how to install the stack. Guess what: it took not even five minutes to configure this notebook for IPv6, connect it to our network, and *ping6* other IPv6 hosts.

Applications

I installed a few IPv6-enabled applications, such as Apache Web Server, Bind 9, and FTP and Telnet servers. To find current information about IPv6 applications, look at the IPv6 Forum homepage at *http://www.ipv6forum. org*. Click on the left side button for Implementations and choose IPv6 Applications. Another reference site for IPv6 application information is *http: //www.ipv6.org/v6-apps.html*. There are HTTP servers and clients, Telnet and FTP applications, chat and email software, firewalls, monitoring tools, and patch links. At *http://www.hs247.com*, you can also find a lot of useful information about IPv6 implementations on different operating systems, as well as IPv6-enabled applications for each operating system—enough to spend quite some time in your lab. And don't forget to send me some trace files.

The IPv6 Technology Preview for Windows 2000 and the Windows XP IPv6 stack contain a set of sample applications that you can use to experiment with IPv6-based traffic beyond the use of standard connection diagnostic tools such as *ping6* and *tracert6*. The following applications are provided:

HTTP client
> The new Internet extensions dynamic link library (DLL), *Wininet.dll*, provides IPv6 capability so that Windows-based Internet browsers, such as Microsoft Internet Explorer or Netscape Navigator, can make connections to both IPv4 and IPv6 web servers.

FTP client
> The new FTP client, *Ftp.exe*, is capable of establishing FTP sessions with IPv4 and IPv6 FTP servers.

Telnet client
> The new Telnet client, *Telnet.exe*, is capable of establishing Telnet sessions with IPv4 and IPv6 Telnet servers.

Telnet server
> The new Telnet server, *Tlntsvr.exe*, is capable of establishing Telnet sessions with IPv4 and IPv6 Telnet clients.

For those of you who love trace files and work with Network Monitor, note that the current version of Network Monitor Version 2 supports the decode of IPv6.

Microsoft is working on IPv6-enabled versions of Internet Information Server (IIS), file sharing, and DNS over IPv6 transport. They are announced for 2002. Please refer to Microsoft's IPv6 site for current information.

Find FTP, Telnet, and HTTP trace files in Chapter 9.

Cisco Router

I had a Cisco router with the latest updates in my lab. Cisco provided the router to support this book, so I will describe the configuration on a Cisco router. Configuration of other routers might be fairly similar. If you are familiar with your routing hardware, you will figure out how to do it or your vendor can provide the necessary information.

Cisco's IPv6 support begins with the Cisco IOS 12.2(2) Technology release. Make sure you are using the latest release because new features will be supported with every update. There is detailed documentation for IPv6 on Cisco's web site, where you can find an overview, configuration descriptions, and commands. For a detailed explanation of configuring your Cisco router for IPv6, refer to the following page: *http://www.cisco.com/univercd/cc/td/doc/product/software/ios122/122newft/122t/122t2/ipv6/ftipv6c.htm*. This link relates to the current IOS. If you are using a later release, you might have to find a different link on the Cisco web site.

Figure 11-3 shows the interface configuration in my lab.

```
Cisco - HyperTerminal                                              _|□|x|
File  Edit  View  Call  Transfer  Help

Enter configuration commands, one per line.  End with CNTL/Z.
client(config)#
client(config)#interface ethernet 0/0
client(config-if)#ipv6 ?
IPv6 interface subcommands:
    address         Configure IPv6 address on interface
    enable          Enable IPv6 on interface
    mtu             Set IPv6 Maximum Transmission Unit
    nd              IPv6 interface Neighbor Discovery subcommands
    rip             Configure RIP routing protocol
    traffic-filter  Access control list for packets
    unnumbered      Configure IPv6 interface as unnumbered

client(config-if)#ipv6 nd ?
    managed-config-flag   Hosts should use DHCP for address config
    ns-interval           Set advertised NS retransmission interval
    other-config-flag     Hosts should use DHCP for non-address config
    prefix-advertisement  Configure IPv6 Routing Prefix Advertisement
    ra-interval           Set IPv6 Router Advertisement Interval
    ra-lifetime           Set IPv6 Router Advertisement Lifetime
    reachable-time        Set advertised reachability time
    suppress-ra           Suppress IPv6 Router Advertisements

client(config-if)#ipv6 nd

Connected 03:46:34    VT100    9600 8-N-1    SCROLL  CAPS  NUM  Capture  Print echo
```

Figure 11-3. Interface configuration on our Cisco router

First, I needed to enable IPv6 packet forwarding. This is not enabled by default (different from IPv4). It is done with the global command *ipv6 unicast-routing* (not shown on the screenshot). Next, I configured the interface Ethernet 0/0. By typing *IPv6 ?*, I received a list of available commands. From this screen, the IPv6 address can be configured, as well as options for linking MTU, neighbor discovery, routing, and filters. The command *IPv6 nd ?* displays the options available for the configuration of neighbor discovery. From this screen, you can configure flags to specify whether hosts on this link should use DHCP for address-related or non-address-related information and different intervals, such as the router advertisement interval. The subnet prefix and the lifetime advertised in Router Advertisement messages are also configured here. I made the first configuration steps and set this router up as a 6to4 tunnel with the Microsoft 6to4 relay router as tunnel destination.

Here are some interesting ND commands that you can use on your Cisco router. This is not a complete list, but it should help you get started and give an idea of how you can configure your routers.

ipv6 nd dad attempts <number>
> Configures the number of Duplicate Address Detection (DAD) and Neighbor Solicitation messages to send before considering an address unique. DAD can be disabled by specifying *ipv6 nd dad attempts 0*.

ipv6 nd ra-interval <seconds>
> Configures the interval between IPv6 Router Advertisement transmissions from this interface. The value for this should be less than or equal to the IPv6 Router Lifetime if this is a default router. The default is 200 seconds. To prevent synchronization with other IPv6 nodes, the actual value used should be randomly adjusted to within plus or minus 20 percent of the specified value.

ipv6 nd ra-lifetime <seconds>
> Configures the lifetime of a Router Advertisement. This value is included in all IPv6 Router Advertisements sent out this interface. If the router is not a default router, this will have a value of zero. If the router is a default router, this value will be non-zero and should not be less than the minimum Router Advertisement interval. The default value is 1,800 seconds.

[no] ipv6 nd suppress-ra
> Controls transmission of IPv6 Router Advertisements on the interface. The default is to send Router Advertisments (RAs) on Ethernet, FDDI, or Token Ring interfaces if IPv6 unicast routing is enabled. Use the command *ipv6 nd supress-ra* to turn off RAs on LAN interfaces. On other

types of interfaces, the default is never to send an RA. Use the command *no ipv6 nd suppress-ra* to send RAs on interfaces such as serial or tunnel interfaces

[no] ipv6 nd prefix <prefix> | default, [[<valid-lifetime> <preferred-lifetime>] | [at <valid-date> <preferred-date>] [off-link] [no-autoconfig]]

By default, all prefixes configured as addresses on the interface are advertised in Router Advertisements. This command allows control over the individual parameters per prefix, including whether the prefix should be advertised. The *default* keyword can be used to set default parameters for all prefixes. A date can be set for prefix expiration. The valid and preferred lifetimes are counted down in real time. When the expiration date is reached, the prefix is no longer advertised.

[no] ipv6 nd managed-config-flag

Defaults to OFF. When OFF, Router Advertisements sent from this interface have the Managed Address Configuration Flag turned off. Hosts are thus permitted to use IPv6 stateless autoconfiguration to create global unicast addresses for themselves.

For a complete list of router configuration commands, refer to your Cisco documentation. For a discussion of routing protocols, refer to Chapter 8.

The next step I performed was to verify my interface configuration. Figure 11-4 shows the output.

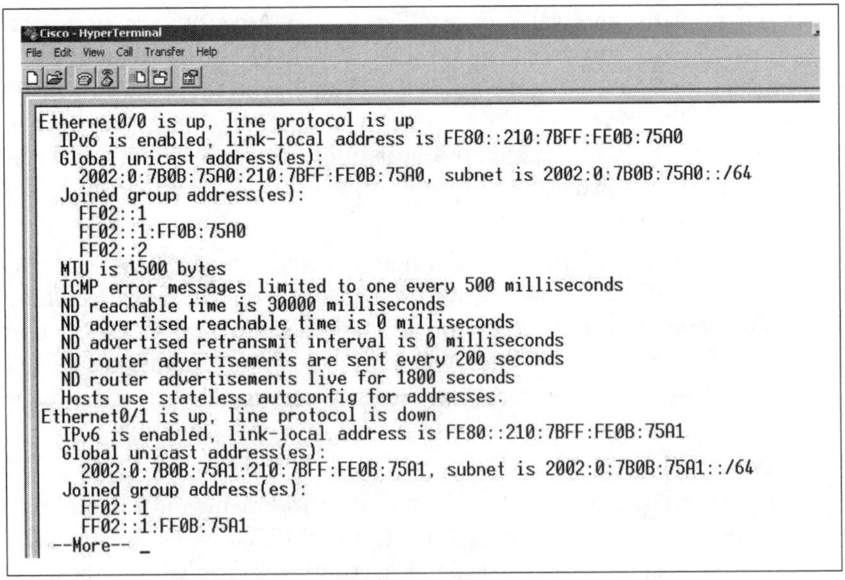
Cisco - HyperTerminal
File Edit View Call Transfer Help
Ethernet0/0 is up, line protocol is up
IPv6 is enabled, link-local address is FE80::210:7BFF:FE0B:75A0
Global unicast address(es):
2002:0:7B0B:75A0:210:7BFF:FE0B:75A0, subnet is 2002:0:7B0B:75A0::/64
Joined group address(es):
FF02::1
FF02::1:FF0B:75A0
FF02::2
MTU is 1500 bytes
ICMP error messages limited to one every 500 milliseconds
ND reachable time is 30000 milliseconds
ND advertised reachable time is 0 milliseconds
ND advertised retransmit interval is 0 milliseconds
ND router advertisements are sent every 200 seconds
ND router advertisements live for 1800 seconds
Hosts use stateless autoconfig for addresses.
Ethernet0/1 is up, line protocol is down
IPv6 is enabled, link-local address is FE80::210:7BFF:FE0B:75A1
Global unicast address(es):
2002:0:7B0B:75A1:210:7BFF:FE0B:75A1, subnet is 2002:0:7B0B:75A1::/64
Joined group address(es):
FF02::1
FF02::1:FF0B:75A1
--More--

Figure 11-4. Verifying the interface configuration

The output shows that I have a link-local address with the prefix FE80 and a global unicast address with the prefix 2002. The multicast group addresses joined are FF02::1 (all nodes), FF02::2 (all routers), and FF02::1:FF0B:75A0 (solicited-node multicast address). A list with all the configuration options follows, stating timers, intervals and address configuration options. Other tools that can be used on Cisco's current IOS are *ping*, *traceroute*, and a DNS client, all operational in IPv6.

Figure 11-5 shows the Router Advertisement in the trace file.

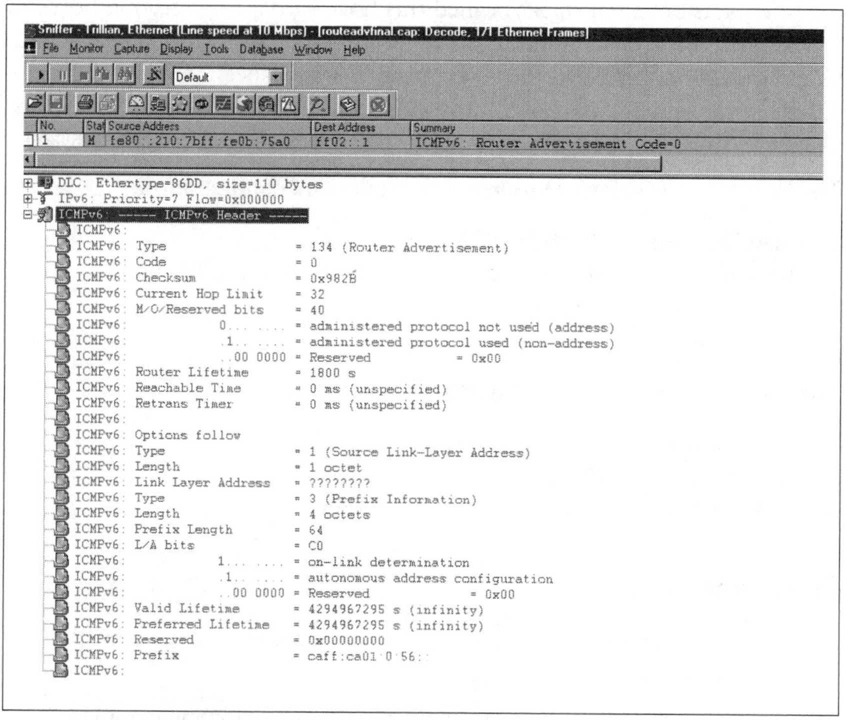

Figure 11-5. Router Advertisement in the trace file

The router sends the advertisement to the all-nodes multicast address ff02::1, so all nodes on the link receive it. Looking at this packet in the detail window, we can see how the router is configured. The hop limit is set to 32. DHCP (administered protocol) is not used for address information, but is used by the hosts to get non-address-related information through DHCP. The lifetime is configured for 1,800 seconds. The Type field is set to 3 for prefix information. The prefix length is 64 bits and the lifetime is set to infinite. The prefix advertised in this case is caff:ca01:0:56::/64. This is what I had configured on the router prior to taking this trace file. All hosts that boot on this link send out a Router Solicitation message and receive this

Router Advertisement. They learn all the parameters, including the prefix information from the router, and autoconfigure for an IPv6 address.

Description of the Tests

You will all go through these steps sooner or later, but I thought I'd share my first tries with you.

I started out with two hosts. One host is a Windows 2000 machine running the Microsoft Research stack. I called this host *Marvin*. The second host is a SuSE Linux host, also running an IPv6 stack. That host's name is *Ford*. Communication between the two hosts has not been an issue. In the absence of a router, they both autoconfigured for a link-local IPv6 address, using the 48-bit MAC identifier to build the address.

The Windows 2000 host *Marvin* has the following configuration:

MAC address	00-02-B3-1E-83-29
IPv4 address	62.2.84.115 (network range of our ISP, public IPv4 address)
IPv6 address	fe80::202:b3ff:fe1e:8329

The Linux host *Ford* has the following configuration:

MAC address	00-A0-24-C5-32-56
IPv4 address	192.168.0.99 (local network)
IPv6 address	fe80::2a0:24ff:fec5:3256

Pinging with IPv6

The first success was the verification of IPv6 communication by pinging each host as follows.

Open a command window on *Marvin* and issue the following command:

```
ping6 fe80::2a0:24ff:fec5:3256
```

Do you want to know what a ping with IPv6 looks like? Have a look at Figure 11-6.

Frame 1 is the Echo Request from *Ford*; Frame 2 is the Echo Reply from *Marvin*. The screenshot shows the two MAC addresses configured for a link-local IPv6 address (prefix fe80). Between the third and fourth byte of the MAC address, fffe is inserted. The Payload Length field tells us the length of the data carried after the header. Remember from Chapter 2 that this field calculates the length in a different way than we are used to from IPv4. The length of the IPv6 header is not included in the calculation. The Next

![Sniffer trace window]

```
Sniffer - Trillian, Ethernet (Line speed at 10 Mbps) - [pingtuxntsel1.cap: Decode, 2/2 Ethernet Frames]
File  Monitor  Capture  Display  Tools  Database  Window  Help

[W2K]

No. Stat Source Address        Dest Address            Summary
  1  M  fe80::2a0:24ff:fec5:3256  fe80::202:b3ff:fe1e:8329  ICMPv6: Echo Request Message Code=0
  2     fe80::202:b3ff:fe1e:8329  fe80::2a0:24ff:fec5:3256  ICMPv6: Echo Reply Message Code=0

DLC:  ------ DLC Header ------
 DLC:
 DLC:  Frame 2 arrived at  22:39:40.5049; frame size is 118 (0076 hex) bytes.
 DLC:  Destination = Station 3Com8 C53256
 DLC:  Source      = Station 0002B31E8329
 DLC:  Ethertype   = 86DD
 DLC:
IPv6:  ------ IPv6 Header ------
 IPv6:
 IPv6:  Version            = 6
 IPv6:  Priority           = 0 (Uncharacterized Traffic)
 IPv6:  Flow Label         = 0x000000
 IPv6:  Payload Length     = 64
 IPv6:  Next Header        = 58 (ICMPv6)
 IPv6:  Hop Limit          = 128
 IPv6:  Source address     = fe80::202:b3ff:fe1e:8329
 IPv6:  Destination address = fe80::2a0:24ff:fec5:3256
 IPv6:
ICMPv6:  ------ ICMPv6 Header ------
 ICMPv6:
 ICMPv6:  Type               = 129 (Echo Reply Message)
 ICMPv6:  Code               = 0
 ICMPv6:  Checksum           = 0xE75E
 ICMPv6:  Identifier         = 39979
 ICMPv6:  Sequence Number    = 0
 ICMPv6:  [56 Bytes of data]
 ICMPv6:
```

Figure 11-6. Trace file with an IPv6 ping

Header field is the same field as the Protocol Type field in IPv4. (The table
with all the protocol numbers can be found in Chapter 2.) Protocol number
58 specifies ICMPv6. The ICMPv6 header shows what type of ICMP message this is. (A table listing all the ICMP message types can be found in
Chapter 4.) Message type 128 is an Echo Request, and 129 is an Echo Reply.
The identifier and sequence number are used to match requests and replies.
All these fields are important when you need to troubleshoot.

To understand ICMPv6 and become familiar with the whole
range of functionality, refer to Chapter 4.

Pinging the 6Bone over the IPv4 Infrastructure

Pinging with IPv6 is cool, but the local ping quickly got boring. So I decided
that I wanted to ping some hosts on the 6Bone and, even more exciting, visit
some IPv6 web sites. Good thought, but how do I get out there? After all,
my ISP still has an IPv4-only infrastructure.

The Microsoft documentation helped me a step further with the description
of how to use *6to4cfg.exe* (replaced by *netsh* on Windows XP), a tool that is
used to configure tunnels for IPv6 to be carried over an existing IPv4 infrastructure. The requirement for this host is to have a public IPv4 address. The

6to4.exe tool autoconfigured a public IPv6 address for my host by using the public IPv4 address and turning it into a public IPv6 address.

Figure 11-7 shows the output of the *6to4cfg.exe* command when autoconfiguring.

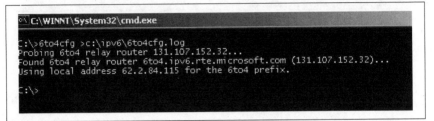

Figure 11-7. Using 6to4cfg.exe on a Windows 2000 host

The screenshot shows a relay router name of *6to4.ipv6.rte.microsoft.com* with an IPv4 address of 131.107.152.32. This is a router that can be used by anyone wishing to establish tunneled IPv6 communication to the 6Bone. It can be found in the Microsoft documentation about the IPv6 research stack. This host has an IPv6 address of 2002:836b:9820::836b:9820. *6to4cfg.exe* uses our local IPv4 address as prefix for 6to4 configuration.

Sometimes things work as expected, so I was able to capture the trace file in Figure 11-8. It shows how the IPv6 ICMP message is encapsulated into an IPv4 packet.

```
Sniffer - Trillian, Ethernet (Line speed at 10 Mbps) - [pingw2k6bone.cap: Decode, 1/8 Ethernet Frames]
 File  Monitor  Capture  Display  Tools  Database  Window  Help
 [  ] [ ] [  ] [M] [A] [W2K        ▼]
 [    ] [    ] [                              ] [  ] [  ] [  ]
 No. Stat Source Address         Dest Address              Summary
  1  M   2002:3e02:5473::3e02:5473  2002:836b:9820::836b:9820  ICMPv6: Echo Request Message Code=0
  2      2002:836b:9820::836b:9820  2002:3e02:5473::3e02:5473  ICMPv6: Echo Reply Message Code=0

 ⊞ DLC: Ethertype=0800, size=114 bytes
 ⊞ IP:    D=[131.107.152.32] S=[62.2.84.115] LEN=80 ID=26173
 ⊟ IPv6: ----- IPv6 Header -----
    IPv6:
    IPv6: Version              = 6
    IPv6: Priority             = 0 (Uncharacterized Traffic)
    IPv6: Flow Label           = 0x000000
    IPv6: Payload Length       = 40
    IPv6: Next Header          = 58 (ICMPv6)
    IPv6: Hop Limit            = 128
    IPv6: Source address       = 2002:3e02:5473::3e02:5473
    IPv6: Destination address  = 2002:836b:9820::836b:9820
    IPv6:
 ⊟ ICMPv6: ----- ICMPv6 Header -----
    ICMPv6:
    ICMPv6: Type               = 128 (Echo Request Message)
    ICMPv6: Code               = 0
    ICMPv6: Checksum           = 0x38E4
    ICMPv6: Identifier         = 0
    ICMPv6: Sequence Number    = 14
    ICMPv6: [32 Bytes of data]
    ICMPv6:
```

Figure 11-8. Pinging the 6bone through an IPv4 infrastructure

The summary line shows the Echo Request and the Echo Reply and the two beautiful IPv6 addresses. The IPv4 layer (highlighted in the detail window) shows a source address of 62.2.84.115, which is my local host's public IPv4 address used to access the Internet. The destination address of 131.107.152. 32 is the IPv4 address of Microsoft's relay router (refer back to Figure Figure 11-7). This router will know how to treat the ICMPv6 packet. The Protocol field in the IPv4 header, which cannot be seen in this screenshot, has the value 41 for IPv6.

Traceroute with IPv6

Skeptical as I am, I decided to check on *traceroute* next. Remember, *traceroute* uses Echo Request and Reply messages. By raising the hop limit by one for every packet, *traceroute* forces all routers on the path to a given destination to send back an ICMP Time Exceeded message. This way, the source host gets a list of all routers along the path. And it worked!

Note that *traceroute* on a Microsoft machine with the current IPv6 research stack is done by issuing *tracert6.exe*, as can be seen in Figure 11-9.

```
C:\>tracert6 3ffe:b00:c18:1::10

Tracing route to www.6bone.net [3ffe:b00:c18:1::10]
over a maximum of 30 hops:

  1    208 ms    323 ms    207 ms   2002:836b:9820::836b:9886
  2    256 ms    290 ms    271 ms   2002:836b:4179::836b:4179
  3    332 ms    329 ms    324 ms   6bone.merit.edu [3ffe:1c00::3]
  4    514 ms    571 ms    484 ms   3ffe:1cff:0:fb::2
  5    475 ms    543 ms    511 ms   www.6bone.net [3ffe:b00:c18:1::10]

Trace complete.
```

Figure 11-9. tracert6 to www.6bone.net

I issued *tracert6.exe* for 3ffe:b00:c18:1::10, which is the IPv6 address of *www.6bone.net*. The first hop 2002:836b:9820::836b:9886 is the endpoint of the tunnel. To get there, any number of hops is possible. *tracert6* cannot provide any information about the tunnel. Only the hops from the end point of the tunnel to the final destination are displayed.

Figure 11-10 shows how this same command looked when tracing it with Sniffer.

The first frame shows the first Echo Request sent to the final destination. This packet has a hop limit of 1. The first router in the path, 2002:836b: 9820::836b:9886, replies with a Time Exceeded message. Frames 2, 4, 6, 8,

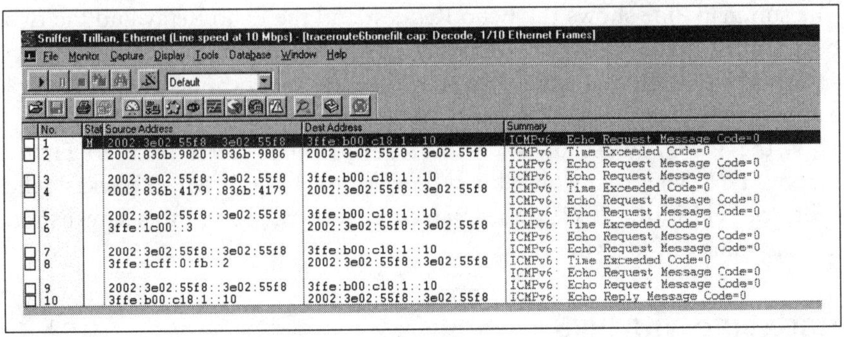

Figure 11-10. tracert6 to the 6Bone in the trace file

and 10 are the replies from the routers along the path to the destination. Compare the source address of these replies with the *tracert6* output in Figure 11-9, and hey, do they match?

Browsing with IPv6

After mastering *ping6* and *tracert6*, I wanted more. How about browsing web sites? I looked for web sites that are accessible over IPv6-only and tried to get there.

On the Microsoft platform, the new Internet extensions dynamic link library, *wininet.dll*, allows web browsers to access IPv6-enabled web servers. For example, *wininet.dll* is used by Microsoft Internet Explorer to make connections with web servers and view web pages. Internet Explorer uses IPv6 to download web pages in the following circumstances:

- The DNS query for the name of the web server in the URL returns an IPv6 address.

- On Windows NT and Windows 2000 with the IPv6 Technology Preview Stack, you can also use an URL in the format for literal IPv6 addresses, as described in RFC 2732. A literal IPv6 address in a URL is the address enclosed in square brackets. For example, to reach the web server at the IPv6 address 2010:836B:4179::836B:4179, the URL is *http:// [2010:836B:4179::836B:4179]*.

For a list of IPv6-accessible web sites, see *http://www.ipv6.org/v6-www.html*. Accessing IPv6-only web sites assumes that you have connectivity to the 6Bone.

Your browser cannot browse IPv6 web sites if it is configured to use a proxy server. When the browser is configured to use a proxy server, all name-resolution requests for web sites are forwarded to the proxy server. Unless the proxy server is IPv6-enabled, proxy-based requests for local or remote IPv6 web pages will not work.

From the list of IPv6-accessible web sites, we chose *http://ipv6.research.microsoft.com*. Figure 11-11 shows the welcome screen at this site.

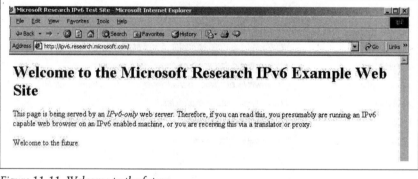

Figure 11-11. Welcome to the future

Let's hope that the future is a little more colorful than this welcome site. But our IPv6 stack is obviously ready to surf the web over IPv6.

I have done many more experiments in my lab, including FTP and Telnet. To see some of those trace files, refer to Chapter 9. But most importantly, play for yourself and make your own trace files. That's much more fun.

Vendor Support

A great number of vendors already support IPv6 and the list grows daily. I had to make a choice for my test network. There are many other vendors and operating systems that you can use to play with. The IPv6 Forum has a list of members with links to the vendor sites. They all have IPv6 position papers published. To get updated information, visit your vendor's IPv6 site. Here is a list of position papers, dated October 2001.

Vendor	Web site
Microsoft	*http://www.microsoft.com/ipv6/*
IBM	*http://www.ibm.com/software/ipv6/*
Cisco	*http://www.cisco.com/ipv6/*
Nokia	*http://www.nokia.com/ipv6/*
Alcatel	*http://www.cid.alcatel.com/ipv6/index.html*
SUN	*http://www.sun.com/solaris/ipv6/*
Trumpet	*http://www.trumpet.com.au/ipv6/*
BITS Pilani	*http://ipv6.bits-pilani.ac.in/case-for-v6/*
6WIND	*http://www.6wind.com/ipv6.html*
Compaq	*http://www.compaq.com/ipv6/*
Consulintel	*http://www.consulintel.es/html/ipv6/ipv6.htm*
Nortel Networks	*http://www.nortelnetworks.com/ipv6/*
Hewlett Packard	*http://www.hp.com/products1/unixserverconnectivity/software/ipv.html*
Mentat Inc.	*http://www.mentat.com/tcp/tcp.html*
Ericsson	*http://www.ipv6forum.com/navbar/position/Ericsson-IPv6-statement.pdf*
Hitachi	*http://www.v6.hitachi.co.jp*
RIPE/NCC	*http://www.ripe.net/annual-report/*
NTT	*http://www.v6.ntt.net/globe/index-e.html*
ETRI Korea	*http://www.krv6.net*
Ipinfusion	*http://www.ipinfusion.com/ipv6_network-processing_white_paper0727.pdf*

For a current list of available implementations, refer to *http://playground. sun.com/pub/ipng/html/ipng-implementations.html* (sorted by vendor) and *http://www.ipv6.org/v6-apps.html* (sorted by application).

RFCs

If you want to learn more about IPv6, you need to read RFCs. This appendix provides an overview of the standards and the RFC process.

Standards

This part of the appendix provides an overview of the important things to know about RFCs and the RFC process. It also includes a list of IPv6-relevant RFCs.

General RFC Information

If you want to understand the role of the IETF and the standardization process, if you need a list of all the organizations involved in the process and a description of what they do, or if you wish to attend an IETF meeting, there is an interesting and humorous RFC that describes the background, processes, and rules: RFC 3160, titled "The Tao of IETF—A Novice's Guide to the Internet Engineering Task Force."

Requests for Comments (RFCs) are written reports describing most of the information regarding TCP/IP and the architecture, protocols, and history of the Internet. There are many sites on the Internet where RFCs are electronically accessible. The sites are very different, but most of them support some form of search mechanism. Find the site that best suits your preferences.

A good starting point is *http://www.rfc-editor.org*. There is a tribute to Jon Postel, father of the Internet, who died in October, 1998. He was *the* RFC editor. Besides this information, there is also an overview of the RFC series and process.

On the search and retrieve page of this site, there are many ways to access the wealth of information. RFCs can be viewed by number or in an index, they can be in forward or reverse chronological order, and they can be searched by author, title, number, or keyword. Of course, there is also a link to alternative RFC repositories.

 RFC 2555 is an interesting overview of 30 years of RFC history and a good description of the contribution of Jon Postel's services to the Internet community. There is even more information about Jon Postel at *http://www.postel.org/remembrances/*.

The first RFC, RFC 0001, was published by Steve Crocker on April 7, 1969. Today the number of RFCs continues to rise quickly and has exceeded 3000. RFCs can have different statuses, such as standard, informational, experimental, and historic. A good overview of the different statuses and current level of standardization can be found at *http://www.rfc-editor.org*. Here's a short list of some important basic RFCs that you should be aware of:

RFC 3000, "Official Protocol Standard"
Known as the Internet Official Protocol Standard, this RFC lists only official RFC protocol standards and is therefore not a complete index. It contains the state of standardization as of October, 2001.

RFC 1700, "Assigned Numbers Document"
This RFC is now outdated. For many years, it has been a reference point, containing a summary of the assignment of protocol parameters for the Internet Protocol Suite. IANA is the central coordinator for the assignment of these parameters. RFC 1700 has been replaced by an updated list at *http://www.iana.org/numbers.html*.

RFCs 1122 and 1123, Host Requirements Documents
These two RFCs are known as Host Requirements Documents and cover the requirements for Internet host software. RFC 1122 covers the communications protocol layers such as link layer, IP layer, and transport layer. RFC 1123 covers the application and support protocols. Many terms widely used throughout all RFCs are defined in these two documents.

RFC 1812, "Requirements for IPv4 Routers"
This RFC is self-explanatory. At the time of this writing, I have not yet found an RFC including requirements for IPv6 routers.

The RFCs ending on xx99 are usually a summary of a range of previous RFCs and their status. For instance, if you need a summary for the RFCs from 3000 to 3099, refer to RFC 3099.

Drafts

I refer to drafts often throughout this book. I always mention that draft numbers may have increased since the writing of the book. Here's a short description of the draft process:

During the development of a specification, draft documents are made available on the IETF's homepage, *www.ietf.org*. If a draft is published as an RFC, the draft is removed from the directory. If the draft is updated, the number increases. A draft is valid for a maximum of six months. If, after that time, it has not been updated or published as an RFC, it is also removed from the directory. So in some instances you might not find a draft mentioned in the book because it has either been removed or published as an RFC.

RFC Index for IPv6

This is a list of all relevant IPv6 RFCs and RFCs regarding related technologies. It is sorted by RFC number.

General IPv6 RFCs

- RFC 1981, "Path MTU Discovery for IP version 6" (August, 1996)
- RFC 2003, "IP Encapsulation within IP" (October, 1996)
- RFC 2080, "RIPng for IPv6" (January, 1997)
- RFC 2185, "Routing Aspects of IPv6 Transition" (September, 1997)
- RFC 2205, "Resource ReSerVation Protocol (RSVP) Version 1 Functional Specification" (September, 1997)
- RFC 2207, "RSVP Extensions for IPSEC Data Flows" (September, 1997)
- RFC 2210, "The Use of RSVP with IETF Integrated Services" (September, 1997)
- RFC 2292, "Advanced Sockets API for IPv6" (February, 1998)
- RFC 2324, "Hyper Text Coffee Pot Control Protocol (HTCPCP/1.0)" (April, 1998) One of my favorites.
- RFC 2373, "IP Version 6 Addressing Architecture" (July, 1998)
- RFC 2374, "An IPv6 Aggregatable Global Unicast Address Format" (July, 1998)
- RFC 2375, "IPv6 Multicast Address Assignments" (July, 1998)
- RFC 2401, "Security Architecture for the Internet Protocol" (November, 1998)

- RFC 2402, "IP Authentication Header" (November, 1998)
- RFC 2406, "IP Encapsulating Security Payload (ESP)" (November, 1998)
- RFC 2407, "The Internet IP Security Domain of Interpretation (DOI) for ISAKMP" (November, 1998)
- RFC 2408, "Internet Security and Key Management Protocol (ISAKMP)" (November, 1998)
- RFC 2409, "The Internet Key Exchange (IKE)" (November, 1998)
- RFC 2411, "IP Security Document Roadmap" (November, 1998)
- RFC 2412, "The OAKLEY Key Determination Protocol" (November, 1998)
- RFC 2428, "FTP Extensions for IPv6 and NATs" (September, 1998)
- RFC 2450, "Proposed TLA and NLA Assignment Rules" (December, 1998)
- RFC 2452, "IP Version 6 Management Information Base for the Transmission Control Protocol"
- RFC 2454, "IP Version 6 Management Information Base for the User Datagram Protocol" (December, 1998)
- RFC 2460, "Internet Protocol, Version 6 (IPv6) Specification" (December, 1998) Obsoletes RFC 1883.
- RFC 2461, "Neighbor Discovery for IP Version 6 (IPv6)" (December, 1998) Obsoletes RFC 1970.
- RFC 2462, "IPv6 Stateless Address Autoconfiguration" (December, 1998)
- RFC 2463, "Internet Control Message Protocol (ICMPv6) for the Internet Protocol Version 6 (IPv6) Specification" (December, 1998)
- RFC 2465, "Management Information Base for IP Version 6: Textual Conventions and General Group" (December, 1998)
- RFC 2466, "Management Information Base for IP Version 6: ICMPv6 Group" (December, 1998)
- RFC 2471, "IPv6 Testing Address Allocation" (December, 1998)
- RFC 2473, "Generic Packet Tunneling in IPv6 Specification" (December, 1998)
- RFC 2474, "Definition of the Differentiated Services Field (DS Field) in the IPv4 and IPv6 Headers" (December, 1998)
- RFC 2475, "An Architecture for Differentiated Services" (December, 1998)
- RFC 2507, "IP Header Compression" (February, 1999)

- RFC 2526, "Reserved IPv6 Subnet Anycast Addresses" (March, 1999)
- RFC 2529, "Transmission of IPv6 over IPv4 Domains without Explicit Tunnels" (March, 1999)
- RFC 2545, "Use of BGP-4 Multiprotocol Extensions for IPv6 Inter-Domain Routing" (March, 1999)
- RFC 2553, "Basic Socket Interface Extensions for IPv6" (March, 1999)
- RFC 2675, "IPv6 Jumbograms" (August, 1999)
- RFC 2710, "Multicast Listener Discovery (MLD) for IPv6" (October, 1999)
- RFC 2711, "IPv6 Router Alert Option" (October, 1999)
- RFC 2732, "Format for Literal IPv6 Addresses in URLs" (December, 1999)
- RFC 2740, "OSPF for IPv6" (December, 1999)
- RFC 2765, "Stateless IP/ICMP Translation Algorithm (SIIT)" (February, 2000)
- RFC 2766, "Network Address Translation-Protocol Translation (NAT-PT)" (February, 2000)
- RFC 2772, "6Bone Backbone Routing Guidelines" (February, 2000)
- RFC 2874, "DNS Extensions to Support IPv6 Address Aggregation and Renumbering" (July, 2000)
- RFC 2893, "Transition Mechanisms for IPv6 Hosts and Routers" (August, 2000) Obsoletes RFC 1933.
- RFC 2894, "Router Renumbering for IPv6" (August, 2000)
- RFC 2921, "6BONE pTLA and pNLA Formats (pTLA)" (September, 2000)
- RFC 2925, "Definitions of Managed Objects for Remote Ping, Traceroute, and Lookup Operations" (September, 2000)
- RFC 2928, "Initial IPv6 Sub-TLA ID Assignments" (September, 2000)
- RFC 3019, "IP Version 6 Management Information Base for The Multicast Listener Discovery Protocol" (January, 2001)
- RFC 3041, "Privacy Extensions for Stateless Address Autoconfiguration in IPv6" (January, 2001)
- RFC 3053, "IPv6 Tunnel Broker" (January, 2001)
- RFC 3056, "Connection of IPv6 Domains via IPv4 Clouds" (February, 2001)
- RFC 3068, "An Anycast Prefix for 6to4 Relay Routers" (June, 2001)

- RFC 3111, "Service Location Protocol Modifications for IPv6" (May, 2001)
- RFC 3122, "Extensions to IPv6 Neighbor Discovery for Inverse Discovery Specification" (June, 2001)
- RFC 3142, "An IPv6-to-IPv4 Transport Relay Translator" (June, 2001)
- RFC 3162, "RADIUS and IPv6" (August, 2001)
- RFC 3177, "IAB/IESG Recommendations on IPv6 Address" (September, 2001)
- RFC 3178, "IPv6 Multihoming Support at Site Exit Routers" (October, 2001)
- RFC 3175, "Aggregation of RSVP for IPv4 and IPv6 Reservations" (September, 2001)
- RFC 3209, "RSVP-TE: Extensions to RSVP for LSP Tunnels" (December, 2001)
- RFC 3226, "DNSSEC and IPv6 A6 aware server/resolver message size requirements" (December, 2001)

RFCs referring to topologies

- RFC 2464, "Transmission of IPv6 Packets over Ethernet Networks" (December, 1998)
- RFC 2467, "Transmission of IPv6 Packets over FDDI Networks" (December, 1998)
- RFC 2470, "Transmission of IPv6 Packets over Token Ring Networks" (December, 1998)
- RFC 2472, "IP Version 6 over PPP" (December, 1998)
- RFC 2491, "IPv6 over Non-Broadcast Multiple Access (NBMA) networks" (January, 1999)
- RFC 2492, "IPv6 over ATM Networks" (January, 1999)
- RFC 2497, "Transmission of IPv6 Packets over ARCnet Networks" (January, 1999)
- RFC 2590, "Transmission of IPv6 Packets over Frame Relay Networks Specification" (May, 1999)
- RFC 3146, "Transmission of IPv6 Packets over IEEE 1394 Networks" (October, 2001)

IPv6 Resources

This appendix contains all the resources mentioned in the book, for easy reference.

Ethertype Field

Table B-1 lists possible values for the Ethertype number. The complete list can be found at *http://www.iana.org/assignments/ethernet-numbers*. Transmission of IP datagrams over Ethernet is defined in RFC 894 and RFC 895. The Ethertype for IPv6 is, as the table shows, 86DD.

Table B-1. Ethertype numbers

Ethertype (hex)	Description
0000–05DC	IEEE802.3 Length field
0000–05DC	IEEE802.3 Length field
0101–01FF	Experimental
0200	XEROX PUP (see 0A00)
0201	PUP Addr Trans (see 0A01)
0400	Nixdorf
0600	XEROX NS IDP
0660	DLOG
0661	DLOG
0800	Internet IP (IPv4)
0801	X.75 Internet
0802	NBS Internet
0803	ECMA Internet
0804	Chaosnet
0805	X.25 Level 3

Table B-1. Ethertype numbers (continued)

Ethertype (hex)	Description
0806	ARP
0807	XNS Compatability
0808	Frame Relay ARP
081C	Symbolics Private
0888–088A	Xyplex
0900	Ungermann-Bass net debugr
0A00	Xerox IEEE802.3 PUP
0A01	PUP Addr Trans
0BAD	Banyan VINES
0BAE	VINES Loopback
0BAF	VINES Echo
1000	Berkeley Trailer nego
1001–100F	Berkeley Trailer encap/IP
1600	Valid Systems
4242	PCS Basic Block Protocol
5208	BBN Simnet
6000	DEC Unassigned (Exp.)
6001	DEC MOP Dump/Load
6002	DEC MOP Remote Console
6003	DEC DECNET Phase IV Route
6004	DEC LAT
6005	DEC Diagnostic Protocol
6006	DEC Customer Protocol
6007	DEC LAVC, SCA
6008–6009	DEC Unassigned
6010–6014	3Com Corporation
6558	Trans Ether Bridging
6559	Raw Frame Relay
7000	Ungermann-Bass download
7002	Ungermann-Bass dia/loop
7020-7029	LRT
7030	Proteon
7034	Cabletron
8003	Cronus VLN
8004	Cronus Direct

Ethertype (hex)	Description
8005	HP Probe
8006	Nestar
8008	AT&T
8010	Excelan
8013	SGI diagnostics
8014	SGI network games
8015	SGI reserved
8016	SGI bounce server
8019	Apollo Domain
802E	Tymshare
802F	Tigan, Inc.
8035	Reverse ARP
8036	Aeonic Systems
8038	DEC LANBridge
8039–803C	DEC Unassigned
803D	DEC Ethernet Encryption
803E	DEC Unassigned
803F	DEC LAN Traffic Monitor
8040–8042	DEC Unassigned
8044	Planning Research Corp.
8046	AT&T
8047	AT&T
8049	ExperData
805B	Stanford V Kernel exp.
805C	Stanford V Kernel prod.
805D	Evans & Sutherland
8060	Little Machines
8062	Counterpoint Computers
8065	Univ. of Mass, Amherst
8066	Univ. of Mass., Amherst
8067	Veeco Integrated Auto.
8068	General Dynamics
8069	AT&T
806A	Autophon
806C	ComDesign

Table B-1. Ethertype numbers (continued)

Ethertype (hex)	Description
806D	Computgraphic Corp.
806E–8077	Landmark Graphics Corp.
807A	Matra
807B	Dansk Data Elektronik
807C	Merit Internodal
807D–807F	Vitalink Communications
8080	Vitalink TransLAN III
8081–8083	Counterpoint Computers
809B	Appletalk
809C–809E	Datability
809F	Spider Systems Ltd.
80A3	Nixdorf Computers
80A4–80B3	Siemens Gammasonics Inc.
80C0–80C3	DCA Data Exchange Cluster
80C4	Banyan Systems
80C5	Banyan Systems
80C6	Pacer Software
80C7	Applitek Corporation
80C8–80CC	Intergraph Corporation
80CD–80CE	Harris Corporation
80CF–80D2	Taylor Instrument
80D3–80D4	Rosemount Corporation
80D5	IBM SNA Service on Ether
80DD	Varian Associates
80DE–80DF	Integrated Solutions TRFS
80E0–80E3	Allen-Bradley
80E4–80F0	Datability
80F2	Retix
80F3	AppleTalk AARP (Kinetics)
80F4–80F5	Kinetics
80F7	Apollo Computer
80FF–8103	Wellfleet Communications
8107–8109	Symbolics Private
8130	Hayes Microcomputers
8131	VG Laboratory Systems

Table B-1. Ethertype numbers (continued)

Ethertype (hex)	Description
8132–8136	Bridge Communications
8137–8138	Novell, Inc.
8139–813D	KTI
8148	Logicraft
8149	Network Computing Devices
814A	Alpha Micro
814C	SNMP
814D	BIIN
814E	BIIN
814F	Technically Elite Concept
8150	Rational Corp
8151–8153	Qualcomm
815C–815E	Computer Protocol Pty Ltd
8164–8166	Charles River Data Systems
817D	XTP
817E	SGI/Time Warner prop.
8180	HIPPI-FP encapsulation
8181	STP, HIPPI-ST
8182	Reserved for HIPPI-6400
8183	Reserved for HIPPI-6400
8184–818C	Silicon Graphics prop.
818D	Motorola Computer
819A–81A3	Qualcomm
81A4	ARAI Bunkichi
81A5–81AE	RAD Network Devices
81B7–81B9	Xyplex
81CC–81D5	Apricot Computers
81D6–81DD	Artisoft
81E6–81EF	Polygon
81F0–81F2	Comsat Labs
81F3–81F5	SAIC
81F6–81F8	VG Analytical
8203–8205	Quantum Software
8221–8222	Ascom Banking Systems
823E–8240	Advanced Encryption Systems

Ethertype (hex)	Description
827F–8282	Athena Programming
8263–826A	Charles River Data Systems
829A–829B	Inst Ind Info Tech
829C–82AB	Taurus Controls
82AC–8693	Walker Richer & Quinn
8694–869D	Idea Courier
869E–86A1	Computer Network Tech
86A3–86AC	Gateway Communications
86DB	SECTRA
86DE	Delta Controls
86DD	IPv6
86DF	ATOMIC
86E0–86EF	Landis & Gyr Powers
8700–8710	Motorola
876B	TCP/IP Compression
876C	IP Autonomous Systems
876D	Secure Data
880B	PPP
8847	MPLS Unicast
8848	MPLS Multicast
8A96–8A97	Invisible Software
9000	Loopback
9001	3Com(Bridge) XNS Sys Mgmt
9002	3Com(Bridge) TCP-IP Sys
9003	3Com(Bridge) loop detect
FF00	BBN VITAL-LanBridge cache
FF00–FF0F	ISC Bunker Ramo
FFFF	Reserved

Next Header Field Values (Chapter 2)

Table B-2 lists the possible values for the Next Header field in the IPv6 Header, as explained in Chapter 2. The complete list can also be found at *http://www.iana.org/assignments/protocol-numbers*.

Table B-2. Next Header field values

Decimal	Protocol	Reference
0	IPv6 Hop-by-Hop Option	RFC 1883
1	Internet Control Message	RFC 792
2	Internet Group Management	RFC 1112
3	Gateway-to-Gateway	RFC 823
4	IP in IP (encapsulation)	RFC 2003
5	Stream	RFC 1190
6	Transmission Control	RFC 793
7	CBT	Ballardie
8	Exterior Gateway Protocol	RFC 888
9	Any private interior gateway (used by Cisco for their IGRP)	IANA
10	BBN RCC Monitoring	SGC
11	Network Voice Protocol	RFC 741
12	PUP	PUP, Xerox
13	ARGUS	RWS4
14	EMCON	BN7
15	XNET, Cross Net Debugger	IEN158,JFH2
16	CHAOS	NC3
17	UDP	RFC 768
18	Multiplexing (MUX)	IEN90,JBP
19	DCN Measurement Subsystems	DLM1
20	Host Monitoring (HMP)	RFC 869
21	Packet Radio Measurement (PRM)	ZSU
22	XEROX NS IDP	ETHERNET,XEROX
23	Trunk-1	BWB6
24	Trunk-2	BWB6
25	Leaf-1	BWB6
26	Leaf-2	BWB6
27	Reliable Data Protocol (RDP)	RFC 908
28	Internet Reliable Transaction (IRTP)	RFC 938
29	ISO Transport Protocol Class 4	RFC 905
30	Bulk Data Transfer Protocol	RFC 969
31	MFE Network Services Protocol	MFENET,BCH2
32	MERIT Internodal Protocol	HWB
33	Sequential Exchange Protocol (SEP)	JC120

Table B-2. Next Header field values (continued)

Decimal	Protocol	Reference
34	Third Party Connect Protocol	SAF3
35	Inter-Domain Policy Routing Protocol	MXS1
36	XTP	GXC
37	Datagram Delivery Protocol (DDP)	WXC
38	IDPR Control Message Transport Protocol	MXS1
39	TP++ Transport Protocol	DXF
40	IL Transport Protocol	Presotto
41	IPv6	Deering
42	Source Demand Routing Protocol (SDRP)	DXE1
43	Routing Header for IPv6	Deering
44	Fragment Header for IPv6	Deering
45	Inter-Domain Routing Protocol (IDRP)	Sue Hares
46	Reservation Protocol (RSVP)	Bob Braden
47	General Routing Encapsulation (GRE)	Tony Li
48	Mobile Host Routing Protocol (MHRP)	David Johnson
49	BNA	Gary Salamon
50	Encapsulated Security Payload for IPv6	RFC 1827
51	Authentication Header for IPv6	RFC 1826
52	Integrated Net Layer Security TUBA	GLENN
53	IP with Encryption (SWIPE)	JI6
54	NBMA Address Resolution Protocol (NARP)	RFC 1735
55	IP Mobility	Perkins
56	Transport Layer Security Protocol (TLSP)	Oberg
57	SKIP	Markson
58	ICMP for IPv6 (IPv6-ICMP)	RFC 1883
59	No Next Header for IPv6 (IPv6-NoNxt)	RFC 1883
60	Destination Options for IPv6 (IPv6-Opts)	RFC 1883
61	Any host internal protocol	IANA
62	CFTP CFTP	CFTP,HCF2
63	Any local network	IANA
64	SATNET and Backroom EXPAK	SHB
65	Kryptolan	PXL1
66	Remote Virtual Disk Protocol (RVD)	MBG
67	Internet Pluribus Packet Core (IPPC)	SHB
68	Any distributed file system	IANA

Table B-2. Next Header field values (continued)

Decimal	Protocol	Reference
69	SATNET Monitoring	SHB
70	VISA Protocol	GXT1
71	Internet Packet Core Utility (IPCU)	SHB
72	Computer Protocol Network Executive (CPNX)	DXM2
73	Computer Protocol Heart Beat (CPHB)	DXM2
74	Wang Span Network (WSN)	VXD
75	Packet Video Protocol (PVP)	SC3
76	Backroom SATNET Monitoring	SHB
77	SUN ND PROTOCOL-Temporary	WM3
78	WIDEBAND Monitoring	SHB
79	WIDEBAND EXPAK	SHB
80	ISO Internet Protocol	MTR
81	VMTP	DRC3
82	SECURE-VMTP	DRC3
83	VINES	BXH
84	TTP	JXS
85	NSFNET-IGP	HWB
86	Dissimilar Gateway Protocol (DGP)	DGP,ML109
87	TCF	GAL5
88	EIGRP	CISCO,GXS
89	OSPFIGP	RFC 1583
90	Sprite RPC Protocol	SPRITE,BXW
91	Locus Address Resolution Protocol (LARP)	BXH
92	Multicast Transport Protocol (MTP)	SXA
93	AX.25 Frames	BK29
94	IP-within-IP Encapsulation Protocol	JI6
95	Mobile Internetworking Control Protocol (MICP)	JI6
96	Semaphore Communications Sec. Protocol	HXH
97	Ethernet-within-IP Encapsulation	RDH1
98	Encapsulation Header	RFC 1241
99	Any private encryption scheme	IANA
100	GMTP	RXB5
101	Ipsilon Flow Management Protocol (IFMP)	Hinden
102	PNNI over IP	Callon
103	Protocol Independent Multicast (PIM)	Farinacci

Table B-2. Next Header field values (continued)

Decimal	Protocol	Reference
104	ARIS	Feldman
105	SCPS	Durst
106	QNX	Hunter
107	Active Networks	Braden
108	IP Payload Compression Protocol	RFC 2393
109	Sitara Networks Protocol (SNP)	Sridhar
110	Compaq Peer Protocol	Volpe
111	IPX in IP	Lee
112	Virtual Router Redundancy Protocol (VRRP)	Hinden
113	Reliable Transport Protocol (PGM)	Speakman
114	Any zero-hop protocol	IANA
115	Layer Two Tunneling Protocol	Aboba
116	Data Exchange (DDX)	Worley
117	Interactive Agent Transfer Protocol (IATP)	Murphy
118	Schedule Transfer Protocol (STP)	JMP
119	SpectraLink Radio Protocol (SRP)	Hamilton
120	UTI	Lothberg
121	Simple Message Protocol (SMP)	Ekblad
122	SM	Crowcroft
123	Performance Transparency Protocol (PTP)	Welzl
124	ISIS over IPv4	Przygienda
125	FIRE	Partridge
126	Combat Radio Transport Protocol (CRTP)	Sautter
127	Combat Radio User Datagram (CRUDP)	Sautter
128	SSCOPMCE	Waber
129	IPLT	Hollbach
130	Secure Packet Shield (SPS)	McIntosh
131	Private IP Encapsulation within IP (PIPE)	Petri
132	Stream Control Transmission Protocol (SCTP)	Stewart
133	Fibre Channel (FC)	Rajagopal
134-254	Unassigned	IANA
255	Reserved	IANA

Reserved Anycast IDs (Chapter 3, RFC 2526)

Table B-3 lists the Anycast IDs that have been assigned so far.

Table B-3. Reserved Anycast IDs

Decimal	Hexadecimal	Description
127	7F	Reserved
126	7E	Mobile IPv6 Home-Agents anycast
0-125	00-7D	Reserved

Values for the Multicast Scope Field (Chapter 3, RFC 2373)

The values listed in Table B-4 have been defined in RFC 2373 for the Multicast Scope field.

Table B-4. Values for the Multicast Scope field

Value	Description
0	Reserved
1	Node-local scope
2	Link-local scope
3, 4	Unassigned
5	Site-local scope
6, 7	Unassigned
8	Organization-local scope
9, A, B, C, D	Unassigned
E	Global scope
F	Reserved

Well-Known Multicast Group Addresses (Chapter 3, RFC 2375)

RFC 2375 defines the initial assignment of IPv6 multicast addresses that are permanently assigned. Some assignments are made for fixed scopes; other assignments are valid in different scopes. Table B-5 lists them.

Table B-5. Well-known multicast addresses with fixed scope

Address	Description
(Interface-local) or Node-local scope	
FF01:0:0:0:0:0:0:1	All-nodes address
FF01:0:0:0:0:0:0:2	All-routers address
Link-local scope	
FF02:0:0:0:0:0:0:1	All-nodes address
FF02:0:0:0:0:0:0:2	All-routers address
FF02:0:0:0:0:0:0:3	Unassigned
FF02:0:0:0:0:0:0:4	DVMRP routers
FF02:0:0:0:0:0:0:5	OSPFIGP
FF02:0:0:0:0:0:0:6	OSPFIGP Designated Routers
FF02:0:0:0:0:0:0:7	ST routers
FF02:0:0:0:0:0:0:8	ST hosts
FF02:0:0:0:0:0:0:9	RIP routers
FF02:0:0:0:0:0:0:A	EIGRP routers
FF02:0:0:0:0:0:0:B	Mobile-agents
FF02:0:0:0:0:0:0:D	All PIM routers
FF02:0:0:0:0:0:0:E	RSVP-encapsulation
FF02:0:0:0:0:0:1:1	Link name
FF02:0:0:0:0:0:1:2	All DHCP agents
FF02:0:0:0:0:1:FFXX:XXXX	Solicited-node address
Site-local scope	
FF05:0:0:0:0:0:0:2	All-routers address
FF05:0:0:0:0:0:1:3	All DHCP servers
FF05:0:0:0:0:0:1:4	All DHCP relays
FF05:0:0:0:0:0:1:1000 to FF05:0:0:0:0:0:01:13FF	Service location

Table B-6 lists the currently assigned multicast group addresses with variable scope. The addresses are noted beginning with FF0X, X being the placeholder for a variable scope value. An updated list can be found at *http://www.iana.org/assignments/ipv6-multicast-addresses*.

Table B-6. Assigned IPv6 multicast group addresses with variable scope

Address	Group
FF0X:0:0:0:0:0:0:0	Reserved multicast address
FF0X:0:0:0:0:0:0:100	VMTP Managers Group
FF0X:0:0:0:0:0:0:101	Network Time Protocol (NTP)
FF0X:0:0:0:0:0:0:102	SGI-Dogfight

Table B-6. Assigned IPv6 multicast group addresses with variable scope (continued)

Address	Group
FF0X:0:0:0:0:0:0:103	Rwhod
FF0X:0:0:0:0:0:0:104	VNP
FF0X:0:0:0:0:0:0:105	Artificial Horizons - Aviator
FF0X:0:0:0:0:0:0:106	NSS - Name Service Server
FF0X:0:0:0:0:0:0:107	AUDIONEWS - Audio News Multicast
FF0X:0:0:0:0:0:0:108	SUN NIS+ Information Service
FF0X:0:0:0:0:0:0:109	MTP Multicast Transport Protocol
FF0X:0:0:0:0:0:0:10A	IETF-1-LOW-AUDIO
FF0X:0:0:0:0:0:0:10B	IETF-1-AUDIO
FF0X:0:0:0:0:0:0:10C	IETF-1-VIDEO
FF0X:0:0:0:0:0:0:10D	IETF-2-LOW-AUDIO
FF0X:0:0:0:0:0:0:10E	IETF-2-AUDIO
FF0X:0:0:0:0:0:0:10F	IETF-2-VIDEO
FF0X:0:0:0:0:0:0:110	MUSIC-SERVICE
FF0X:0:0:0:0:0:0:111	SEANET-TELEMETRY
FF0X:0:0:0:0:0:0:112	SEANET-IMAGE
FF0X:0:0:0:0:0:0:113	MLOADD
FF0X:0:0:0:0:0:0:114	Any private experiment
FF0X:0:0:0:0:0:0:115	DVMRP on MOSPF
FF0X:0:0:0:0:0:0:116	SVRLOC
FF0X:0:0:0:0:0:0:117	XINGTV
FF0X:0:0:0:0:0:0:118	microsoft-ds
FF0X:0:0:0:0:0:0:119	nbc-pro
FF0X:0:0:0:0:0:0:11A	nbc-pfn
FF0X:0:0:0:0:0:0:11B	lmsc-calren-1
FF0X:0:0:0:0:0:0:11C	lmsc-calren-2
FF0X:0:0:0:0:0:0:11D	lmsc-calren-3
FF0X:0:0:0:0:0:0:11E	lmsc-calren-4
FF0X:0:0:0:0:0:0:11F	ampr-info
FF0X:0:0:0:0:0:0:120	mtrace
FF0X:0:0:0:0:0:0:121	RSVP-encap-1
FF00X:0:0:0:0:0:0:0:122	RSVP-encap-2
FF0X:0:0:0:0:0:0:123	SVRLOC-DA
FF0X:0:0:0:0:0:0:124	rln-server
FF0X:0:0:0:0:0:0:125	proshare-mc

Address	Group
FF0X:0:0:0:0:0:0:126	dantz
FF0X:0:0:0:0:0:0:127	cisco-rp-announce
FF0X:0:0:0:0:0:0:128	cisco-rp-discovery
FF0X:0:0:0:0:0:0:129	gatekeeper
FF0X:0:0:0:0:0:0:12A	iberiagames]
FF0X:0:0:0:0:0:0:201	"rwho" Group (BSD) (unofficial)
FF0X:0:0:0:0:0:0:202	SUN RPC PMAPPROC_CALLIT
FF0X:0:0:0:0:0:2:0000 to FF0X:0:0:0:0:0:2:7	FFD Multimedia Conference Calls
FF0X:0:0:0:0:0:2:7FFE	SAPv1 Announcements
FF0X:0:0:0:0:0:2:7FFF	SAPv0 Announcements (deprecated)
FF0X:0:0:0:0:0:2:8000 to FF0X:0:0:0:0:0:2:FFFF	SAP Dynamic Assignments

ICMPv6 Message Types and Code Values (Chapter 4, RFC 2463)

Table B-7 lists ICMPv6 message types and their type numbers.

Table B-7. ICMPv6 message type numbers

Type	Name	Reference	Chapter
1	Destination Unreachable	RFC 2463	Chapter 4
2	Packet Too Big	RFC 2463	
3	Time Exceeded	RFC 2463	
4	Parameter Problem	RFC 2463	
128	Echo Request	RFC 2463	Chapter 4
129	Echo Reply	RFC 2463	
130	Multicast Listener Query	MC-LIST	
131	Multicast Listener Report	MC-LIST	
132	Multicast Listener Done	MC-LIST	
133	Router Solicitation	RFC 2461	
134	Router Advertisement	RFC 2461	
135	Neighbor Solicitation	RFC 2461	
136	Neighbor Advertisement	RFC 2461	
137	Redirect Message	RFC 2461	

Table B-7. ICMPv6 message type numbers (continued)

Type	Name	Reference	Chapter
138	Router Renumbering	Crawford	
139	ICMP Node Information Query	Crawford	
140	ICMP Node Information Response	Crawford	

Table B-8 lists the code values of the Destination Unreachable Message (Type 1).

Table B-8. Code values for the Destination Unreachable message (Type 1)

Code	Description
0	No route to destination.
	This message is generated if a router cannot forward a packet because it does not have a route in its table for a destination network. This can only happen if the router does not have an entry for a default route.
1	Communication with an administratively prohibited destination.
	This type of message can, for example, be sent by a firewall that cannot forward a packet to a host inside the firewall because of a packet filter, or if a node is configured not to accept unauthenticated echo requests.
2	Not assigned; used to be defined as "not a neighbor" in RFC 1885, which is now obsolete.
3	Address unreachable.
	This code is used if a destination address cannot be resolved into a corresponding network address or if there is a data-link layer problem preventing the node from reaching the destination network.
4	Port unreachable.
	This code is used if the transport protocol (e.g., UDP) has no listener and if there is no other means to inform the sender. For example, if a DNS query is sent to a host and the DNS server is not running, this type of message will be generated.

Table B-9 lists the code values for the Time Exceeded message (Type 3).

Table B-9. Code values for the Time Exceeded message (Type 3)

Code	Description
0	Hop limit exceeded in transit
	Possible causes: The initial hop limit value is too low or there are routing loops.
1	Fragment reassembly time exceeded
	If a packet is sent fragmented by using a fragment header (refer to Chapter 2 for more details) and the receiving host cannot reassemble all packets within a certain time, it notifies the sender by issuing this ICMP message.

Table B-10 shows the values for the Parameter Problem message (Type 4).

Table B-10. Code values for Parameter Problem (Type 4)

Code	Description
0	Erroneous header field encountered
1	Unrecognized Next Header type encountered
2	Unrecognized IPv6 option encountered

Multicast Group Addresses and Token Ring Functional Addresses (Chapter 7)

Table B-11 shows how IPv6 multicast addresses are mapped to Token Ring functional addresses.

Table B-11. Mapping IPv6 multicast addresses to Token Ring functional addresses

MAC functional address (canonical)	Multicast addresses
03-00-80-00-00-00	All-nodes (FF01::1 and FF02::1)
	Solicited-node (FF02:0:0:0:0.1:FFxx:xxxx)
03-00-40-00-00-00	All Routers (FF0X::2)
03-00-00-80-00-00	Any other multicast address with three least-significant bits = 000
03-00-00-40-00-00	Any other multicast address with three least-significant bits = 001
03-00-00-20-00-00	Any other multicast address with three least-significant bits = 010
03-00-00-10-00-00	Any other multicast address with three least-significant bits = 011
03-00-00-08-00-00	Any other multicast address with three least-significant bits = 100
03-00-00-04-00-00	Any other multicast address with three least-significant bits = 101
03-00-00-02-00-00	Any other multicast address with three least-significant bits = 110
03-00-00-01-00-00	Any other multicast address with three least-significant bits = 111

Multicast Addresses for SLP over IPv6 (Chapter 9)

Table B-12 lists the multicast addresses that have been defined for SLP over IPv6.

Table B-12. Multicast addresses for SLP over IPv6

Multicast address	Description
FF0X:0:0:0:0:0:0:116	Service Agent (SA)
	Used for Service Type and Attribute Request Messages.
FF0X:0:0:0:0:0:0:123	Directory Agent (DA)
	Used by User Agents (UAs) and SAs to discover DAs. Also used by DAs for sending unsolicited DA Advertisement messages.
FF0X:0:0:0:0:0:1:1000 to FF0X:0:0:0:0:0:1:13FF	Service Location
	Used by SAs to join the groups that correspond to the Service Types of the services they advertise. The Service Type string is used to determine the corresponding value in the 1000 to 13FF range, which has been assigned by IANA for this purpose. For an explanation of the algorithm used to calculate the group ID, refer to RFC 3111.

The X in FF0X is the placeholder for the multicast scope to be used for this group ID. For instance, 2 is link-local scope and 5 is site-local scope.

Protocol Translation (Chapter 10, RFC 2765)

Table B-13 shows how IPv4 header fields are translated to IPv6 header fields.

Table B-13. Translated IPv6 header fields

Header field	Information
Version	6
Traffic Class	All 8 bits from the Type of Service and Precedence Field are copied.
Flow Label	Zero
Payload Length	The Total Length from the IPv4 header field minus the size of the IPv4 header (including options, if present).
Next Header	Protocol Field copied from IPv4 header.
Hop Limit	TTL value copied from IPv4 header. Since the translator is a router, the value has to be decremented by one (either before or after translation) and the value checked. If zero, an ICMP TTL exceeded message has to be generated.
Source Address	Combination of IPv4-mapped address prefix and the IPv4 address in the 32 low-order bits, for example: ::ffff:0:0:192.168.0.1.
Destination Address	Combination of IPv4-translatable address prefix and the IPv4 destination address, for example: 0::ffff:0:0:192.168.0.99.
IPv4 Options	If any IPv4 options are present, they are ignored. If a source route option is present, the packet must be discarded and an ICMPv4 "destination unreachable/source route failed" (Type3, Code 5) error message should be returned to the sender.

Table B-14 shows the header fields when a translated packet needs to be fragmented.

Table B-14. IPv6 header fields with fragmentation

Header field	Information
Header fields	
Payload Length	The Total Length from the IPv4 header field minus the size of the IPv4 header (including options if present) plus 8 bits for the size of the Fragment header.
Next Header	44 (Fragment header)
Fragment header fields	
Next Header	Protocol field copied from IPv4 header.
Fragment Offset	Fragment Offset field copied from IPv4 header.
M-Flag	More Fragments bit copied from the IPv4 header.
Identification	The high-order 16 bits set to zero, the low-order 16 bits copied from the Identification field in the IPv4 header.

Table B-15 shows how the fields in ICMPv4 Query messages types are translated to ICMPv6 message types.

Table B-15. Translation of ICMPv4 query messages

Message type	Translation
Echo and Echo Reply (types 8 and 0)	Adjust the type to 128 or 129, respectively and adjust the ICMP checksum to take the type change into account and include the ICMPv6 pseudo-header.
Information Request/Reply (types 15 and 16)	Obsoleted in ICMPv6. Silently discard.
Timestamp and Timestamp Reply (types13 and 14)	Obsoleted in ICMPv6. Silently discard.
Address Mask Request/Reply (types17 and 18)	Obsoleted in ICMPv6. Silently discard.
Router Advertisement (type 9)	Single hop message. Silently discard.
Router Solicitation (type 10)	Single hop message. Silently discard.
Unknown ICMPv4 types	Silently discard.

IGMP messages are single-hop messages and should not be forwarded over routers. They therefore do not require translation and are silently discarded.

Table B-16 shows the translation for ICMP error messages.

Table B-16. Translation of ICMPv4 error messages

Message type	Translation
Destination Unreachable (Type 3)	For all codes not listed here, the type is set to one.
Code 0/1, Network/Host Unreachable	Type 1, Code 0 - No Route to Destination.

Table B-16. Translation of ICMPv4 error messages (continued)

Message type	Translation
Code 2, Protocol Unreachable	Type 4, Code 1 - Port Unreachable. Make the pointer point to the IPv6 Next Header field.
Code 3, Port Unreachable	Type 1, Code 4 - Port Unreachable.
Code 4, Fragmentation needed but DF set	Type 2, Code 0 - Packet Too Big. The MTU field needs to be recalculated to reflect the difference between the IPv4 and the IPv6 header sizes.
Code 5, Source Route Failed	Type 1, Code 0 - No Route to Destination (note that source routes are not translated).
Code 6, 7, Destination Network/Host Unknown	Type 1, Code 0 - No Route to Destination.
Code 8, Source Route Isolated	Type 1, Code 0 - No Route to Destination.
Code 9, 10 Communication with Destination Administratively Prohibited	Type 1, Code 1 - Communication with Destination Administratively Prohibited.
Code 11, 12, Network/Host Unreachable for TOS	Type 1, Code 0 - No Route to Destination.
Redirect, Type 5	Single hop message. Silently discard.
Source Quench, Type 4	Obsoleted in ICMPv6. Silently discard.
Time Exceeded, Type 11	Type 3 - Time Exceeded. Code field unchanged.
Parameter Problem, Type 12	Type 4 - Parameter Problem. The pointer needs to be updated to point to the corresponding field in the translated and included IP header.

The following tables show how IPv6 is translated to IPv4. Table B-17 shows how IPv6 header fields are translated to IPv4 header fields.

Table B-17. Translated IPv4 header

Header field	Information
Version	4
Internet Header length	5 (no options)
TOS and Precedence	All 8 bits from the Traffic Class are copied.
Total length	Payload Length from the IPv6 header plus length of the IPv4 header.
Identification	Zero
Flags	More Fragments Flag set to zero; Don't Fragment Flag set to one.
Fragment Offset	Zero
Time to Live	Hop Limit value copied from the IPv6 header. Since the translator is a router, the value has to be decremented by one (either before or after translation) and checked on the value. If zero, an ICMP TTL exceeded message has to be generated.
Protocol	Next Header field copied from the IPv6 header.
Header Checksum	Computed after generation of the IPv4 header.

Table B-17. Translated IPv4 header (continued)

Header field	Information
Source Address	If the IPv6 address is an IPv4-translated address, the low-order 32 bits of the IPv4-translated source address are copied to the IPv4 Source Address field. Otherwise, NAT will assign an IPv4 address out of the configured address pool and copy it into the IPv4 Source Address field.
Destination Address	The low-order 32 bits of the IPv4-mapped destination address are copied to the IPv4 Destination Address field.
Options	If an IPv6 Hop-by-Hop Options header, Destination Options header, or a routing header with the Segments Left field equal zero to are present, they are not translated. In this case, the Total Length field and the Protocol field have to be adjusted accordingly. If a routing header is present with a Segments Left field of non-zero, an ICMPv6 Parameter Problem message (Type 4, Code 0) has to be returned to the sender with the Pointer field pointing to the first byte of the Segment Left field.

If the IPv6 packet contains a Fragment header, the respective fields are translated as shown in Table B-18.

Table B-18. Translating the Fragment header

Header field	Information
Total Length	Payload Length from the IPv6 header, minus 8 for the Fragment header, plus the size of the IPv4 header.
Identification	Copied from the low-order 16 bits in the Identification field in the Fragment header.
Flags	The More Fragment flag is copied from the M flag in the Fragment header. The Don't Fragment flag is set to zero so IPv4 routers can fragment the packet.
Fragment Offset	Fragment Offset field copied from IPv6 header.
Protocol	Next Header value copied from the Fragment header.

Table B-19 shows how ICMPv6 message types are translated to ICMPv4 message types.

Table B-19. Translation of ICMPv6 informational messages

Message Type	Translation
Echo Request and Echo Reply (types 128 and 129)	Adjust the type to 8 and 0, respectively, and adjust the ICMP checksum to take the type change into account and to exclude the ICMPv6 pseudo-header.
MLD Multicast Listener Query/Report/Done (types 130, 131, 132)	Single-hop message. Silently discard.
Neighbor Discover Messages (types 133 to 137)	Single-hop message. Silently discard.
Unknown Informational Messages	Silently discard.
Address Mask Request/Reply (types 17 and 18)	Obsoleted in ICMPv6. Silently discard.

Table B-19. Translation of ICMPv6 informational messages (continued)

Message Type	Translation
Router Advertisement (type 9)	Single hop message. Silently discard.
Router Solicitation (type 10)	Single hop message. Silently discard.
Unknown ICMPv4 types	Silently discard.

Error messages are treated as shown in Table B-20.

Table B-20. Translation of ICMPv6 error messages

Message Type	Translation
Destination Unreachable (type 1)	Set the Type field to 3 and the code field as follows:
Type 1, Code 0 - No Route to Destination	Type 3, Code 1 - Host Unreachable.
Type 1, Code 1 - Communication with Destination Administratively Prohibited	Type 3, Code 10 - Communication with Destination Administratively Prohibited.
Type 1, Code 2 - Beyond Scope of Source Address	Type 3, Code 1 - Host Unreachable.
Type 1, Code 3 - Address Unreachable	Type 3, Code 1 - Host Unreachable.
Type 1, Code 4 - Port Unreachable	Type 3, Code 3 - Port Unreachable.
Packet Too Big (type 2)	Type 3, Code 4 - Fragmentation Needed but DF set. The MTU field needs to be adjusted for the difference between the IPv6 and IPv4 headers, including a Fragment header, if present.
Time Exceeded (type 3)	Type 11, Code field unchanged.
Parameter Problem (type 4)	If the Code field is set to 1, translate to a Type 3, Code 2 - Protocol Unreachable; otherwise, to Type 12, Code 0 - Parameter Problem. The pointer needs to be updated to point to the corresponding field in the translated and included IP header.
Unknown Error messages	Silently discard.

Current Prefix Allocations

Table B-21 lists the prefixes initially assigned in RFC 2373.

Table B-21. List of assigned prefixes

Allocation	Prefix binary	Prefix hex	Fraction of address space
Reserved	0000 0000		1/256
Reserved for NSAP allocation	0000 001		1/128
Reserved for IPX allocation (deprecated in later draft)	0000 010		1/128
Aggregatable global unicast addresses	001		1/8

Table B-21. List of assigned prefixes (continued)

Allocation	Prefix binary	Prefix hex	Fraction of address space
Link-local unicast addresses	1111 1110 10	FE80	1/1024
Site-local unicast addresses	1111 1110 11	FEC0	1/1024
Multicast addresses	1111 1111	FF	1/256

Table B-22 lists the current TLA allocations.

Table B-22. Current TLA allocations

Prefix	Allocated to	RFC
2001::/16	Sub-TLA Assignments	RFC 2450
	ARIN 2001:0400::/29	
	RIPE NCC 2001:0600::/29	
	APNIC 2001:0200::/29	
2002::/16	6to4	RFC 3056
3FFE::/16	6Bone Testing	RFC 2471

As of February, 2002, over 120 production networks have been allocated IPv6 address prefixes. For a current list, refer to *http://www.dfn.de/service/ipv6/ipv6aggis.html*.

Vendor Support

A great number of vendors already support IPv6, and the list grows daily. The IPv6 Forum releases a list of members with links to the vendor sites. They all have published IPv6 position papers. So in order to get updated information, visit your vendor's IPv6 site. Here is a list of position papers, dated October, 2001.

Vendor	Web site
Microsoft	*http://www.microsoft.com/ipv6/*
IBM	*http://www.ibm.com/software/ipv6/*
Cisco	*http://www.cisco.com/ipv6/*
Nokia	*http://www.nokia.com/ipv6/*
Alcatel	*http://www.cid.alcatel.com/ipv6/index.html*
SUN	*http://www.sun.com/solaris/ipv6/*
Trumpet	*http://www.trumpet.com.au/ipv6/*
BITS Pilani	*http://ipv6.bits-pilani.ac.in/case-for-v6/*

Vendor	Web site
6WIND	*http://www.6wind.com/ipv6.html*
Compaq	*http://www.compaq.com/ipv6/*
Consulintel	*http://www.consulintel.es/html/ipv6/ipv6.htm*
Nortel Networks	*http://www.nortelnetworks.com/ipv6/*
Hewlett Packard	*http://www.hp.com/products1/unixserverconnectivity/software/ipv.html*
Mentat Inc	*http://www.mentat.com/tcp/tcp.html*
Ericsson	*http://www.ipv6forum.com/navbar/position/Ericsson-IPv6-statement.pdf*
Hitachi	*http://www.v6.hitachi.co.jp*
RIPE/NCC	*http://www.ripe.net/annual-report/*
NTT	*http://www.v6.ntt.net/globe/index-e.html*
ETRI Korea	*http://www.krv6.net*
Ipinfusion	*http://www.ipinfusion.com/ipv6_network-processing_white_paper0727.pdf*

For a current list of available implementations, refer to *http://playground. sun.com/pub/ipng/html/ipng-implementations.html* (sorted by vendor) and *http://www.ipv6.org/v6-apps.html* (sorted by application).

Recommended Reading

This appendix provides a list of books that I recommend.

DNS and BIND, by Paul Albitz and Cricket Liu (O'Reilly).

Ethernet: The Definitive Guide, by Charles E. Spurgeon (O'Reilly).

Guide to Service Location Protocol, by Silvia Hagen (podbooks.com).

Internetworking with TCP/IP: Principles, Protocols and Architectures, by Douglas E. Comer (Prentice Hall).

IPv6: The New Internet Protocol, by Christian Huitema (Prentice Hall).

Novell's Guide to LAN/WAN Analysis, by Laura A. Chappell (John Wiley & Sons).

Novell's Guide to Troubleshooting TCP/IP, by Silvia Hagen and Stephanie Lewis (John Wiley & Sons).

Routing in the Internet, by Christian Huitema (Prentice Hall).

Index

Numbers

10 Gigabit Ethernet (10GE), 121
3ffe::/16 address prefix for 6Bone, 5
6Bone, 4
    addressing, 5
    growth of, 5
    joining, 5
    pinging over IPv4, 273–274
    structure of, 5
6Net (IPv6 research network), 10
6Ren (research and education network
        coordination), 10
6to4, 235–241
    network design (example), 243
    relay routers, 231
    routers, configuring as gateways, 135
    TLA identifier for aggregatable global
        unicast addresses, 38
    (see also interoperability, IPv6/IPv4;
        tunneling)
6to4cfg.exe utility, 262, 265

Symbol

:: (double colon) in IPv6 addresses, 30

A

A6 records, 215, 216, 219
AAA (Authentication, Authorization,
        Accounting) process, 127
AAAA records, 215, 216, 219
AAL5 (ATM Adaptation Layer), 127

abbreviating IPv6 addresses, 29
ABRs (area border routers), 155
    Area LSDB, 186
    cost from the ABR to the ASBR, 180
    prefixes for IPv6 addresses,
        configuring, 156
Access Control (AC) field, Token Ring
        header, 125
Address Resolution Protocol (ARP), 45,
        59
addresses
    IPv4
        mapping private to public, 34
        network ID in subnet mask, 30
        types of, 28
    IPv6, 3, 12, 28–44
        aggregatable global unicast, 34
        anycast, 29, 39
        autoconfiguration for
            hosts, 69–73
        Destination Address field, 16
        format prefixes, 31
        global routing prefix, 30
        ISATAP, 38, 241–243
        link- and site-local, 34
        loopback, 32, 37, 44, 237
        mixed with IPv4 addresses, 30
        multicast, 28, 41–44
        notation, 29
        privacy issues, 33
        required, 44
        Source Address field, 16
        special, 36

We'd like to hear your suggestions for improving our indexes. Send email to *index@oreilly.com*.

ATM (Asynchronous Transfer
Mode), 127
ATMARP server, 128
traffic classes, 117
web site resources for, 128
attacks
authentication, preventing with, 91
flooding or clogging, preventing in
Diffie-Hellman key
exchange, 100
IPSEC protective measures, needed
improvements in, 104
man-in-the-middle, 85
preventing with encrypted
identification tokens, 100
pings, ignoring nonauthenticated, 55
rate-limiting function for ICMPv6
messages, 56
types of, 77–79
disruption or denial of service, 78
electronic eavesdropping, 78
fabricating, modifying, or deleting
information, 78
attributes, BGP, 202
AS_PATH, 194, 196
LOCAL_PREF, 196
MP_REACH_NLRI path
attribute, 204
MP_UNREACH_NLRI path
attribute, 206
NEXT_HOP, 196
audio, transmitting high-quality, 107
authentication
application, 86
Authentication, Authorization,
Accounting (AAA)
process, 127
Authentication Extension headers, 92
Authentication header, 17, 89
order in multiple header
processing, 18
binding updates from mobile nodes
by Home Agent, 133
client, 85
data in trailer for ESP header, 96
extensions for, 3
ICMPv6 Echo Request and Reply
messages, 55
of information, using asymmetric
cryptography, 81

IPv6, 91–95
combining with encryption, 98
payload and header, 93
noninteroperable systems, problems
with, 87
in OSPF, 153
routing exchanges, RIPng, 151
SAs (Security Associations) and, 90,
100
user identification and password,
security problems with, 84
authenticity of information
providers, 79
autoconfiguration, 69–73
host link-local address on Ethernet
interface, 32
IPv6 mechanisms for, 3
stateful and stateless, 69
stateless, 59, 122
FDDI networks, 124
automatic IPv6 address definition on
Solaris, 257
automatic tunneling, 229, 233
combining with configured, 234
ISATAP, 241–243
autonomous address configuration,
using prefix information in ND
messages, 66
autonomous system border router
(ASBR), 158, 180
autonomous systems (AS), 137
AS-External-LSAs
blocking in stub areas, 159
replacing with Type-7-LSAs in
stub areas, 160
flooding scope, 154
types of, 193

B

backbone area, 156
backbone networks (6Bone)
addressing, 5
growth of, 5
joining, 5
structure of, 5
backup designated routers (BDRs), 152
election of, 168
forming adjacencies, 165

ISPs, regional registry for IPv6
addresses, 36
iterated tunneling, 90

J

joining the 6Bone, 5
Jumbogram Extension header, 14

K

KEEPALIVE messages, BGP, 195, 203
Kerberos authentication services, 86
key exchanges (modes), 99
Keyed Message Digest No. 5 (MD-5)
checksum algorithm, 93
keys, cryptographic
in asymmetric encryption, 80
DES encryption algorithm, 96
distribution problems, 79
generation, distribution, and
management system for
email, 86
IPSEC management of, 89
managing for SAs, 98–102

L

labeling, flow labeling in IPv6, 3, 109
Layer 2 (see Data Link layer)
layers, security services and, 87
LCP (Link Control Protocol), 127
leaf sites, 6Bone, 5
length
Extension headers, 17
Header Extension Length field, 19,
21, 26
IPv6 headers, 11
Length field in neighbor discovery
options, 66
Length of Payload field,
Authentication Extension
header, 92
Payload Length field, 14
Link Control Protocol (LCP), 127
Link LSDB, 186
Link State Acknowledgment
packets, 172, 191
Link State Advertisements (LSAs), 154,
174
with area flooding scope, 155
AS-External-LSA, 158, 181–183

format changes from IPv4, 153
headers, 175–177
Inter-Area-Prefix-LSAs, 156, 179
Inter-Area-Router-LSA, 180
Intra-Area-Prefix-LSA, 184
Link-LSA, 183
Network-LSA, 155, 178, 186, 191
Router-LSA, 155, 177, 186, 191
Type-7-LSAs in stub areas, 160
unknown types, handling, 153
link state databases (LSDBs), 173–185
Area LSDBs, 186
AS LSDB, 186
AS-External-LSA, 181–183
contents of, 173
Inter-Area-Prefix-LSAs, 179
Inter-Area-Router-LSA, 180
Intra-Area-Prefix-LSAs, 184
Link LSDB, 186
Link-LSA, 183
LSA headers, 175–177
LSAs, 174
Network-LSA, 178
reducing size by blocking external
routes, 159
Router-LSA, 177
Link State Request packets, 172
LSAs responding to, 190
link state types, 176
Link State Update packets, 172
link states in OSPF for IPv6, 154
link types, OSPF, 165
supported in Router-LSA, 178
link-layer addresses
ICMPv6 messages and, 51
neighbor cache entries,
overriding, 64
next-hop router, 65
Options field, Neighbor Solicitation
message, 63
resolution with Neighbor Solicitation
and Advertisement, 63
router, in Router Advertisement, 59
link-local addresses, 33, 34, 39
forming on PPP links, 126
host requirement for in IPv6, 44
next hop IPv6 address, 146
OSPF, use in, 153, 161
prefix fe80:, 57
Token Ring networks, 125

U

U-bit (handling bit for flooding
    unknown LSAs), 159
UDP, 210–212
    packet with a zero checksum,
        IP/ICMP translation and, 250
    ports used with DHCPv6, 213
    protocol number in Next Header
        field, 14
    RIPng routing protocol, based
        on, 143
    stateless IP/ICMP translation
        and, 248
unicast addresses, 28
    aggregatable global, 5, 34
        anycast addresses, 39
    global aggregatable
        TLA, address allocations
            made, 36
    hosts, required in IPv6, 44
    IPv6, 28
        assigning one to multiple
            interfaces, 29
        IPv4-compatible, 37
        prefixes for, 32
    LSAs, sending to, 190
    SA management mechanisms for, 91
    TLA identifier for 6to4
        operations, 38
unicasts, end-to-end QoS, 108
unique identifiers
    EUI-48 format, assignment with
        OUIs, 39
    EUI-64 format, 32, 241
unique stable IP addresses, 33
universal/local bit of MAC address,
    complementing, 32
Unix, configuring name server on, 217
unknown error message type,
    processing, 56
unknown informational message type,
    processing, 56
unknown LSAs, handling, 192
Unnumbered Information (Control
    field)
    FDDI header, 124
    Token Ring header, 126
unreachability detection, neighbor, 60
unreachable routes, 142

unrecognized IPv6 option encountered
    message, 53
unrecognized next header type
    encountered message, 53
Unsolicited and Solicited Response
    messages, RIPng, 149
unsolicited Neighbor Advertisement
    messages, Target Address
    field, 64
unspecified addresses, 32, 37
    ICMPv6 messages and, 56
UPDATE message, BGP, 194, 200
    IPv4 information in, 204
update messages
    RIPng routing protocol, 139
    RTEs within single updates, 145
updating routing tables, Bellman-Ford
    algorithm for, 140
Upper-Layer header, order in multiple
    header processing, 18
user identification and passwords,
    security problems with, 84
utilities for IPv6
    Linux, 259
    Solaris, 257
    Windows NT 4.0 and Windows
        2000, 261
    Windows XP, 264

V

Valid Lifetime field (prefix information
    in ND messages), 67
variable scope multicast
    addresses, 296–298
variable-length fields (TLVs), 208
vendor support for IPv6, 255, 277, 306
    position papers, web sites for, 277
verifying neighbor reachability, 63
Versatile Secure Key Exchange
    Mechanism for Internet
    (SKEME), 99
Version field, 13
    RIPng messages, 144
virtual links in OSPF, 157, 165

W

"web of trust" scheme, 86
web servers, 225
web sites, IPv6-accessible, 226, 276

About the Author

Silvia Hagen has worked in the networking industry since 1990. She became a CNE and CNI in 1992. Silvia began her career as an instructor and has trained hundreds of system engineers. Today she is CEO of Sunny Connection AG in Switzerland and works as a senior consultant and analyst for many mid-sized and large-sized companies.

Her area of expertise is directory services and protocol analysis. She is the coauthor of *Novell's Guide to Troubleshooting TCP/IP* (John Wiley & Sons) and the author of *Guide to Service Location Protocol* (podbooks.com). She gives presentations on various networking topics for universities and companies around the world, including Novell's Brainshare and NetWare Users International Conferences. She also offers customized corporate presentations and training sessions. For more details and information, visit her web site at *http://www.sunny.ch*.

Colophon

Our look is the result of reader comments, our own experimentation, and feedback from distribution channels. Distinctive covers complement our distinctive approach to technical topics, breathing personality and life into potentially dry subjects.

The animal on the cover of *IPv6 Essentials* is a rigatella snail. The rigatella snail, or *Eobania vermiculata*, is native to the Mediterranean region, especially to Turkey and Crete. The snail lives in gardens, hedges, and dunes, where it feeds on vegetation. The snail got its scientific name because the rings on its shell resemble vermicelli (a type of pasta). It is also sometimes called the "noodle snail."

Rigatella snails commonly have about five brown rings on their cream-colored shells. Their eyes sit on stalks, or tentacles, which protrude from their heads. The snails are 17 to 21 millimeters high and 20 to 25 millimeters wide. They move by rhythmically contracting their muscular base, or foot. As they move, the snails secrete a colorless discharge that creates a type of carpet, which protects them from the surfaces on which they travel. This discharge is so effective that a snail could crawl along the blade of a razor and not be cut.

Rigatella snails are edible. They are one of the most popular types of snail used to make the European delicacy, escargots.

Claire Cloutier was the production editor for *IPv6 Essentials*. Leanne Soylemez and Claire Cloutier were the copyeditors. Ann Schirmer was the proofreader. Sarah Sherman provided editorial assistance. Ann Schirmer, Emily Quill, and Jeffrey Holcomb did quality control checks. Claire Cloutier, Sarah Sherman, Philip Dangler, Leanne Soylemez, Darren Kelly, and Judy Hoer were the compositors. Ellen Troutman-Zaig wrote the index.

Hanna Dyer designed the cover of this book, based on a series design by Edie Freedman. The cover image is a 19th-century engraving from *Cuvier's Animals*. Emma Colby produced the cover layout with QuarkXPress 4.1, using Adobe's ITC Garamond font.

David Futato designed the interior layout. This book was converted to FrameMaker 5.5.6 with a format conversion tool created by Erik Ray, Jason McIntosh, Neil Walls, and Mike Sierra that uses Perl and XML technologies. The text font is Linotype Birka; the heading font is Adobe Myriad Condensed; and the code font is LucasFont's TheSans Mono Condensed. The illustrations that appear in the book were produced by Robert Romano and Jessamyn Read, using Macromedia FreeHand 9 and Adobe Photoshop 6. The tip and warning icons were drawn by Christopher Bing. This colophon was written by Linley Dolby.

Other Titles Available from O'Reilly

Network Administration

DNS and BIND, 4th Edition

By Paul Albitz & Cricket Liu
4th Edition April 2001
622 pages, ISBN 0-596-00158-4

DNS and BIND, 4th Edition, covers the new 9.1.0 and 8.2.3 versions of BIND as well as the older 4.9 version. There's also more extensive coverage of NOTIFY, IPv6 forward and reverse mapping, transaction signatures and the new DNS Security Extensions; and a section on accommodating Windows 2000 clients, servers, and Domain Controllers.

Internet Core Protocols: The Definitive Guide

By Eric Hall
1st Edition February 2000
472 pages, Includes CD-ROM
ISBN 1-56592-572-6

Internet Core Protocols: The Definitive Guide provides the nitty-gritty details of TCP, IP, and UDP. Many network problems can only be debugged by working at the lowest levels—looking at all the bits traveling back and forth on the wire. This guide explains what those bits are and how to interpret them. It's the only book on Internet protocols written with system and network administrators in mind.

Network Troubleshooting Tools

By Joseph D. Sloan
1st Edition August 2001
364 pages, ISBN 0-596-00186-X

Network Troubleshooting Tools helps you sort through the thousands of tools that have been developed for debugging TCP/IP networks and choose the ones that are best for your needs. It also shows you how to approach network troubleshooting using these tools, how to document your network so you know how it behaves under normal conditions, and how to think about problems when they arise so you can solve them more effectively.

TCP/IP Network Administration, 3rd Edition

By Craig Hunt
3rd Edition April 2002
746 pages, ISBN 0-596-00297-1

This complete hands-on guide to setting up and running a TCP/IP network starts with the fundamentals: what protocols do and how they work, how addresses and routing are used, and how to set up your network connection. The book also covers advanced routing protocols and provides tutorials on configuring important network services. The expanded third edition includes sections on Samba, Apache web server, network security, and much more.

Managing NFS and NIS, 2nd Edition

By Hal Stern, Mike Eisler & Ricardo Labiaga
2nd Edition July 2001
510 pages, ISBN 1-56592-510-6

This long-awaited new edition of a classic, now updated for NFS Version 3 and based on Solaris 8, shows how to set up and manage a network filesystem installation. Managing NFS and NIS is the only practical book devoted entirely to NFS and the distributed database NIS; it's a "must-have" for anyone interested in Unix networking.

sendmail, 3rd Edition

By Bryan Costales with Eric Allman
3rd Edition December 2002 (est.)
1000 pages (est.), ISBN 1-56592-839-3

Versions 8.10 through 8.12 of the sendmail program differ so significantly from earlier versions that a massive rewrite of our best-selling reference was called for. With so many web sites now seeking to make mail delivery efficient, there's a new chapter on performance tuning, and because sendmail 8.10 and above are now rich in anti-spam features, a chapter on handling spam has been added. Also new to this edition is coverage of other programs supplied with sendmail, such as vacation and makemap. These additional programs are pivotal to sendmail's daily operation. Altogether, versions 8.10 through 8.12 include dozens of new features, options, and macros, and this greatly expanded edition thoroughly addresses each.

O'REILLY®

Network Administration

Essential SNMP

By Douglas Mauro &
Kevin Schmidt
1st Edition July 2001
326 pages, ISBN 0-596-00020-0

This practical guide for network
and system administrators introduces SNMP along with the
technical background to use it effectively. But the
main focus is on practical network administration:
how to configure SNMP agents and network management stations, how to use SNMP to retrieve
and modify variables on network devices, how to
configure management software to react to traps
sent by managed devices. Covers all SNMP versions through SNMPv3.

Unix Backup & Recovery

By W. Curtis Preston
1st Edition November 1999
734 pages, Includes CD-ROM
ISBN 1-56592-642-0

This guide provides a complete
overview of all facets of Unix
backup and recovery and offers
practical, affordable backup and recovery solutions
for environments of all sizes and budgets. It
explains everything from freely available backup
systems to large-scale commercial utilities.

T1: A Survival Guide

By Matthew Gast
1st Edition August 2001
304 pages, ISBN 0-596-00127-4

This practical, applied reference
to T1 for system and network
administrators brings together in
one place the information you
need to set up, test, and troubleshoot T1. You'll
learn what components you need to build a T1
line; how the components interact to transmit data;
how to adapt the T1 to work with data networks
using standardized link layer protocols; troubleshooting strategies; and working with vendors.

Cisco IOS in a Nutshell

By James Boney
1st Edition December 2001
608 pages, ISBN 1-56592-942-X

This two-part reference covers
IOS configuration for the TCP/IP
protocol family. The first part
includes chapters on the user
interface, configuring lines and
interfaces, access lists, routing protocols, and dial-
on-demand routing and security. The second part
is a classic O'Reilly-style quick reference to all the
commands you need to work with TCP/IP and the
lower-level protocols on which it relies, with lots of
examples of the most common configuration steps
for the routers themselves.

Cisco IOS Access Lists

By Jeff Sedayao
1st Edition June 2001
272 pages, ISBN 1-56592-385-5

This book focuses on a critical
aspect of the Cisco IOS—access
lists, which are central to securing routers and networks.
Administrators cannot implement access control
or traffic routing policies without them. The book
covers intranets, firewalls, and the Internet. Unlike
other Cisco router titles, it focuses on practical
instructions for setting router access policies rather
than the details of interfaces and routing protocol
settings.

Hardening Cisco Routers

By Thomas Akin
1st Edition February 2002
192 pages, ISBN 0-596-00166-5

This small, handy reference
helps system and network
administrators make sure their
Cisco routers are secure. Because
it's about securing the routers themselves, and not
the entire network, it's highly practical. The book
includes Cisco Router Security Checklists for
quick reference, not to mention value-added topics
that incorporate the most current thinking about
security: DoS attack mitigation, router auditing,
and FBI recommendations on incident response.

Network Administration

The Networking CD Bookshelf, Version 2.0

By O'Reilly & Associates, Inc.
Version 2.0 May 2002
752 pages, Included CD-ROM
ISBN 0-596-00334-x

Seven best selling O'Reilly Animal Guides are now available on CD-ROM, easily accessible and searchable with your favorite web browser: *TCP/IP Network Administration*, 3rd Edition; *DNS & Bind*, 4th Edition; *Building Internet Firewalls*, 2nd Edition; *SSH, The Secure Shell: The Definitive Guide*; *Network Troubleshooting Tools*; *Managing NFS & NIS*, 2nd Edition; and *Essential SNMP*. As a bonus, you also get the new paperback version of *TCP/IP Network Administration*, 3rd Edition.

Solaris 8 Administrator's Guide

By Paul Watters
1st Edition, January 2002
400 pages, ISBN 0-596-00073-1

This guide covers all aspects of deploying Solaris as an enterprise-level network operating system, with a focus on e-commerce. Written for experienced network administrators who want an objective guide to networking with Solaris, the book covers installation on the Intel and Sparc platforms, and instructs you how to setup Solaris as a file server, application server, and database server.

Designing Large-Scale LANs

By Kevin Dooley
1st Edition, January 2002
400 pages, ISBN 0-596-00150-9

This unique book outlines the advantages of a top-down, vendor-neutral approach to network design. Everything from network reliability, network topologies, routing and switching, wireless, virtual LANs, firewalls and gateways to security, Internet protocols, bandwidth, and multicast services are covered from the perspective of an organization's specific needs, rather than from product requirements. The book also discusses proprietary technologies that are ubiquitous, such as Cisco's IOS and Novell's IPX.

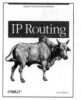

IP Routing

By Ravi Malhotra
1st Edition, January 2002
240 pages, ISBN 0-596-00275-0

This concise guide offers the basic concepts of IP routing, free of hype and jargon. It begins with the simplest routing protocol, RIP, and then proceeds in successive chapters to IGRP, EIGRP, RIP2, OSPF, and finally to the most complex, BGP. By the end, you will have mastered not only the fundamentals of all the major routing protocols, but also the underlying principles on which they are based.

Using SANs and NAS

By W. Curtis Preston
1st Edition, February 2002
218 pages, ISBN 0-596-00153-3

Storage Area Networks (SANs) and Network Attached Storage (NAS) allow organizations to manage and back up huge file systems quickly. W. Curtis Preston's insightful book takes you through the ins and outs of building and managing large data centers using SANs and NAS. Whether you're a seasoned storage administrator or a network administrator charged with taking on this role, you'll find all the information you need to make informed architecture and data management decisions.

How to stay in touch with O'Reilly

1. Visit our award-winning web site

http://www.oreilly.com/

★ "Top 100 Sites on the Web"—PC Magazine
★ CIO Magazine's Web Business 50 Awards

Our web site contains a library of comprehensive product information (including book excerpts and tables of contents), downloadable software, background articles, interviews with technology leaders, links to relevant sites, book cover art, and more. File us in your bookmarks or favorites!

2. Join our email mailing lists

Sign up to get email announcements of new books and conferences, special offers, and O'Reilly Network technology newsletters at:

http://www.elists.oreilly.com

It's easy to customize your free elists subscription so you'll get exactly the O'Reilly news you want.

3. Get examples from our books

To find example files for a book, go to:

http://www.oreilly.com/catalog

select the book, and follow the "Examples" link.

4. Work with us

Check out our web site for current employment opportunites:

http://jobs.oreilly.com/

5. Register your book

Register your book at:
http://register.oreilly.com

6. Contact us

O'Reilly & Associates, Inc.
1005 Gravenstein Hwy North
Sebastopol, CA 95472 USA
TEL: 707-827-7000 or 800-998-9938
        (6am to 5pm PST)
FAX: 707-829-0104

order@oreilly.com
For answers to problems regarding your order or our products. To place a book order online visit:

http://www.oreilly.com/order_new/

catalog@oreilly.com
To request a copy of our latest catalog.

booktech@oreilly.com
For book content technical questions or corrections.

corporate@oreilly.com
For educational, library, and corporate sales.

proposals@oreilly.com
To submit new book proposals to our editors and product managers.

international@oreilly.com
For information about our international distributors or translation queries. For a list of our distributors outside of North America check out:

http://international.oreilly.com/distributors.html

O'REILLY®

To order: *800-998-9938* • *order@oreilly.com* • *www.oreilly.com*
Online editions of most O'Reilly titles are available by subscription at *safari.oreilly.com*
Also available at most retail and online bookstores.